Business Travel

Conferences, Incentive Travel, Exhibitions, Corporate Hospitality and Corporate Travel

Rob Davidson and Beulah Cope

FT Prentice Hall
FINANCIAL TIMES

An imprint of **Pearson Education**
Harlow, England • London • New York • Boston • San Francisco • Toronto • Sydney • Singapore • Hong Kong
Tokyo • Seoul • Taipei • New Delhi • Cape Town • Madrid • Mexico City • Amsterdam • Munich • Paris • Milan

Pearson Education Limited

Edinburgh Gate
Harlow
Essex CM20 2JE

and Associated Companies throughout the world

Visit us on the World Wide Web at:
www.pearsoneduc.com

ISBN 0582 40444 4

British Library Cataloguing-in-Publication Data
A catalogue record for this book is available from the British Library.

10 9 8 7 6 5 4 3 2 1
05 04 03

Typeset by 68 in 10/13 pt Sabon
Printed and bound in China
SWTC/01

Contents

Preface

Cinderella finally gets to the ball.

Despite its huge economic importance and its very considerable contribution to the development of world trade and commerce, business travel in its many forms has remained, until recently, the Cinderella sector of the travel and tourism industry – at least in academia.

While courses in leisure travel have proliferated in universities the world over, it is only relatively lately, in higher education in the UK and continental Europe, that the various sectors of business travel have received the recognition they deserve. Previously, we have seriously lagged behind the level of provision offered in this discipline by universities in North America and Australasia, where institutions such as George Washington University and the University of Nevada, Las Vegas, have led the way in establishing business travel firmly in higher education curricula.

Now, thankfully, travel and tourism undergraduate and postgraduate courses that completely ignore business travel are increasingly rare, as academics – and the students they teach – have gradually come to appreciate the importance of understanding a market that in most countries accounts for between one-quarter and one-third of all travel-related spending.

In the past few years in the UK and Europe a great number of imaginative initiatives have been taken in response to the growing demand for courses in business travel-related subjects. These include the HNC in Business in Conference and Event Management, offered by the City of Westminster College in partnership with the University of Westminster; Colchester Institute's BA in Hospitality Studies with Conference Management; Buckinghamshire Chilterns University's BA in Conference, Events and Facilities Management; Cheltenham and Gloucester College of Higher Education's HND in Sports and Corporate Hospitality Management; and the European Masters in Congress Management offered by Sheffield Hallam University, Universidad de Deusto, Berufsakademie Ravensburg and Università degli Studi di Bologna. In addition, universities such as Leeds Metropolitan have included the study of exhibitions and trade shows in their events management courses at undergraduate and postgraduate levels.

While the teaching of business travel-related subjects expands in the higher education sector, a number of professional qualifications are offered by the various associations that are active in improving the knowledge and skills of their members. Organisations such as the Association for Conferences and Events (ACE), the International Association of Professional Congress Organisers (IAPCO), Meetings Professionals International (MPI) and the Society of Incentive Travel Executives

(SITE) provide a wide range of vocational education and training opportunities for those already employed in the industry or seeking to prepare themselves for careers in business travel.

Until recently, academic interest in business travel education had been frustrated by the absence of an introductory textbook on this subject, written with the higher education student in mind. To date, lecturers, researchers and students have had to rely for their information on a variety of trade journals and more technical works dealing with only one sector of the business travel industry. A textbook dealing with all sectors of business-related travel in an analytical manner, and providing a sound practical and theoretical context for the study of this subject, has been significant by its absence.

This book has been written to fill that gap.

Business Travel is an updated version of my 1994 book of the same name. However, whereas the first edition was aimed at students of this subject in further education (in which, at the time, the study of this subject was much more widespread than in our universities), this new edition has been written specifically for use in the higher education sector. The change in readership is reflected throughout the book, not only in the level of analysis but also in the more wide-ranging breadth and depth of approach to the subject and the presentation of those complex issues that the student of business travel at the higher education level must consider.

This book follows a sectoral structure, with a chapter devoted to each of the main segments of the business travel industry: individual business travel, meetings, incentive travel, exhibitions and corporate hospitality. Preceding and following these chapters are two others, the first providing a general introduction to the topic and the final chapter exploring the interface between travel for leisure and travel for business-related purposes. Chapters 1–6 begin with a list of learning objectives and end with case studies followed by questions. There is a glossary of technical terms used in the text at the end of the book.

The sectoral chapters present the particular market segment in detail, examining supply, demand and intermediaries. The main players are presented, and each chapter also explores the principal issues and trends affecting the segment under discussion. With the comparative wealth of research that has been carried out into the meetings industry, Chapter 3 is substantially longer than the chapters dealing with the other sectors of business travel. All chapters, however, cover the relevant sector in detail, reviewing much of the research that has been undertaken into the relevant constituent.

Geographically speaking, this book deliberately takes a 'fish-eye lens' approach, with the UK market given most prominence but set firmly in its European context. However, examples are also drawn from world regions beyond the European continent, with a number of comparisons being made, in particular with the North American market for business travel.

It is my avowed intention that *Business Travel* should not only inform students of this important and fascinating subject but also inspire them. Behind all of its technical and commercial aspects, business travel, in all of its forms, is quite simply about direct communication between people: a handshake with a colleague or client and face-to-face interaction at the end of a journey. In addition, the innumerable range of topics discussed at meetings and conferences, together with the multifarious nature of the products and services presented at exhibitions, testify to mankind's diversity, creativity and ingenuity. This book has been written as a celebration of those most human of qualities.

Rob Davidson

Acknowledgements

Our sincere gratitude is due to the great number of people who have generously helped in making this book possible. They have been particularly helpful in providing information on their own companies, organisations and associations operating in the various sectors of the business travel industry. Many have also provided invaluable and constructive comments on the content of the chapters that follow. We would like to thank all of the following for their cooperation and, in all cases, encouragement throughout the period of researching and writing this book:

Adam Bates, BTA; Steve Bedlow, The Delegate Group; Ingrid Behaghel von Flammerdinghe, HCCE; Nigel Dale, BTI UK; Renate Dobler, Austria Center, Vienna; Colette Doyle, Conference & Incentive Travel; Steve Gunn, National Starch & Chemical; Austen Hawkins, AEO; Penny Jenkins, Legoland, Windsor; Rósbjörg Jónsdóttir, Iceland Convention & Incentive Bureau; John Keenan and Martin Lewis, Meetings & Incentive Travel; Jana Leitner, Deutsche Messe AG; Wendy Moffat, Spectra; Sydney Paulen, Incentive Travel & Corporate Meetings; Marianne de Raay, AIPC; Tony Rogers, BACD; Gill Smillie, Conference Centres of Excellence; Dennis Speet, ICCA; Mandy Torrens, Reed Travel Exhibitions; and John Williams, GBTA.

Publisher's Acknowledgements

We are grateful to the following for permission to reproduce copyright material:

Figure 1.2 from *Business & Conference Tourism in the EEA*, published by the Office for official publications of the European Communities, 1996; Figure 1.3, Tables 1.4, 1.5 and 1.6 (a)–(g) published by Reed Travel Exhibitions; Tables 2.1 and 2.2 © Crown copright 2002. Reproduced with the permission of the Controller of Her Majesty's Stationery Office (HMSO); Table 2.3 from *Travel and Tourism Analyst* No.4/Mintel's Travel Intelligence; Figure 2.2 adapted from Palmer, A. (2001) *Principles of Service Marketing*, 3rd edition, McGraw-Hill, Maidenhead, p.97. Reproduced with the permission of McGraw-Hill; Figure 6.1 adapted from Christopher, M., Payne, A. and Ballantine, M. (1991), *Relationship Marketing*, Butterworth-Heinemann, London, in Palmer, A. (2001), *Principles of Services Marketing*, 3rd edition, McGraw-Hill, Maidenhead, p. 126. Reproduced with the permission of McGraw-Hill; Figure 2.3 © Ted Dewan. Reproduced with the permission of Ted Dewan, www.wormworks.com; Figures 2.4 and 2.5 from IATA Corporate Air Travel Survey 2000; Table 2.4 from *Travel Trade Gazette* UK Ireland; Tables 3.1 and 3.2 and Figures 3.1, 3.2, 3.3 and 3.4 from the UK Conference Market Survey 2000, published by the Meetings Industry Association; Tables 3.7, 3.8 and 3.9 published by ICCA (2001), www.iccaworld.com; Figure 3.5 and Table 3.10 published by the Austria Center Vienna; Table 4.1 from *Travelstyles: Americans as international travellers*, published the Menlo Consulting Group, Inc. (1999) and the British Tourist Authority; Table 4.2 from 'The incentive travel market to the UK and Ireland' (O'Brien, K., 1997), in *Insights*, September, published by the English Tourism Council (Tel: 0208 563 3362); Figure 5.1 reproduced with the permission of the Association of Exhibition Organisers; Tables 5.1 and 5.2 published by EMECA; Table 5.3 reproduced with the permission of the Exhibition Venues Association (EVA); Table 5.4 and Figures 5.2, 5.3 and 5.4 published by National Starch & Chemical; Table 6.1 adapted from Burton, J. (1999), *Business Development and Account Management*, London, GBTA. Reproduced with the permission of the Guild of Business Travel Agents; Figures 6.2 and 6.4 reproduced with the permission of Legoland, Windsor; Figure 6.3 reproduced with the permission of Swindon Town Football Club; Table 7.1 from ' "Travelling workers" and "working tourists": variations across the interaction between work and tourism', in *International Journal of Tourism Research*, Vol. 3, pp. 1–8. © John Wiley & Sons Limited. Reproduced with permission; Figure 7.2 reproduced with the permission of St. Andrews & Kingdom of Fife Convention Bureau.

Box 2.1 published by *Business Traveller Magazine*, March 1999; Case study 'The Guild of European Business Travel Agents and the UK's Guild of Business Travel Agents' in Chapter 2 reproduced with the permission of GBTA Ltd; Case study 'Business Travel International: meeting the demands of corporate travel clients' in Chapter 2 reproduced with the permission of BTI UK; Box 3.3 published by the Austria Center Vienna; Case study 'Meeting in Madrid' in Chapter 3 based on an article by Roberta Etter in *Conference & Incentive Travel*, May 1999, Haymarket Marketing Publications; Case study 'Golf developments in Scotland' in Chapter 4 incorporates material from the article 'Bunkered by Mr Big' which appeared in *The Guardian* newspaper on 28 July 2001 © John Burnside; Box 5.1 published by Inside Communications Ltd; Box 7.1 reproduced with the permission of the National Association of Pension Funds.

In some instances we have been unable to trace the owners of copyright material, and we would appreciate any information that would enable us to do so.

Chapter 1

Introduction to business travel

Objectives

On completion of this chapter, you should be able to:

- *understand the principal definitions in business travel;*
- *appreciate the differences between business travel and leisure travel;*
- *understand the structure of the business travel market;*
- *recognise the links between business travel and the economy;*
- *discuss the main impacts of business travel, as well as the major opportunities, challenges and threats affecting this industry.*

Business travel in the twenty-first century

- 800 delegates attended the three-day International Conference on Health Research for Development at Bangkok's Shangri-La Hotel, organised by the Council for Health Research and Development. Among the topics discussed was an agreement on a framework for improved international cooperation in health research.
- 1500 publishers from 76 countries exhibited their books and multimedia products at the Bologna Children's Book Fair, held at the Fiere Internazionali di Bologna. Over four days, they introduced their latest products to over 4000 literary agents, librarians, printers and booksellers in a 22 000-m² exhibition hall.
- As a reward for outstanding sales figures, Novell, a UK-based provider of Internet services software, sent 130 of their top sales executives and their partners on a two-day incentive trip to Madeira. On the first day, participants chose either to play golf on the Palheiro championship course or go on a luxury coach tour to explore the island's natural beauty and heritage. A jeep safari on the second day drove through the Laurisilva Forests and the Rieviro Frio nature park.
- The UK's Industrial Society published figures showing that in one year, the British spent almost 46 million nights away from home travelling on business.
- Kempton Park, Sandown Park and Epsom Downs racecourses in south-east England hosted corporate hospitality events for companies using their private entertaining facilities. Guests were able to watch the racing live from their tables while enjoying à la carte dining in the racecourses' restaurants.

Introduction

When, in the 1990 film *Pretty Woman*, the streetwalker character played by Julia Roberts attempts to solicit the Richard Gere character with the question, 'So, what brings you to Los Angeles – business or pleasure ?', she was concisely identifying the two main motivations underlying travel today.

Many centuries before the practice of taking holidays and participating in other forms of travel for pleasure became as widespread as it is now, travel for the purposes of trading in distant markets and attending meetings to discuss issues of common concern was widespread. These historical antecedents of modern business travel indicate that our forebears recognised long ago that economic prosperity depends upon entrepreneurs and businesspeople travelling in order to conquer new markets, and that understanding and harmony between nations require the representatives to travel regularly in order to meet and discuss diplomatic and strategic issues.

It is clear, therefore, that the need to meet and negotiate face to face with others constituted one of the earliest motivations behind our apparently irresistible urge towards mobility, which, by the twenty-first century, had created the world's largest industry: travel and tourism.

● ● ● ● **Definitions**

Although for the layperson the terms 'travel' and 'tourism' may be synonymous with leisure and pleasure, the importance of business travel is widely acknowledged in official and technical definitions. The World Tourism Organisation's (WTO) official definition of tourism, for example, suggests that people travelling for business or professional purposes can also be considered as tourists (WTO, 1993).

In broad terms, business travel comprises all trips whose purpose is linked with the traveller's employment or business interests. These trips may be necessary in order to enable the actual work to be carried out; or they may enable the employee to learn how to do their job more effectively; or they may be given by the employer as a reward for a job well done. Most of the forms of travel covered in this book are, therefore, work-related. They are as follows:

- *Individual business travel*: comprises the trips made by those whose employment requires them to travel in order to carry out their work. From journalists and politicians to talent-spotters and accident investigators, there is a wide range of jobs that can be done effectively only when those who do them are prepared to accept being away from home and their workplace base regularly as a normal feature of their work.
- *Meetings*: includes the vast range of events, such as conferences, training seminars, product launches and annual general meetings, that are held by companies and associations in order to facilitate communication with and between their employees, customers, shareholders and members.
- *Exhibitions*: also known as trade fairs, trade shows and consumer shows. Exhibitions of this type are events to which businesses send sales staff in order to display their products – from farm machinery to wedding dresses – to potential customers, who attend in order to buy and/or receive expert information about the goods being exhibited, usually straight from the manufacturers.
- *Incentive trips*: comprises those trips – usually luxurious and often to attractive destinations – that employees receive from their employer as a prize for winning a competition related to their job, e.g. selling more life insurance policies than anyone else on the staff, or being part of the sales team that increases its sale of photocopiers by a higher percentage than all other teams.
- *Corporate hospitality*: consists of the often lavish entertainment that companies extend to their most valuable clients or potential clients at prestigious sporting and cultural events, such as the Rugby League World Cup or the Glyndebourne opera festival. Companies mainly use this form of entertainment as a way of creating goodwill and building rapport with VIP customers and potential customers.

In many cases, the terms 'business tourism' and 'business travel' are used interchangeably as generic terms to describe these different sectors. But for those, including most Americans, who regard tourism and business as diametrically opposed activities, the term 'business tourism' is somewhat perplexing and even something of a contradiction in terms. For reasons of logic and clarity, the term 'business travel' will be used here to represent the full range of activities that this book encompasses in its scope. Each of those activities will be considered in turn as a discrete sector within the business travel industry. These sectors will be subdivided into 'individual business travel' and 'business tourism', the latter including the meetings, exhibitions, incentive travel and corporate hospitality sectors. This subdivision is not arbitrary: it highlights two separate types of activity sharing quite distinct characteristics.

Individual business travel is composed of trips made to carry out duties that are a regular and necessary part of the traveller's employment. Such trips are most often made by the individual travelling alone, and the destination is usually predetermined by the demands of the job to be done: the traveller must go to wherever the client to be visited is based, or to where the problem is to be solved, or to where the contract is to be signed, i.e. the destination is fixed. This is the only nondiscretionary sector of business travel: the destination is not chosen, but is determined by the object of the work that has to be carried out.

The other sectors, which may be grouped together as business tourism, are discretionary. The destinations for most meeting events, exhibitions, incentive trips and corporate hospitality events are 'floating', i.e. there is a degree of flexibility in the decision as to where they may be held. For this reason, these sectors are 'the prime focus of marketing activities by venues and destinations, because decisions about where the events take place are open to influence' (Rogers, 1998; p.19). Attendance at such events, which constitute a more occasional aspect of working life, often takes the form of group travel, with colleagues travelling together or meeting there.

An alternative term being used increasingly to describe some of these business tourism sectors is the MICE industry, an acronym for 'meetings, incentives, conferences and exhibitions'. But quaint and eye-catching though the term may be, many of those working in these sectors are uncomfortable with the MICE designation, as they are of the belief that it is not helpful in earning business travel the respect and recognition it deserves from politicians and other opinion-formers. The use of the term MICE in this book will therefore be kept to a minimum.

Figure 1.1 shows the structure of the business travel industry.

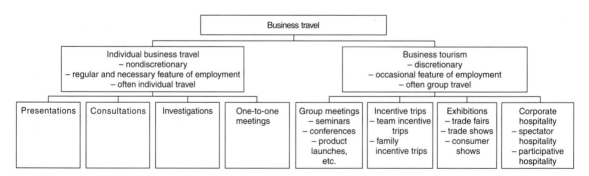

Figure 1.1 Business travel sectors

Before moving on from the issue of the categorisation of business travel products, there are two paradoxical factors relating to this umbrella term that must be acknowledged. Referring back to the wide range of activities and events included here under the term 'business travel', it is clear that:

● there are forms of business travel that are not business related;
● there are forms of business travel that involve very little travel.

An example of the former case would be any conference where the motivation to meet is not to discuss issues related to the delegates' jobs or profession. For instance, many associations meet regularly because their members share an interest in voluntary or charity work (Rotary International), the same faith (the Association of Independent Methodists) or the same hobby (Harley Davidson Riders' Club of Great Britain).

Business travel sectors that involve very little actual travel would be, for example, one-day meetings held in the seminar room of a local hotel, or a group of London-based clients spending an afternoon drinking Pimms, eating strawberries and watching tennis at a corporate entertainment event at Wimbledon.

However, despite their apparent status as exceptions to the rule, all of the above events and activities will be considered as lying firmly within the scope of this book's subject matter. They would certainly all be regarded by suppliers such as conference centres, hotels and catering companies as being in the same general market as the other types of business travel already discussed. And while transport operators such as airlines and high-speed train companies may call into question the use of the term 'business travel' to describe events attended by people who live or work locally, it is unlikely that taxi companies and operators of public transport, for example, would share their concern.

A final point to be emphasised regarding the classification of business travel activities as shown in Figure 1.1 is that, very often, elements of two or more categories are combined in the same event. For example, a motivational conference held for a dozen company executives in Monte Carlo clearly contains aspects of a classic incentive trip in addition to the meeting element. Indeed, in the company's desire to use the event as a reward for its executives, the 'conference' element may simply be a short pep talk from the managing director flown in on the final day for the occasion.

The same type of hybrid events is found in the growing number of conferences that are accompanied by an exhibition on the same theme and usually in the same venue. For example, organisers of a conference on the theme of an aspect of medical research may invite representatives of pharmaceutical companies to buy exhibition space for their stands in a hall adjacent to the conference room. There are three potential advantages of combining events in this way:

● The exhibition earns revenue, which offsets the cost of the conference for organisers and delegates.
● It gives the exhibiting companies the opportunity to present their products to an interested market.
● It provides the delegates with an additional reason for attending the event.

Smith (1990; p.73) notes the trend towards adding exhibitions to conferences: 'There have been changes in the relation of conferences with exhibitions; nowadays they are increasingly found together ... The significant element is that while exhibitions are profitable, conferences usually are not, so an associated exhibition can often subsidise the meeting.'

In the same way, many exhibitions have a related conference or a series of seminars on topics related to the theme of the exhibition. Such elements can add value to exhibitions by, for example, featuring industry experts who present their views to the trade show visitors and exhibitors gathered for the event.

● ● ● ● Business travel and leisure travel

While most people reading this book will be familiar with the various forms of leisure travel through their experiences of holidays, short breaks and daytrips, many will be far less acquainted with the general characteristics of travel for business. A convenient starting point, therefore, is a comparison of the two. Table 1.1 summarises the contrasts between them.

What soon becomes apparent is how difficult it is to generalise about business travel when the many different types of event and activity that compose it mean that there are often exceptions to the rule. Nevertheless, Table 1.1 highlights a sufficient number of differences between leisure and business travel to indicate that the two are dissimilar in many ways. The significance of some of these differences will be considered in greater detail in the course of this chapter.

However, the emphasis on the contrasts between the two types of travel ought not to be allowed to obscure two important issues that serve as a reminder that, despite the differences between them, the strict segmentation of the market into leisure travel and business travel may not always be meaningful and clear-cut.

Those travelling on business often make use of the same services and facilities as leisure travellers. For example, with the exception of charter flights, most airlines carry a combination of leisure and business passengers on most routes, and most hotels accommodate a combination of business and leisure guests; the building that serves as a concert hall one day can be used the next day as a venue for an international conference; and who can tell which of the diners in a hotel restaurant are visiting the city on business and which are there simply for their own pleasure? In particular, those on incentive trips may on occasion appear almost indistinguishable from leisure visitors in terms of the services and facilities they use.

Moreover, all visitors may have need of the destination's information and advisory services, telecommunications networks and medical services. And all appreciate an attractive and safe environment.

The 'all work and no play' dictum applies absolutely to those travelling on business-related matters. Leaving aside the hours spent conferencing, negotiating and generally getting the job done, most business travellers, delegates and visitors to trade shows find themselves with time to spare in the places they are visiting. Very

Table 1.1 Comparison of leisure and business travel

	Leisure travel	Business travel	But ...
Who pays for the trip?	The traveller	The employer	Self-employed people and those attending association events pay for themselves
Who or what determines the destination?	The traveller	The organiser of the event, or the location of the work to be done	Organisers take participants' wishes into account for discretionary forms of business travel
When do trips take place?	In leisure time	In working time	Many business trips extend into the travellers' evenings and weekends
	Classic holiday periods and at weekends	Mainly outside holiday periods, Monday–Friday	
	Relatively infrequently, but (holidays) last longer	Relatively frequently, but for short periods	
Planned how far in advance (lead times)?	Holidays booked a few months in advance; short breaks booked a few days in advance	Large events organised years in advance	Individual business travel can happen at very short notice
Who travels?	Anyone with the money and time to travel	Adults; largely managerial level, or those with technical/specialist skills not available locally	Associations draw their memberships from a wider range of people of different ages and backgrounds
What type of destination?	Mainly coastal, mountain, urban and rural	Largely centred on cities in stable, industrialised destinations	Incentive travel destinations are similar to leisure destinations
What type of travelling companions?	Friends and family	Usually unaccompanied in the case of individual business travel; or with colleagues in the case of business tourism	Family members may be included in incentive trips or in conference attendance

often, social and cultural elements are programmed into conferences, for example, to give delegates the opportunity to relax and network together. Thus, business visitors engaging in activities such as sightseeing excursions, shopping, and cultural pursuits add to the level of leisure consumed at the destination.

In addition, many of those travelling on business choose to extend their trip by, for example, spending a few extra days at the destination for leisure purposes before or after the event they are there to attend. Similarly, many of those attending a business tourism event decide to take along a friend or partner with them on the trip. That friend or partner will normally be free during the event to enjoy the attractions that the destination has to offer, thus adding to the number of those who visit for leisure-related reasons. The question of how business travel can generate additional leisure tourism is the theme of Chapter 7.

● ● ● ● Structure of the business travel market

Although, as has been stated, business travel and leisure travel share many facilities and services, the business travel sectors depend, for their effective functioning, on a considerable number of stakeholders whose role is concerned largely or exclusively with providing the facilities and services for this market.

Throughout this book, the main buyers, intermediaries and suppliers for each of the business travel sectors will be identified, and their roles examined in detail. Table 1.2 shows the structure of this market.

Private companies, large and small, are clearly the main consumers and providers of business travel services, although they are by no means the only types of organisation active in this market. For example, representatives and employees of government bodies and agencies also need to travel and meet regularly in order to function effectively; members of associations of all types are important consumers in the conferences sector; and organisations such as universities attend specialist consumer shows to present the courses they teach, with the aim of recruiting students.

The public sector is also present in this market as both supplier and intermediary. For example, many conference centres are owned by local authorities, and destination marketing organisations are almost always funded through a combination of public and private sector support. The need for public and private sector players to work together effectively in partnership in order to ensure the success of the business travel industry in any destination is paramount, a point underlined by Dwyer and Mistilis (1997; p.230): 'Strategies and solutions for developing the [business travel] industry will be generated in some combination of both the public and private arenas; an overarching constraint could be the nature of the interplay between these sectors, including their ability to work together in a proactive way for shared goals.'

Regarding the suppliers and intermediaries in the business travel and tourism market, Table 1.2 shows that many are common to almost all sectors: destination marketing organisations, transport providers, accommodation and catering operators, and suppliers of leisure and recreation facilities. In addition to these, however, each sector has its own specialist suppliers of the products and services it requires in order to function effectively, as well as its own specialist intermediaries. The role of these suppliers and intermediaries will be explored in the sectoral chapters that follow this one. In the meantime, it is worth noting that the great number and variety of these suppliers and intermediaries provides some indication of the extent of the challenges that must be met in coordinating their activities in order to provide buyers with a quality service.

The end consumers of business travel

Not included in the range of players shown in Table 1.2 are those who constitute another key category of stakeholders in the business travel market, the *end consumers* of business travel – those who make the trips and attend the seminars and trade fairs, for example, that their employers pay for. While in the leisure travel

Table 1.2 Players in the business travel market

Business travel sector	Buyers	Intermediaries	Suppliers
Individual business travel	Corporate sector and other types of organisation (voluntary sector, government bodies, etc.) Possibly through their own: • in-house travel managers/travel coordinators • secretaries/PAs	Business/corporate travel agencies Travel management companies Possibly through: • implants • dedicated online booking services	Transport providers Accommodation and catering operators Leisure and recreation suppliers
Meetings	Corporate sector Governmental sector • local • regional • national • intergovernmental Associations • professional • trade • fraternal • religious, etc. Possibly through their own: • in-house travel managers • in-house conference organisers • secretaries/PAs	Professional conference organisers/meeting planners Venue-finding agencies Production companies Destination management companies/ground handlers Specialist marketing consortia Destination marketing organisations	Transport providers Accommodation and catering operators Leisure and recreation suppliers Conference centres Management training centres Hotels' meetings facilities Universities Unusual venues Audiovisual contractors Telecommunications companies (video/satellite conferencing facilities) Interpreters
Incentive travel	Corporate sector, possibly through: • in-house travel managers • in-house conference organisers	Incentive travel houses Business travel agencies Destination management companies/ground handlers Destination marketing organisations	Transport providers Accommodation and catering operators Leisure and recreation suppliers
Exhibitions	Manufacturers and service providers	Exhibition organisers Exhibition contractors Destination marketing organisations	Transport providers Accomodation and catering operators Leisure and recreation suppliers Exhibition centres Stand contractors
Corporate hospitality	Corporate sector	Corporate hospitality agents PR companies Event management companies	Marquee contractors Caterers Historic and unusual venues Sporting/cultural events promoters Activity operators

Source: Based on Davidson, R. (2001), 'Distribution channels for business travel', in Laws, E. and Buhalis, D., *Tourism Distribution Channels: practices, issues and transformations*, London, Continuum.

market the purchaser is usually also the end consumer, in the business tourism market this is not necessarily the case. Apart from self-employed people and those paying to attend certain types of association meeting, the person who travels is rarely the person who is financing the trip.

As continuing success in this market clearly depends upon satisfying not only the buyers but also the end consumers of the services, the vital question arises: who are the business travellers upon whose activities this industry depends?

As always, generalisations are difficult in a market as diverse as this one. But, contrary perhaps to much public opinion, business travellers are not always white-collar workers employed in the upper echelons of their organisations. As shown in Table 1.2, those in possession of technical or specialist skills are often called upon to travel in order to carry out tasks away from their normal places of employment. For example, the contributions of the photographers who travel to a major sports event to capture it on film are just as important to their employers as the written text of the accompanying article produced by their journalist colleagues.

Almost by definition, however, a large percentage of those travelling on business are managerial and sales staff, who have the power either to make decisions or to influence the decisions of others. They have the authority to negotiate on behalf of their companies, governments or professional bodies, for example, and the work they are employed to do is of such a complex or sensitive nature that it can only be carried out face to face with others.

Contributing further to the question of who actually travels on business, Middleton (1994; p.B-10) asks: does the business travel market comprise a relatively small number of individuals who make a large number of business trips, or a relatively large number of individuals making fewer visits? His answer, admittedly based on partial evidence, suggests that the former possibility is the case, and that there is a vital core of frequent repeat visitors: 'At the top end of the business market, individuals are making over 20 business trips per annum. It seems probable that less than 5% of adults are responsible for the great bulk of business travel.'

Business travel destinations

It has already been indicated that most business travel is to urban destinations. Cities are where head offices, factories, and conference and exhibition centres are located; they are also where the majority of the facilities that support the business travel market are to be found, e.g. hotels, transport termini and cultural/entertainment resources used by business visitors.

However, there are a number of differences between the use of cities by business visitors and their use by leisure tourists. While leisure visitors are principally attracted to a select group of cities offering a wealth of heritage/shopping/entertainment attractions, business travellers' trips require them to visit a wider range, including towns and cities of a largely commercial or industrial character. It may, therefore, be argued that business tourism brings economic benefits to places untouched by leisure visitors.

Within cities, leisure visitors in their choice of accommodation and activities tend to remain in close proximity to the city centre, whereas business visitors may be much more dispersed in respect of where they stay and where they go to carry out their business. Depending on their mode of transport, for example, they may use airport hotels or motels close to major roads. Their business may also take them far from the city centre to industrial estates or to exhibition centres, which are often situated between the city itself and its airport, where land is cheaper.

Just as the vast majority of business travel is undertaken by a small percentage of the general population, the destinations in which the lion's share of the world's total business travel takes place are concentrated in a small number of countries. While developing countries are enjoying growing rates of success in attracting holiday-makers to their beaches and for cultural diversion, industrialised nations continue to dominate the business tourism market in terms of both demand and supply. The immense volume of commerce carried out between and within the world's main trading blocs provides the motivation for much of the world's business travel. The industrialised countries are often those that are best placed to provide the services and security upon which business tourism depends.

Even within the countries of the industrialised world, the amount of business travel is distributed unequally. Figure 1.2 shows how, for example, the principal destinations for Europe's meetings and exhibitions industry are concentrated into a few zones within the continent.

It is interesting to note that many of Europe's principal leisure tourism regions find themselves outside the zones indicated in Figure 1.2 as the continent's major business travel destinations.

●●●● Business travel and the economy

In common with most industries, business travel is affected directly and indirectly by the state of the economy in which those who buy it and sell it operate. At the same time, business travel has a considerable impact upon the economy of the destinations to which its consumers make their trips.

Before we consider the impact that this industry has on destinations, however, we will discuss the ways in which features of the general economic environment can affect demand for business travel.

Demand for business travel

There is a general consensus of opinion among commentators that, as for most industries, the level of demand for business travel is determined in part by the buoyancy of the national and, increasingly, global economy. Bull (1995; p.20) emphasises that 'economic cycles in generating areas ... may influence patterns of business demand for tourism, through both the ability of businesses to meet travel costs and businesses' desire to maintain or restrict travel elements of their promotional or training budgets'.

Figure 1.2 The meeting and exhibition industry in the European Economic Area

Source: *Business & Conference Tourism in the EEA*, Office for official publications of the European Communities, 1996.

As an unambiguous illustration of this, the drastically shrinking budgets for business travel witnessed on a global level during the economic downturn at the beginning of the 1990s are still a vivid memory for many of those employed in this industry.

However, many would also agree with Middleton (1994; p.B-13) that 'although business travel volume ebbs and flows with the growth and decline of the ... economy, it is inherently more stable than holiday travel and less influenced by fashions'. Rogers (1998; p.77) elaborates further on this point, with an illustration from the meetings sector:

One of the positive characteristics of the conference industry is its resilience, even in times of economic downturn. While there may be a trading down, many events still go ahead: public companies are required to hold an Annual General Meeting for their shareholders, senior managers need to engage in management retreats to explore ways of reviving their business, new products are launched, staff still have to be trained and motivated, sales forces need to be brought together for briefings, and many other types of conference take place, albeit with reduced budgets.

Some industry analysts have gone further, maintaining that in some cases spending on business travel can actually rise when the economy is slowing down. Bull (1995; p.116), for example, writes: 'With business tourism, demand may be generated when other sectors are *in depression*, as producers decide they need to send sales forces out to generate demand for their products ... When most sectors are booming, there may be less of a desperate need to put sales people on the road'.

Part of the explanation for the apparent resilience of the spending that fuels this industry is the nature of the demand for business travel in its various forms. While leisure travel is what economists call a *final demand* – travel that is an end in itself, undertaken for its own ends – most business travel activities fall into the class of those commodities whose production is driven by *derived demand*. These are goods and services that are purchased only because they are inputs that are necessary elements in the course of producing other goods or services. Other classic examples of derived demand are machine tools, catering equipment and insurance policies.

Therefore, although business tourism is driven by derived demand and is not usually something purchased to be enjoyed as an end in itself, it is regarded by those who pay for it as vital to, for example, the training or motivating of staff to improve their efficiency, or the provision of networking opportunities to create goodwill and new sales opportunities for the company.

This indispensable quality of much business travel means that in general it displays a different level of *elasticity of demand* to that which characterises leisure travel, such as the annual family holiday. Since business travel is usually considered as something that is undertaken because it is necessary to the effective functioning of the company that purchases it, it is generally acknowledged to be relatively income-inelastic: moderate increases in air fares, for example, will not generally dissuade business travellers from making their journey (and, conversely, no fare reductions will tempt them to travel unless their business interests demand it). It is this income-inelasticity that means that, on the whole, business travel volume is fairly stable. By way of contrast, demand for holidays, short breaks and daytrips tends to display a much greater degree of elasticity, often fluctuating considerably according to the buyer's level of disposable income.

This is not to say, of course, that levels of spending on business travel do not vary. Clearly, as mentioned previously, these are linked to, on the one hand, the assets and incomes of the companies (and, in the case of some conferences, the individuals) who purchase business travel products, and on the other hand, the prices of business travel services. One theme of this book is how buyers of business travel products are modifying how they purchase and what they purchase in this market, in order to obtain value for money in the face of rising prices in many sectors of this industry.

Another demand determinant for business travel, to which Bull (1995) draws attention, is the level of government taxation of business expenses. Companies usually meet the cost of at least some of their spending on business tourism by claiming it as an expense against corporate income for tax purposes. Therefore, government policy on the extent to which these expenses may be allowed against tax may, in theory at least, alter the effective prices of tourism products and hence demand. In other words, despite the relatively inelastic nature of demand for business travel products, any change to the level of tax-deductibility for business travel expenses allowed by governments will have an impact on demand: the greater the level of deductibility, the greater the potential increase in the level of demand for business travel.

However, as Bull (1995; p.42) writes:

> In practice, governments use tax deductibility much more selectively. The United States government for example varies the dollar limit of tax-deductible travel expenses per person per day, and can allow greater deductibility for, say, domestic tourism than international tourism spending (and the daily allowances vary considerably between overseas countries visited). This changes relative effective prices, and can be used as a balance of payments policy weapon.

Economic impacts of business travel

There is no doubt that just as destinations the world over have invested in infrastructure and marketing as a way of attracting leisure visitors and the economic benefits their presence brings, the principal motivation underlying investment in facilities and services for the business travel market is a financial one.

The potential earnings from the various forms of business travel can be considerable, both for the individual companies who supply this market and for the towns and cities to which people travel on business. For this is the high-quality, high-yield end of the tourism spectrum, often characterised by lavish spending, and often bringing large numbers of high-spending visitors who, by the time the event is over, have left many of the destination's cash registers full to the brim. Smith (1990; p.68) expresses this effect vividly when he quotes the US city mayor who once said: 'When we have a convention in town, it is as if an airplane flew overhead dropping dollar bills on everyone.'

It has long been recognised that due to the higher spending levels associated with business travel, it has a greater per capita value than leisure travel in securing employment and other economic benefits.

As a rule of thumb, the ratio of daily expenditure by business travellers to that of leisure visitors is generally situated somewhere between 2:1 and 3:1. It has been estimated, for example, that business visitors to the UK spend three times more per day on average than leisure visitors. Figures from the International Passenger Survey show that in 2000 an estimated 851 000 conference visitors from abroad brought £591 million to the UK, on a spend-per-day basis spending £177   almost three times as much as the average for all visitors. In the same year, overseas attendees at UK trade fairs delivered an average daily yield of £151–£89 more than the average for all visitors to the UK (ONS, 2001).

Table 1.1 provides some indication of why these higher spending levels should be so. Most of those people travelling on business are high-spending as they themselves generally bear only a fraction of the costs. Those who are travelling in the knowledge that their expenses will be refunded usually tend to be as generous to themselves as company policy will allow.

In addition to the volume of direct turnover, business tourism in the European Economic Area (EEA) has considerable induced effects, generated, for example, by the large number of ancillary activities linked to conferences and exhibitions: space hire, stand construction, security staff and so on. In total, this induced activity is estimated to be 1.5–2 times the direct turnover of the sector (European Commission, 1996).

From the point of view of the destination and the suppliers operating there, a further advantage of business travel is that as it is less susceptible to peaks and troughs of demand than is leisure tourism: the spending is spread more evenly throughout the year, with only a slight dropping-off in demand during the peak holiday periods. This complementary pattern of demand between leisure and business travel makes the possibility of serving both markets an enticing prospect for many destinations, and a considerable number have leapt at the opportunity to move into the business tourism market. Many UK seaside resorts, for instance, have used business travel as a way of extending their season. Grant et al. (1997) give the classic examples of Brighton and Bournemouth, which have been particularly successful in developing conference tourism that is not dependent on weather and main holiday period factors.

A further advantage offered by business travel is that as it tends to occur midweek, between Monday and Thursday, its pattern of demand is also complementary to that of the short-break and daytrip markets, which tend to be concentrated at weekends. As Middleton (1994; p.B-13) remarks:

> The obvious focus of business on weekday rather than weekend travel provides a sound economic base from which leisure products can be developed and marketed. An important synergy exists between business markets and the growing short break leisure market, especially over Friday, Saturday and Sunday nights when business travel demand is lowest. A growing business travel market typically generates and sustains leisure markets in the same facilities for reasons of operating economics.

Other impacts of business travel

Although the direct economic impacts of business travel on destinations are the most prominent consequence of any city's success in attracting meetings, trade shows, incentive trips and corporate hospitality events, as well as individual business travellers, there are several other positive effects that may also motivate local and national politicians to target this market.

Image

It is clear that important events of the type discussed in this book can be an effective way of putting the destinations where they take place firmly on the political map. For example, Rogers (1998) points out that the prestige that can result from the hosting of a high-profile event such as a summit conference of heads of state or business leaders can earn the destination a considerable amount of credibility and acceptance on the international political stage.

But, pleasant though it may be for politicians to bathe in the reflected glory of having their city visited by the distinguished and the influential, destinations often have a more matter-of-fact reason for seeking to attract the business tourism market. Blank (1996; p.224) notes:

> Cities seek conventions not only for the direct income but because, in this way, they can focus the attention of key groups of decision-makers upon the city's potential for professional and business location and development. These are prominent among the reasons why nearly all large cities have located convention centres downtown in close juxtaposition to a high-amenity offering of activities to help make a good impression upon these visitors.

Thus, many destinations have recognised that business tourism can stimulate future inward investment if businesspeople see the attractions of a destination while travelling on business and then return to establish business operations there. They can also become unpaid 'ambassadors' for a destination by communicating to colleagues and others their positive impressions and favourable experiences (BTF & BTAC, 1999).

But ambassadors can also serve to establish or reinforce the image of the destination as a place to visit for leisure purposes. As Abbey and Link (1996; p.175) point out, for example, 'Through conventions, a large number of potential repeat visitors become acquainted with a tourism area. If they are treated well and pleased, they will not only advertise with word of mouth, but will also likely visit the area on other occasions.'

Environmental and social impacts

At a time when consumer concern over the potential and actual negative impacts of mass leisure tourism upon the natural, built and human environments of destinations is gaining prominence, and interest groups are putting growing pressure upon the holiday industry to display more environmental awareness, attention must also be paid to how business travel affects those towns and cities where it takes place.

Much comment on this issue is upbeat, favourably comparing the impacts of business travel with those of leisure visitors. In favour of the former, it has been argued that as business tourism tends to have a good geographical spread, it does not create the detrimental impact on the environment sometimes brought by mass leisure tourism to the holiday or daytrip 'honeypots'. Middleton (1994; p.B-13) elaborates upon this point:

> Much of business travel is accommodated in towns and cities ... where it makes minimal impact on fragile natural environments. Business visitors are typically indistinguishable from residents in dress, behaviour and use of facilities. Much of business travel is fundamentally more sustainable than many sectors of the leisure travel market.

An argument sometimes advanced in support of the more sustainable nature of business travel over its leisure equivalent is that since many business visitors use public transport, such as trains, to reach their destinations, they are supporting less polluting forms of transport than the family car, which is used so extensively for leisure travel.

But while this argument may hold some weight for much domestic business travel, it is clear that most international business-related trips are made by air, the most highly polluting mode of transport. Aviation is known to be the fastest-growing source of greenhouse gas emissions and a major contributor to climate change. A report published for the Green Party of England and Wales (Whitelegg and Fitz-Gibbon, 2001) indicates how, since the fuel that aircraft burn is not taxed, aviation's polluting impact translates into hidden economic costs that are paid not by the industry itself but by society as a whole.

The report argues that since, unlike most goods, aircraft and aviation fuel and airline tickets are zero-rated for value-added tax (VAT), this means that society as a whole is subsidising air transport. It has been estimated that if aviation's VAT zero-rating were removed, this would raise a further £1.8 billion a year (HMC&E, 2001), and that if aviation fuel were taxed at the same rate as unleaded petrol, then this would raise about £5 billion a year (Sewill, 2000). In the absence of such fiscal measures, air transport – for all purposes – continues to be subsidised by the public, regardless of whether they ever use it.

The hidden subsidies to the aviation sector are also said to include:

● health costs associated with noise and air pollution;
● costs of building and maintaining the transport infrastructure that serves airports;
● direct and indirect subsidies to the industries that supply the air transport sector, including oil and aircraft manufacturing.

Putting VAT on air travel, fuel and aircraft purchases would inevitably lead to a significant increase in airfares for business and leisure travellers alike. As the real cost of flying became more apparent, it is reasonable to expect that demand would be affected. However, as discussed earlier in this chapter, the price-elasticity of business travel means that any cutback in demand would be much more likely to come from the leisure sector – representing roughly two-thirds of all passengers using UK airports – rather than business travel.

But with one-third of air passengers travelling on business, many believe that businesses should bear some of the responsibility for aviation's negative externalities. Many businesses derive a direct economic advantage from flying their employees to meetings and missions. The net effect of the current taxation system is that those who do not fly, either for business or leisure, are subsidising those who do, and those who fly occasionally are subsidising those who fly a lot. Society's effective subsidising of those businesses that generate air travel is hardly compatible with any government's belief in both economic level playing fields and social justice.

The costs of being a business destination

It is often remarked that the costs incurred by destinations in their efforts to attract business visitors are mainly incidental, as many already have an existing leisure tourism infrastructure of hotels, airports, tourist boards, etc. that can also serve as suppliers or intermediaries for business travel.

While this may be the case for certain sectors, such as individual business travel, incentive trips and corporate hospitality, other sectors, including conferences and trade fairs, require substantial investment in specialist facilities in which such events may be held. In the case of conference centres, in particular, the investment may be subsidised wholly or partly from public funds, creating what are, in effect, often substantial opportunity costs for the host community.

To the direct costs of investing to attract business visitors must be added the cost to destinations of the various externalities which can arise as a result of hosting certain types of event. The most extreme example of this may be the cost of preparing cities for large government-related meetings. For instance, stringent security measures meant that the Italian port of Genoa was practically turned into a warzone for the G8 Summit of July 2001. Surface-to-air missiles were deployed at the airport, with sharpshooters standing by near strategic targets, and 18 000 police were posted throughout the city, which was ringed with reinforced concrete barricades and wire fences. As a result, Genoa's residents lived under siege conditions during the summit, and many left town.

The cost of these preparations, and that of putting right the damage caused by protesters during the summit, must be weighed against the financial gains that accrued to the city as a result of hosting this event. In this case, the impact on Genoa's reputation and image must also be entered on the negative side of the balance sheet.

While the Genoa example is an extreme one, it is by no means an isolated case. In the UK, the annual political party conferences, often hosted by resorts such as Blackpool, Torquay and Brighton, are accompanied by substantial security operations and disruption to the lives of local residents. Brighton police have estimated that the cost of their security measures for a single political party conference ranges between £1.5 million and £2 million (Ward, 2001).

The subject of business travel's impacts on the host community is a severely under-researched issue. While Middleton's assertion that the sociocultural impact of business tourism is minimal – since business visitors and residents closely resemble each other in appearance, behaviour, etc. – might be true for most major cities in the industrialised world, it seems highly probable that there are many examples of destinations where very visible business tourism activities and events impact directly on various personal aspects of the lives of residents. The apparently ubiquitous association of business travel with prostitution is perhaps the most obvious example. On a more subtle issue, more needs to be known about the impacts on the self-image of more disadvantaged residents seeing groups of high-spending, incentive award winners descend on their town for a few days of extravagant indulgence. In this context, it would be interesting to test whether Fredline and Faulkner's (2000) study of residents' reactions to large sporting events might be used to determine host reactions to major business travel events.

Challenges facing the business travel market

In the mid-1990s, Horwath Axe Consultants were commissioned by DG XXIII of the European Commission to measure the scope of business travel in 150 venues across 17 European countries and to identify major challenges affecting those sectors. The results, published in 1996, highlighted a number of factors that needed to be addressed if business travel in Europe was to reach its full potential. The issue of skills training for business travel was highlighted as a challenge, and this has already been discussed in the preface to this book. Some of the other major challenges identified will now be considered, and progress towards meeting those challenges will be reviewed.

Political challenges

It is generally accepted that there needs to be a greater recognition by government of the contribution that business tourism plays in the economic prosperity of communities, at national and local level. The Horwath Axe report confirmed that despite many efforts to raise the industry's profile, business tourism still suffered from a lack of identity within the wider context of European tourism (European Communities, 1996).

Rogers (1998; p.190) is among those commentators who believe that the situation, in the UK at least, has improved at the level of local government: 'Generally speaking, local government has woken up to the potential which this young industry offers, but central government is still not fully committed.' The progress made at the local authority level is acknowledged by Smith (1990; p.68), who believes that the UK can learn from the example of France on this issue:

A promotional gathering in France may find the chief promoter is the Mayor, who behaves as if he is used to going on the promotional trail to win meetings. It is a concept that has not sufficiently taken root in British town halls. But there are exceptions. Belatedly, city halls across the nation are beginning to see the benefit of meetings and are unrolling the red carpet, offering a civic reception and unlocking the drinks cupboard when a meeting comes to town.

For Smith (1990; p.66), a local authority that effectively encourages the meetings market is one that 'sees itself as a meeting place, promotes its facilities for conferences and seminars, pays at least a little attention to the search for friends among meetings planners, welcomes their delegates, and provides overt and covert inducements which can range from a free deckchair to a no-charge convention centre for 1000 people for a week'.

At the national level, much remains to be done before most European countries can be seen to be fully supportive of their business travel sectors. However, recently a number of initiatives have been taken to raise the profile of the various sectors of business travel. For example, in the attempt to highlight the value to the UK economy of the meetings industry and its contribution to the balance of payments, the major trade bodies, venues, conference organisers and suppliers launched the first National Meetings Week (www.meetpie.com/nmw) in June 2001. Another of the week's objectives was to encourage the government to recognise the importance of the meetings industry when considering future infrastructural developments. The organisers enlisted the participation of politicians and celebrities who often play a role in the meetings sector as after-dinner speakers. Much of the activity during National Meetings Week centred around the Meetings & Incentive Travel Show, a trade show held at ExCeL in London's Docklands.

Market intelligence

Linked to the issue of business travel's lack of recognition by governments are two other issues identified by Horwath Axe: the lack of standardised and properly defined terminology for the various business travel sectors, and the need for reliable statistics and regular research. Without these, it is argued, it is impossible to obtain the rigorous market intelligence required to lend credibility to this industry and to demonstrate its size and value with any degree of accuracy.

Middleton (1994; p.B-2) describes the problem:

> All interested in business travel will be fully aware of the difficulties with interpreting published data. It is a fact of life that there is no consensus on the size and value of the overall market, and no agreement even in the relatively well-defined areas of conferences, exhibitions and incentive travel. Different surveys adopt different definitions and strict comparability is impossible.

It would seem that little progress appears to have been made since Smith (1990; p.70) described how business travel terminology often confuses rather than illuminates, using the meetings sector as an illustration: 'People speak of conventions, congresses, conferences, meetings, seminars, and symposia. Efforts to clarify these terms never seem to bring lasting results and the words are fairly interchangeable.'

The challenge of terminology is linked directly to the wider issue of market research. As Rogers (1998; p.15) indicates, the shortage of statistics based on standardised terminology:

> ... has meant that governments have not taken the industry seriously as a major benefactor to national economies because it has been impossible to demonstrate clearly the economic impact that conferences can have ... What is important is the need to ensure that statistics are being collected and interpreted in a standardised way on a worldwide level, as befits a truly global industry ... This is crucial to the national and international recognition and support which the industry now deserves and demands.

The need for agreement on common definitions in the business travel sectors has become even more pressing as the first step in providing the foundation for effective research into business travel, measured from both the demand side and the supply side.

An initiative of the European Masters in Conference Management group, led by the Berufsakademie Ravensburg (www.ba-ravensburg.de), was launched in 2001, proposing to make a contribution to defining the terminology of at least one aspect of business travel, the meetings sector. Using a three-stage Delphi research method, the aim of the project was to pool the opinions of industry specialists in order to arrive at a consensus as to terminology for the meetings sector.

Technology

From the Internet to global distribution systems, unprecedented advances in information and communications technology (ICT) are having a profound impact on every aspect of how business is conducted, including business travel in all of its forms. The widespread use of technology in the business travel industry has enabled companies to increase their efficiency and profitability by being more responsive to their clients' needs and better equipped to serve them. ICT support services are playing a major role in improving back-office efficiency and the service standards extended to business travellers.

But, for an industry whose whole *raison d'être* is based on individuals' and groups' needs to communicate with each other, the question arises as to whether ICT has the potential to present itself as an actual substitution for business travel. The challenge posed by ICT is a major one indeed. With every advance in the speed and image and sound quality of satellite link-ups, and as fibre-optic cables extend their reach into more homes and offices, the potential for communication via on-screen images may gain in appeal when compared with the inconvenience, expense, consumption of time and, particularly since the events of 11 September 2001, the potential danger that business travel can involve.

Already, at the click of a mouse it is possible to download a recorded presentation in words and images from a conference in another continent, view goods being presented at a distant trade fair, or have a videoconference discussion with a client on their desktop computer.

For a number of years, the question has been asked: to what extent will ICT actually obviate the need for physical travel by replacing it? Seaton and Bennet (1996) stress that even a 15% reduction in business travel would have an immense impact on hotels, airlines, travel agents and all the other services involved in business travel on a worldwide basis. They point out that some business travel agencies are already adapting to the potential change by offering videoconferencing as an alternative to travel, and that some hotel chains are offering the same facility to their business guests.

Throughout this book, for each sector of business travel examined, we shall return to this issue of the extent to which ICT represents a friend or foe for the business travel industry.

Opportunities for the business travel industry

While the business travel industry grapples with the challenges facing it, it is important not to lose sight of the fact that there are a number of elements in the market and the market environment that provide grounds for optimism.

Supply side

Several factors are acknowledged to constitute assets for Europe as a supplier of facilities and services for the various business travel sectors. These have been identified as (European Communities, 1996):

- its attractive diversity in terms of destinations and cultures;
- its level of market maturity due to its historical position;
- the expertise and professionalism of its specialists, and the quality of its products;
- the presence of many company head offices, institutions and associations, which generates an important need for meetings and exchanges of information.

In addition, an important supply-side asset for intra-European business travel is the rapidly expanding transport infrastructure within Europe, whose high-speed trains and budget airlines continue to expand their networks, making travel for all purposes, including business, more convenient and rapid, and, in many cases, increasingly affordable. As long as the problem of major European gateways approaching their air traffic control capacities can be overcome, the continent's transport infrastructure should continue to ease the business traveller's path.

The Howarth Axe report sets all of these assets in the context of an upbeat outlook for the business tourism industry, which it has predicted will grow globally at a rate superior to that of the tourism market in general.

However, a recurrent theme of the sectoral chapters of this book is that of the growing competition that European suppliers face from other world regions for the discretionary business travel market. Just as growing numbers of leisure tourists are being tempted to visit new destinations in world regions where enthusiasm levels and promotional budgets for tourism are high, so business tourism buyers and intermediaries are increasingly being targeted by destinations eager to capture a share of this lucrative market.

Asia and Australasia in particular continue to equip themselves with the facilities and services they need in order to establish firmly their hold on the international business tourism market. And the business tourism suppliers in those world regions appear to have considerable support at the national government level. Dwyer and Mistilis (1997; p.219), for example, write:

> A former Australian government placed so much emphasis on this market that it developed a National Strategy to ensure the long term growth of the sector and to maximise the economic and social benefits to the country. Japan and Singapore have government plans to increase the number of international conventions hosted.

It is clear that in the face of such competition, which has novelty value and the falling real costs of long-haul airfares to its advantage, European cities will need to make increasing efforts to maintain their share of the global business tourism market.

Demand side

The increasing volume of world trade since the end of the Second World War has ensured the growth of business travel in line with it. Within Europe, the level of demand for business travel has also been encouraged by a relaxation of border controls and, more recently, by a harmonisation of most European Union (EU) member states' currencies.

More widely, there has been a process of internationalisation of not only businesses but also associations. Schlentrich (in Seaton and Bennett, 1996) claimed that the elimination of international trade barriers had resulted in a global marketplace, making business travel one of the most important profit and growth sectors of the tourism industry. The conclusions of the General Agreement on Free Trade (GATT) and the North American Free Trade Agreement (NAFTA) have resulted in the further breaking down of trade restrictions and have set the stage for over 120 nations to compete freely and internationally. The trend towards free market economies in the former Eastern bloc countries and moves by China towards a liberalised market economy should further encourage favourable international business travel.

As long as the trend towards growth in world trade and the internationalisation of businesses and associations continues, there will be a role for a travel industry that responds effectively to the near-universal need to meet with others face to face in order to do business.

●●●● Business travel in times of turmoil

On 11 September 2001, the global business travel industry was presented with the greatest challenge it has had to face in its entire history. Already facing the almost certain prospect of a worldwide recession, suppliers from airlines to hotels, from conference centres to car-hire companies, were preparing with all their ingenuity to weather the economic storm ahead. But nothing – not the recession of the 1990s, nor the Gulf War, nor the antiglobalisation demonstrations that turned conference cities into bloody battlefields – had had an impact on business travel comparable to that resulting from the terror attacks on New York and Washington DC that day.

Having witnessed on their computer monitors and TV screens the very symbol of business travel – jet aircraft – being turned into weapons of mass destruction, vast numbers of travellers the world over reacted in a wholly understandable manner: by cancelling their trips and finding other ways of carrying out their business. In the immediate aftermath of the events of 11 September, many companies ordered their staff to stay grounded, as they did when, a decade earlier, war broke out in the Gulf. There were widespread reports of companies seeking technological alternatives to travel, such as videoconferencing and Web-conferencing. The value of shares in such companies soared immediately.

Airlines were the first suppliers to feel the effects of reduced business traveller numbers, with one carrier, Swissair, going out of business within three weeks of the terror attacks. But city hotels in countries around the world also suffered, with some closing down entire floors as business travellers stayed away.

Despite the superficial similarities between the Gulf War and the war against international terrorism, it was not a sense of déjà vu that characterised the mood of the days immediately following the attacks. With the world in a ferment of speculation as to how events would develop, there was a near-universal feeling that the world had changed irrevocably, and that some things – yet to be defined – would never be the same again. Uncertainties multiplied and forecasts of all types become little more than a best guess.

This book has been written in the belief that the desire to travel in order to meet distant colleagues, clients and collaborators face to face and to shake the hand of friendship with them is so deep-rooted in mankind that it will inevitably triumph over the anxiety and distrustful fear of others that the forces of terror attempt to propagate. The freedom to travel on business, to meet and communicate with others, which enriches so powerfully the working lives of so many people, all over the world, is too precious a gift to be surrendered.

This book does more than describe and analyse business travel: it positively celebrates it in the names of those business travellers whose flights ended in tragedy that fateful Tuesday morning.

Case study

EIBTM: a new look for the twenty-first century

Since 1987, the European Incentive and Business Travel and Meetings (EIBTM) exhibition (Figure 1.3) has been one of the major global events for this industry. The exhibition's organisers are Reed Travel Exhibitions (RTE), which took over the event in 2000 from EIBTM Holdings Ltd, the company that ran the event for its first 13 years. RTE also organises EIBTM's sister event, Asia-Pacific Incentives & Meetings Expo (AIME) in Melbourne,

Case study *continued*

Figure 1.3 EIBTM exhibition
Source: Reed Travel Exhibitions.

Table 1.3 Attendance at EIBTM

	1988	2001
Number of countries exhibiting	54	110
Number of visitors	2850	5950

Source: Reed Travel Exhibitions.

Australia. Table 1.3 shows how the EIBTM has grown since its first year.

The three-day event held at the Palexpo Exhibition Centre in Geneva in May each year is a vital business-to-business forum that plays a key role in bringing together those who buy in the business travel, meetings and incentive markets with those who supply or promote facilities and services in these sectors: the exhibitors. Like all trade fairs, EIBTM creates an event where buyers and suppliers can meet each other, exchange information and do business together.

In general, those attending EIBTM fall into one of two main categories: exhibitors (those who are selling) and visitors (those who are buying) (Table 1.4).

In 2001, there were 3250 exhibitors present at EIBTM, from 110 countries, booking 12 220 m² of exhibition space – 14% more than in 2000.

But exhibitions only function well if the right buyers are there to meet and do business with the exhibitors. A major advantage for the exhibitors at this event is that EIBTM guarantees the attendance of key buyers from all over the world. So how are these vital participants encouraged to attend?

The Hosted Buyers' Programme

The answer lies in a unique feature of the EIBTM exhibition: its Hosted Buyers' Programme. This is a highly effective method used by EIBTM to ensure that the right buyers attend each year – and it is planned meticulously.

▶

Case study *continued*

Table 1.4 Exhibitors and visitors at EIBTM

Exhibitors	Visitors
Airlines	Visitors are responsible for organising, influencing or making budgetary decisions for:
Conference venues	
Convention and visitor bureaux	
Cruise lines/luxury train companies	• annual conventions
	• conferences and seminars
Destination management companies	• corporate meetings and hospitality
Ground transportation	• corporate travel
	• incentive travel campaigns
Health resorts/spas	• international congresses
Hotels/hotel groups	• product launches
Incentive destinations	• special events
Incentive houses/specialists	• staff motivation
	• training programmes
Meeting and conference planners	
National tourist organisations	
Publications	
Technology providers	
Trade associations	

First, the organisers liaise with industry experts to identify exactly the leading buyers in the fields of business travel, meetings and incentives – those decision makers who have the level of authority to choose, for example, venues for their organisations' meetings, or agencies to arrange business travel arrangements or incentive trips for their staff.

Once identified, these key buyers are invited to attend EIBTM at no charge to themselves, with the exhibition organisers funding their flights to Geneva (from European cities) and their hotel accommodation there for the duration of the event.

In return, Hosted Buyers agree to attend a number of 25-minute prescheduled appointments that EIBTM organises for them with exhibitors, who use their time allocated with the buyers in order to present their destination or the facilities and services they offer. Each buyer is committed to attending a set number of such appointments – three for those attending for only one day, six for

two days' attendance, and seven for those staying longer than two days. In order to maximise the appointments' usefulness, buyers and exhibitors are matched according to the interests that each party has specified.

The EIBTM team endeavours to match the interests and needs of both Hosted Buyers and exhibitors to ensure that their mutual business interests are maximised and long-term business relationships are forged. In 2001, of a total 5950 visitors to the exhibition, 3286 were Hosted Buyers, a 5.69% increase over 2000.

However, it is the interaction and discussions between all buyers and exhibitors that create the thousands of business leads and new contacts, which in turn generate sales for the suppliers and agencies who exhibit at EIBTM.

A predominantly European event

The event is first and foremost European in character. In 2001, 64% of the exhibitors and 88.52% of the visitors were from Europe. North America was the next best represented region, with 10% and 3.56%, respectively. Table 1.5 provides further details of the origins of EIBTM's visitors.

Twenty-first-century innovations

RTE's strategy for EIBTM was to make no changes to the event during its first year as its organisers, but simply to observe closely how it operated, before making any radical modifications. After the 2000 event, RTE decided that a major market research initiative was required to determine what the exhibitors and visitors thought of

Table 1.5 Geographical breakdown: visitors

Area	Attendance (%)
Europe (EU)	67.71
Europe (non-EU)	20.81
Asia	0.81
Middle East and North Africa	2.33
North America	3.56
South/Central America	0.87
South/Central Africa	0.99
South-East Asia	0.81
Australasia and Pacific	0.87
Other/blank	1.24

Source: Reed Travel Exhibitions.

Case study *continued*

EIBTM and whether any improvements were necessary. The research highlighted a number of problems, which RTE was determined to solve in time for the following year's event. The modifications and innovations introduced in 2001 were:

- *New EIBTM website*: launched to keep visitors and exhibitors up to date with advice, information and news leading up to and during the event. The site had more than 182 500 page views in the four weeks before the event, with visitors spending an average of 13 minutes on the website. Online buyers were able to conduct business via the website for the first time.
- *Better traffic flow*: following criticism of the traffic flow and signage at the exhibition in previous years, a series of improvements were made, including moving the visitor entrance and investing in detailed and very visible signage. Separate visitor and exhibitor entrances meant that queuing for badges was kept to a minimum. This was alleviated further by the introduction of pre-registration and mailing badges in advance.
- *More customer-focused approach*: EIBTM aimed to provide a higher level of customer service, using a range of innovations, from the bright yellow shirts worn by all staff so that they could be spotted easily, to the free coffee offered each morning to exhibitors before opening.
- *Second-generation Hosted Buyers' Programme*: research from the 2000 event showed that the Hosted Buyer concept was outdated and that measures to tighten and control the quality, attendance and matching of buyers to exhibitors were necessary. There was particular concern over no-shows (Hosted Buyers failing to attend appointments programmed for them) and the actual quality of some of the buyers (too many were considered to lack the authority to make real purchasing decisions on behalf of their organisations). Investment in new technology was used in order to match appointments more efficiently, monitor no-shows, and allow the whole appointment system to be coordinated online.

The customers' response

The improvements introduced by RTE were met with an overwhelmingly enthusiastic response from the vast majority of visitors and exhibitors. Typical of the exhibitors'

reactions to the changes was that of the Manager of Overseas Promotions of the Government of Dubai's Department of Tourism and Commerce Marketing:

> We participate in 28 exhibitions every year all over the world, but EIBTM is the top. There is no other event to compare. There was a big change at EIBTM this year and it was much better. We have been exhibiting here for 12 years now, going from just 18 m² and three participating companies to 250 m² and 53 participating companies, with nearly 100 representatives from Dubai.

> We saw more trade buyers and had 20 Hosted Buyer groups from Germany, the UK, France and Australia on the stand – that's 270 people – who seemed to love the relaxed atmosphere and the fact that we did not bombard them with information. The free time in the afternoon is a very good idea, as buyers came in the morning and then returned later to conduct serious detailed business with the suppliers.

As a follow-up exercise after the 2001 EIBTM, the company sent out market research questionnaires to all main standholders seeking their continuing feedback on the event.

Buyers attending the EIBTM in 2001

Tables 1.6 (a)–(g), based on RTE's research, provide data on the profile of the buyers who visited the event in 2001.

A new host city for EIBTM?

In 2001, RTE announced that since EIBTM first began, it had grown beyond all recognition in size and scope. For this reason, the company decided to ask major European cities with appropriate facilities if they wished to tender to

Table 1.6(a) Type of company

Company	Attendance % (multiple answers given)
Corporate	14.34
Association	5.68
Incentive house/agency	27.50
PR/marketing/advertising agency	5.44
Sales promotion agency	2.72
Conference organiser/ meeting planner	13.46
Outbound travel agency	10.27
Other/blank	25.01

Source: Reed Travel Exhibitions.

▶

Case study *continued*

host the exhibition post-2003, when the contract with the Palexpo Exhibition Centre in Geneva expired. The decision was to be taken in 2002, based on the views of exhibitors, the EIBTM Advisory Council, and post-event visitor and exhibitors research.

Table 1.6(b) Job title

Job title	Attendance %
President/owner/MD	24.44
Director/general manager	15.77
Manager	18.97
Executive	2.34
Coordinator	1.39
Organiser/planner	17.80
Administrator/assistant	2.76
Other/blank	16.53

Source: Reed Travel Exhibitions.

Table 1.6(c) industry/business area

Industry	Attendance % (multiple answers given)
Automobiles	16.08
Electronic/communication/IT	23.03
Pharmaceutical/medical/chemical	27.19
Food/beverage/tobacco/cosmetic	19.48
Engineering/building	3.01
Industrial goods (general)	12.19
Financial/insurance/banking	23.13

Source: Reed Travel Exhibitions.

Table 1.6(d) Level of responsibility

Level of responsibility	Attendance %
Final decision	22.17
Recommend	14.14
Research	8.82
Plan/organise	35.80
Blank/unspecified	19.07

Source: Reed Travel Exhibitions.

Table 1.6(e) Product interest

Product interest	Attendance % (multiple answers given)
Airlines	34.62
Conference venues	43.59
Convention and visitor bureaux	33.60
Cruise lines/luxury train companies	23.79
Destination management companies	40.99
Event management specialists	33.89
Ground agents	22.47
Hotel/hotel groups	53.87
Incentive destinations	49.16
National tourist organisations	26.20
Publications	9.47
Technology providers	10.48
Health resorts and spas	19.69

Source: Reed Travel Exhibitions.

Table 1.6(f) Type of events organised

Type of event	Attendance % (multiple answers given)
Conference/meeting	62.91
International convention	34.91
Incentive travel	55.05
Product launch	25.83
Staff training/special events	33.22
Business travel	30.01

Source: Reed Travel Exhibitions.

Table 1.6(g) Number of events organised per year

Number of events	Attendance %
1–5	19.24
6–10	14.51
10+	48.27
Blank/unspecified	17.98

Source: Reed Travel Exhibitions.

Case study *continued*

Questions

1 What reasons can be given for the geographical profile of EIBTM being so dominated by Europe and North America? How would it compare with the geographical profile of AIME?

2 From the data presented on the buyers' profile in Tables 1.6 (a)–(g), what evidence is there that the EIBTM has been successful in attracting the right type of buyers?

3 Regarding a possible new host city for EIBTM, what are likely to be the 'appropriate facilities' required?

4 Undertake research to find out which city won the new contract to host EIBTM – and why.

5 A new meetings and incentive travel exhibition – IMEX, based in Frankfurt – was launched, for 2003. How does it seek to differentiate itself from EIBTM? (www.imex-frankfurt.com)

References

Abbey, J.R. and Link, C.K. (1996), 'The convention and meetings sector – its operation and research needs', in Ritchie, J.R.B. and Goeldner, C.R. (eds), *Travel, Tourism and Hospitality Research*, New York, John Wiley & Sons.

Blank, U. (1996), 'Tourism in United States cities', in Law, C.M. (ed.), *Tourism in Major Cities*, London, Routledge.

BTF & BTAC (1999), *Business Tourism Leads the Way*, London, Business Tourism Forum & Business Tourism Advisory Committee.

Bull, A. (1995), *The Economics of Travel and Tourism*, Melbourne, Longman.

Davidson, R. (2001), 'Distribution channels analysis for business travel', in Laws, E. and Buhalis, D., *Tourism Distribution Channels: practices, issues and transformations*, London, Continuum.

Dwyer, L. and Mistilis, N. (1997), 'Challenges to MICE tourism in the Asia-Pacific region', in Opperman, M. (ed.), *Pacific Rim Tourism*, Wallingford, CAB International.

European Communities (1996), *Business and Conference Tourism in the European Economic Area*, Brussels, European Commission.

Fredline, E. and Faulkner, B. (2000), 'Host community reactions: a cluster analysis', *Annals of Tourism Research*, Vol. 27, p. 3.

Grant, M., Human, B. and Le Pelley, B. (1997), 'Seasonality', *Insights*, July, pp. A5–9.

HMC&E (2001), Annual Report, London, HM Customs & Excise.

Middleton, V.T.C. (1994), 'Business tourism in the UK', *Insights*, July.

ONS (2001), *International Passenger Survey*, London, Office for National Statistics.

Rogers, T. (1998), *Conferences: a twenty-first century industry*, Harlow, Addison Wesley Longman.

Seaton, A.V. and Bennett, M.M., (1996), *Marketing Tourism Products*, London, Thomson Business Press.

Sewill, B. (2000), *Tax Free Aviation*, London, Aviation Environment Federation.

Smith, G.V. (1990), 'The growth of conferences and incentives', in Quest, M. (ed.), *Horwath Book of Tourism*, London, Macmillan.

Ward, L. (2001), 'Blockade faces Blair at Brighton', *The Guardian*, 15 August.

Whitelegg, J. and Fitz-Gibbon, S. (2001), *Aviation's Economic Downside*, London, Green Party.

WTO (1993), *Definitions Concerning Tourism Statistics*, Madrid, World Tourism Organisation.

Chapter 2

Individual business travel

Objectives

On completion of this chapter, you should be able to:

- *explain the relationships between the three component parts of the individual business travel sector – clients, travel suppliers and intermediaries;*

- *identify the principal factors influencing the development and dynamics of the individual business travel sector;*

- *explain the complexity of individual business travel purchasing decisions, identifying the range of decisions to be made and the individuals and groups involved in making them;*

- *analyse the impacts on suppliers and intermediaries of the service characteristics of individual business travel products and review strategies in use to address them;*

- *describe responses by individual business travel suppliers and intermediaries to changes in demand and in their operating environments.*

Individual business travel in the twenty-first century

- Two employees working in the legal department of IBM fly to Sao Paulo on a two-day trip to discuss the details of a supply contract between their company and its Brazilian subsidiary.
- At very short notice, a journalist flies to Aberdeen and hires a car to take him to a secluded Highland castle, where an American actor and his wife are on holiday. He carries out an exclusive interview with the actor and returns to London the following day.
- A government minister travels by TGV from Paris to her constituency in Lyon for a press conference, and travels back to Paris the same day.
- A telephone engineer flies from London to Belgrade to work for three weeks with a team of engineers repairing and replacing phone systems damaged during the conflict in Serbia.

Introduction

It is fashionable to speak of a *hypermobile* world: one in which at any moment there are over 360 000 people in the air and where, every day, at least four million people catch a plane (Doyle and Nathan, 2001). Yet the increases in mobility – for both work and leisure – are spread far from evenly, and there is growing evidence of a yawning mobility gap in society. At one extreme, there is a supermobile elite spending its time shuttling between global cities, airport lounges and opulent hotels; at the other extreme, there is a practically immobile group. For it is a startling fact that even in an economy as industrialised as the UK's, 50% of its population still lives and works within 5 miles of where they were born (Doyle and Nathan, 2001).

One important contributing factor to determining anyone's place along the mobility spectrum is whether they are in work. This chapter focuses on those people in employment whose work obliges them to travel routinely and regularly: the 'road warriors' of business travel.

Individual business travel refers to any trip away from the traveller's normal workplace undertaken in the course of doing his or her job. For reasons of convenience, it is often referred to as 'corporate travel', although it includes not only the travel of those employed by companies but also travel undertaken on behalf of other organisations, such as governments and universities. It can involve domestic or international travel, by air, sea, road or rail. It can involve overnight stays and the purchasing of extra services at the destination, such as car rental or interpretation and secretarial services. Figure 2.1 illustrates the three key components of this sector – suppliers, customers ('corporate clients') and intermediaries.

The roles of, and relationships between, these three components are subject to constant change. Suppliers, intermediaries and corporate clients all operate

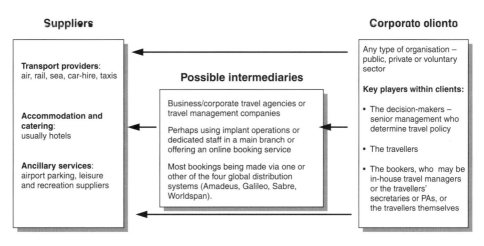

Figure 2.1 The three components of the individual business sector

in a fast-evolving market environment in which they must adapt to political, economic, social and technological changes in order to survive and succeed. As each of the three types of players in the chain attempts to adapt, the others are affected directly and indirectly, creating a dynamic that makes corporate travel an exciting and constant challenge for all involved.

This chapter investigates the roles of the three main components of the individual business travel sector. First, the nature and needs of the corporate client will be explored. The remainder of the chapter will focus on the respective responses of corporate travel suppliers and intermediaries to changes in demand and to external forces and influences.

The development of corporate travel

Work-related travel is not a new phenomenon. As soon as an organisation looks outside its home base for new markets or new suppliers, or whenever it contemplates setting up additional operations in new locations, the need for corporate business travel is created. As international trade barriers have diminished, so international business and thus corporate travel have expanded. The corporate travel sector grew substantially in the latter part of the twentieth century and is poised to continue this expansion into the twenty-first century. The World Travel and Tourism Council, as cited in O'Brien (1998), forecast a 3.7% annual growth rate (in real terms) in business travel spending across Europe alone in the period between 1998 and 2010. Some of the growth in this sector can be attributed to increases in business-class airfares, but the main reason is the tremendous expansion in numbers of people travelling on business.

As we mentioned in Chapter 1, increasing globalisation means that few companies can afford *not* to travel on business. Even in periods of slow growth or even recession, it is now generally accepted that the global nature of business is such that the number of business trips taken is unlikely to decline dramatically. As the director of American Express Consulting put it, 'A business that needs people to travel so they can generate revenue can't afford to cut out travel' (Rice, 2001; p.15).

Business travel patterns

It is widely acknowledged that establishing accurate numbers of people travelling, let alone distinguishing between those doing so for business or for leisure purposes, is not an exact science, and surveys of all kinds need to be treated with a certain amount of caution.

One useful contribution to the data currently available is the International Air Transport Association (IATA) annual survey of international airline passengers travelling on business, the Corporate Air Travel Survey (www.iata.org/air/cats.htm). This is based on the responses of 1000 frequent business travellers surveyed at airports worldwide and via the Internet. In a sector that is low on reliable data, the IATA findings are welcomed by both suppliers and intermediaries, even though the limited number of respondents necessarily creates an incomplete picture of the sector and excludes the views of a number of important players. For example, the responses of the business passengers questioned may not reflect exactly the views of their company directors, who are more likely to be the people making the key decisions concerning corporate travel policy; likewise, the views of those business travellers in Europe who may have transferred allegiance from short-haul air travel to high-speed intercity train are also unvoiced in the IATA survey.

Research into corporate business travel is also commissioned by a wide range of interested parties, including agencies, consultancies and suppliers, all of whose interests, sampling techniques and selection criteria necessarily influence their final survey findings.

One source from which useful data can be extrapolated for business travel to and from the UK is the International Passenger Survey, published by the Office for National Statistics (www.statistics.gov.uk). Table 2.1 provides a comparison between outbound and inbound travel to the UK for the years 1998–2000, showing the numbers of business trips taken and whether they were by air or by surface (sea or tunnel). The figures reveal that while both outbound and inbound busines

Table 2.1 International business trips from and to the UK

	Total UK outbound business trips	UK outbound business trips by air	UK outbound business trips by sea and tunnel	Total inbound business trips to the UK	UK inbound business trips by air	UK inbound business trips by sea and tunnel
1998	8 032 000	6 077 000	1 955 000	6 883 000	5 555 000	1 328 000
1999	8 161 000	6 400 000	1 761 000	7 044 000	5 480 000	1 564 000
2000	8 872 000	6 946 000	1 926 000	7 321 000	5 776 000	1 545 000

Figures have been rounded to the nearest 1000.

Source: International Passenger Survey © Crown copyright 2002. Reproduced with the permission of the Controller of Her Majesty's Stationery Office (HMSO).

Table 2.2 International business trips from the UK, by destination area

Year	North America	EU	Other Western Europe	Other	Total
1998	771 000	5 878 000	466 000	917 000	8 032 000
1999	810 000	5 871 000	499 000	981 000	8 161 000
2000	965 000	6 420 000	477 000	1 010 000	8 872 000

Figures have been rounded to the nearest 1000.

Source: International Passenger Survey © Crown copyright 2002. Reproduced with the permission of the Controller of Her Majesty's Stationery Office (HMSO).

travel are growing, the number of outbound trips made by UK residents regularly exceeds the number of inbound trips made by overseas business travellers (in 1998 by 17%, in 1999 by 16%, and in 2000 by 21%). Over 75% of all busines trips, whether outbound or inbound, are made by air rather than surface.

Further details of outbound corporate travel are given in Table 2.2. It can be seen that over the three years covered by the data, this increased to North America, the EU and the rest of the world, with the greatest number of trips by far being to Europe. Indeed, the authors of a business report published by Key Note Ltd commented that the UK had witnessed a 'change in business culture, which accepts that a trip to the near continent is little different from a trip to other parts of the UK' (Key Note, 2000; p.21).

Additional information on the European corporate travel market in particular is provided by the World Travel and Tourism Council, whose data, shown in Table 2.3 compare the corporate travel spending of 15 European countries, including spending on domestic business trips, and indicate corporate travel spending as a percentage of total travel expenditure in each country.

It is interesting to note that the countries for whom business travel represents a higher proportion of their total spending on travel (e.g. Turkey, Greece, Portugal) are often those that have correspondingly lower gross national products (GNPs) and populations that spend far less per capita on leisure travel than those living in countries such as Germany, the UK and the Netherlands, where business travel's share of total travel spending is much lower.

The purchasing process

A key feature of the corporate travel market is that travel purchasing decisions are taken at two different levels:

● *Company-wide travel policy decisions*: these set the context within which the second level of decisions are taken, and may take the form of a written company travel policy

● *Day-to-day purchasing decisions*: travel arrangements for individual business trips are taken within the parameters and conditions set by the company-wide travel policy.

Table 2.3 Corporate travel in Europe

	Business travel spending (US dollars, billions)	Comparative share of spending (%)	Business travel spending (% share of total travel spending)	Forecast annual growth in business travel 1998–2010 (%)
France	32.2	17.3	24.9	3.1
Italy	27.5	14.8	28.5	3.8
Germany	26.7	14.4	13.2	3.3
UK	26.4	14.2	17.6	3.6
Spain	17.7	9.5	34.6	5.4
Switzerland	7.5	4	26.5	3.1
Netherlands	6.7	3.6	18.1	2.4
Turkey	5.7	3.1	37.3	11.5
Sweden	4.7	2.5	25.7	3.1
Denmark	3.5	1.9	25.2	2.5
Greece	3.5	1.9	33.6	5.5
Finland	3.1	1.7	26.5	4
Norway	2.9	1.6	24.4	3.3
Portugal	2.5	1.3	32.3	4.4
Ireland	1.7	0.9	35.6	5.5
Total (including others)	**186**	**100**		

Source: O'Brien, K. (1998), 'The European business travel market', *Travel and Tourism Analyst*, No. 4, 1998/Mintel's Travel Intelligence.

Clearly, travel purchasing decisions require the involvement of many different groups within companies, and are usually the product of the combined (and sometimes conflicting) needs, wants and influences of a range of contributors. Figure 2.2 suggests a depiction of the roles of the various participants in the decision-making unit (DMU).

Each of these roles will now be explored. However, it is important first of all to recognise that:

● for some simple purchasing decisions, one person could conceivably combine several of the roles shown in Figure 2.2, whereas for more complex issues the number of people involved in the process is likely to be higher;
● given the distinction between policy decisions and day-to-day travel planning, the relative level of power and importance of the various roles contributing to the DMU will vary considerably.

Buyers

This role is played by the companies and organisations that purchase individual business travel for their employees. They provide the funds that ultimately fuel the

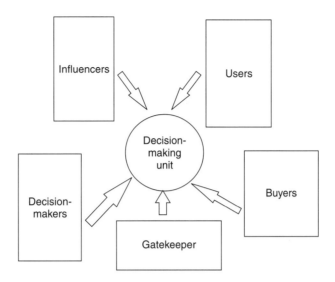

Figure 2.2 Roles contributing to the decision-making unit

Source: Adapted from Palmer, A. (2001), *Principles of Services Marketing,* 3rd edn, McGraw-Hill, Maidenhead, p.97. Reproduced with the permission of McGraw-Hill.

whole individual business travel market. This is not to say, of course, that their spending on travel is not open to the scrutiny of others. In the case of listed companies, for example, their shareholders, among others, have access to company accounts, which include mention of the spending on this item. Public organisations, such as universities and local authorities, are also open to scrutiny by auditors, for example, who can examine in detail the spending on trips made by staff.

With expenditure on corporate travel now representing the third highest element of companies' expenditure after salaries and data-processing (American Express, 1999), travel has come to represent a very significant cost for many buyers.

End users

As we stated in Chapter 1, the end users or end consumers of business travel services are rarely the same people who are responsible for purchasing these services. Most of the end users in the corporate business travel sector are those employees who travel on company business. Who are they and what do they need in terms of service?

Although the classic image of the business traveller is the senior manager comfortably ensconced with a glass of complimentary champagne in business class, this is only one aspect of the reality of who the end users of individual business travel effectively are. Although senior managers may represent a significant percentage of the *international* business travel market (followed closely by middle and junior management), when domestic corporate business travel is taken into account, it is a company's field and sales staff who constitute the largest single group of end users (Davidson, 1994).

Reflecting the gender profile of management in general, most of those travelling on company business are male. Within Europe, it has been estimated that the average proportion of women among business travellers is 13%. However, it is generally recognised that the UK, with its relatively high proportion of women in employment, has the highest percentage of female business travellers. Collis (2000) estimates that women account for over 20% of the UK market.

For comparative purposes, the findings from two surveys conducted in the USA provide a profile of business travellers in that country: the Runzheimer Survey and Analysis of Business Travel Policies and Costs 2000 (www.runzheimer. com/tmc/scripts/satravel.asp) and the OAG Market Research and TIA Survey of Business Travellers 1998, which incorporates the National Travel Survey 1998 (www2.oag.com). Their results reveal that:

- one in five (22%) adults in the USA makes at least one business trip per year; the number of people travelling for business has increased by 14% since 1994 and 2% since 1996;
- business travellers take an average of five trips a year;
- the business sectors that generate most corporate travel are:
  - health
  - law
  - education
  - manufacturing
  - finance
  - banking
  - real estate
- the proportion of women business travellers has risen from 34% in 1994, to 38% in 1996, to 41% in 1998;
- men take more business trips than women (an average of seven for men compared with four for women);
- the average age of the business traveller is 42;
- the key destinations of US business travellers are domestic rather than international.

The most striking contrast is the very high proportion of US business travellers who are women. It seems likely, however, that as European economies continue to shift away from manufacturing towards the service sector, where women are better represented in management structures, the gap between Europe and the USA in this respect will narrow.

What do business travellers need in terms of service? Generally, their priorities are focused on the effectiveness and quality of the travel products purchased. They seek convenience, comfort, reliability, stress-free travel arrangements and prompt resolution of any service failure.

It is often said that business travel appears glamorous and exciting only to those who never do it. In general, for most people, travelling for work-related purposes, with all the pressures which that can entail, often becomes more of a chore than a pleasure, with any problems occurring during a business trip likely to be perceived as a major aggravation. Box 2.1 shows an extract from a letter published in the trade press demonstrating the types of frustration experienced by two colleagues travelling on business.

The fact that a presumably busy person has devoted time and energy in order to express his criticisms in this way confirms that service-level expectations of business travellers are extremely high. Since their companies are usually paying handsomely for the services that end users need, they are all the more intolerant of disappointing experiences such as this.

Gatekeepers

Gatekeeper roles are assumed by people who can use their influence and authority within the company or organisation in order to limit the options available to DMUs. They are generally people at a very senior level within the company management who intervene occasionally to impose their will on policy-level purchasing decisions.

Box 2.1

Road warrior rage

Dear Sirs,

I stayed at the ******** Airport Hotel, Heathrow, recently and would rate it the worst of the 20 or so airport hotels I have experienced in 12 cities in eight countries … Our complaints include the following:

No late-opening restaurant/coffee shop (we arrived at 11.30 p.m. having missed connections and meals as a result of disruptive weather); room service offering only sandwiches.

A queue at check-in (although check-out was good).

An extremely poor room: no wake-up alarm; no safe; only one of the four lamps worked; no desk and the only possible area to work in was unlit; only two tea bags and two milk sachets.

When we paid our bill, the desk clerk asked if everything was all right. When I explained that the room was sub-standard, the clerk apologised and asked what I would like done about it. Clearly, the original question was asked purely as lip service to customer care, not to elicit a genuine response, otherwise the desk clerk would have known what should have been done. (Incidentally, the staff we dealt with were uniformly efficient and polite.)

Yours etc. . . .

Source: Business Traveller Magazine, March 1999.

For example, a senior manager in the role of gatekeeper may intervene in a policy-level decision such as the choice of a business travel agent to serve the company, by insisting that the agency currently servicing the company's travel account is not invited to retender for that account. This might happen, for example, when the senior manager has been dissatisfied with the agency's service provision.

Decision-makers

The role of decision-makers in the purchasing process is played by those people who have the authority to select specific suppliers and intermediaries. This can occur at the two levels already described: the company-wide and the day-to-day levels. At the former level, decision-makers would be those within the company's management team who set the company's travel policy or designate specific airlines, hotel groups and car-rental firms to be used by individual travellers. If an intermediary is to be used, then the choice of which one to contract is also made by the decision-makers. This role may be played by the company's procurement manager or its managing director, for example. Alternatively, it is a role that may fall to the company's travel manager if there is one. Companies that have a large travel spend often employ a travel manager (or travel coordinator) to negotiate centrally with suppliers and intermediaries on behalf of the entire company. If an intermediary is used, then it is part of the travel manager's responsibility to liaise directly with them.

At the day-to-day level of decision-making, choices are made by those in the company who are given the task of booking hotel rooms, airline tickets and car-hire for the end users. These decisions are occasionally made by the end users themselves, but more commonly the business traveller's secretary or PA makes the arrangements for them. As it is usually these people rather than the actual travellers who have direct contact with the travel agency, their priorities are concerned with the ease, effectiveness and reliability of the booking and ticket-delivery process.

However, the choices made by the secretaries, PAs and end users are rarely made at their complete discretion. This is largely because the priorities of the decision-makers often differ in some respects from those of the end users who actually make the trips. For example, a key concern of decision-makers is usually cost control, whereas the priority of the business travellers may well be maximum luxury, prestige and comfort. Increasingly, cost-conscious decision-makers are attempting to drive down travel-related costs, while still ensuring that their employees arrive at their destinations fit, prepared and motivated to do the job required of them.

Where one exists, end users, secretaries and PAs have to work within the company's *travel policy*, which is in general compiled by those decision-makers who have a company-wide role and who use their authority to influence the choices made by the other decision-makers.

A clearly written, comprehensive travel policy is seen by a growing number of employers as the cornerstone in controlling and reducing their travel-related expenses. Such documents provide staff with a vital point of reference for determining their company's policy on business travel and enabling them to make travel arrangements within clearly defined guidelines. Most company travel policies offer guidelines on issues such as which suppliers are to be used and what class of travel and category of hired car are permitted. They may contain specifications such as:

- no-frills (or low-cost) airlines to be used for short-haul flights whenever possible;
- business-class air travel only permitted on flights of more than three hours' duration;
- hotel bookings in no higher than three-star accommodation;
- preferred airlines, hotels and car-hire companies (with whom corporate discounts may have been arranged) to be used whenever possible;
- a ban on employees using business travel to accumulate personal air miles.

According to a report compiled by Carlson Wagonlit Travel (1999), 80% of companies employing over 500 people have a formal travel policy in place. Others may use informal guidelines, although these are generally considered to be less effective in controlling travel costs.

Influencers

Purchasing choices made by people in the roles already discussed – end users, buyers, gatekeepers and decision-makers – will be subject to a range of influences based on:

- their own personal experience and perceptions of corporate travel;
- the recommendations and criticisms of other people within their own company and other companies;
- press articles and media broadcasts;
- the sales and marketing undertaken by the travel suppliers and agencies themselves.

For key policy-level decisions, such as which intermediary to contract or which airline to use, those involved in the process will seek guidance from colleagues in other companies and from influential bodies such as the Institute of Travel Management (ITM) (www.itm.org.uk) in the UK or the National Business Travel Association (NBTA) (www.nbta.org) in the USA, both of which are organisations set up by and for corporate travel managers, partly with the aim of researching and providing their members with information so that their purchasing decisions can be as well-informed as possible.

The importance of the media as influencers means that constant efforts are made by business travel agents to retain a high press profile in order that the buyers who are their current and potential customers become aware of any prestigious new accounts they gain and of their high client satisfaction ratings. For example, excellent public relations would have been gained from the headline 'Rosenbluth wins British Aerospace account', followed by an article naming the four other major business travel agencies that Rosenbluth had beaten in the competition for the £45 million account (Young, 1999a).

● ● ● ● Suppliers

A great number of different suppliers are involved in providing services for the corporate travel market. Those travelling on business need a range of different forms of accommodation, from hotels and motels to bed-and-breakfasts and, for the longer-term business visitor, self-contained flats. Taxis, rented cars, trains and airlines transport business travellers to their destinations and back. Many city-centre restaurants and bars depend for their economic survival upon their business clientele's expense accounts. In this section, however, we shall concentrate on those two types of supplier identified most closely with the business travel market: airlines and hotels.

Airlines

The relationship between air travel suppliers and those who use their services has been, at times, a turbulent one. Much of the tension between the buyers and suppliers in this market arises from, on the one hand, the need of the airlines to maximise their profit from business passengers and, on the other, the wish of the buyers to spend less on this major item of expenditure.

Until the recession of the early 1990s, companies spent liberally on sending executives to their overseas destinations by air. The general pattern was that upon entering the aircraft, business travellers (and the very rich) would turn left for first- and business-class seats, while leisure travellers would turn right to take up their places in economy class (Figure 2.3).

However, the recession brought this neat arrangement to an end: most businesses were forced to reduce travel costs, and many traded down from business class to

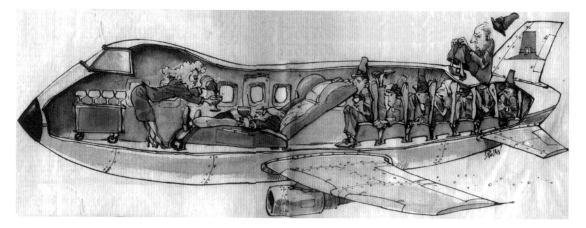

Figure 2.3 Some airlines try to entice the corporate traveller to choose business class

Source: © Ted Dewan. Reproduced with the permission of Ted Dewan, www.wormworks.com.

economy class for their employees. For short-haul flights in particular, company managers realised that the considerable difference in fares between the two classes of travel could not be justified and so continued to use economy class even after the economic situation had improved. American Express's 1999 Global Travel and Entertainment Expense Management Survey found that even by the end of the 1990s, economy fares still accounted for 72% of business travel (Young, 1999b).

In the attempt to persuade corporate clients to abandon economy class and return to the front of the plane, the strategy of most airlines has been to shower increasingly lavish facilities on to their business-class passengers – larger seats, extra facilities in the lounges and on the aircraft, fast-track check-ins, improved loyalty schemes, etc. In order to justify the continuing high cost of seats in business class, Upton (2001) describes some of the enhancements that some airlines are introducing, particularly into their long-haul business-class cabins, to make them appear more attractive and better value for money for passengers. In 2001, for example, a number of carriers, including SAS, Singapore Airlines and Cathay Pacific, introduced beds in business class following the initiative taken first by British Airways (BA) in 1999. Cathay Pacific's beds are two inches longer than those of BA and half an inch wider. Like BA's, they come with an adjustable privacy screen, adjustable headrest, and an extra collapsible table. They also offer an in-seat laptop power source, telephone and USB socket, a 10.5-inch TV screen to watch videos on demand, a bar and a reception area for passengers to mingle in-flight, and a dressing room.

However, corporate consumers, continuing to tighten their travel budgets, have shown great reluctance to return to spending considerable sums on business-class air travel. In fact, the cost-conscious corporate market has been more tempted by the products offered by suppliers more in tune with their need to make economies. These products usually take one of two forms:

- No-frills flights offered by low-cost carriers, such as easyJet, Ryanair, Go, Buzz and Virgin Express. The success of such airlines in the corporate travel market came as a surprise to many commentators in the industry, who originally believed that they would be used only by the leisure travel segment. Collis (2000; p.134) notes that 'No-frills is the fastest-growing sector of the airline industry in Europe, which, analysts say, could triple in the next five years'. As support for his statement, he cites the Mintel 'No-Frills/Low Cost Airlines' report, which, in February 1999, predicted that the sector would grow from 5.4 million passengers in 1998 to 15 million in 2003.
- New classes of travel that offer the flexibility of a business-class-type ticket – no amendment or cancellation charges and a full refund if travel plans change – as well as greater comfort than economy class. Such in-between products include BA's World Traveller Plus service, which, for a relatively small addition to the standard economy fare, provides the opportunity to sit in improved accommodation on the plane separate from the other economy passengers (Davies, 2000). Virgin Atlantic's Premier and SAS' Economy Extra are further examples of this trend.

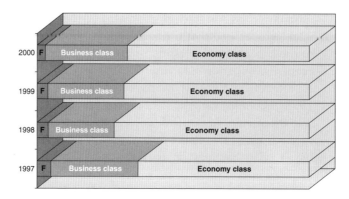

Figure 2.4 Passengers' usual class of travel on short-haul flights

Source: IATA Corporate Air Travel Survey 2000.

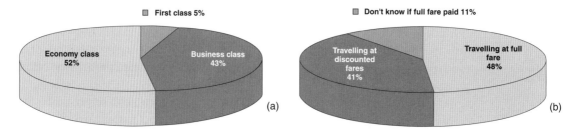

(a)

(b)

Figure 2.5 (a) Long-haul class of travel for business travellers; (b) travellers on discounted fares in first and business class on long-haul flights

Source: IATA Corporate Air Travel Survey 2000.

Those companies who are still prepared to pay for business-class travel for employees do so mainly for those who are travelling long distances and who must go straight to work on arrival at their destination, since the increased comfort and facilities usually ensure that they arrive in a better state of mind and health, as well as having had the opportunity to work en route.

Figure 2.4 shows the habitual use of the three classes of travel by airline passengers. After regular falls in the proportion of passengers using business class during the early 1990s, the situation appears to have stabilised.

However, what Figure 2.4 does not reveal is that more companies have been negotiating discounted fares in business class, thus directly affecting the airline's yield. Findings from the IATA Corporate Air Travel Survey 2000 indicate that while almost half the long-haul business air travellers surveyed were using the premium classes (first or business), over 40% of those had negotiated discounted fares. Figure 2.5 illustrates this.

Hotels

Like the airlines, the hotel sector has had to adapt to the changing needs of business travellers, with the optimum balance between cost, convenience and comfort constantly being sought by the corporate customer. Wishing – or needing – to be more industrious and productive while travelling on company business, many business guests in hotels have come to require much more than a quiet room. They increasingly want hotels to be not so much home from home but offices away from the office; in response, major hotel chains and independent hotels have introduced a range of in-room facilities, such as computers, modems and fax machines. At the Hilton, Heathrow, for example, for a time-based fee, guests can use a high-tech personal computer built into a stylish desk in their rooms, giving them fax/email/Internet access, together with scanning, printing and CD sound facilities. Translation and photocopying services are among the additional services that may be made available in hotels' business centres, which offer guests the full range of secretarial and support services during their stay.

However, the need to drive down travel budgets has meant that many companies are seeking the hotel equivalent of the no-frills airline. This has assisted the growth of low-cost hotel brands such as Travelodge and Travel Inn in the UK, and the French budget chains Formule 1 and Campanile. These brands, successfully serving the growing cost-conscious market segment of the business travel market, have carved out a place for themselves in the portfolios of a number of major hotel groups.

Brand loyalty is something that most chains recognise as a highly desirable quality in their business guests; in the attempt to foster this, chains are increasingly creating their own loyalty clubs for the frequent traveller. The principal benefits of belonging to such clubs are said to be substantial savings of both time and money for members. For example, the late check-out or early check-in facilities offered to certain hotel loyalty cardholders can mean avoiding the expense of paying for an extra night's accommodation, while express check-in/check-out facilities make for valuable time savings. Free room upgrades, discounts on laundry and telephone surcharges, and free accommodation at weekends are among the other perks proffered by hotel chains in their effort to create loyal clients out of their business guests (Davidson, 1994).

Suppliers and their female clients

As their business clientele have come to include more women, both airlines and hotels have had to respond to the needs of the increasing numbers of female business travellers. Personal security and hotel facilities are both major considerations. A recent Expotel 'Women Aware' survey indicated that women's top ten list of needs from hotels were, in order of importance (Collis, 2000):

1 Well-lit, secure carparks or valet parking.
2 Room security locks.
3 Permanently lit corridors during the hours of darkness.
4 Security peepholes in room doors.
5 Issuing of room numbers in a discreet manner by reception staff.

6 Rooms that are not on the ground floor.
7 Hairdryers.
8 Ironing boards.
9 More workspace.
10 Full-length mirrors.

It is generally believed that airlines too could do much more to make their female business passengers feel looked after. Collis (2000; p.98) cites the results of a survey of female business travellers conducted by Total Research Corporation of Princeton, New Jersey, in which all airlines received low image and performance scores, mainly because of 'rudeness and lack of help from staff, and the perception that men get preferential treatment'. Only 18% of the women polled felt that airlines made special efforts to cater for women travellers. Conclusions drawn by the researchers were: 'There's a mindset among airlines, hotels and car-rental firms that they are delivering what women travellers want: but the reality is they are not: they do not understand the special needs and concerns of women.'

There are, however, examples of organisations addressing the needs of female travellers. The Red Carnation hotel group (www.redcarnationhotels.com), for example, has created a list of Safety Points for the Female Traveller, giving advice on hotel choice, room security, and personal safety in transit and at the destination. The magazine *Executive Woman* has also developed a scheme called Facilitator, which hotels 'prepared to go that extra mile to be woman-friendly' (Collis, 2000; p.100) are invited to join. The names and locations of the member hotels are then publicised through the magazine.

The challenges faced by suppliers

As service providers, all suppliers in the corporate travel market need to address the five service characteristics identified by Palmer (2001): intangibility, inseparability, variability, perishability and lack of ownership.

Intangibility

Of the five characteristics identified by Palmer (2001), this is the one that least concerns corporate travel suppliers. While leisure travel providers must provide reassurance to their customers, for whom holidays can be perceived as a risk purchase (since they cannot be sampled in advance), intangibility is rarely a cause of concern to business travellers, who usually have a clear idea of what to expect of the business travel product from the information available to them and from their prior experience.

Inseparability and variability

These service characteristics are closely linked. Because a service is inseparable – produced and consumed simultaneously – clients are affected directly by any service failures To this challenge must be added the element of variability, sometimes referred to as heterogeneity – the fact that the experiences of service processes and encounters are unlikely to be the same for all clients as a result of a range of factors, including human fallibility (on the part of service providers, for example), the variability of natural surroundings (such as the weather), occasional equipment failure, and variations in clients' taste, mood, perceptions, etc.

To address the combined challenges posed by inseparability and variability, corporate travel suppliers adopt a range of strategies. These include:

- *Attempting to separate production and consumption*: e.g. car-hire companies prepare all the documentation in advance of a client coming to collect a car so that the formalities and queuing can be reduced to an absolute minimum. Another example can be seen at the Peninsula Hotel Group, where telephones in clients' rooms are preprogrammed with a range of information so that, for instance, incoming calls are diverted automatically to their mobile phones when they are out of the room (Fox, 1999).
- *Improving the service delivery system*: by analysing the processes and streamlining them. United Airlines, for example, has announced the introduction of mobile check-in facilities at Heathrow Airport following trials in the USA (Noakes, 2001a).
- *Managing the service-consumption process*: the service can be broken down into critical incident points (CIPs) – those moments when customers are in direct contact with what they believe to be the service provider. Once these CIPs have been identified, strategies can be developed to ensure that the consumer's experience is a positive one at each of them. One strategy adopted frequently in this regard is to train staff to adhere to a script, providing them with a blueprint of how best to respond in different situations. While this does create consistency in service quality, care has to be taken not to offend clients by dealing with them mechanically, and not to demotivate employees by dictating their responses (Bateson and Hoffman, 1999).
- *Selecting, training and motivating staff*: while the extensive use of critical incident point analysis and blueprinting might suggest that standardisation of staff input is a specific goal of the organisation, this is generally not the case. Most business travel suppliers would echo the view of Travelstore sales director Bill Kirkwood, who claimed that 'staff are the key to business expansion' (Fox, 2000; p.19). Well-trained, motivated staff who share their company's organisational goals can generally be relied upon to respond appropriately in a range of situations.
- *Industrialising the service process*: this can occur in two ways:
  - by increasing the client's own contribution to it, e.g. hotels have successfully introduced automated check-out facilities using PCs in the guests' rooms, and automated check-in is now common for corporate air travellers; in the air transport sector, passengers using e-tickets are becoming used to amending their bookings from their laptops should they need to make changes to their original plans. It is something of a paradox that many corporate travellers, whose expectations of service quality are understandably high, have embraced

the opportunity to complete work hitherto done for them by travel suppliers. Mill (1992) described business travellers as likely to become frustrated with the numerous demands of travel over which they have no control, and it could be that by contributing to the service process, they feel that they have regained more control of their travel arrangements;
– by using technology to supplant the need for staff involvement in the service encounter.

Until recently, the first few CIPs for an airline were (Palmer, 2001):

- initial telephone enquiry
- making reservation
- issue of ticket
- check-in of baggage
- inspection of ticket
- issue of boarding pass.

With the arrival of e-tickets, five of these CIPs no longer need to involve airline or airport staff. According to the IATA Corporate Air Travel Survey 2000, 25% of business travellers used e-tickets in the year 2000, and the use by business travellers of automated check-in doubled between 1999 and 2000.

Perishability

Perishability, or the inability to store services for use at a later date, is a crucial issue for corporate travel suppliers from the perspectives of both profitability and service quality. It means, first, that unsold flight seats, hotel rooms and hire cars represent revenue lost for ever, and second, that organisations need to manage the quality of service encounters at times of both peak and slack demand. As we stated in Chapter 1, business travel is less prone to seasonal variations than leisure travel, but the fact that it tends to be concentrated on weekdays means that suppliers are likely to be left with spare capacity at the weekends.

Strategies traditionally adopted by service providers to address perishability include:

- *Attempting to schedule capacity to meet demand.* Car-rental companies do have some flexibility of supply. Provided they can anticipate periods of high demand in particular rental locations, they can ensure that vehicles are available to meet client needs. However, hotels and airlines do not enjoy this elasticity of supply and so must adopt other techniques, such as using staff rostering effectively to ensure that there are sufficient staff at times of high demand.
- *Using price and promotion to attract off-peak usage,* a technique that is becoming more effective as cost-conscious client companies encourage their employees to take advantage of lower prices. In American Express's first corporate travel barometer of the year 2000, it found that 79% of respondents had flown at weekends to save money. According to the head of corporate travel at American Express, 'Companies chasing cheap leisure fares are incentivising weekend travel

by offering employee benefits such as extra money or travel or accommodation for a partner' (Huddart, 2000; p.2).

- *Targeting complementary markets*: as discussed in Chapter 1, when corporate travel destinations are also leisure travel destinations, suppliers will target both markets, offering prices and services appropriate to each.

Lack of ownership of ideas

In order to maintain their competitive edge, suppliers must always be striving to innovate and improve their services. But the fifth service characteristic concerns suppliers' lack of ownership of ideas: their inability to patent their innovations and stop others from imitating them. Examples of service innovations that have been imitated in the corporate travel sector include:

- low-cost, no-frills airlines
- premium economy seats for the cost-conscious corporate client
- frequent-flyer programmes
- business facilities within airport lounges
- laptop computer power ports in business class
- in-flight telephones.

Airline loyalty programmes provide an excellent illustration of the challenge presented to service businesses by the lack of ownership of ideas. Competitive edge was undoubtedly gained by the first airline to devise a scheme whereby travellers could earn free miles every time they travelled with that company, eventually accumulating enough miles for a free flight. But as other airlines were quick to imitate the concept, all carriers have tended to increase the benefits offered to loyal travellers in order to remain competitive and attractive. This has created a typical service business paradox in that a technique designed to forge a lasting relationship with clients has actually encouraged those clients to shop around.

● ● ● ● Intermediaries

Bringing together the buyers and suppliers already described are the intermediaries, who play a key role in the individual travel market.

Not all companies use an intermediary: corporate travel arrangements can be made directly with suppliers. In many cases, especially when the company spends relatively little on travel, or when it has employed a business travel manager, no intermediary is involved. Alternatively, some companies choose to use their local generalist travel agency who, as well as booking holidays and short breaks for their private clientele, will book airline and train tickets and hotel accommodation for corporate clients.

More often, however, organisations outsource the purchasing and negotiating functions to a specialist business/corporate travel agency or travel management company. Such an intermediary may handle the company's account in several ways:

- through an implant operation (a satellite branch of the agency based directly on the premises of the corporate client);
- through a main branch where specific members of staff are assigned to particular accounts (outplants);
- through a main branch where there is a pool of staff to handle a range of different accounts;
- through an online booking service.

Table 2.4 shows the intermediaries used by the FTSE top 100 companies.

Table 2.4 FTSE top 100 companies' choice of agency

Company	Agent	2000 spend
3i	Carlson Wagonlit Travel	£3.5m
Abbey National	98% BTI UK; the rest is shared between American Express, Chelsea Village Travel and Protravel	£5m
Alliance & Leicester	Lonsdale Travel Group	£2m
Allied Domecq	American Express	£7m
Amvescap	Reed & Mackay	£2m
Anglo American	Select World Travel	Less than £1m
ARM Holdings	Seaforths Travel	£500 000 on air travel
Associated British Foods	No central agency – various UK subsidiaries have their own travel arrangements	
AstraZeneca	BTI UK	More than £22m
Autonomy Corporation	Confidential	Not available
BAA	American Express	£2.5m
Bank of Scotland	Travel Management Group	£4m
Barclays	Split between Barclays and BTI UK Barclays Capital: Carlson Wagonlit Travel	Combined spend of about £24m, of which Barclays capital is an estimated £4m
Bass	BTI UK	£5m
BG	American Express	£7m
Billiton	World Travel Management	More than £1m
Blue Circle Industries	Carlson Wagonlit Travel has a global contract	£4m in UK
BOC	Rosenbluth International	£9m

Table 2.4 *continued*

Boots	Carlson Wagonlit Travel, Expotel for UK hotels and coach hire	Carlson: £4m Expotel: £4.5–£5m
BP Amoco	Carlson Wagonlit Travel for Europe, the Middle East, Africa, the Americas and Pacific-Asia	£270m globally, £50m in UK
British Aerospace	Mainly with Rosenbluth International, hotels with BSI	£40–£45m
British Airways	Business travel is done in-house by staff travel department	Not available
British American Tobacco	BTI UK	£9m
BSkyB	The Travel Company	£4.5m
BT	BTI UK	£40m
Cable & Wireless	American Express	More than £10m
Cadbury Schweppes	Britannic Travel	£5m
Canary Wharf Group	Confidential	Confidential
Capita Group	Gray Dawes Travel	£3m
Carlton Communications	50% BTI UK, 50% arranged in-house	£10m
Celltech Group	P&O Business Travel	About £1m
Centrica	Lonsdale Travel	£3m
CGNU	BTI UK	£7m
CMG	Navigant International UK	More than £2m
Colt Telecom Group	Hillgate Travel	£1.5m
Daily Mail and General Trust	No consolidated travel policy – 'many and various' agencies used	Not available
Diageo	BTI UK	£20m
Dimension Data Holdings	In-house agency Leading Travel, based in South Africa. Individual travellers also make own arrangements	Not available
Dixons	Gray Dawes Travel	£3m
EMI Group	Travel by Appointment	£6m
Electrocomponents	American Express	£2m (estimated)
Energis	Gray Dawes Travel	About £1m, most of which is air travel
Exel	Individuals make own arrangements	Not available
GKN	American Express	£20m
GlaxoSmithKline	Glaxo: BTI UK SmithKline Beecham: Carlson Wagonlit Travel	Combined spend of more than £60m: Glaxo, £35m; SmithklineBeecham, £28m

Table 2.4 *continued*

Company	Agent	2000 spend
Granada Compass	American Express for three divisions	£4m
Granada Media	American Express	£2m (estimated)
Great Universal Stores	Great Universal Stores Travel	£2.5m
Halifax Group	Britannic Travel for air and rail, hotels booked in-house	£3m
Hanson	American Express for head office, group uses individual agents	Not available
Hays	Hourds Travel	Not available
Hilton Group	BTI UK	£4m
HSBC	BTI UK	More than £23m
ICI	American Express	More than £15m
Imperial Tobacco Group	Lonsdale Travel, BSI for hotels	£2m (estimated)
International Power	Carlson Wagonlit Travel	£2.5m
Invensys	Carlson Wagonlit Travel	£5m (estimated)
Kingfisher	The Travel Company, hotel and conference business with First Option	More than £5m
Land Securities	Parador	£125 000
Lattice Group	BTI UK	£1m (estimated)
Legal & General Group	In tender process – does not want disclosed	Confidential
Lloyds TSB Group	Gray Dawes Travel	£20m
Logica	Rosenbluth International	£3m
Marconi	Rosenbluth International	More than £25m
Marks & Spencer	American Express	£6m
Misys	The Travel Company	£4m
National Grid Group	BTI UK	£5m
Nycomed Amersham	BTI UK	£3m
Old Mutual	Not consolidated, although most is with P&O Business Travel	£650 000 total, £450 000 air only
Pearson	The Travel Company	£5.5m
PowerGen	BTI UK	£4.2m
Prudential	Most with Phoenix Travel, some with Rosenbluth International	£7m
Railtrack Group	Expotel for hotels, conferences and training; Travel Force for all other business travel	£2–£2.5m each
Reckit Benckiser	Echelon Travel	£4–£5m
Reed International	BTI UK	£6m
Rentokil International	Most with American Express, First Option for hotels	£2.5m

Table 2.4 *continued*

Reuters Group	Gray Dawes Travel	£10m
Rio Tinto	Carlson Wagonlit Travel	More than £6m
Rolls-Royce	BTI UK	More than £17m
Royal & Sun Alliance Insurance	BTI UK Hillgate Travel has World Group office	£10m
Royal Bank of Scotland Group	Carlson Wagonlit Travel holds RBoS business, The Travel Company has former Natwest business	£30m, split between both agencies
Safeway	Fleet Street Travel	£2.5m
Sage Group	Norseman Travel	Not available
Sainsbury	BTI UK	£4m
Schroders	Rosenbluth International	More than £10m
Scottish & Southern Energy	Carlson Wagonlit Travel	£2m
Scottish Power	BTI UK	£2m (estimated)
Shell Transport & Trading	Carlson Wagonlit has 80%, American Express has 20%	More than £30m
Shire Pharmaceuticals Group	BTI UK	£4m (estimated)
Smiths Group	Confidential	Confidential
South African Breweries	Global Travel Management, Woking	£113 000
Spirent	American Express	£2m (estimated)
Standard Chartered	Gray Dawes Travel	£9m
Telewest Communications	Britannic Travel	£600 000
Tesco	Ayscough Travel, First Options for UK hotels	£7m
Unilever	BTI UK: 51%; Carlson Wagonlit: 44%; Ian Allan Travel and Co-op Travelcare share the rest	£28m on air travel
United Business Media	Rosenbluth International	£15m
United Utilities	Uniglobe	About £2m
Vodafone Group	BTI UK	£4m on air travel
WPP	Currently tendering	Not available

Source: *Travel Trade Gazette*, 29 January 2001.

With so many to choose from, how do companies decide which is the best agency to serve their needs? The choice is often made at the end of a formal tendering process, during which candidate agencies are considered against specific criteria. The list of criteria upon which corporate clients can base their selection of a business agency to handle their account can be extensive, including (Burton, 1999):

- possibility of having an implant on site (the corporate client may even stipulate the number of staff and levels of qualifications);
- staff in main agency dedicated to corporate client's account (the client may specify numbers and qualifications);
- level of cost-savings achieved on travel spend;
- level of rebates earned on sales;
- guarantee of a share in any supplier incentive schemes such as override commission (paid to the agency by suppliers when sales targets achieved);
- possession of quality kitemark, such as ISO9002 or Investors in People;
- service provision and service level indicators, such as ticket delivery, 24-hour access to booking service, processing of passport and visa applications, provision of foreign exchange and travellers' cheques facilities, response rates to enquiries and bookings, reliability, accuracy, personal profiling of travellers, adherence to company travel policy, airport representation, global representation, provision of training, familiarisation visits for travel bookers in company, proximity of agency to company, favourable credit limits and payment terms, supply of timetables, travel information, supply of management information on travel trends, travel savings and travel spending within different cost centres in company.

Business agencies tendering for a corporate travel account must attempt to identify the selection criteria that are important to that client and then assess accurately the weightings or priorities allocated to each criterion. During the tendering process, the agency is provided with information about the company's travel requirements, which should ensure that the service it ultimately offers in its sales documentation and presentation is the most appropriate for that account. The process can last several months, with at least four stages involved:

1 *Invitation to tender*: the corporate client invites travel agents to prepare a tender for the business, usually several months before its contract with its current agent is due to expire. The current agent is usually, although not always, invited to tender to renew its contract at the same time as prospective alternative agents are preparing their bids for the business. Sometimes, corporate clients only invite tenders from specified agents; sometimes, they will accept tenders from any agent wishing to offer its services.
2 *Presentations and submissions of tender documents*: normally, the corporate client requests to see the documents before the agency sales team makes a formal presentation, so that issues can be clarified during the presentation (or sometimes to eliminate some agencies from the competition).
3 *Assessment of the alternative agency proposals*: this process can be very quick if the corporate client has clear and weighted criteria on which to base its selection of an agency and if there are discernible differences between the service promises of the agencies tendering for the business. When the agencies' offers are very similar and/or the client's wish list is not precise, then this can be a drawn-out stage of the process.

4 *Negotiation of contract*: inevitably, the corporate client is likely to seek extra advantages from its prospective agent. For example, rebate levels may be negotiated up from an original tender, or dedicated staff levels may be increased. Very often, since the offers in other agents' proposals can give corporate clients new ideas of what they can demand from an agent, the procurement manager or travel manager may present the prospective agent with the conditional promise of the contract, provided the agency offer is amended somewhat – in favour of the company, of course.

Business travel agencies compete intensely to manage clients' accounts because of the potentially considerable earnings these can bring them. Until recently, corporate travel represented what would seem to be an ideal market for intermediaries. As airlines, for example, benefited from business travellers choosing one of the very high-cost flexible fares, business travel agents, whose commission was calculated on a percentage basis of the airfare, earned much of their income from these high-yield travel purchases. On the face of it, booking a flexible £2000 round-trip business-class fare between London and the USA, for example, took less time and fewer resources to process than finding and booking a suitable non-flexible cheap fare for a fraction of that price, say £400. Based on the classic 9% commission payment level, the respective business travel agency incomes would be £180 compared with £36.

However, even when the fortunes of business travel agents were at their apogee, earning their revenue was not as effortless as the example of the London–USA airline ticket appears to suggest at first glance. It may have been a much more complex transaction because:

- the booking may have been amended at least once or twice before departure as the business commitments and personal plans of the traveller changed;
- the booking, or changes to it, could well have been requested out of hours when most leisure-oriented travel agencies would not be open;
- there may have been a misunderstanding between the traveller and the colleague booking on his or her behalf that led to further amendments in the booking;
- the travel agency may have had to seek advice or approval from the traveller's superior in the client company if the journey requested did not conform with the company's travel policy;
- the agency would have been expected to deliver the travel documents to the traveller or arrange for them to be available at the airport;
- the client company would possibly also require the agency to provide regular management information reports on its overall travel spend.

In addition, if the agent were receiving 9% commission from the airline, then the likelihood is that the corporate client would have negotiated a share of that commission (known as a rebate) for themselves, as part of the agency–client contract set up during the account tendering process described previously.

Furthermore, the corporate travel agency would have been expected to respect and enforce their client's travel policy – even when the employee making the booking requested, for example, an airline, class of travel or hotel not authorised by their company's travel policy. In those circumstances, the travel agent would respond in one of two ways:

- The agent would seek exceptional authorisation from the company's decision-maker before processing the booking.
- Where a company adopts a more laissez-faire approach to their employees, the agent would show in the regular management information returns to the company that arrangements that fell within the company travel policy had been offered and rejected by the particular traveller or booker. Then the company could deal directly with its own employee, if necessary.

On occasions, business travellers have been so keen to deviate from company travel policy that they have introduced a last-minute change to their business commitments necessitating a modification to their itinerary or carrier. Anecdotal evidence suggest that in many cases this often occurs because the traveller wishes to switch to an airline that, although unauthorised by the company's travel policy, has a frequent-flyer programme of which he or she is a member. The 1999 Carlson Wagonlit *Frequent Traveller Analysis* revealed that 25% of bookers and 13% of travellers had deviated from company policy due to membership of a frequent traveller scheme (Carlson Wagonlit, 1999).

Issues and trends

While corporate clients are seeking better value travel products, their suppliers are operating in a market environment characterised by a number of opportunities and constraints, the most important of which are:

- cutting their own distribution costs;
- advances in information and communication technology.

Cutting distribution costs

Commission capping

For suppliers, the use by corporate travel agencies from the early 1980s onwards of computer reservation systems (CRS) and then later global distribution systems (GDS) – Galileo International, Amadeus, SABRE and Worldspan – provided two key profit improvement opportunities: first, the need to employ large numbers of reservation staff to deal with telephone bookings from agents was eliminated; second, the opportunity to develop effective yield-management techniques was created. Airline load factors, for example, could be improved simply because the supplier was able to display availability directly to travel agencies via the system. However, the cost to the suppliers of linking their own reservation systems to these GDSs was high, with a charge made by the GDS for every booking. The cost to suppliers has not gone down; indeed, all four systems have recently announced increases of 4–9.5% (Noakes, 2001b).

In addition to the expense of paying GDS fees, suppliers also had to meet the costs of paying commission to travel agencies. Historically, airlines had paid travel agencies 9% commission on international air sales and 7.5% commission on domestic air sales. By the end of the 1990s, distribution costs worldwide were estimated to account for 25% of airline's sales and marketing budgets – and close to two-thirds of this took the form of commission paid to travel agents (O'Brien, 1998).

The combined burden of agency commission together with GDS fees has led to airlines actively seeking to reduce their distribution costs. One technique being used increasingly is commission capping – cutting the rate of commission paid to travel agencies.

From the airline's viewpoint, the reductions were justified by changes in the nature of the work undertaken by travel agents reserving and ticketing flights. The argument went that by the late 1990s, the work involved was considerably less than it was when the standard commissions were introduced. Reservations are now made online, and tickets and itineraries can be printed in seconds, compared with the complex manual processes involved in the days before CRS.

Travel agency commission capping has now been introduced by many airlines; US carriers began the trend in their home market, and by 2001 were paying only 5%, with a maximum of $US50 per booking (Macefield, 2001). The practice spread to Europe in the 1990s, beginning with the budget airline Ryanair, which reduced its commission rate from 9% to 7.5%. Other airlines followed, with the results that they made considerable savings – at business travel agencies' expense. United Airlines, for example, claimed in 2000 that it would save $US150 million a year through its commission capping (Davidson, 2001).

The situation is a difficult one for the airlines. On the one hand, they are seeking cost savings by reducing travel agency commission payments; on the other, they run the risk of alienating the travel agents, who could, in retaliation, promote those competitor airlines who have not (yet) reduced commissions. For example, 85% of BA sales come via travel agencies (Noakes, 2002), so the airline's introduction in the UK of reduced commission rates, then a flat booking fee, and subsequently a reduced booking fee has been a high-risk strategy. Business travel agents have not always been passive in their acceptance of commission capping. Travel agents in the Caribbean stopped selling tickets for American Airlines in protest when the airline cut commission payments from 9% to 6%. Agents in Argentina, Peru, South Africa and Australia have all protested against commission-cutting airlines (Davidson, 2001).

It is likely, however, that the corporate travel buyers will react differently to the airlines' commission-capping policy, as it should, in theory at least, lead to reductions in the standard long-haul fares, which have hitherto had a higher agency commission built in. For example, BA's fee structure in 2001 ranged from £6 to £20 per booking according to the type of ticket sold. Thus, for booking a £6000 business-class ticket, the difference for a travel agency between the 7% commission rate (paid before 31 March 2001) and the £20 fee paid after that date was £400.

The question from the point of view of the buyers will inevitably be, how many of these savings are passed on to customers?

Fees instead of commission

With commission paid by suppliers to intermediaries being severely reduced, the relationship between business travel agents and their clients is changing radically, with a move towards the client paying fees for the services provided by the agency.

Agencies are increasingly proposing one of two types of fees to be paid to them by the client in return for servicing their travel account: management or transaction fees. Both are based on the client paying only net prices for travel services purchased, but with a fee added to cover the agency's overheads and provide a profit margin (Cope, 2001).

If the agency opts to charge a management fee, then it will allocate overhead costs to the account in proportion to that account's use of the agency, taking into account staff time, premises, rates, electricity, telephone, etc. Some of these costs are relatively straightforward to apportion to particular clients, especially where dedicated staff are used. For this reason, a management fee is considered suitable for implant operations, where the agency costs can be identified reasonably easily. When an account is being serviced from a central office, however, the allocation of costs becomes much more complex.

A common feature of management fee arrangements is that the client has access to the relevant figures for agency overheads, which demonstrate the amount of work involved in providing the range of services demanded by the client. However, this degree of transparency may expose any underuse of resources. Increasingly, therefore, agencies are looking at new ways to save costs, e.g. by consolidating several branches into large booking centres, outsourcing certain functions such as ticket delivery, and centralising other activities such as credit control and rail bookings (Cope, 2001).

In some cases, agencies are adopting transaction fees rather than management fees, especially for smaller accounts. Using this system, every service is attributed a charge, which will cover the overheads required to complete it and build in a profit margin. To determine the range of fees, the agency uses historical data on time and resources required for every type of service. However, different interpretations of the term 'transaction' are in use. Some agencies are applying a charge for every contact made by the client, be it to book, amend, check a detail, or cancel. Others apply one charge for each booking made, to include any extra contacts made in relation to that booking.

The business travel sector is divided over which system will prevail. One prediction is that made by the UK vice president of Carlson Wagonlit Travel: 'The rush to transaction fees will diminish in favour of more straightforward management fees' (Tweedie, 2001; p.33). American Express, on the other hand, has embraced the concept of transaction fees, introducing in January 2001 five levels of reservation fee according to the type of service used. The lowest fee of £13 per booking is for companies using its interactive, online travel planning, booking and payment service. Those companies booking via one of its call-centre operations are charged £23 per booking. Those using outplants (dedicated staff working within an American Express branch) are charged £30 per booking. Finally, those companies requiring a specialised priority and VIP service are charged £62. For corporate clients where there is an implant operation, there will be a management fee (Reynolds, 2001).

Whether an agency continues to try to survive on commissions alone or moves over to charging management or transaction fees to their clients, cost control has become an overriding concern. Some companies, such as American Express in the UK, have consolidated their operations into fewer, very large call centres, made possible through the advent of e-tickets and electronic communications. Some, including American Express, BTI UK and Rosenbluth, have developed online booking services tailored to the needs of individual corporate accounts, where the need for direct personal contact with bookers is reduced. And some, like Gray Dawes, have moved their offices outside expensive capital city locations. Without exception, all monitor their outgoings with extreme care, constantly balancing the value of, for example:

- having their own ticket delivery service or using courier services according to need;
- employing permanent staff or making use of temporary recruitment agency staff at busy times.

Timely collection of payment from corporate clients has also become a key to business travel agency survival. An agency is debited automatically on the 17th of the month for any IATA scheduled air tickets issued during the previous month. Thus, if it has not been paid by its clients, it will lose interest on the net price of the tickets sold. But while agencies encourage their corporate clients to pay by Lodge Card, a form of credit card for travel transactions, or, even better, direct debit, many clients still prefer the old system of payment following a monthly statement.

Advances in e-commerce

Reduced travel agent commission rates are linked closely with the development of e-commerce. Innovations in this field are creating new distribution channels for a wide range of products and services, including travel. Travel is the second biggest-selling product on the Web, behind PC hardware, and is set to overtake PC hardware by 2002, according to Jupiter Communications, the IT market research group (Davidson, 2001). A new electronic marketplace has emerged with its own rules. It is efficient, fast, transparent and borderless. It is a place where everyone can see, and compare, all available prices. For example, Internet search engines can locate flights and lowest fares, and these same services can be used to book flights and to generate tickets or e-ticket surrogates.

Using this technological solution, suppliers can now reach their customers directly using online Internet booking services. Already well established in the

USA, such services were first introduced in Europe in 1995. That year, British Midland launched the first fully bookable European air travel Internet site, and Holiday Inn became the first hotel chain to provide an online booking service (O'Brien, 1998).

Despite its obvious business travel distribution applications, growth in the use of the Internet for booking travel and accommodation has been fuelled overwhelmingly by leisure travel, a market in which the traveller's dates, times and even destinations are relatively flexible. There is extensive debate over the suitability of using e-commerce to book business travel. Business travellers can rarely choose their travel dates or destinations. They need great flexibility in the service they receive to enable them to book, then cancel and change, their itineraries if necessary; they also often need advice on related topics such as vaccinations and visa requirements, which websites, unlike travel agents, rarely provide.

Because of these limitations, the use of the Internet for booking business travel services is still fairly restricted: 89% of companies taking part in the 1999 Carlson Wagonlit Travel Business Travel Survey reported that they did not book air travel electronically. Nevertheless, the same survey found that three-quarters of travellers and bookers would, in principle, be prepared to book flights on their computer system. Furthermore, four out of ten travellers and bookers said that they had been content to use the Internet as a source of travel information (Carlson Wagonlit Travel, 1999).

Reflecting the apparent readiness of travellers and bookers to use the Internet for this purpose, extensive growth in online business travel is widely predicted. Inevitably, the American market will lead the way. The USA-based Association of Corporate Travel Executives, which represents suppliers as well as travel managers, predicts that 32%, or $US39 billion (£24.6 billion), of US corporations' travel expenditure will be online by 2003. The figure currently stands at $US5 billion. Equivalent figures for Europe are very low by comparison. The research company, The Gartner Group, estimates that the market for all online travel booking was worth £12 million in the UK in 1998 and that this will grow to £1.9 billion in 2003 (Davidson, 2001).

Further, business travel displays a number of characteristics that make it eminently suitable to purchase through e-commerce. In the area of business travel, information is largely standardised and free of emotional involvement, so that the attributes of the travel products required can be understood completely, simply by knowing the destination, travel dates and times, quality classification and price (Schertler and Berger-Koch, 1999). The same authors argue that business travel is an example of what are known as 'search goods' – goods that can be judged entirely before purchase (after collecting the adequate information) and after consumption. Goods with a high share of search qualities generally offer a high potential for 'disintermediation', the bypassing of mediators/intermediaries.

It is certainly true that the Internet enables airlines and hotels to sell directly to the public for a relatively low cost. Currently, the use of e-commerce for business travel services appears to be more potential than actual, even though that potential may be very significant. To take BA as an example, its aim is that half its tickets will be sold online by 2003. At the moment, however, only 1% of its tickets are distributed online. Travel agents account for 85% of its sales, with the remainder being sold over the telephone (Daneshkhu, 2000).

Nevertheless, airlines appear to be determined to capitalise fully on the Internet's potential. In 2000, nine European flag carriers caused consternation among both travel agencies and the GDSs when they announced plans to launch a joint website – OPODO – over the years 2001–2003, providing direct online booking access to 80% of European route coverage (www.opodo.co.uk). A similar project has been developed in the USA, with airlines combining forces to create the Internet travel service ORBITZ (www.orbitz.com).

Hotels, too, have embraced the new technology, with considerable growth in the use of e-commerce. In 1999, the European director of sales and marketing of the Marriott hotel chain announced that: 'Online reservations have increased dramatically over the last year, with online generated business growing by 213%' (Weinberger, 1999; p.61). However, this growth would appear to have generated its own teething problems. A survey conducted by O'Connor and Horan (1998) of the Institut de Management Hôtelier International in Paris found that 55% of the hotel groups covered quoted a cheaper room tariff over the telephone than from their online booking facilities. The survey found that, on average, Web rates were 12% higher than the rate quoted by the central reservations office. As O'Connor and Horan point out, there is no scope for negotiating with an online booking site that only usually processes bookings at rack rates. By way of contrast, the central reservations office tends to be up to date on supply-and-demand trends and will adjust the price accordingly (Edmunds, 1999a). The same survey also highlighted inconsistencies in availability given by both types of reservation systems. Of the central reservation offices contacted, 23% said that there was no availability on the nominated night even though the company's website had processed the booking.

Current thinking on the use of e-commerce for business travel, at least in Europe, would appear to be characterised by a combination of resignation and cautious optimism that this will be a major element of distribution in the near future. Nevertheless, the path is far from smooth, and there are a number of challenges still to be met.

Don Lunn, chairman of the Guild of Business Travel Agents (GBTA), highlights some of these: 'There are still greater hurdles to be overcome in the business travel environment, like interchangeability of tickets on multi-sector itineraries and compliance with corporate travel policies.' Crucially, he asks: 'Will major corporations really permit their employees to book through their PCs whatever they wish? And, in any case, how sensible is it for a well-paid executive to be spending company time arranging his own travel?' (Daneshkhu, 2000; p.1).

Although it might be expected that someone representing the interests of business travel agencies might emphasise the disadvantages of using direct distribution through e-commerce, similar concerns have been expressed by the buyers themselves. British Aerospace's travel manager has questioned the wisdom of allowing employees self booking facilities, since every direct booking to an airline or hotel was one less arrangement that had previously been part of the company's bulk buying power. Moreover, he also pointed out that there was no way of controlling such bookings to ensure that they were in conformity with company travel policy (CIMTIG, 1999).

A *Financial Times*, contributor concurs (Edmunds, 1999b; p.VII):

> Europeans, and in particular the British, have been slower to switch to fully-integrated online booking than the Americans ... In Britain, corporate culture has been more resistant to multi-tasking, with a passionately held belief that senior executives are not being paid big salaries to complete menial administrative tasks such as travel reservations.

However, even taking these concerns into account, there does appear to be a degree of unanimity that there is a role for the use of the Internet in the purchase of business travel. Most commentators agree that the Internet is suitable for the booking of simple journeys. A single-destination return trip, such as London to Paris and back, may be straightforward enough to be booked in this way. Moreover, the airlines have everything to gain from using the Internet to sell this simple type of product directly to the client, since the profit margin tends to be quite low and the further deduction of a commission makes it even lower. Arguably too, business travel agents may not miss this type of business, given how little they earn on low-cost travel.

It would, of course, be a mistake to regard e-commerce and business travel agencies as two separate and incompatible intermediaries in the business travel distribution chain. The larger agencies, in particular, have embraced the technology and put it to use to enhance the service they provide to clients.

American Express, for example, has instituted its own online reservation system, AXI, which allows corporate travellers to make policy-compliant trip arrangements from their laptops (Weinberger, 1999). The agency's decision to develop AXI for its corporate customers is also important in ensuring that American Express retains its market presence as a progressive travel management company. Another example was the acquisition in 2000 by Travelstore.com of Amersham Travel, whose managing director described the move as 'the way forward ... We expect on-line business to be the future of travel' (Giles, 2000; p.80). The launch by easygroup of their Flightbusters website (www.easyvalue.com), which seeks out the sort of back-to-back flight combinations hitherto only possible through the expertise of an experienced agent, reinforces this view.

The move towards agencies offering these products seems unstoppable. O'Brien (1998; p.50) expressed the view that 'the development of agency Internet booking capabilities, and the provision of company Intranets featuring travel itineraries and other relevant data will enable corporate travel agents to position themselves as technically advanced providers of travel services to their corporate clients'.

However, business travel agencies are not alone in the development of such products, as GDS companies are also developing integrated business solutions for the corporate market. For example, Amadeus's suite of products, Corporate World, has been developed in order to answer what the company describes as 'the growing demand from companies for integrated business solutions offering self-booking, travel information management and decision support'. Using Corporate World, travellers can book online following company policy and with the company's preferred suppliers. The business travel agency issues the tickets and bills the company directly. The travel manager is happy that no one is going outside company travel policy, and the agents are happy because the easy point-to-point bookings are taking care of themselves, allowing them time to look after the management of accounts and deal effectively with complicated itineraries (Scales, 1999).

Given all of these radical changes in the market environment in which they function, what is the outlook for intermediaries in this key sector of business travel?

It would appear that those best placed to survive will be those who are seen by their clients to be saving them money. They will be the agencies who 'manage' the travel budget of the client rather than simply act as a shopping service. And they will collect a fee for this service, in the same way that solicitors, consultants and other professions do. The GBTA's recognition of this can perhaps be seen in its deliberations over whether to drop the word 'agents' from its title. Indeed, its investment over the last decade in improving the training, development and qualifications of business travel personnel is a clear indicator that it views its membership as a profession rather than an industry.

Case study

The Guild of European Business Travel Agents and the UK's Guild of Business Travel Agents

A coalition of autonomous guilds of business travel agents across Europe, the Guild of European Business Travel Agents (GEBTA) (www.gebta.org) includes more than 300 business travel agents in ten European countries, with a total turnover in excess of $US13 billion. GEBTA's mission is to speak and act in unity for the benefit of the European business travellers and the travel agents who serve them. Its objectives are to:

- ensure that the business traveller receives the very best service and assistance from business travel suppliers;

- maintain a dialogue with suppliers and regulation authorities in Europe to speak across national boundaries on behalf of business travellers and their agents;
- raise standards of professionalism of the business travel agents throughout Europe by initiating European qualifications geared specifically to the business travel industry;
- actively address and support issues concerning the improvement of the European travel infrastructure.

The ten countries whose national business travel agency guilds combine to form GEBTA are Belgium,

▶

Case study *continued*

Denmark, France, Germany, Ireland, Italy, the Netherlands, Portugal, Spain and the UK. GEBTA was formed in 1990 at the instigation of the UK's GBTA, whose members were keen for there to be a pan-European voice that could represent both agents and business travellers to the organisations that supply, service and regulate the business travel market. The need by 1990 for this combined approach simply reflected the changing operating environment for business travel, where airlines as well as reservation systems were embarking on strategies of mergers and alliances, and where the impacts of legislation initiated in Brussels were being felt throughout Europe.

Emphasising the importance to the European economy of business travel, GEBTA sees it as vital that travel infrastructure should be improved and costs be contained. In its own words, it 'maintains a continued pressure on suppliers and regulators to make special provisions for the business traveller'. Its activities also include research into key issues affecting both members and travellers. For example, working with ECTAA (the EU National Travel Agents and Tour Operators Association), and co-financed by the EU, it published in 2000 the results of a Deloitte Consulting study in five member countries to determine the average cost for a travel agency of scheduled air-ticket issue. Its activities reflect on a pan-European scale the activities and interests of its member guilds, the most active of which is undoubtedly the UK's GBTA – understandably so, since it has been established the longest (since 1967) and since it represents by far the largest outbound international business travel market in Europe.

Representing agencies that handle around 80% of business air bookings made in the UK, and whose combined turnover in 1998 was £7.64 billion, the GBTA (www.gbta-guild.com) is well established and influential in the UK travel sector. Its mission is:

- to be a committed and respected organisation representing the interests and requirements of the business travel market;
- to be recognised as delivering the best standard of service, quality and value to the business traveller.

According to its website, on which it describes itself as 'the world's most influential travel trade organisation', the GBTA is extremely active in several spheres and has achieved much since it came into existence. Its members include all leading multiples handling business travel, most medium-sized independent agencies, and many small specialists – in total around 1500 branches employing around 15000 people. The activities for which it is best known include:

- working parties
- professional qualifications, training and development
- links with business travel suppliers
- services for members
- lobbying with governments, regulators and suppliers
- information provision to the corporate travel market
- organisation of conferences and meetings on behalf of members.

Its working parties address key issues for business travel. Five different working parties meet to focus on air transport, hotels, surface travel, technology and human resources. The membership of each working party comprises agency representatives who have particular expertise in the sector concerned. Thus, for example, in the human resources working parties, the human resource managers from a range of member agencies will be working together.

The GBTA professional qualifications, training and development are now well established within the UK travel industry. Four levels of qualifications are used:

- *Introductory*: for people who have not yet joined a business travel agency. Some colleges of further education offer classes in preparation for this level. Additionally, the GBTA has produced self-study materials. The assessment for this level involves two open-book, three-hour examinations and the completion of a logbook.
- *Consultant*: for people already working within the industry who have two years' practical experience. Like the introductory qualification, candidates must pass two open-book, three-hour examinations and submit a logbook to obtain a certificate at this level.
- *Supervisory*: for people in, or aspiring to be in, a senior role within an agency. Whereas the two previous-level qualifications focus entirely on practical travel skills and knowledge, this level introduces general business and organisation theory and analysis. It is assessed through a closed-book, three-hour

Case study *continued*

examination and an assignment of no less than 4000 words.

- *Management*: for people already in a management role. The three key components of this level are staff management, financial management and marketing. Each component is tested separately through an assignment and a three-hour, closed-book examination.

The GBTA works in partnership with the City and Guilds of London Institute to award these qualifications, which have now been established for a decade. An education committee meets regularly to update the syllabuses, and a final level, equivalent to a masters degree, may soon be added to the GBTA portfolio.

Links with business travel suppliers are negotiated on behalf of members. An example of the support the GBTA can provide is its arrangement through Pegasus Commission Processing for hotel commissions to be paid through a central system, eliminating the need for agencies to track payments. It has also negotiated special rates for members with certain suppliers. And even though many business travel agents are unhappy about BA's introduction of booking fees for flights, the transition has been made smoother as a result of the GBTA's technology team working with the airline and computer reservations systems teams to manage the collecting, charging and reporting of the new fees.

Services for members include the provision of Guildfare, the GBTA's own low airfares unit, and its Hotel Guide, offering special rates worldwide. Members whose clients require a 24-hour contact line can also make use of the GBTA's out-of-ours service rather than be on call themselves.

Lobbying with governments, regulators and suppliers has become an important function of the GBTA, which has its own parliamentary consultant. Key concerns expressed by the GBTA on behalf of its members include increased levels of Air Passenger Duty for business travellers, congestion at Heathrow, air-traffic-control delays, and the threat of introducing taxation on aviation fuel.

Information provision to the corporate travel market is a key role for the GBTA, especially at a time when so much is changing for both business travel sellers and buyers. Given the likelihood that many other carriers will follow the BA example and replace travel agency commission with a flat fee, the need for members to start charging clients for their services is inevitable. Thus, press statements issued by the GBTA, targeted at the business travel reader, provide a full explanation of the imminent changes and their effects. Points made in the statements can also be used by agents when explaining to clients why a move to management or transaction fees is necessary.

The GBTA's organisation of conferences and meetings on behalf of members provides a regular forum for members to exchange views and ideas. Each year, members can attend both the Annual General Meeting, held in London, and the Annual Conference, held in different international business locations. Additionally, the GBTA arranges meetings and seminars according to need. For example, when some US agents began the move towards management and transaction fees in the mid-1990s, the GBTA invited these US pioneers to lead a series of seminars for members in the UK to alert them to the advantages and pitfalls they were likely to encounter.

Source: Reproduced with the permission of GBTA Ltd.

Questions

1 Explain why several national associations for business travel agencies have combined forces to form GEBTA.

2 Discuss the advantages for UK business travel agencies of enrolling their staff for GBTA training courses and qualifications. What, if any, are the risks of doing so?

3 All the business travel guilds in Europe aim to represent travellers as well as agents. Discuss how they aim to do both.

Business Travel International: meeting the demands of corporate travel clients

Business Travel International (BTI) operates in over 80 commercial countries, with more than 4000 offices in Europe, the Americas, Asia-Pacific, the Middle-East and Africa. Proud of its combination of 'substantial global capabilities and local expertise', its member company in the UK, BTI UK was awarded 'Business Travel Agent of the Year, 2002' by *Business Travel World*.

Business travel agencies face different types of competition. First, they are in competition with suppliers such as airlines and hotels who are keen for business travellers to book direct. Second, they are in competition with other business travel agencies to win the contracts to manage companies' travel accounts. On-line agencies, not necessarily specialising in business travel, have emerged as a third level of competition. And looking to the future, a fourth level of competition may well emerge from management consultancy firms as they recognise the value to businesses of providing advice on managing travel activities and budgets. To be successful, an agency must deliver the appropriate balance of cost, comfort and convenience for each of their corporate accounts. This case study focuses on how BTI agencies are approaching the challenges for survival and success in the twenty-first century.

The optimum mix of cost, comfort and convenience is likely to be achieved by the travel agency that can provide the following for the corporate client:

- *Time-savings* both in the booking process and during the trips themselves.
- *Cost-savings* through travel policy management, cheap fare searches, advice on internal process improvements and managing the BTI cost of service.
- *Global management information* to help the company in its planning and control.
- *Convenience* in providing services quickly and easily for both bookers and travellers.

Time savings

BTI boasts three key factors that guarantee time savings: the expertise of its staff, the capacity and flexibility of its information technology systems and the sensitivity of both to the particular priorities of its clients. An example of BTI UK's commitment to recruiting and training only the highest calibre staff is its involvement in its parent company's graduate development scheme, in which all trainees spend time in different areas of the business before making their career choice. BTI agent expertise is combined with information technology (IT) applications to ensure maximum service speed at the times of booking, checking details and even making changes once a business trip is underway. BTI offers a number of self-service booking solutions, so that travellers can book and amend their trips online, with their managers assured that company travel policy, including any route deal preferences, will be adhered to and that full management information will be available to them automatically. The systems also provide comprehensive information on airlines, hotels and destinations.

Cost savings

Corporate clients need to know that their travel agent is providing the best value for money, but as BTI recognises, 'value means different things to different people'. Thus, each corporate client's needs are analysed and account servicing arrangements tailored to suit their needs.

BTI's partners around the world work toward the same goal: providing local purchasing power and negotiation strength for the benefit of their international customers. Working on a day-to-day basis, BTI's staff expertise and IT capabilities mean that selection of travel arrangements should provide the best value for the company and traveller concerned, but working also at a strategic level, BTI offers a consultancy service for companies 'to help identify, control and reduce cost in all areas of travel related activity'. At this level, BTI not only helps shape clients' policies on travel and expense management, but also advises on the implementation of these policies and the management of the changes involved.

Different corporate clients require different types of service from their travel agents: some want no more than a simple booking service, while others outsource the

Case study *continued*

entire management of their travel policy to the agent. Thus, agency remuneration arrangements need to reflect the service levels provided. To cope with the range of agency–client agreements, BTI tailors the payment arrangements for each company. In some countries, the traditional commission and rebate system can still be used. However, this is now obsolete in most developed markets, such as the UK and US, due to reductions in/elimination of commission by suppliers. In others, management fees have been introduced, where BTI passes all the commissions on to the client, receiving a fee in return for the services it provides – a fee that will vary according to the levels of service agreed. Another option used by BTI is that of transaction fees, where the client pays a set charge for each service, an arrangement often favoured by small and medium-sized client companies, for whom the scope of the service required tends to best fit this pricing structure.

savings made for the client through the agency's use of specialist fares and knowledge. It is also standard practice for the account manager from the agency to meet with the client on a regular basis to offer analysis of the travel management reports and provide suggestions regarding further lowering of travel expenses and negotiating or managing airline deals where appropriate. In those agreements where agency fees are linked to performance and cost-efficiency standards, an open-book approach to the agency–client relationship enables clients not only to see their own spending (cost centre by cost centre, if required) but also any savings made thanks to the agency; they also have the opportunity to see and discuss the agency's operating costs of servicing their accounts. Effectively, BTI clients may have whatever management information they require to help them in the planning and control of their travel budget.

Global management information

BTI focuses on working with clients to achieve mutual profitability, so systems have been developed with the capacity and flexibility to provide whatever management information may be required by individual client companies. BTI *GEMS*, for example, 'allows travel managers to analyse consolidated global management information from every angle at their desktop'. For each client, management information reporting requirements are agreed and then supplied accordingly, on a monthly, quarterly or annual basis. Standard now, for example, are the savings reports, showing levels of

Convenience

BTI tailors its service provision so that each company's needs are incorporated into the service design. According to need, it offers implant or outplant operations, online bookings and local booking centres. It provides ticket deliveries and has a 24-hour emergency service. Its international network means that it is both globally strong and locally responsive. At a time when corporate client needs can vary from high-tech communication systems to traditional telephone bookings, BTI's flexible and consultative approach ensures that an appropriate service mix is provided in all cases.

Source: Reproduced with the permission of BTI UK.

Questions

1 What advantages does being global bring to a BTI agency when negotiating for travel accounts?

2 Bearing in mind the changes in commission agreements between suppliers and travel agents, consider the types of corporate accounts that are best suited to:
- paying gross prices and receiving an agency rebate (or discount);
- paying net prices plus a management fee;
- paying net prices plus transaction fees.

3 Suggest strategies that could be adopted by independent business travel agencies in the face of competition from the large multinational chains such as BTI, American Express, Carlson Wagonlit, etc.

References

American Express (1999), *Global Travel & Entertainment Expense Management Survey*, London, American Express.

Bateson, E.G. and Hoffman, K. (1999), *Managing Services Marketing*, 4th edn, Fort Worth, Dryden Press.

Burton, J. (1999), *Business Development and Account Management*, Vol. I, London, GBTA.

Business Traveller Magazine (1999), Letters to the Editor, *Business Traveller Magazine*, March.

Carlson Wagonlit Travel (1999) *Business Travel Annual Survey*, Potters Bar, Carlson Wagonlit Travel.

CIMTIG (1999), *Airlines and Corporate Travel – Whatever Next ?* Proceedings of the Chartered Institute of Marketing Travel Industry Group meeting, 8 June, London.

Collis, R. (2000), *The Survivor's Guide to Business Travel*, London, Kogan Page.

Cope, B. (2001), *Financial Management Issues in the Travel Industry*, London, GBTA.

Daneshkhu, S. (2000), 'Extinction is fear of agents around the world', *Financial Times*, 10 February.

Davidson, R. (1994), 'European business travel and tourism', in Seaton, A. *et al.* (eds), *Tourism: the state of the art*, Chichester, Wiley.

Davidson, R. (2001), 'Distribution channels analysis for business travel', in Laws, E. and Buhalis, D. (eds), *Tourism Distribution Channels: practices, issues and transformations*, London, Continuum.

Davies, P. (2000), 'BA adds fourth class', *Travel Trade Gazette*, 7 February.

Doyle, J. and Nathan, M. (2001), *Whatever next? Work in a mobile world*, London, Industrial Society.

Edmunds, M. (1999a), 'Bargains slipping through the net', *Financial Times*, 1 November.

Edmunds, M. (1999b), 'Efficiency relies heavily on policy', *Financial Times*, 9 September.

Fox, L. (1999), 'High-tech phones at Peninsula', *Travel Trade Gazette*, 22 March.

Fox, L. (2000), 'Staff are the key to business expansion', *Travel Trade Gazette*, 22 May.

Giles, D. (2000), 'On-line agency buys Amersham Travel', *Travel Trade Gazette*, 13 March.

Huddart, G. (2000), 'Business travellers are cost conscious', *Travel Trade Gazette*, 13 March.

IATA (2000), *Corporate Air Travel Survey 2000*, London, IATA.

Key Note (2000), *Business Travel Market Assessment Report*, London, Key Note Ltd.

Macefield, S. (2001), 'Service fees still causing ripples across the pond' , *Travel Trade Gazette*, 8 January.

Mill, R.C. (1992), *The Tourism System: an introductory text*, Englewood Cliffs, Prentice Hall.

Noakes, G. (2001a), 'Mobile check in at Heathrow with United', *Travel Trade Gazette*, 8 January.

Noakes, G. (2001b), 'Sabre hits airlines with 9pc hike', *Travel Trade Gazette*, 8 January.

Noakes, G. (2002), 'BA web snares agents', *Travel Trade Gazette*, 18 February.

O'Brien, K. (1998), 'The European business travel market', *Travel and Tourism Analyst*, No. 4.

O'Connor, P. and Horan, P. (1998), *An Analysis of Web Reservations Facilities in the Top 50 International Hotel Chains*, Paris, Institut de Management Hôtelier International.

Palmer, A. (2001), *Principles of Services Marketing*, 3rd edn, Maidenhead, McGraw-Hill.

Reynolds, P. (2001), 'Outplants favoured', *Travel Trade Gazette*, 26 March.

Rice, K. (2001), 'A more inventive way to fly', *Financial Times*, 17 April.

Scales, J. (1999), 'Getting there by net', *The Irish Times*, 14 April.

Schertler, W. and Berger-Koch, C. (1999), 'Tourism as an information business: the strategic consequences of e-commerce for business travel', in Buhalis, D. and Schertler, W. (eds), *Information and Communication Technologies in Tourism: Proceedings of the International Conference in Innsbruck, Austria*, Vienna, Springer.

Tweedie, J. (2001), 'What's in store for the trade in 2001?', *Travel Trade Gazette*, 8 January.

Upton, G. (2001), 'Airlines rearrange seats in the sky', *Financial Times*, 4 September.

Weinberger, R. (1999), 'Trimming the fat: slimmed down corporate budgets and cost cutting policies are revolutionising the business of travel', *Time*, 21 June.

Young, H. (1999a), 'Rosenbluth wins Bae account', *Travel Trade Gazette*, 22 March.

Young, H. (1999b), '72 pc of fares in economy', *Travel Trade Gazette*, 26 April.

Chapter 3

The meetings industry

Objectives

On completion of this chapter, you should be able to:

- *identify the main sources of data on the meetings market;*

- *distinguish the various types of demand for meetings and the main characteristics of each;*

- *classify suppliers in the meetings market according to type of venue and recognise the strengths and weaknesses of each type;*

- *understand the roles of the key intermediaries;*

- *identify the principal trends in the meetings market and the factors contributing to them;*

- *understand the key ethical and political issues raised by the ways in which meetings are organised and conducted.*

▶ ● Meetings events in the twenty-first century

- The International Association of Physicians in AIDS Care held its fifth international conference on healthcare resource allocation for HIV/AIDS and other life-threatening illnesses over four days in Rio de Janeiro.
- 150 delegates attended a conference at the Renaissance Hotel, Heathrow Airport, hosted by ERA Technologies' Avionics. One-third of the delegates arrived by air.
- The National Merchants Buying Society held a three-day conference for 260 of their members in Edinburgh's Sheraton Hotel. A gala dinner was held in the Royal Museum of Scotland, and there was a Caribbean-themed evening on the last night at the Dynamic Earth visitor attraction.
- Barclays Financial Management chartered the *Radisson Diamond,* a cruise ship that caters exclusively for meetings at sea, with a multipurpose auditorium, simultaneous translating facilities and videoconferencing.
- 100 clients were invited to the Grand Hotel in Monaco to witness the launch by the telecommunications company Fusion of its new product, Onesea, a multi-terabit-capacity network connecting southern Europe, North Africa and the Middle East using cables under the sea.

● ● ● ● Introduction

Human beings are, by nature, social animals. It seems inconceivable that our evolution as a species could have taken place at the same extraordinary rate without our natural predisposition to congregate regularly in order to exchange our ideas and experiences, enhance our knowledge and skills, and celebrate our most laudable achievements.

The practice of meeting to exchange and disseminate information, once so vital to our collective survival, remains an essential feature of the professional, political, spiritual and recreational lives of a significant proportion of the population. Now, several hundred million people travel each year in order to attend meetings. Some, such as the 1992 Earth Summit in Rio de Janeiro or the Population and Development Conference in Cairo in 1994, are truly global in nature, amassing tens of thousands of delegates and media representatives from all over the world. Others may consist of a mere handful of colleagues spending a one-day brainstorming session in a meeting room in a local hotel. But whatever the scale and location of the event, the fundamental motivations underlying the arranging of the meeting are invariable: to combine the knowledge, talents and ideas of those present in order to solve problems, share enthusiasms or simply find a way of doing things better.

This chapter examines the principal features of supply and demand in the meetings market, including the roles played by those who are active in it – those who attend meetings, those who organise and pay for them, as well as those who provide the facilities and services that make such events possible: the meetings industry. The dominant trends are also considered in the context of key changes in the meetings market environment.

In order to set the current situation in its proper chronological context, however, this chapter begins with a brief overview of the history of organised meetings.

● ● ● ● Historical background

It is only in the past 50 years or so that the burgeoning scale of meetings activity, coupled with its geographical expansion across the globe, has resulted in the development of a specialised meetings industry, created to serve the needs of men and women who travel in order to congregate with those with whom they share a common interest. Smith (1990; p.66) notes that in recent times, meetings 'have become a major profit centre, an essential part of the communications process on which our global village depends', adding, however, that '"meetings industry" is a relatively new phrase. Few people in the 1950s would have used such a term.'

The history of organised meetings is much longer than that of the meetings industry itself. Large-scale, formal meetings held for strategic and diplomatic purposes, such as the 1814 Congress of Vienna, which re-established the territorial divisions of Europe after the defeat of Napoleon I, or the 1822 Congress of Verona, which convened to discuss the major European powers' military strategy, are early examples of how meetings have been an important element of political life in Europe and beyond for almost 300 years.

On a less grandiose scale, meetings of the merchant and professional classes of Europe had an established place in public life even before the Industrial Revolution. Shone (1998) notes that, at that time, fashionable Georgian towns such as Bath, Buxton and Cheltenham provided assembly rooms for such events. Rooms were also available, then as now, for public meeting purposes in some of the buildings of the scientific societies, such as the Royal Society and the Royal Geographical Society in London.

However, more generally, inns and hotels were the venues for the vast majority of meetings, which were held either in dedicated meetings rooms or in the premises' ballrooms if they were attended by large numbers.

But the growth in demand that was eventually to create the need for the modern meetings industry owes much to the influence of the Americans. Smith (1990) reports that the historian Alexis de Tocqueville, in his early nineteenth-century analysis of the political and social system of the USA, notes how keen Americans were to get together in associations and hold meetings. Rogers (1998) also links the origins of today's meetings industry to the trade and professional association conventions in the USA during the latter part of the nineteenth century. The number of such associations was to accelerate during the early decades of the twentieth century on both sides of the Atlantic.

In the USA, between 1900 and 1920, the white-collar workforce more than doubled in size, from 5.1 million to 10.5 million, more than twice the growth rate for the workforce as a whole (Boyer *et al.*, 1993). As the number of professional workers grew in Europe and the USA, so too did their sense of professional identity. As a result, long-established professional societies such as the American Bar Association and the British Medical Association saw their membership expand rapidly during those years. Scores of new professional groups and business associations were also formed, from the American Association of Advertising Agencies (established in 1917) and the National Association of Accountants (1919) to the Institute of Directors (1903) and the Association Française des Femmes Ingénieurs (1929).

Observant witnesses to this expansion were quick to understand that there were vast potential benefits for those towns and cities chosen as the venues for these associations' meetings. It was inevitable then that, as Rogers (1998) remarks, in due course a number of committees were created to lure the growing convention business from these expanding and thriving associations. It was in the creation of these committees – the convention bureaux of their day – that the modern meetings industry found its genesis, and the first elements of the vast human and physical infrastructure that we now know as the meetings industry were established.

Sources of data on the meetings industry

Across the world, how many people are, at this very minute, involved in attending a meeting of some kind – and where are these meetings being held? The truth is that despite its huge economic importance – both as a cost item to buyers and as a profit centre for suppliers – it is still extremely difficult to estimate the size and location of the world's meetings industry with any reliable degree of accuracy. Nowhere is the dearth of statistical data for business travel and tourism – highlighted in Chapter 1 – felt more acutely than in the meetings sector.

It has often been lamented that few other multimillion dollar industries have such a meagre database as that of the meetings industry – even in Europe itself, a mature and lively marketplace for meetings of all types and sizes. Although some excellent data are available on meetings attendance and spending in several individual European countries and in some cities, the statistical basis for the meetings industry taken as a whole is still at best erratic and deficient in many aspects. To the regret of those responsible for measuring and predicting trends in the meetings industry, there is still no single barometer or uniform methodology that gauges the activity in this market within Europe. Instead, researchers, marketeers and planners have to rely on an incomplete and irregular collage of meetings statistics and reports in order to estimate the size of the industry and the main trends that characterise it.

One valuable piece of this statistical patchwork, however, is comprised of the data provided by the Brussels-based Union of International Associations (UIA) (www.uia.org). Based on the findings of its annual survey of over 25 000 international associations, the UIA publishes figures on one specific category of meetings only – the annual meetings of international associations (although some national meetings with international participation are also included). The association's International Congress Calendar includes details of over 15 000 such meetings each year. Numerically, international associations' meetings are a small section of the total market, but it is a section of particular interest to the countries, cities and towns active in this marketplace on account of the considerable prestige and economic benefits that they can bring to the places in which they are held.

As Smith (1991; p.120) has commented:

> These congresses are only a fraction of the world meetings market, but the sector most eagerly contested by conference towns throughout Europe, the Orient and elsewhere. Even in the North American conference marketplace, usually regarded as self contained, several bigger US city convention bureaux from time to time identify this sector of the market and work to win a share of it.

Nevertheless, as the strict criteria for being included in the UIA data include there being a minimum of five nationalities represented among the delegates, major events such as the American Society of Travel Agents (ASTA) Convention and the meetings of the American Bar Association, which are from time to time held in the UK, are excluded. Similarly, religious, commercial and sporting events, of which the UK has a major share, are not counted, thus putting the UK's ranking in the UIA league tables at a disadvantage (BTF & BTAC, 1999).

Another valued contributor to the statistical base for meetings is the International Congress and Convention Association (ICCA) (www.icca.nl), which, from its headquarters in Amsterdam, maintains a database on the location of past and future meetings of international associations. Like those of the UIA, the ICCA's data enable comparisons to be made over a long time and are indicative of trends and changes in market shares. ICCA data are based on the meetings of international associations that have at least 50 participants, are organised on a regular basis, and move between at least three different countries. The ICCA stresses that its goal is to collect accurate information but that it does not claim to have data on all meetings that meet these criteria. For this reason, it is generally accepted that the ICCA's qualitative data are more representative than its quantitative data.

Although the ICCA's figures are not directly comparable with those of the UIA, taken together both sets of data provide reliable measurement of the international meetings they track over the years. As such, they will be used to illustrate some of the trends that are discussed at the end of this chapter.

It is precisely because the meetings included in UIA and ICCA data represent only a tiny fraction of the overall market that many European countries have chosen to conduct their own surveys in order to measure demand for meetings in their cities more comprehensively.

An example of a national survey in the UK is the annual British Conference Market Trends Survey (BCMTS), commissioned by the British Tourist Authority and its partner sponsors with the aim of providing a monitor of the trends and levels of activity of the UK conference industry. The BCMTS defines a conference as an event that involves 15 or more people and occupies the venue for six hours or more during the course of one or more days. Participating venues complete an annual questionnaire detailing all the conferences that they have held during the preceding year. Since 1994, data have been collected on who uses the facilities, how many delegates attend the events, the revenue earned by the venue, the conference duration, and whether the event involves an overnight stay.

It is acknowledged even by those carrying out the survey that the sample size of the BCMTS is too small to allow a reliable extrapolation of the figures for the size or value of the whole UK conference market (Shallcross, 1998). Nevertheless, despite this limitation, the BCMTS is generally considered to be a value-for-money survey, and, in a research area of relative scarcity, a welcome contribution.

Another key source of meetings data for the UK is the UK Conference Market Survey, an in-depth annual survey carried out by market researchers, The Right Solution, on behalf of the Meetings Industry Association and sponsored by the British Tourist Authority, the British Association of Conference Destinations, CAT Publications, Conference Centres of Excellence and Pannell Kerr Foster and the Sundial Group. The Right Solution carries out in-depth telephone research with 300 corporate conference organisers from *The Times* top 1000 companies and, since 1998, 300 UK-based association conference organisers, in order to determine trends in the characteristics of the events they hold as well as their destination- and venue-selecting criteria.

But while national surveys play a valuable role in measuring the level of activity in the meetings market for countries as a whole, it is at the level of individual cities competing for business within those countries that success in this market also needs to be monitored effectively. Given the high level of public-sector investment required at the local level in order to attract and maintain a vigorous meetings market, it is not surprising that cities should wish to assess their success, not only in terms of market share but also by surveying delegates and seeking to calculate economic returns of meetings of all kinds.

In response to the need of cities to be able to measure the benefits they obtain from meetings and compare these accurately with other cities in the same country, a number of European nations have created statistical modelling schemes that enable individual cities to assess the value of the meetings business they succeed in attracting.

In the UK, the first organised attempt to create a benchmark for the industry was the Conference Delegate Expenditure Survey, which gives destinations a reliable base against which to carry out their own economic impact studies. In 1998, the consultants System Three were commissioned by the National Tourist Boards to undertake a study in order to gain more information on the volume and value of the UK conference market. The specific objectives were:

- to provide estimates of volume and value data for conference delegate expenditure in England, Scotland, Northern Ireland and Wales;
- to provide comparative expenditure information by type of conference, size, duration, origins of delegate and venue;
- to provide market profile data and an assessment of market needs.

A two-strand approach to this research was adopted: a survey of conference delegates and a survey of conference organisers. The study has since become a UK benchmark used by towns and cities to produce comparable data on local spend by visiting corporate, association and academic delegates.

Another example of this approach to data collection is found in France, where the national association of conference towns, France Congrès, in 1998 developed a model that enables conference centres to calculate the economic impact they have on the cities in which they are situated. Based on the calculation of delegates' spending, the use of the model produces estimates of the revenue created by conferences in each city and the number of jobs created or supported by them, taking into account the direct, indirect and induced economic impacts of such events (*Gazette Officielle*, 1998). When the first results were published in 2000, it was shown, for example, that in Cannes, 10% of the population was employed in that town's meetings industry (Cossardeaux, 2000).

One important issue is the extent to which meetings can be said to generate economic benefits for their host cities. Many models differ in their definition of what constitutes the full impact of meetings activity. Ryan (1999), for example, describes how Auckland City Council has developed an 'events economic impacts model', which incorporates calculations of indirect and induced impacts as well as the direct effects of visitor spending. White (1998) makes a case for meetings-related exhibition statistics also being included in the overall figures, claiming that in the case of Harrogate, for example, associated exhibitions running alongside conferences are an integral part of the market share being analysed and evaluated, and that to measure only the conference element is neither relevant nor practical.

A further important contribution to the meetings database of many countries is that made by the trade press through their annual surveys of market trends. In the UK, for example, *Meetings & Incentive Travel* magazine's annual Trends and Spends Survey examines the activities of the major UK-based agencies specialised in outbound conferences and incentive trips. Similarly, *Conference & Incentive Travel* magazine conducts its own regular surveys of UK conference destinations, national tourist offices' involvement in conference promotion, and hotel chains.

However, despite the variety of different organisations contributing to the overall supply of data available on this sector of business tourism, several commentators (Smith, 1990; Rogers, 1998; Rockett and Smillie, 1994) have compared the situation in Europe unfavourably with that currently found in the USA, where, they claim, the quantification and qualification of meetings activity are much more advanced.

Sadly, little appears to have changed in the years that have passed since Smith (1991) first lamented that 'Europeans feel they lag behind the US in the development of a statistical basis for the meetings and convention industry'. In that article, Smith speaks admiringly of the figures produced by the International Association of Convention and Visitor Bureaux (IACVB) (www.iacvb.org) for the USA, on delegate spend and length of stay, adding that no comparable European data exist. Similarly, the Meetings Outlook Survey produced by the American Society of Association Executives and Meetings Professionals International (MPI) provides valuable data, but with a strong North American focus.

However, on a more positive note for Europe, a recent Eurostat initiative to develop guidelines for the collection of conference sector data has resulted in a methodological manual for use by organisations that are active in this field (Eurostat, 2000). The objective underlying the production of the manual is to establish a common methodology, which, through the creation of definitions and criteria, might bring about greater compatibility and comparability between statistics produced using this system. Time will tell whether this initiative will result in the considerable improvement still needed in the database for meetings in Europe.

Meanwhile, a range of useful data on the worldwide meetings industry may be accessed via the DOME (Data on Meetings and Events) Internet database (www.domeresearch.com), a welcome, relatively new source of information in this area.

Buyers

The meetings market is the most diverse of all the sectors of business travel and tourism. Demand for meetings facilities and services originates from a multitude of different types of customers, all extremely varied in terms of the sizes and purposes of the meetings they hold. These can range from a small manufacturing business in search of a local venue in which to hold a sales strategy seminar for six people, to the United Nations inspecting cities all over the world with a view to choosing a destination for its 2001 summit on racism, with 10 000 delegates, including several hundred heads of state. It is, therefore, vital for those responsible for providing and marketing venues and other services for the meetings industry to be able to segment the market in a meaningful and operational manner.

Market demand is usually synonymous with the buyers in that market. However, in the context of the meetings industry, the term 'buyer' is ambiguous. On the one hand, 'buyers' may refer to the actual initiators of the meetings events – those organisations whose needs create the demand for meetings of all kinds. On the other hand, the word 'buyer' is also used to describe those individuals who are employed directly or indirectly by these organisations to select destinations and venues and to plan the meetings events themselves.

For the purposes of clarity, in this context the term 'buyer' will be reserved to describe the organisations that are the initiators of meetings, while the term 'meetings planner' will be used to describe the individuals employed by those organisations to organise their events. Demand in terms of buyer organisations will be considered first.

Segments of the market

It is possible to envisage several alternative segmentations of the overall demand for meetings. For example, the market could be segmented by size into small and large meetings; or it could be segmented according to the main purpose of the event – educating, motivating, informing; or even according to the types of people who attend the events – local residents, out-of-towners, visitors from overseas, etc.

However, the system of segmentation used most commonly defines the different types of demand primarily according to the type of buyer involved, i.e. the actual initiators of the meetings. Under this system, the two main segments – meetings of business corporations and meetings of professional or trade associations – between them account for most of the overall demand by far in this sector.

Corporate demand

It is generally recognised that the corporate sector, consisting essentially of private businesses of all sizes, dominates in terms of the sheer number of meetings it needs in order to function effectively. Smith (1990), for example, goes as far as to estimate that about 90% of all meetings are in fact corporate events, although the general consensus is that this proportion is somewhat exaggerated. This market can be usefully subdivided into 'internal' and 'external' meetings. The former are generally aimed at the employees of the company, and often take the form of relatively small, one-day meetings, held for staff training purposes, or as management seminars or board meetings.

External corporate meetings are, by contrast, aimed primarily at the wider market in which the company operates, and consequently involve the company's external partners and associates. Such meetings events may be held for the purpose of bringing together the company's dealers and distributors for product presentations, or its own shareholders for annual general meetings. Attendance at such events may run to many hundreds of delegates. Some corporate meetings involve both internal and external delegates, a good example of this being events organised in order to launch a new product. At such meetings, the company must convince both its own sales force and external distributors of the new product's value. These are generally very striking, spectacular events at which the product – which can be anything from a new model of combine harvester to the latest perfume from a fashion house – is unveiled with great ceremony and its strongest selling points explained to all of those present.

Although practically every industry sector needs to hold meetings from time to time, certain sectors are generally recognised as producing a higher-than-average level of demand. According to Rogers (1998; p.25), the buyers that are particularly prominent in generating corporate conference business include:

- oil, gas and petrochemicals
- medical and pharmaceuticals
- computing and telecommunications
- engineering and manufacturing

- financial and professional services
- retail and wholesale distribution
- travel and transport.

Association demand

Association demand derives from the meetings held by the countless sectoral organisations that operate on behalf of their members. Such organisations may be professional or trade associations (e.g. the British Dental Association, the International Federation of Newspaper Publishers), or they may serve to bring together those with a common cause or leisure interest (e.g. the League Against Cruel Sports, the US Military Veterans' Motorcycle Club). They may be local, regional, national, continental or international in the scope of their membership and activities.

But, whatever its common purpose or geographical range, the broad aim of any association is to serve its members' interests. According to the American Society of Association Executives (ASAE), this means taking measures to (Seaton and Bennett, 1996):

- advance the status and image of the members;
- provide for peer interaction and exchange of information;
- evaluate and project future trends;
- lobby and advance the association members' interests (political, economic, social);
- emphasise the value of membership;
- provide entertainment and informal interaction.

It is clear that a number of these objectives can be met most effectively through the provision of regular opportunities for association members to gather together in order to discuss issues of common interest. Such meetings may be annual or biannual (but rarely less frequent), their rate of recurrence generally depending on the extent of their membership and how geographically dispersed it is. Consequently, although in number there are far fewer of them than corporate meetings, association events constitute a very significant share of the meetings market. According to Greenhill (2000), there are approximately 7000 such associations in the UK alone, and it is estimated that nearly half of these hold events on a regular basis.

For the international association meetings market, most demand tends to be generated by the same sectors each year. For 2000, the ICCA (2001) report demonstrates that medical sciences, science, industry and technology remained the big four areas in terms of subject matter, adding that education and agriculture were also important, followed by social sciences and economics.

It is clear that medical conferences – and the exhibitions that often accompany them – represent a vast area of demand, both from individual companies and associations. As a result, a number of associations have been formed to identify and disseminate best practice in this specialised field of events. The Healthcare Convention and Exhibitors Association (www.hcea.org), the International Exhibitors Association on Radiological Congresses, and the International Pharmaceutical Congress Advisory Association (www.ipcaa.org) are examples of membership-based organisations that exist to promote high standards in the medical conferences and exhibitions sector.

Other categories

Apart from corporate and association buyers, other categories often identified in segmentation systems include government bodies (local authorities, central government departments and agencies), intergovernmental structures (the EU, the G8 group of nations), as well as religious and trade union agencies, none of which fits convincingly into the two main market segments.

Some of these types of buyers are occasionally subsumed within the association sector with which they share certain characteristics. Indeed, Seaton and Bennett (1996) use the term 'avocational associations', which they define as organisations whose members share sport, recreational, hobby, fraternal, cultural, civic or other social interests. When discussing the segmentation of the North American meetings market, Kotler *et al.* (1996) use the acronym 'SMERF' (social, military, educational, religious and fraternal) organisations, a term that is not found frequently outside the USA.

Characteristics of the main buyer segments

Size

Association and corporate buyers may be distinguished by a number of characteristics of the types of demand they generate for meetings. Perhaps the most striking contrast between the two segments is seen in the size of their respective events. Since many association events generate high delegate volumes, it is in this sector that a relatively high proportion of the largest meetings is to be found. In the UK meetings market, for example, Shallcross (1998) remarks that a significantly higher proportion of association conferences have more than 200 delegates than any other sector.

Length

Most surveys demonstrate that association meetings tend to be longer than corporate events, and are more likely to be residential. For example, the UK Conference Market Survey for 2000 indicated that in that year, the average length of an association meeting event was 2.49 days, as compared with 1.63 days average duration for a corporate meeting (MIA, 2000).

It is due to the combination of association events being, generally speaking, larger and longer than corporate meetings that lead times (the period of time that passes from the date a decision is made to organise a meeting until the time when the meeting is actually held) are, on average, longer for association events than for corporate events. This difference is most marked in the case of international meetings: ICCA observes that while the lead time for (international) association meetings is two to three years, and sometimes longer, corporate meetings are planned over a shorter period, usually less than one year (ICCA, 2001). Rogers (1998; p.78) links the difference in length of lead times between the association and corporate markets to the fact that corporate demand for meetings appears to follow changes in the economy more closely than association demand: 'Fluctuations in conference demand are more noticeable in the corporate sector than in the association sector, often because of factors such as lead times. Corporate events, with relatively short lead times, can quickly respond to changing economic situations.'

Spending

It has traditionally been assumed by many that, in terms of actual spending, the more cost-conscious association market usually budgets for lower delegate rates (the cost of venue hire plus meals and accommodation, if required). Whereas this may be true of many association meetings – in particular, where most delegates are paying out of their own pockets – it is by no means the case that all associations are parsimonious in their approach to spending on meetings. Rogers (1998) observes that delegates attending an annual surgeons' conference would expect to stay in accommodation of at least three-star hotel standard, whereas a charity or religious conference would be more likely to require more modest accommodation at the budget end of the spectrum.

The revenue generated by association meetings takes on even greater dimensions when the spending of delegates' guests is taken into account. Although certain types of corporate meetings welcome the partners of those attending, this is much more common in the association market, where attendance is usually voluntary and where delegates' guests are often actively encouraged to attend, as a means of increasing attendee numbers. This theme is elaborated upon in Chapter 7.

Location

Corporate buyers have a greater tendency than those in the association sector to return to the same destination or venue. As these are often determined by the location of the company's own headquarters or its representations, there tends to be a limited range of possible options from which a venue may be chosen. Consequently a hotel, for example, situated close to one of the company's premises may find that it has a regular contract to provide meetings facilities for that company – on condition, of course, that it delivers consistently satisfactory service. Mill (1992) elaborates on this point:

> Attendance at corporate meetings is required. As a result the choice of destination has no effect on the number of people attending. Many corporate meetings are held at the same place year after year if the host hotel can show it can deliver quality service... Since the accent at a corporate meeting is on work, privacy and a lack of distractions are appreciated more than recreational facilities and sightseeing opportunities.

In the association sector, there is greater flexibility of choice, as attendance at association events is usually voluntary. The choice of a different venue each time can add to the attractiveness of the conference package and therefore boost attendance. Ryan (1999; p.49) underlines this point: '[Association] conference organisers are not destination-loyal; indeed, changing venues is a means of sustaining interest in a series of conferences over time.'

However, one important constraint for locating association events is the obligation to rotate destinations in order, over time, to share out the costs, in terms of time and money, which members have to bear in order to attend. In order to maximise attendance, an association may alternate between different parts of the country, or within a continent, or even globally, depending on the geographical distribution of its members. For instance, for its annual conferences, the International Lesbian and Gay Association (ILGA) has, since 1991, alternated between northern-hemisphere and southern-hemisphere destinations, such as Mexico (1991) and Brazil (1995). In 1999, the nineteenth ILGA World Conference was held for the first time in an African country, when 200 delegates from 40 countries gathered in Johannesburg to discuss the theme of 'Building Partnerships for Equality'.

A consequence of the system of rotating destinations is that once a particular city has been used as the venue for an association meeting, the same association is unlikely to return there for a number of years.

Buying/decision-making process

From the point of view of those supplying and promoting meetings facilities and venues, one of the most striking contrasts between the corporate and the association markets is the way in which their respective buying processes and buying patterns differ so extensively.

In seeking to attract new business, two key questions that suppliers must endeavour to answer are *who* within the buyer organisation is responsible for organising meetings, and *how* is the decision as to where the meeting will be held actually taken within the buyer organisation?

The first question raises the issue of the meetings planners or meetings organisers who have a degree of influence on which venues are considered for conferences, seminars and other events. Who are they? To whom within organisations should suppliers and destination marketing organisations, for example, direct their marketing efforts? Identifying exactly who the meetings planners are is often far from simple.

Part of the complexity of the issue arises from the fact that large organisations, whether in the corporate or the association sector, may either have a single, specialist meetings planner – one person with the responsibility for all decisions on meetings-related matters for that organisation – or, alternatively, following a more decentralised system, each branch, division or chapter of the organisation may be responsible for purchasing its own meetings facilities and services, in which case there will be a number of different individuals with responsibility for planning meetings.

A third option for both corporate and association organisations is to give the responsibility for arranging meetings to an external intermediary, who will undertake all or some of the planning of the event on behalf of the buyer. The use and role of intermediaries will be examined later in this chapter. First, however, it is important to return to the questions posed earlier: who within the buyer organisation is responsible for organising meetings, and how is the decision as to where the meeting will be held actually taken?

Regarding the buyers encountered in the corporate sector, Rogers (1998) notes that, in the UK at least, relatively few companies have a dedicated conference or event management department, and that staff involved in organising meetings appear in a whole range of guises and job titles.

Greenhill (2000) develops this issue:

It is very difficult to establish the actual universe of [meetings planners]. The changing nature of companies' structures affects the number of organisers. There are many people who organise a meeting or conference just once a year, and their main professional responsibility is entirely different. However, there are also those for whom it is a full-time responsibility. They are very experienced events organisers and have specialist skills that contribute greatly to the success of their events.

Those responsible for planning meetings for the companies who employ them can have any one of a wide range of functions within their organisations, as shown by the variety of their principal professional responsibilities listed in Table 3.1.

It is clear that those marketing venues and destinations need to be able to identify the people within companies who are responsible for organising meetings in order to target their marketing efforts directly at those corporate buyers. However, the question is complicated further by the fact that often it is not the actual meetings planner who has the final say on selecting the venue or destination.

Table 3.1 Principal professional responsibilities of meetings planners in the corporate sector

Job title/department	Percentage
Secretary/PA	33
Administration	6
Sales and marketing	21
Corporate communications	8
Conference/meetings/event coordinator	8
Public relations	5
Travel organiser	4
Training	3.5
Personnel/human resources	3.5
Manager	3
Director	2
Services/facilities organiser	2
Other	1
Total	**100**

Source: *UK Conference Market Survey 2000*, published by the Meetings Industry Association.

Shone (1998; p.129) illustrates this point:

> Let us suppose the buyer of a large multinational company is the UK training division. The buyer is the Chief Training Manager within the division. He or she may actually be part of a committee responsible for organising the annual conference; and while the Chief Training Manager and the committee supposedly have the responsibility, in practice, they have to report their choice of venue to the UK Divisional Director, who has the final say. In some organisations, this type of reporting may be a simple rubber-stamping; in others the real power [to decide] may lie with the Divisional Director.

Finding out, therefore, exactly who within companies has the power to decide on where corporate meetings will take place is a complex yet crucial matter for suppliers. The situation is, if anything, more complex in the case of associations.

One feature hardly ever encountered in the corporate sector but that often characterises the buying process in the international association sector in particular is the bid process. This arises from the fact that, in the association market, the hosting of a meeting in a particular city or venue often takes place as the result of an initiative taken by a local or national branch or chapter of the association in question. This is particularly the case for the international association meetings market. Lawson (2000; p.19) claims that: 'Most of the decisions affecting the choice of venue for international associations stem from invitations made through their national branches or chapters.'

When several chapters of the same association are in competition to host the same event, each is invited to bid for the privilege of doing so. In that case, each one will compile a bid proposal detailing the advantages of the event being hosted in their particular city or country, in very much the same way as, on a grander scale, countries bid to be the venue for the Olympic Games.

An example of an event won in this way is seen in the successful joint bid made by Edinburgh and Glasgow in 1999 to host the four-day international Velocity 2001 conference of the European Cyclists' Federation. The bid, put together by a consortium including the two cities' councils and local cycling campaign groups, made a convincing enough case for the two Scottish cities to be selected in preference to the competing bids submitted by Dublin, Gothenburg and Strasbourg.

As the local authorities of each competing destination usually have a clear interest in their city being the winner in this process, they usually support the bid by contributing to the proposal document. Rogers (1998; p.30) outlines the content of a typical bid proposal:

> A bid document is likely to contain a formal invitation, often signed by the Mayor or other civic dignity, a full description of the destination highlighting its attractions, access and communications details ... information on the support services available in the destination ... a list of the services provided by the convention and visitor bureau or conference office, details of hotel and other accommodation and, of course, full details of the venue being proposed to stage the conference.

Assistance with any presentations and/or the inspection visits that can also form part of the bid procedure may also be provided by the destination's own marketing organisation. The need to provide such support and assistance can add up to a substantial investment in terms of the amount of work and expense. But most destinations understand that it is vital to participate when the consequence of coming first in the competition is such a tremendous boost to their economy and image. Indeed, the more proactive destination marketing organisations do not wait until associations' local contacts contact them for assistance. Understanding that local contacts can be strong allies in getting their city or country on the initial list of possible destinations, and then lobbying for it to be selected, many destination marketeers make active efforts to identify such groups and convert them into valuable conference leads.

The decision-making process in the association market is complicated further by the issue of exactly who within the organisation is responsible for arranging the event and choosing the destination and venue. In common with the corporate sector, many associations have no specific, specialised member or members of staff responsible for organising meetings events. But one difference is that, as Shone (1998; p.28) notes, the organisation of conferences for the association market often relies heavily on the efforts of unpaid volunteers, and that, as a result:

> This poses a challenge for venue managers and sales teams, n1ot only in identifying who, in an association, is likely to be the conference organiser, but also in terms of dealing with organisers who lack the necessary experience and skills. In consequence, sales teams may have to exert greater efforts to ensure an association conference goes smoothly than might be the case when dealing with ... a contact within a commercial organisation whose specific duties include conference organisation.

Regarding the choice of destination and venue, whereas in the corporate sector it is frequently the case that the decision as to where a meeting is to be held is made by one individual, in associations the decision is more likely to be made by a number of people working together. A Travel & Tourism Intelligence (TTI, 2000) report cites research that indicates that association meeting planners have the power to decide upon a meeting venue approximately 40% of the time, but for the remaining 60% it is usually the decision of groups of people internal to professional and trade associations. Such groups may take the form of a special organising committee or the association's secretariat, for example. Whatever its composition, in consumer terminology, the group constitutes a 'buying centre'.

Two or even three different, but connected, buying centres may be involved in the different stages of the decision-making process linked to the location and organisation of a large association meeting:

● The destination may be chosen by a specialist committee representing the association as a whole – typically including the meeting planner, the association's executive, its president, and members of the executive committee.

- The venue and other local suppliers may be chosen by the local organising committee – representing the local branch that won the bidding process, if there was one.
- The actual programme for the event may be organised by a specialist programme committee, which may be part of the local organising committee or a separate body.

Clearly, a much wider range of players may be involved in the decision-making process in associations than is the case for corporate meetings. For those responsible for marketing venues and destinations, this inevitably raises the point that while meeting planners are important players in the process, marketing to them alone is unlikely to be entirely effective. The situation is complicated further by the fact that not all players in the process have equal influence over the final decision as to where the event is to be held.

This was demonstrated vividly by Clark *et al.* (1997), who undertook a study of how the various association players use their power (or influence) to shape the outcome of the decision-making process. They demonstrated how different buying-centre participants play different roles in the decision-making process. The roles identified approximate closely to those described in the case of corporate travel purchasing in Chapter 2: 'users', 'influencers', 'buyers', 'deciders' and 'gatekeepers'. Within these roles, Clark *et al.* showed how some members of the buying centre can – and do – exert influence based on their roles and the power they hold, particularly in the initial part of the buying decision, i.e. when the group is generating a shortlist of five or six potential cities for consideration (an 'evoked set') or deciding upon the result of the bidding procedure. The study concluded that group members used their individual power and influence in different ways to affect the joint decision-making process. The different types of power, and how they may be used, are shown in Table 3.2.

The conclusion of the authors is that those who are responsible for marketing destinations and venues would be best served by first identifying the power sources within the association they hope to attract, and then designing a specific strategy

Table 3.2 Categories of power in buying centres

Power	The ability to ...
Reward	... bestow a reward on other members of the committee
Coercive	... punish other members if they do not go along with his/her wishes
Referent	... influence others by sheer personal magnetism
Legitimate	... influence based on position or hierarchical relationship
Expert	... influence based on personal knowledge, skills, abilities or experiences
Information	... influence by providing or withholding selected information from the group
Departmental	... influence resulting from association with a particular department or unit

Source: Clark, J.D., Evans, M.R. and Knutson, B.J. (1997), 'Selecting a site for an association convention: an exploratory look at the types of power used by committee members to influence decisions', *Journal of Hospitality & Leisure Marketing*, Vol. 5, pp. 81–95.

aimed at convincing the committee member holding/mediating the most power. In marketing terms, they recommended the use of a laser approach to marketing rather than shotgun marketing. However, at the same time, Clark *et al.* (1997; p.91) do admit that this is an involved and ongoing process:

> It is not uncommon in associations to have a new chairperson every year ... Therefore marketing strategies not only need to be aimed at the current chair or president, they need to identify and court future leaders. A long-term relationship between the hospitality marketer and the association chair(s)-to-be can impact how they use their influence in your favour for the year they are in power.

Seasonality and periodicity of demand

Just as for leisure tourism, most commentators claim to detect seasonal patterns of demand for meetings, demonstrated by months and days of the week when demand is predictably higher or lower than at other times. For example, concerning the UK meetings market, Shallcross (1998; p.B-48) writes:

> The conference market is highly seasonal with pronounced and relatively predictable peaks ... Conference activity peaks in March and in September, October and November, while activity tails off significantly in December. Trends in seasonality are essentially common to all venue types. The months of least activity are July and August, coinciding with general holiday preferences as one would expect.

The seasonal spread of meetings held in the UK is shown in Figure 3.1.

Witt and Moutinho (1995) note that Fighiera (1985) also documented a noticeable tendency to seasonality in the distribution of demand for meetings, and speculate that a partial explanation for these patterns might be the indirect impact of 'natural' factors related to climate – principally the availability of accommodation at relatively cheap rates in holiday resorts at times of the year that lie outside their normal peak season for leisure tourism.

But while this particular supply-side factor undoubtedly plays a part in determining levels of demand for meetings held in resorts such as those on the French Mediterranean coast, there are different factors contributing to the seasonal distribution of meetings in other types of venue. For example, Shallcross (1998) notes that peaks in meetings activity in educational establishments coincide with periods of student vacation.

Witt and Moutinho (1995; p.94) acknowledge this, concluding that predicting the seasonality of demand for meetings is far from straightforward:

> It is clear from Fighiera's data, however, that the matter is more complex ... in that climatically similar regions (for example, the Netherlands and the UK) do not report the same cycles in the distribution of meetings. Moreover, national and international events follow quite distinguishable cycles. Evidently any explanation will have to concentrate principally on configurations of institutional factors (timetables for the parliamentary year, for example) which will interact with more conventionally seasonal factors.

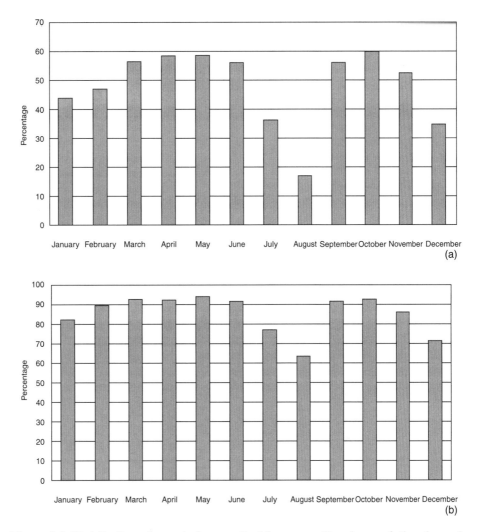

Figure 3.1 Distribution of events by month: (a) seasonality of associations' events; (b) seasonality of corporate events

Source: MIA (2000), *UK Conference Market Survey 2000*, published by the Meetings Industry Association.

Figure 3.2 shows how meetings held in UK venues are distributed throughout the week.

It would seem that conference facilities are most in demand on Thursdays, which is the most popular day of the week with both the association and corporate sectors. This is followed closely by Wednesday and Tuesday. It is interesting to note that almost half of associations are also holding events on Saturdays, while the percentage of companies asking their employees to give up part or all of their weekends in order to attend meetings is far lower.

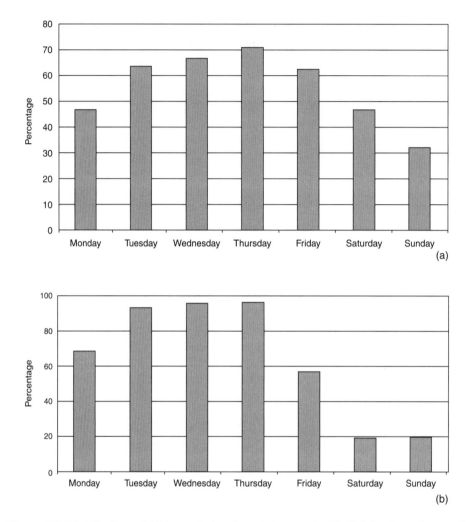

Figure 3.2 Distribution of UK events by day of the week: (a) distribution of associations' events; (b) distribution of corporate events

Source: MIA (2000), *UK Conference Market Survey 2000*, published by the Meetings Industry Association.

●●●● Suppliers

In order to respond to the extensive and varied demand for meetings of all kinds, a comprehensive infrastructure of suppliers offering a wide range of facilities and supporting services must operate efficiently and in harmony. The suppliers in this market are those who make available for hire the venues and other services that make it possible for meetings to take place. Although most of this section concentrates on the actual buildings in which meetings are held, it is important to bear in mind that an equally vital role is played by the suppliers of the other types of services that also contribute to the success of meetings. These include the audiovisual contractors who rent out specialist equipment, the telecommunications companies whose video/tele/satellite conferencing services can extend the number of participants for meetings, interpreters and translators, speciality caterers, floral contractors, and exhibition contractors.

But while the importance of these auxiliary services cannot be overestimated, the fact is that the choice of a suitable type of venue is one of the most crucial decisions to be taken in the organisation of any meeting. The meetings facility market is represented by a wide range of venues of differing sizes and levels of equipment and services. To a large extent, this variety reflects the differing needs of meetings organisers. For example, a trade union holding its annual general meeting has very different needs from a corporate brainstorming session (Shallcross, 1998).

The principal types of meetings venues are examined below. The specific characteristics of each type of venue is demonstrated, with emphasis on the segments of the meetings market that each serves most effectively. Many of the types of venue described below have formed their own marketing consortia through which they engage in collaborative marketing activities in order to give themselves a higher market profile; these will also be identified.

Hotels

As stated in the brief history of organised meetings at the beginning of this chapter, hotels have traditionally supplemented their role as accommodation and catering providers with that of suppliers of rooms where meetings may be held.

During the past few decades, hotels have increasingly recognised the advantages of supplying meetings facilities. As Smith (1990) indicated, even those hoteliers who not so long ago regarded meetings as a minor, low-season activity, useful in quiet months as an adjunct to the banqueting department, now often see conferences as a profit centre in their own right.

Despite the rise of many different, competing forms of venue, hotels are still where the bulk of meetings take place. They account for over 70% of the provision of meetings space in the UK, according to Shone (1998). In terms of demand, Greenhill (2000) showed that in the UK, city-centre hotels were the most popular type of venue for both the association and the corporate market, with airport hotels coming in second place as venues for corporate meetings.

For hotels, the attraction of offering conference facilities – which can range from a single seminar room to a whole conference wing – is easily explained, since it often represents the opportunity to take profitable advantage of underutilised resources and infrastructure. Better still, residential conferences increase occupancy rates and can often generate higher room rates than the leisure market. Under the eternal pressure of increasing occupancy, many hotels may even have come to depend on conference revenues to a substantial degree (Shallcross, 1998).

For the organiser, the attractiveness of hotels as meetings venues is also manifest. While once conferences may have been low on many hotels' priority list, with badly lit rooms, and a flipchart and an indelible marker being described as 'comprehensive facilities', many now offer sophisticated technology and staff who are trained to provide a dedicated service. One point of contact, a money-back guarantee if clients are not satisfied with either service or catering, and all-inclusive quotes ensuring a bill with no surprises, are all commonplace (Chetwynd, 1998). However, it is clear from buyers' reactions that service is also of fundamental importance, and no amount of elaborate facilities will compensate for mediocre staff skills and attitudes. Greaves (1998b; p.38) quotes the words of a Halifax Financial Services course coordinator listing her priorities when choosing a hotel for training sessions: 'The quality of service is the most important factor for us. We will not use a hotel again if the trainer is dissatisfied with it; and we also look at the service in the restaurant and whether the hotel has additional facilities such as a business centre or health suite.'

To match the first-rate conference facilities in which, over the years, private hotels and hotel chains have invested, many of their staff have also acquired specialist marketing and organisational skills, enabling them to offer a proficient one-stop shop to meetings organisers.

In short, all of the evidence appears to suggest that considerable progress has been made in the level of professionalism and service that meetings organisers can expect from hotels in Europe since Smith wrote:

> European hotels trail behind many hotels in North America, where convention managers offer personal attention to meeting planners from the first inspection visit through to the event ... Meetings planners in Europe say those friendly faces they first meet have often disappeared before they bring delegates some time later, and many hotels admit they see conferences as secondary to banqueting – even properties which advertise themselves as outstanding conference venues. (Smith, 1990; p.72)

To their afore-mentioned strong selling points must be added another clear advantage offered by hotels as venues: namely, that if an overnight stay is involved, the delegates are all in one place, with everything they need, from leisure and catering facilities to accommodation and occasionally even shops under one roof. As delegates have no need to travel between their accommodation and the venue, this can amount to considerable time-savings for them, as well as greater security, particularly in cities with high street-crime levels.

Hotels located at airports have the potential of offering an additional time-saving advantage. Chetwynd (1998) points out that for organisers bringing delegates to the UK from around Europe or the world, the advantage of keeping them near to the airport are enormous savings of both time and temper – no sitting in traffic jams trying to reach the city centre. She goes on to describe how 12 hotels at London's busiest airport have grouped together to form the consortium 'Destination Heathrow', to market themselves as a serious contender to the capital's city-centre properties.

Shallcross (1998) makes the point that levels of one-day conference activity are much higher at city hotels than at country hotels. However, for the more lucrative residential conferences, country hotels are proving to be equally as attractive – perhaps reflecting the perceived benefits of 'getting away from it all'. He adds that country hotels seem to get a larger proportion of their business from association and government users than city hotels do.

Hotels situated close to conference centres and other types of non-residential venue are well placed to benefit as providers of accommodation for delegates. Rogers (1998; p.36) adds that 'additionally, the bigger association conferences often choose one hotel as their "headquarters" hotel and there can be significant public relations benefits with the hotel being featured in national and sometimes international television and media coverage'.

A final, not inconsiderable factor in favour of hotels as meetings venues is identified by Chetwynd (1998), who maintains that for their meetings events, Americans very often prefer hotels to dedicated conference facilities, because of the more personal service and atmosphere that they believe hotels can offer.

However, hotels are by no means ideally suited to hosting every type of meetings event. For example, the limited size of meetings facilities in many hotels is a factor that can restrict the number of large events they are able to accommodate. While hotels may excel as the venues for meetings events for several hundred delegates, those European hotels that can match the capacity of Disneyland Paris's Hotel New York, with its 5000 m^2 of conference space accommodating up to 5000 delegates (Greaves, 1999), are very few in number.

But more important than problems of capacity may be a hotel's lack of flexibility in the types of meetings space it can offer. For example, many hotels remain vulnerable to the criticism that their standard multipurpose function rooms are inadequate to meet all the needs of the contemporary conference organiser. Even in London, with its extensive supply of hotels, this particular limitation of hotels appears to present difficulties. In an article on this subject, Trelford (1999; p.78) quotes the Director of Travel Operations of a major meetings planning agency, who claims that: 'London is deficient when it comes to decent conference space coupled with bedroom space. The problem is that hotels tend to have one available meeting space – usually a wonderful ballroom – and that's it.'

In the same article, Trelford highlights what she perceives as another limitation of hotel conference facilities: the fact that they often lack syndicate rooms, which are now a major requirement for practically all large conferences. Chetwynd (1998) concurs, citing another meetings planner:

> [Hotels] may be happy to host a standard conference, classroom-style with a lectern, but many do not understand what a big convention is about. If I want to use a conference room for a breakout session and a ballroom for a plenary session, for an event that may take one or two days to set up – something complicated – even big properties do not want to take it.

Branding

Since the early 1990s, many hotel chains have branded their conference product to assist in the promotion of their facilities and services and to build customer loyalty.

Examples of some of the best-known hotels' conference brands are Forte's Conference Privilege, Marriott's Meeting Edge and Thistle Hotels' Conferenceplan. Branding works by guaranteeing buyers that they will receive the same quality-assured level of service whichever hotel in the chain is used. The branding of hotel conference packages is usually accompanied by a money-back guarantee if a hotel fails to deliver on any aspect of its quality-assured services.

From the point of view of the buyers, branding brings a number of advantages, not least of which is the security of knowing that their meeting will be planned and will take place according to a number of assured, written standards. Such standards may, for example, state how promptly the initial enquiry will be dealt with, exactly how hotel staff will assist on the day of the event, how the meetings room will be set up, how the bill will be calculated, and how soon after the event it will be sent to the client. Moreover, the buyers know that exactly the same standards will apply, whether they are hiring a room in the chain's London hotel or in its Lusaka property.

A further advantage for the buyers is that most of these branded meeting packages are often marketed directly at them, therefore bypassing the need to use an agency or intermediary. This issue will be examined in more detail when trends are considered at the end of this chapter, but the growth in availability of directly marketed hotel meetings packages is clearly a challenge for those who make their living through finding and organising meetings on behalf of buyers.

The widespread practice of hotels branding their conference product points to the considerable success of this method of serving the meetings market. However, as Rogers (1998; p.130) has indicated, the very homogeneity of hotel chains' branded conference products may not be to every buyer's or planner's taste:

> Conference organisers are constantly looking for somewhere new, somewhere a little different to make their event live long in the memory of their delegates. If delegates find that their surroundings and the type of service received are more or less identical at each conference, regardless of where it is being held, delegate perceptions of the event may not always be as favourable as the organiser would have wished.

By way of summary, it is interesting to review the results of Riley's survey (cited in TTI, 2000) of those hotel attributes that play the most important role in determining the selection of such venues for the meetings market. Table 3.3 compares the opinions of meetings planners with those of hotel managers in response to the question: 'What are the attributes of a hotel that are most significant in determining its suitability for the meetings market?'

Conference centres

It is not for nothing that conference centres, with their striking architecture, vast dimensions and often prominent locations, are called 'palaces' in several European languages. Whether purpose-built or converted from buildings originally used for

Table 3.3 Attributes of a hotel that are the most significant in determining its suitability for the meetings market

Meetings planners' opinions (descending order of importance)	Hotel managers' opinions (descending order of importance)
High quality of food	Helpful staff
Cleanliness of hotel	High quality of food
Experienced conference manager to deal with	Cleanliness of hotel
Comfortable seating in conference room	Comfortable seating in conference room
Good sound insulation in conference room	Experienced conference manager to deal with
Complete blackout available in conference room	Availability of basic audiovisual equipment
Hotel able to accommodate all delegates in house	Good acoustics in conference room
Helpful staff	Hotel experienced and specialised in conferences
Efficient check-in and check-out procedures	Efficient check-in and check-out procedures
Good acoustics in conference room	Hotel able to accommodate all delegates in-house
Air-conditioned conference room	Good road links
Hotel experienced and specialised in conferences	Good sound insulation in conference room
Availability of syndicate rooms	Good parking facilities
Competitive room rates	
Purpose-built conference room	

Source: Riley, M. and Perogiannis, N. (1990), 'The influence of hotel attributes on the selection of a conference venue', *International Journal of Contemporary Hospitality Management*, Vol. 2.

other purposes, a conference centre usually provides the most visible indication that the city in which it is located is an active player in the meetings market.

The rise of conference centres as venues is linked to the explosive growth of the association market from the 1960s onwards. As associations grew larger and more international in scope, requiring much more meeting space, the stage was set for the construction of conference centres on a large scale. Rogers (1998) traces the development of conference centre construction, globally: during the 1960s and 1970s, in cities throughout Europe and North America, sophisticated conference facilities were constructed in response to the needs of this rapidly developing market. In the 1980s and 1990s, similar large-scale conference centre projects were undertaken throughout much of Asia and the Pacific Rim, with locations such as Hong Kong and Singapore developing state-of-the-art facilities to compete with established centres in Europe and North America. During the same period, new conference centres were built in a number of Eastern European countries, such as Hungary and the Czech Republic, as well as in South Africa following the end of its apartheid system.

Other world regions are less well served with large, modern conference centres. In the rest of Africa and in Central and South America, according to Graf (2001a), there have been no projects of international relevance for decades. He also cites the examples of China, Russia, Indonesia and Brazil as evidence of countries which, despite the size of their populations, their land and political weight, are relatively poor in their supply of state-of-the-art conference facilities.

Although their illustrious and often imposing exteriors are important, not least for the image they portray to visiting delegates as well as the city's own residents, it is the extensive space that they provide inside that sets conference centres apart from other types of venue. The principal advantage of conference centres is that they have the vast space required to accommodate the largest types of meetings events, such as annual meetings of international associations, where the number of those attending can run to several thousands. They are typically well-equipped, with features such as the latest audiovisual equipment and booths for simultaneous translators, as well as a wide range of areas that may be used as breakout or syndicate rooms or for catering (Shallcross, 1998).

In Europe, the vast majority of purpose-built conference centres are municipally owned, and some have been financed in part with state, federal or EU grants. In many cases, however, the actual management of conference centres takes the form of a public-sector/private-sector partnership. This system is widespread in France, for example, as explained by Tuppen (1996; p.67):

> In many cases, it is the municipalities themselves that have invested directly to ensure the construction of conference centres. Their subsequent management is then often placed under the responsibility of a mixed economy company, in which the municipality is usually still a major shareholder. However, direct intervention by the municipal authorities may also occur due to the need to subsidise the often substantial running costs of the centre, for it is relatively rare that the revenue from lettings covers these costs.

Tuppen's last point is of key importance, and is emphasised by, among others, Inskeep (1991) and Lawson (2000, p.18), who writes, of conference centres in general:

> In most cases, a loss is experienced on the operating costs and/or debt charges, which has to be borne by local tax contributions or levies on other properties (hotels, restaurants, etc). Against this must be measured the economic benefits to the area in attracting more visitors, higher tourist expenditures and greater room occupancies in hotels, along with the resultant multiplier effects.

The traditional argument in support of the public subvention of conference centres runs thus: as a rule, investment in conference centres cannot be based on a project–cost feasibility analysis alone, since the direct revenue generated is often inadequate to meet operational costs, let alone service the debt incurred in borrowing money to fund the building of such centres. But conference centres' dependence on the public purse is justified by the wider objectives that cities and towns may have in building conference centres.

What are those wider objectives? As well as the economic benefits already mentioned by Lawson (2000), he also suggests other possible motivations of destinations choosing to invest in the construction of conference centres:

● To provide a catalyst for regeneration of run-down city-centre areas, leading to private investment in hotels, restaurants and other commercial developments.

- To revitalise traditional resorts by extending market opportunities and encouraging investment in upgrading hotels and other facilities.
- To contribute to the image and prestige of the city as a leading cultural and commercial capital.
- To support the role of the city as a focus for business, trade, technology and/or research.
- To emphasise the independence and maturity of the country as a meeting place for nations.

Most of these aims may appear worthy in themselves and uncontroversial, but in fact they are by no means accepted universally as being entirely valid reasons for the building of conference centres. One dissenting voice, among many, is that of the Editor-in-chief of *Tagungs Wirtschaft*, the Germany-based trade publication for meeting and incentive professionals. With particular reference to venues built to host large international events, he disagrees wholeheartedly with the concept of 'the conference venue as an image factor, financed by the taxpayer' (Graf, 2001a):

> City fathers are all too fond of setting up their own 'monuments' in an unholy alliance with architects blessed with more creativity than experience. No demand analyses are carried out ahead of the project, which is condemned to dependence on public subsidies, with 'induced earnings' being advanced as the classical, rather dubious but still much-worn justification …

> A variation on this theme is the conference venue put in place for just one event [which is] deemed politically and/or strategically important – a World Bank meeting, a top-drawer political conference … the world is full of them. That was how the Philippine International Convention Centre in Manila, Asia's first convention venue, came into being. Today, it is very much a wallflower. Venues in Bangkok or Nicosia on Cyprus are similar 'one-event wonders'.

> Investment in the construction of international conference venues has often been prompted by hoped-for signal effects: 'Look! We're not a developing country any more.' At best, [such venues] will hook some association meeting rotating around the world – which, as a rule, does more to boost some politician's image than fill the venue's kitty.

Such reservations surrounding the construction of conference centres for 'image' reasons notwithstanding, the most frequently encountered motivation for constructing such venues is, undoubtedly, regeneration and revitalisation.

Examples abound of destinations that have pinned their hopes for the revival of their fortunes partly on attracting conference business. Some of the most striking are to be drawn from the UK's former coastal and spa resorts, such as Brighton and Harrogate, whose conference centres have helped to reinvent them as business travel destinations. In Harrogate, tourism supports around 7000 jobs, an estimated 68% of which are sustained by non-leisure visitors (Goodhart, 1998). The same author describes a more recently constructed facility, Belfast's Waterfront Hall Conference and Concert Centre, opened in 1997, with a capacity for 2200 delegates. She states that, along with the many hotel developments built to meet the increase in demand for business tourism, the conference centre is 'the most visible sign of regeneration in the city'.

The actual name, the 'Belfast Waterfront Hall Conference and Concert Centre', indicates another important characteristic of a considerable number of conference centres. Many are intended to serve not only as meetings venues but also to cater for the entertainment, recreational and cultural needs of local people and leisure visitors. Lawson (2000) explains how such multipurpose buildings function: 'The main auditoriums are adaptable for concerts or other theatrical performances; flat-floored halls are invariably equipped to be used for meetings, exhibits and/or functions (receptions, dinners, banquets). In some cases, tiered seating can be removed to leave a flat floor for alternative requirements.'

In support of such facilities, Lawson (2000; p.18) provides an economic justification:

> It makes economic sense to provide for dual or alternative use. Congresses and conventions tend to be held outside the peak tourist seasons, which can then benefit from the entertainment attractions. Meetings mainly occur on weekdays whilst weekends and the evenings are times for leisure and entertainment.

Indeed, some commentators, including Smith (1990; p.70), have gone as far as to claim that, in reality, it is fair to say that 'there is almost no such thing today as a conference centre. All are multi-purpose facilities, and are indeed only rightly described as conference centres when there is a conference actually taking place inside them.' However, although this is certainly true of a certain category of conference centre – the municipal venue catering mainly for a local or regional market, and having a commitment to providing services, such as cultural events, to the local community – it is not the case for all conference centres. As regards venues serving the international market, in particular, many would agree with Graf (2001a; p.8) that:

> The smooth implementation of international meetings requires enormous management know-how and special technical, room-arrangement, architectural and other considerations. Municipal, sports and multipurpose centres or hotel ballrooms are not convention centres, and most certainly not on an international scale, fond as they may be of marketing themselves as such.

Moreover, many would argue that it is indeed fortunate that conference centres *are* capable of being used for a variety of purposes, for it is a fact that some of them have been criticised severely as being poorly designed for the hosting of actual meetings events. Part of the problem arises from the difference between what the architects may consider to be a triumphant expression of their art and what the users of the buildings consider to be a success in practical, operational terms.

Shone (1998; p.69) draws parallels between the conception of some conference centres and the example of the Lloyds Building in London, which was lauded by architects for its design but was deeply unpopular with those who had to work in it. Tactfully, he does not name names of conference centres whose design has a negative impact on conference proceedings, but instead lists the types of problem encountered: rooms with no natural light, low ceilings, stuffy atmospheres, confusing layouts and colour schemes 'that would shame a Nevada brothel'.

Shallcross (1998; p.B-45) suggests a further feature of conference centres occasionally neglected by their architects, to the despair of meeting planners:

> An important factor which is sometimes overlooked is the value of medium-sized breakout rooms (capacity 20–100 delegates). While a large hall is required for plenary sessions, these are often only used to capacity for a very small proportion of the total conference duration. The ability to break the total delegation into smaller groups quickly and easily is valued highly by professional conference organisers.

A Hamburg-based meeting planner adds to the list of frequently encountered deficiencies as follows (Lau-Thurner, 2001; p.46):

> Unfortunately, many venues forget that we need an average of at least five working rooms in addition to the actual function rooms: for speakers, the organiser, the programme committee, the organisation team and, last but not least, the press. Added to which, at multilingual conferences, the interpreters also need a rest room.

Areas for accompanying exhibitions also come in for criticism: 'Foyer areas are often used for shows, but in many cases, they are also required for coffee breaks. If they are too full of booths, delegates can find themselves uncomfortably cramped.'

Finally, a consultant to the international meetings industry identifies what he considers to be some significant weaknesses of conference centre design. After criticising the near-uniformity of design of many such structures as 'box-like stages within box-like constructions', he uses ample doses of humour to point out some serious shortcomings shared by many venues (Carey, 2001; p.48):

> Low-rise conference centres make up in length for what they lack in height, so delegates can take three days to move from one hall to another, and some may die of exhaustion en route. At the Ernest N. Morial Centre in New Orleans, the staff travel around by scooter and tricycle, to the envy of the trudging delegates. But my final salvo is aimed at architects who seem not to realise that in our emancipated world, there are almost as many women attending conferences as men. It seems to me obvious that, as women take three times as long as men on routine ablutions, they need more toilets than men. Until centre designers wake up to this fact, long lines of irritated and uncomfortable women will remain a feature of conventions.

It is clear that a considerable gap exists between the aesthetic conception of some conference centres and the practical requirements of those who will use them (or not). Smith (1990; p.69) sums up the problem thus:

> With monotonous regularity, the design of our major conference facilities has changed during construction and even afterwards, leading to a general discontent with the approach of architects to the realities of conference management. They are

accused of designing grandiose structures suitable for coffee table books, rather than researching to establish how their buildings will be used in practice and thus to produce facilities truly suited to purpose.

Slightly more sympathetic to the architectural profession, Rogers (1998; p.8) suggests an alternative reason for the problem:

> The challenge for those planning major, new purpose-built conference centres ... is to anticipate future demand accurately. Lead time from the initial idea for a conference centre until its opening can be as much as 10 years. The process involves, *inter alia*, identification of a suitable site, design and planning stages, assembly of the funding package, construction of venue and related infrastructure, recruitment and training of staff. In such a period, substantial changes in the wider marketplace may have occurred.

In the last few years, however, an increasingly experienced and professional approach to the commissioning of conference centres has evolved, with much more research and more consultation between meetings planners and conference centre designers than was the case several decades ago. Much of the credit for this development is owed to the International Association of Congress Centres (known as the AIPC, from its French name, Association Internationale des Palais de Congrès; www.aipc.org). Since its creation in 1958, this organisation, whose members are the directors and managers of 115 of the world's leading conference centres, has worked to improve the way in which such venues are designed and equipped. Through its Technical Commission, the AIPC commissions and publishes studies and runs its own training courses on conference centre design.

The AIPC's mission extends, however, beyond issues of conference centre design. For its members, it serves to improve their skills and knowledge in the fields of conference centre management and operation, marketing and environmental issues. It also provides them with an effective networking forum and lobbies actively on their behalf. For meetings planners holding events in conference centres that are members of the AIPC, the association provides a formal guarantee of high standards.

Another international association active in promoting conference centres is the Historic Conference Centres of Europe (HCCE) alliance (www.historic-centres.com). The very exclusive membership of the HCCE comprises 18 conference facilities housed in historic buildings, such as former monasteries and palaces, in 12 European countries. The alliance was set up in October 1996, and in May 1997 the members created a joint marketing organisation with a central database to promote their properties. To qualify as an HCCE member, a conference centre must meet strict criteria:

- The building must be at least 100 years old, with state-of-the-art technology in all halls and meeting rooms.
- It must be located in a European city famous for its architectural heritage and cultural life.

- It must be situated in or near the city centre.
- It must be able to provide easy access to hotels, shops, restaurants and city life.

Such centres serve, for the main part, the low-volume, high-class segment of the meetings market, with buyers who want to profit from the special atmosphere of a historic building. Members include the Hofburg Congress Centre in Vienna, a former imperial palace; the Popes' Palace International Congress Centre in Avignon, Europe's largest surviving medieval palace; Dublin Castle Conference Centre; Amsterdam's former stock exchange, the Beurs van Berlage; and the Conference and Exhibition Centre of Cordoba, a Moorish-style monastery and infirmary with nine conference halls.

Based in Graz, Austria, the HCCE attracts new business for its members through its website and by exhibiting at major trade fairs such as the EIBTM. It also has a permanent sales office in the USA.

Academic venues

In the UK in particular, academic venues, especially universities, have played a significant role in both stimulating and responding to the development of the meetings market, while earning vital income for educational establishments.

In the early 1970s, before most municipal conference centres were built or hotels had recognised fully the opportunities of the meetings business, several universities actively began to market themselves as vacation conference venues (Paine, 1993). The 1980s were a period of considerable investment in upgrading facilities, accompanied by an increase in levels of marketing activity.

Universities are built with 'learning spaces' – auditoria, lecture theatres, classrooms – which are highly suited to the meetings market. Moreover, during vacation periods, universities can offer residential conferences, making use of campus accommodation. Smith (1990; p.74) summarises the strengths and weaknesses of academic venues thus: 'Accommodation may be somewhat Spartan, the sleeping rooms may be less than five star, the plumbing may not be quite post-Victorian, but the ambience is great and dinner in the Hall can be attractive with all the college's portraits on the wall – especially if the price is right, which it usually is.'

However, at least part of Smith's sketch is now thankfully outdated. Truly Spartan conditions are becoming much rarer, as many universities have made considerable investment in upgrading student residences to a standard where they can be marketed competitively as comfortable residential conference accommodation. Moreover, as Pemble (1998; p.55) points out, this constant cycle of upgrading and renovating means that the students reap the rewards in term time. She gives the example of universities installing technology facilities in their halls of residence to make them more attractive to conference delegates, quoting a sales executive of Keele University Conference Park: 'All rooms at the university have ISDN lines and we hope to have cable links as well by the end of the year.'

Many educational establishments have taken measures to expand their conference business fairly rapidly, making noticeable efforts to improve not only their facilities but also their standards of service and professionalism. Building on their success in this market, several have also built conference facilities that operate independently from the student facilities and run year round as management training centres.

Just how much academic venues have accomplished in the meetings market can be seen in the figures for investment, events and delegate numbers for a wide range of educational institutions. In a typical year, the University of Warwick, in the heart of England, plays host to 60 000 delegates. In the year 2000, it was the venue for a conference at which Bill Clinton gave his last speech outside the USA as the American President, to an audience of 1000, including staff from the White House, Downing Street, the security forces and the international press. In June 2001, the University of Durham embarked on a £1 million project to refurbish 15 lecture theatres with seating capacities of between 100 and 300, to be ready for conference bookings from March 2002.

Paine (1993) sums up the advantages and disadvantages of academic venues in the UK, as shown in Table 3.4.

Several of the advantages make universities particularly attractive to the association meetings market. Greenhill (2000) demonstrated that in the UK Conference Market Survey for that year, academic venues came second after hotel venues in popularity with associations. Shallcross (1998; p.B-46) quotes data that suggest

Table 3.4 Advantages and disadvantages of academic venues

Advantages	Disadvantages
Nationwide locations, from Aberdeen to Exeter; many campus universities are set in beautiful grounds and in attractive parts of the country	Lack of standard hotel amenities, such as direct-dial telephones, TV, alarm clocks; few twin-bedded rooms; cafeteria-style catering
Architectural styles range from early medieval to modern, from traditional to purpose-built	The extent of the campus is often disorienting and tiring for delegates; can be long walks between buildings.
Size and range of facilities: large halls for plenary sessions and lecture rooms, seminar rooms, etc. for breakout sessions	Only available during the 17 or 18 weeks of vacation; rules out the attractive periods of May, June and October
Learning environment: conducive to serious discussion	
Technical support: audiovisual equipment and specialist technical support	
Value for money	
Total product: free on-site parking, accommodation, catering facilities, bars, sport facilities	

Source: Paine, A. (1993), 'The university conference market', *Insights*, May.

that educational establishments are heavily dependent on trade from this market, especially for residential conferences:

> This can be primarily attributed to the capacity of university venues to hold large numbers of delegates but is also related to the fact that university venues can add prestige to an annual meeting of a company or an association at a competitive price ... On average, universities generate much lower revenue per delegate per day than venues such as hotels, but delegate volume tends to be much higher.

Plainly, the revenue that conferences earn is the main motivation behind the involvement of academic institutions in this market. But Paine (1993) argues convincingly that as well as bringing financial benefits to a university, conferences and symposia can be seen as a legitimate extension of the university's core activity and purpose. They can, for example, create important links between the university and the local community and industry. Despite the apparent tension between academic purpose and commercial use, he claims, universities have come to rely on conference business as a means of ensuring more efficient utilisation of buildings, continuity of employment for domestic, catering and portering staff, and contributing to overheads.

Marketing

Most universities have full-time trained staff running their conference business through dedicated conference offices, which are usually entirely separate from other academic activities. One example is Oxford University, which, in 1994, set up Conference Oxford, a conference marketing office offering assistance with enquiries on a choice of 37 Oxford colleges and over 6000 rooms (Pemble, 1998).

Academic venues in the UK have a long history of joint marketing. For 20 years, two consortia, BUAC and Connect Venues, successfully raised the profile of academic venues in the meetings market, providing valuable marketing and central reservations services to their members. In 2001, both organisations merged to form Venuemasters (www.venuemasters.co.uk), with over 100 members drawn principally from UK colleges and universities active in this market. Venuemasters provides a free venue-finding service based on the database of its members, and works to attract not only business tourists but also leisure tourists with an interest in making use of university facilities during vacations. The organisation runs an annual trade show in London, the Venuemasters Exhibition, providing an event where meetings planners can do business with, and find out about, academic venues from locations all over the UK.

Residential conference centres

In contrast with the academic venues favoured largely by the association market, residential conference centres – also known as management training centres – have traditionally attracted a mainly corporate market.

Training is essential to the continuing success of all businesses, and new technology, a more flexible workforce, more demanding employees and the growing recognition from managers of the importance of investing in staff have all contributed to an increase in staff training. The venue in which this training is carried out is critical to its success, and residential conference centres, with their focused environment in which to learn, are playing an important part in providing venues for this activity.

Such centres are usually situated in their own grounds in rural locations that are close to motorway, rail and airport links. Their aim is to concentrate on providing a purposeful and business-like atmosphere where everything is geared to make life easier for the company organising the event, the trainer running it, and the delegates attending.

In providing meetings facilities and accommodation under one roof, residential conference centres are often considered to be in direct competition with hotel conference venues. Wakely (1997; p.11), in her comparison of the two types of venue, emphasises that in residential conference centres there are not the distractions or conflicts of interest sometimes found in hotels, such as leisure groups or weddings. She adds that residential conference centres generally offer an extensive range of professional meetings rooms (with natural daylight, unlike many hotel function rooms) and an abundance of syndicate rooms (not converted bedrooms). Regarding the actual accommodation, she claims:

> The wide divide between hotels and management centres is narrowing. Gone are the days of sparse single bedrooms, shared bathrooms and canteen meals [in residential conference centres]. At the upper end of the market, bedrooms are now all en-suite offering tea and coffee, trouser presses, televisions, message systems and study areas. Leisure takes a higher profile as it is recognised how important it is for delegates to be able to relax after a possibly stressful day in the training room.

Gosling (1998a) points out another advantage that residential conference centres may have over hotels, claiming that at a time when organisations do not wish to be seen as frivolous or ostentatious, the serious image of the former is likely to create a more favourable impression in the minds of company shareholders and customers.

The ownership and management of residential conference centres can take a variety of forms. 'In the past, the majority ... were spin-offs from academic institutions, and some of the best-established centres are still those which are firmly based in the academic world' (Gosling, 1998a; p.59). Although they may be situated far from the main site of the institution, a number of successful residential conference centres are run by universities, including Aston Business School, Cranfield Management Development Centre and Radcliffe House.

However, as Shone (1998) states, most are operated by private companies, whose *raison d'être* is management development or conference centre provision as a commercial activity. Moreover, many of these privately owned venues are owned or leased by blue-chip organisations to ensure exclusive use. Through this arrangement, the parent company will have priority in booking space or courses but will offer the venue's spare capacity on the open market. Gosling (1998a) gives the examples of Latimer House in Chesham, which is leased by Coopers & Lybrand; Uplands near

High Wycombe, which belongs to the Nationwide Building Society, and Durdent Court in Uxbridge, which is a wholly-owned BP conference and training centre.

Despite all of their apparent advantages for the purchaser, however, one disadvantage of residential conference centres is the fact that, in the UK at least, there is still no official grading system. But even that may be about to change in response to market demand. In the same article, Gosling (1998a; p.60) states:

> Now that dedicated conference and training venues are fully established in their own niche, there are moves in the meetings industry to grade them in the same way as hotels. According to a 1997 survey of UK organisations, 82% of buyers of conference and training venues were in favour of a grading system to help them judge the quality of facilities.

In the meantime, however, buyers and meeting planners are assisted in their decision process by the services provided by the marketing consortium, Conference Centres of Excellence (CCE; www.cceonline.co.uk), whose members are 29 UK dedicated residential conference centres. Membership of the group is via a very rigorous accreditation process, which requires the candidate centre to produce documentary evidence and to undergo an inspection visit by an independent assessor. Successful candidate centres guarantee to provide a range of facilities and services, from 'dedicated meeting rooms with natural daylight and purpose-built conference furniture, designed for comfort and concentration' to 'ensuite bedrooms with well-lit study areas'.

The CCE consortium's main benefit to its members is to provide them with new business through its venue-finding service, although there are other spin-off benefits, including benchmarking, networking and staff education. More generally, the CCE consortium jointly markets residential conference centres to raise their profile as an alternative to the hotel product.

Unusual venues

Often classed (erroneously) as the 'everything else' category, unusual venues have been defined more precisely as 'comprising a wide range of facilities that are used for conferences, including museums, historic houses, art galleries and a number of other buildings normally used for quite different purposes' (Leask and Hood, 2000). Listed buildings, theatres, sports venues, ships and theme parks are further examples of venues where, in addition to their primary use – as visitor attractions, cultural resources, sports facilities and so on – the hosting of meetings provides an additional income stream.

Rogers (1998; p.39) sums up the allure of such venues:

> The attraction of unusual venues is they can give an event a special appeal and can make it memorable for years afterwards. Some have very high quality meeting and conference facilities; others may be quite limited in this respect. But the setting in which the event is being held compensates for such shortcomings in the eyes of the conference organiser (and, it is hoped, of the delegates).

The main appeal of unusual venues, then, is the high recall and entertainment value they can bring to events held in them.

Leask and Hood (2000) concur, insisting that it is the uniqueness of many unusual venues that helps make them memorable, especially for meetings-weary delegates for whom yet another event held in a conference centre or hotel holds little attraction. Gosling (1999a; p.73) also highlights the motivating factor, which explains why organisers wishing to attract greater numbers to a conference, or to reward employees with something more innovative, are opting for unusual venues. She adds: 'At most events, communication is the objective. If the venue itself is a talking point, it may well promote interaction, and delegates are more likely to remember the event.'

The motivation of meeting planners to use unusual venues is more than matched by the motivation of property owners and managers to enter the meetings market. In the UK, a number of supply-side factors have encouraged a range of different types of facilities to promote themselves as venues for the meetings market. Changing funding systems and increased competition for leisure spending has resulted in many properties having to generate more revenue or look to alternative revenue mixes. In particular, museums and galleries have been hit by decreased central and local government funding (Leask *et al.*, 2000). Shallcross (1998) highlights another contributing factor, underlining the importance of a particular mechanism of National Lottery funding, whereby development grants for facilities are often made conditional on the venue taking action to generate income from new sources.

As a result of these supply-side factors, much investment has gone into adapting historic buildings or attractions such as zoos, museums and gardens for occasional use as meetings facilities. Gosling (1999a) mentions a range of UK examples. In Morecambe, an Edwardian railway station on the promenade has been fully restored into The Platform, a new conference and meeting venue for groups of between 60 and 300. Newcastle's unusual venues include Blackfriars Monastery, a restored thirteenth-century friary, and the Newcastle Discovery, a museum dating back to 1899, housing engineering, transport and maritime exhibits.

In the same article, Gosling points out that occasionally new, out-of-the-ordinary venues are created from scratch, such as London's Vinopolis, primarily a visitor attraction based on the history and heritage of wine. The Vinopolis project was unusual in that one of the primary focuses for the developers was to design the venue to meet the needs of the corporate market. Its galleries and wine cellars can be hired for meetings of up to 900 delegates or a seated dinner for up to 650.

A profile of the type of facilities offered by unusual venues in the UK is given by Leask and Hood (2000). In general, they provide small meeting room facilities, with catering services available in-house or contracted in, and an equipment base often limited to only an overhead projector (OHP) and a flipchart. Only 8% of unusual venues in the UK offer facilities for residential conferences.

However, one type of unusual venue where accommodation is plentiful is the cruise ship. These, too, are increasingly being designed to cater for business tourism clients, incorporating in their design dedicated meeting space with state-of-the-art audiovisual equipment. Gosling (1999b; p.84) gives the example of the 142 000-tonne *Voyager of the Seas*, which entered service in 1999. This offers dedicated facilities for up to 400 delegates, capable of converting into six breakout rooms. It also includes an executive boardroom, a multimedia screening room, videoconferencing and classroom training facilities, and floor space large enough to accommodate exhibition or trade shows. She goes on to quote the Marketing Services Manager of Silversea ships, whose vessels *Silver Shadow* and *Silver Mirage* were launched in 2000 and 2001 respectively: 'Quality meeting facilities are becoming a really valuable commodity. New ships cannot really enter the conference and incentive industry unless they have the facilities to justify it.'

It is clear that the most convenient itineraries for incentive and conference groups are short cruises, since very few corporate clients are prepared to let their key staff remain out of the office for more than seven nights. Cruise lines are therefore adapting to this need by offering more three- and four-night cruises. As examples, Gosling cites Celebrity Cruises' *Horizon*, which has offered shorter itineraries since 2000, including a four-night trip from Southampton to Amsterdam and the Channel Islands, and a four-night cruise that starts and finishes in Barcelona.

Estimating the level of actual demand for meetings in unusual venues is more difficult than tracking growth in supply. And the task is often made more difficult by the practice of combining unusual venues with other types of venue under the 'miscellaneous' category in surveys. However, one snapshot is produced by Leask and Hood (2000), who use British Conference Market Trends Survey data to demonstrate a rise from 125 large conferences at unusual venues in 1994 to 225 in 1997. In their own research, the same authors portray a buoyant market, with nearly all of their unusual venue-operating respondents predicting growth well into the twenty-first century.

Although quantitative data on this market are scarce, more is known about the type of demand that unusual venues attract. One of the few in-depth pieces of research in this sector suggests that the biggest single-user categories for unusual venues is the corporate sector, but that association and academic users were also important (Leask and Hood, 2000). Clearly, unusual venues are well suited to business-related events, such as promotional days and product launches, which need to be distinctive to make a lasting impression. Confirming this, Gosling (1999a; p.73) quotes Newcastle upon Tyne's tourism and conference officer: 'This is especially true for events such as product launches where there is no immediate obligation to attend. Surprisingly, using different venues can also boost local attendance. You would be amazed how many local people have not visited some of our more unusual venues.'

However, despite a measure of growth and success in the meetings market, unusual venues are not without their disadvantages, and the occasional use of properties for meetings events presents its own challenges. Conflicts between the primary uses of the properties and the demanding needs of the meetings market were highlighted in the research undertaken by Leask and Hood (2000). Most of these related to the structure of the properties and problems with staff: a lack of breakout rooms, restriction and inflexibility of the actual buildings, lack of up to date equipment, lack of staff availability, logistical problems, and balancing daytime use of the facility with conference use. Gosling (1998b; p.47) quotes one event organiser who has encountered such difficulties: 'Unusual events still need a level of practicality. Some London venues are too rigid in their primary function to be flexible enough for state-of-the-art meetings. One cannot easily do a large-scale conference at the Natural History Museum, for example, because the museum cannot close to give time and space to set up.'

Shallcross (1998; p.B-47) concurs:

There is a danger that after an initial period of growth, [unusual venues'] conference business will become limited by venue design and facilities such as the absence of breakout rooms and the expense of providing an irregular catering service. The venue is then faced with the decision of whether to invest, which may be difficult to justify if conference hosting is a peripheral business.

Another weakness of unusual venues may arise from the fact that much of their appeal appears to be based on their novelty value, an asset obviously prone to producing rapidly declining returns. If a client's main motivation in booking an unusual venue for a meeting is to surprise the delegates and make the conference stand out from other meetings they have attended, then it may be unlikely to book the same venue again for a long time. Without this type of repeat business, unusual venues may be required constantly to spread their marketing nets wider in order to reach new potential clients.

Given these limitations of unusual venues, it remains to be seen how they will perform in a less buoyant market. But in the meantime, unusual venues continue to play a key part in the overall infrastructure of supply in the meetings market.

A summary of the main advantages and disadvantages of the types of venue reviewed in this section is given in Table 3.5.

Venue selection criteria

The emphasis of this section of the current chapter has been on the supply of venues and the facilities they offer in the meetings market. But when faced with such a plethora of venues, what are the main criteria that buyers and suppliers use to decide which venue is the right one for their event? It is interesting to compare the factors that are most important for the corporate sector with those that matter most to association meeting planners. Rankings of the main factors for both market segments are shown in Figure 3.3.

The most conspicuous, although unsurprising, difference between the two parts of Figure 3.3 is the difference between the factors that each market segment regards as the most important: the corporate sector's overriding need to hold its meetings in premises of the highest quality, contrasting with the associations' focus on value for money for their members. But what is also striking is how often the same selection criteria appear in both lists. Some of these will now be considered.

Table 3.5 Summary of the advantages and disadvantages of venues

Type of venue	Advantages	Disadvantages
Purpose-built conference centres	Space for large events Extensive range of technology available, plus technical know-how Many offer exhibition space	May not always be suitable for the growing number of smaller events No on-site accommodation
Hotels	Everything under one roof All-inclusive quotes American preference Airport hotels: time-savings	Mixing leisure and business guests Can appear too frivolous Unsuitable for very large events Lack of flexibility with syndicate rooms, etc.
Universities	Good value for money Learning ambience Everything on site Ancient/modern styles Range of sizes of meeting rooms	Lack of comfort and facilities May be limited to vacation periods Large sites – problems of orientation between buildings
Residential management training centres	Business-like ambience Few distractions – more focused	
Unusual venues	Memorable, novelty value Cruise ships: all-in prices	Limited by design restrictions due to primary function Unlikely to be used several times by same client – novelty value fades No on-site accommodation

Capacity and flexibility of meetings facilities

In order to be able to capitalise on their accessibility, it is clear that venues also need to offer the full capacity required by meeting planners and delegates. The number of delegates that any venue is capable of holding is of fundamental importance in respect of what type of meetings event it can hope to attract. Generally, the larger the event, the fewer available venues there will be for consideration at the planning stage. Meeting planners seeking a venue that can host an event for several thousand delegates face a fairly restricted choice, due to the limited supply of venues capable of accommodating such numbers. Consequently, for such meetings, the decisions about the selection of the destination and the venue are often made together, and one can strongly influence the other. Greenhill (2000) highlights this point:

> The availability of a purpose-built conference centre with facilities of a suitable size will strongly influence an association's decision to hold their annual event in a particular town. For example, the political parties are limited in the choice of

Factor	Percentage rating in survey 2000	Position in survey 1999
1 Price/value for money	80.5	1
2 Location	77.3	2
3 Access (road, rail links)	70.5	4
4 Capacity of conference facilities	64.9	5
5 Availability	57.5	6
6 Previous experience of venue	55.2	N/A
7 Quality of conference facilities	45.5	3
8 Quality of service	44.2	N/A
9 Quality of food	40.9	N/A
10 Staff awareness of needs	35.4	8
11 Cleanliness of venues	34.1	7
12 Quality of bedrooms	25.3	9

(a)

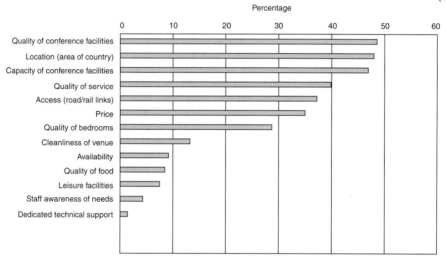

(b)

Figure 3.3 Factors influencing venue selection: (a) ranked by association buyers; (b) ranked by corporate buyers

Source: MIA (2000), *UK Conference Market Survey 2000*, published by the Meetings Industry Association.

destinations for their annual conferences since only a few destinations have very large venues supported by sufficient infrastructure to accommodate many thousands of delegates.

Related to capacity are issues of flexibility. Planners investigating potential venues for their events may, in addition to knowing the venue's capacity, wish to find out whether syndicate rooms are available; whether on-site catering is a possibility; and whether it is possible to run an exhibition alongside the conference itself. Such factors will often pay a crucial role in the selection process.

Facilities

Nevertheless, the right capacity is only part of what venues must offer in order to succeed in this market. In his list of site location criteria for conference centres, Murphy (cited in Inskeep, 1991) draws attention to other indispensable facilities:

- Central location and accessibility to good-quality hotels and an intercity transportation terminal for domestic delegates.
- Close to major shopping and entertainment districts, the prime location being in a downtown or regional business district.
- Availability of parking spaces on site or nearby for people driving to the conferences.
- Proximity to recreation facilities and attractive surroundings as delegates want to maintain their exercise routines and the cities want to encourage sightseeing within the city and environs.

Murphy's last point is reinforced by Mieczkowski (cited in Qu and Li, 1999), who points out that a successful venue should offer a flexible, attractive product to the participants, a mixture of offerings creating optimal conditions not only for work and mutual contacts but also for relaxation, entertainment and fun. By offering facilities and services that satisfy delegates' wishes – and those of their guests, if they are accompanied – to fulfil their leisure and culture pursuits while at the destination, cities are not only adding to their business tourism appeal but are also enabling themselves to maximise the revenue to be made from residential meetings events.

Service

The appropriate services and, indeed, excellent service generally, are also key prerequisites for success in this market. Therefore, venue staff's ability to provide accurate information, demonstrate creativity and resourcefulness, and draw on first-rate organisational skills is valued very highly by meetings planners. Shallcross (1998; p.B-51) puts it succinctly: 'PCOs [professional conference organisers] know the features and facilities necessary to make a particular event work. Competent staff and overall reliability are key qualities, often over cost.'

Destination selection criteria

It is clear from what we have already said about selection criteria that however good a venue's facilities are, its fortunes are linked intrinsically to those of the destination in which it is situated. Location came second in both segments' lists of factors influencing their choice of venue. For that reason, this section will end with a consideration of the most important criteria used by meeting planners and buyers when choosing a destination for their event.

One factor has already been mentioned: the existence in the destination of a venue offering the capacity required to host the meeting being planned. When a large meeting event is being planned, which only a limited number of venues would be capable of hosting, the choice of destination and choice of venue will be made together.

However, most of the time, the destination, in the sense of the host city, is decided upon first. Greaves (1998b; p.38) illustrates this point when she reports that in a survey of the UK market, it was found that 78% of corporate buyers choose the location before considering individual venues. She goes on to quote a training course coordinator from Halifax Financial Services: 'We tend to look at the destination first and take into account where most people will be travelling from and the cost. Then we look at the venues.'

What, then, are the criteria that buyers and meeting planners use when selecting a destination? Two of the most important are considered here.

Accessibility

As indicated in the words of the Halifax training coordinator, the destination's accessibility to those invited – or instructed – to attend the event is a key consideration. In almost every case, the speed, ease and cost of accessing the destination are more important than the actual distance between the delegates' homes and the place where the meeting is to be held. For this reason, being served by an efficient transport infrastructure is more important for a destination than its actual geographical location. Convincing evidence of this may be seen in the example of the city of Lille in north-eastern France, whose fortunes as a meetings destination received a massive boost in the mid-1990s when it found itself at the hub of the newly opened Channel Tunnel and high-speed train network linking Paris, London and Brussels. The city's conference centre, Lille Grand Palais, which opened in 1994, signed a partnership with Eurostar enabling customers to buy a single transport and meetings package. With three auditoria for 1500, 500 and 300 delegates, 16 committee rooms, an arena for 5000 and a banqueting hall for 1200, its ease of accessibility makes it very well placed to compete for business.

However, as regards meetings that are to be attended by delegates from countries situated all over the world, the vital transport criterion is straightforward access by air. Murphy (cited in Inskeep, 1991), for example, emphasises the importance of locating major convention centres in gateway cities that have major national and international airline connections to participants' generating areas around the world. Convenience and speed, in particular, are essential qualities sought by those travelling by air to meetings events, as delegates are no longer prepared to tolerate long, time-consuming connections at airports to get to the destination.

It is, however, worthy of note that there is one category of meetings for which lack of accessibility is an advantage rather than a drawback. Events characterised by the confidential or sensitive nature of the discussions to be held – whether by politicians, financiers or the military – often seek isolated venues, well away from the public and the media. For example, following the violent disturbances at the summit of the G8 group of nations in Genoa in 2001, the decision was taken to hold the 2002 summit in the remote mountain village of Kananaskis, situated at the end of a country road in Alberta, Canada.

Image

Taking Paris as an example of a successful destination in the meetings market, it is clear that a key factor for its success is undoubtedly its extremely positive image. Even those who have never been to Paris conceive of it as an exciting destination, which is rich in culture and heritage and relatively safe, an image carefully maintained and fostered by those responsible for marketing it for all types of tourism, including meetings.

The perception of any destination will always have a strong influence on the decision of whether to hold a meeting there. A destination with no particular image or, worse, with a decidedly negative image in the public's perception, will have to struggle to appeal to this market. Images can be formed through various means, including personal experience, but most are created through the media, from novels and cinema to news bulletins and newspaper reports. Nor are images, once established, necessarily stable. A destination's image can receive a boost from, for example, a hallmark event, such as the Olympic Games – as experienced by Australia in the years following Sydney's hosting of the Games in 2000. Equally, cities and countries can gain instant notoriety from widely publicised events, such as Rio de Janeiro's treatment of its street children in the 1990s, or the Italian police brutality at the 2001 G8 summit in Genoa.

However, despite the importance of image as a criterion in the destination selection process, very little research has been carried out in this field. Oppermann (1996) remarks that research into destination selection criteria has centred almost exclusively on the importance to meeting planners of various destination attributes such as cost, accommodation stock and supply of venues.

Nevertheless, as Oppermann (1996a; p.176) points out, image perception plays an important part in not only the process by which the planner selects a destination for the event, but also, in the case of association meetings events in particular, the process by which those invited to the event decide upon whether or not to attend:

> While corporate meetings are usually a must for all selected participants, association members attend at their own leisure and frequently own expense, while corporate meeting expenses are paid by the employer. Thus, the association meeting sector resembles to a large extent the pleasure tourism sector, especially with regard to the participation and destination selection aspects. Association conference organisers may be viewed as tour operators who select destinations and are trying to sell them to their customers … Potential convention participants are like tourists because they have a wide choice of different conferences at different locations, at varying cost and different times.

Therefore, for those invited to association events, the image of the destination can be just as important a determining factor as it is for those considering it as a place to spend a holiday.

One of the rare destination image studies carried out is included in Oppermann's own survey of the importance of meetings destination attributes to association meeting planners, in which he evaluated general destination images of 30 North American convention destinations. The results of his North American convention destination study are presented in Table 3.6, which shows how cities were ranked according to their image.

Apart from the obvious temptation to speculate to what extent Miami and Los Angeles' low ratings are due to the association of violence with both cities, one other observation can be made immediately from Table 3.6. Without exception, scores are higher, or at least the same, when they are given by those meetings planners who are already familiar with the destination. This suggests that once a meeting planner has experience of a particular destination, then they are extremely likely to have an improved image of it. Conversely, this means that destinations of which the planner has no experience are at a disadvantage in the selection process – a clear argument in support of destinations investing in familiarisation trips for planners and buyers.

It is highly possible that the same phenomenon of 'familiarity breeds contentment' also applies to individual venues, with planners needing to be thoroughly convinced of a venue's ability to deliver before using it for the first time, but then being likely to use it again and again. In Figure 3.3, previous experience of the venue is highlighted as a selection criterion by the association sector. Shallcross (1998; p.B-51) emphasises this point:

> Professional conference organisers tend to choose from a selection of preferred known venues, and reputation is of the highest importance ... Unknown venues are at a disadvantage when competing for this business, though repeat business and referral can be achieved once the venue has demonstrated its abilities.

Support from the destination

A final factor that can play a part in determining the choice of venue is the degree to which the destination itself receives financial support from its own local or regional government for use in enticing meetings planners to choose that particular destination over others. Often known as *subvention*, this type of support can take a number of different forms of financial inducement, from offering the venue on a rent-free basis to providing a free civic reception for delegates. Concern over the ethics of offering such inducements and their compromising effect on what ought to be a level playing field do not appear to have diminished municipalities' enthusiasm for providing this type of sweetener. One example chosen from many is that of the Dutch town of Maastricht, where, for a group comprising 500+ delegates, 'the mayor will happily throw a complimentary drinks reception at the town hall and the city officials will allow you to adorn lampposts and public buildings with signage and corporate images' (Olliver, 2002; p.71).

Table 3.6 North American convention destination image survey

Rank	Destination	Overall mean	With previous experience	Without previous experience
1	San Diego	12.5	12.6	12.1
2	San Francisco	11.8	12.1	9.0
3	New Orleans	11.4	12.0	7.9
4	Orlando	11.4	11.8	7.2
5	Washington, DC	10.6	10.7	9.3
6	Chicago	10.4	10.5	7.0
7	Boston	10.4	10.8	5.9
8	San Antonio	10.1	11.4	7.4
9	Seattle	9.9	10.8	7.4
10	Atlanta	9.7	9.8	8.0
11	Toronto	9.5	9.7	8.9
12	Vancouver	9.5	12.0	8.0
13	Phoenix	9.2	10.1	7.3
14	Dallas	8.8	8.8	8.8
15	Denver	8.7	9.1	7.5
16	Honolulu	8.2	8.7	7.2
17	Las Vegas	8.1	10.3	4.7
18	Montreal	8.0	8.6	7.5
19	Philadelphia	7.7	8.9	5.3
20	Nashville	7.7	8.5	5.8
21	New York	6.4	7.0	3.5
22	St Louis	6.3	6.4	5.9
23	Salt Lake City	6.1	7.1	5.3
24	Houston	5.8	5.8	5.8
25	Los Angeles	5.8	5.9	4.8
26	Portland	5.8	6.8	5.4
27	Quebec City	5.6	6.0	5.5
28	Miami	5.6	5.9	4.9
29	Calgary	4.9	6.4	4.6
30	Atlantic City	3.2	3.2	3.2

Mean scores are derived from scaling of destinations on a scale from 1 to 15.

Source: Oppermann, M. (1996a), 'Convention destination images; analysis of association meeting planners' perceptions', *Tourism Management*, Vol. 17, pp. 175–82.

Intermediaries

Earlier in this chapter, we mentioned that meeting planners could either be employees of the buyer company or association, or they could be intermediaries – employees of agencies specialised in organising meeting events on behalf of clients.

In addition to – or instead of – using their own staff to organise meetings, buyers may employ the services of various kinds of intermediaries and agencies to assist them in the planning and running of such events. These intermediaries undertake a buying role on behalf of their clients, who may be companies, associations or any other type of initiator of meetings.

Such meetings planners represent one type of intermediary: those working on behalf of the buyers. But there is another type of intermediary: those working on behalf of the suppliers, in the sense of the destinations and venues where meetings are held. Both types act as important links in the chain joining buyers with suppliers, and their roles will be examined in this section.

However, it is worth emphasising here that although the two types of intermediary appear to have loyalties to different players in the meetings market, they share a common aim – for the event to go well. With the vast sums often being spent on holding meetings, much is at stake, and intermediaries can play a key role in contributing to the smooth and successful functioning of this market.

Intermediaries working on behalf of buyers

Companies in search of someone to organise all or part of a meeting for them can draw on a multitude of agencies who will use their specialist skills and knowledge to provide this service. Travel agencies, tour operators, hotels, public relations companies and production houses are among the many types of agencies that will occasionally undertake the task of finding a venue and planning all or part of a meeting on behalf of the client. In this section, however, only the roles of those intermediaries and agencies that actually specialise in planning meetings will be discussed.

Professional conference organisers

One of the main types of intermediaries used, especially for national and international association events and governmental conferences, is the professional conference organiser (PCO). A PCO approximates to an independent meetings planner in North America, and the term may be used to describe either the individual or the agency they work for.

The PCO acts as the project manager for the whole event, as well as, from time to time, a consultant advising on aspects such as communications techniques, marketing and public relations, tax and insurance. PCOs are also able to give advice on the additional, complex needs of high-level governmental events, such as adherence to strict rules on protocol and VIP treatment, tight security and the extensive media facilities.

The range of services that PCOs can offer can extend to as little or as much as the client requires. Their professional association, the International Association of Professional Congress Organisers (IAPCO, www.iapco.org), lists the following aspects of meeting planning with which their members can assist:

- assistance with conference bids
- help in defining objectives
- advice on congress taxation liabilities
- preliminary outline plan
- draft income and expenditure budget
- finance consultancy – pre-finance, sponsorship, exhibitions, loans, registration fees
- book-keeping
- control of bank accounts, income and expenditure ledgers
- venue negotiation
- organisational structure
- meetings with organising committees
- registration processing systems
- secretariat and office facilities, including mailing addresses
- liaison with production companies
- scientific or technical programme support
- abstract handling
- exhibition and poster sessions
- speaker liaison
- marketing and public relations
- press office
- staffing on site
- social events
- liaison with airlines
- delegate transportation
- closure of conference accounts
- post-event evaluation.

Providing a valuable insight into the complex tasks that are involved in organising a major meeting event, this list makes it clear why many buyers use intermediaries to undertake the planning on their behalf. PCOs have, in many countries, formed their own associations that act as forums for the exchange of ideas as well as providers of in-service training for this profession. In the UK, objectives of the Association of British Professional Conference Organisers (ABPCO, www.abpco.org) include working to increase standards of professionalism throughout the meetings industry, as well as increasing the volume and value of business being won by its members through a range of marketing activities.

Venue-finding agencies

Venue-finding agencies, or venue-placement agencies, as they are sometimes called, have a much more limited role than the PCO. For the company or organisation whose only need is to identify a suitable venue for its meeting, these intermediaries carry out research to find venues that meet the buyer's criteria for location, cost, size, etc. They usually produce a shortlist, from which the buyer makes the final decision. Their income comes from the commission that they earn from the venues selected by their clients – generally around 10%.

The commission system on which their services are based occasionally leaves these agencies open to the suspicion that they tend to shortlist those venues that offer the highest rates of commission. They must therefore be able to demonstrate to their clients that they are acting objectively in recommending particular meetings facilities, since most venue-finding agencies are small businesses that rely on the knowledge and integrity of their staff for continuing success.

Destination management companies

Destination management companies (DMCs), or ground handlers, are key intermediaries whose strength lies in their extensive and detailed knowledge of the destination where the meetings event is to be held. Generally based at the destination where the event is to take place, these are the agencies who can find accommodation for delegates, organise transfers from the airport to the hotel and from the hotel to the conference centre, suggest exciting pre-conference and post-conference tours and excursions, identify local celebrities to act as after-dinner speakers ... in short, take care of all local arrangements essential to the success of the event.

DMCs often work in collaboration with the PCO or meeting planner who has been given responsibility for the overall organisation of the event. However, it is evident that, in many cases, the roles of the two types of agency may not always be delineated clearly, and that there is scope for competition between them. Smith (1990) has remarked that 'DMCs have traditionally not competed with PCOs, but things are changing. Life is tougher and the grey area between the two is fading. Many PCOs will accept every aspect of an event – and so will some DMCs.'

Conference production companies

High-profile or very elaborate meeting events, such as product launches, if they are to be of a professional standard, require specialist input from agencies with the skills and knowledge to, for example, design and build a conference set and backdrop, and provide audiovisual support and special effects. This is where conference production companies play an essential role.

They are most often employed in connection with events that are highly theatrical in nature and that have to be visually striking and memorable in content in order to achieve their objectives. In addition to the functions mentioned above, conference production companies can also raise the presentation standards of the event by, for example, preparing computer graphics and videos or even writing the scripts and training speakers in delivery techniques and autocue use.

Alternatively, as Shone (1998) points out, conference production companies can also be used to stage an event when an organisation wishes to take over a unique venue, such as a museum or National Trust property, for a conference, and requires expertise to be brought in that the venue itself might not normally possess.

Like DMCs, conference production companies often work in partnership with the PCOs and other meeting planners who invite them to make their specialist contribution to the organisation of an event.

Intermediaries working on behalf of suppliers

Destination marketing organisations

The tendency for buyers to consider individual venues only after they have first chosen the destination for their event means that suppliers such as conference centres and hotels must ensure that the countries and cities in which they are located are presented prominently and positively in the meetings market. For this reason, a number of organisations exist at various geographical scales to bring destinations to the attention of potential buyers and the intermediaries working on their behalf.

With titles such as 'convention and visitor bureau', 'convention bureau' or 'conference desk', these organisations represent the destination in the marketplace, offering buyers a one-stop shop enquiry point. Rogers (1998) emphasises that their role is to sell the destination, highlighting all its strengths and facilities, generating and converting enquiries into confirmed business. They are also involved in product development, identifying weaknesses in venues and facilities and in general infrastructure, and working to rectify such faults.

As well as promoting their countries to the leisure market, many national tourist organisations (NTOs) also target business tourism buyers and intermediaries. There is clear evidence that a growing number of NTOs are putting more time and effort into marketing their countries as destinations for business tourism activities, often acting as the link between buyers and local convention bureaux or DMCs.

The trade publication *Conference & Incentive Travel* carries out annual surveys of NTOs' involvement in conference- and incentive travel-related (CIT) activities, focusing on their representatives in the UK. Although the trend is clearly towards increased involvement in business tourism, many NTOs still concentrate exclusively on leisure tourism promotion.

Conference & Incentive Travel's 2001 survey of NTOs with representation in London showed that the number of those with a dedicated CIT department stood at 64%, 4% up on the 1999 figure. For most, the decision of whether to employ staff specialised in dealing with the CIT market seems to depend primarily on budgetary considerations (Creevy, 2001). However, the level of priority given by NTOs to CIT promotion is indicated by earlier *Conference & Incentive Travel* surveys, which have highlighted the fact that many NTOs have only one member of staff per office dealing with business travel-related enquiries.

Budget permitting, NTOs' CIT-related spending is used mainly for the following purposes:

● arranging familiarisation trips for buyers, intermediaries and journalists, to demonstrate the destination's facilities for CIT
● including material relevant to CIT on the NTO's website
● attending exhibitions, such as IT&ME and the EIBTM
● advertising
● mailings.

Further detail on NTOs' CIT-related marketing activity is given by Greaves (1998a; p.18), who, in a *Conference & Incentive Travel* survey of London-based NTOs, notes that:

> To promote their product more effectively to the corporate market, NTOs use a variety of marketing tools. Over half have promotional videos targeted at the CIT market, while 98% provide a slide or photographic service for use in presentations and campaigns. Some 85% have also set up a website on their destination, although only 56% of sites are relevant to the CIT market.

Despite being often under-resourced and understaffed, NTOs are appreciated by many agencies and intermediaries for the impartial advice they give. However, some buyers claim that they are not selective enough in the information they give out. Creevy (2001; p.29) quotes one such agency: 'It's great when we can work with a tourist board and they can honestly tell you which suppliers to use. In most cases, though, they are not allowed to be subjective and just talk you through every one-star hotel upwards.'

The overall verdict from the agencies' point of view would appear to be somewhat inconclusive. While some of them found NTOs' business tourism departments to be highly effective and proactive, others preferred to deal directly with DMCs. In the latter case, this was often because they found that either NTOs were too slow in responding to requests for information or that they did not have access to the detailed information required. One agency representative is quoted as saying that, in some cases, proactive DMCs have superseded the NTO (Creevey, 2001; p.50): 'One example of this is the DMC, Green Route, in Zimbabwe. It is making massive efforts at the moment to pull in business so that when the country's political situation stabilises, agencies will go to them to plan a trip rather than to the NTO.'

Because of the revenue generation and prestige that meetings can bring, a great number of local and regional authorities have also taken an active role in the development and marketing of their meetings facilities. Many such cities and regions have created destination marketing services, part of whose role it is to generate awareness of the conference facilities and to deal with enquiries from potential clients. For example, in its 1999 survey, the Meetings Industry Association found that 82% of UK local tourist authorities had established dedicated conference marketing organisations; the 18% that did not had at least one person in the general tourism marketing team dedicated to this sector (MIA, 1999).

The genesis of these organisations, most commonly known as convention bureaux, was mentioned at the beginning of this chapter. Smith (1990) notes that they emerged in North America at the end of the nineteenth century when railroad junction cities were the sites for most large meetings. Rogers (1998; p.2) elaborates:

> As more and more cities became aware of the value of convention business, it was inevitable that the solicitation of these conventions would be assigned to a full-time salesperson; and while this may have happened in any one of many major cities, history records that it first happened in Detroit, Michigan, when a group of businessmen

decided to place a full-time salesperson on the road to invite conventions to their city. Thus, in 1896, the first convention bureau was formed, and an industry emerged.

The main aim of convention bureaux is to market destinations effectively to increase visitor numbers and business tourism expenditure. They see themselves as a focal point of meetings marketing and usually provide a venue-finding service that will research and locate appropriate venues for a buyer or meeting planner, and provide costings. Some will even arrange an inspection visit for a potential client. Greaves (1998b; p.38), describing UK bureaux, gives more detail of their activities:

> The overwhelming majority of convention bureaux now offer a wide range of services, including suggesting conference venues and incentive ideas, making hotel reservations, recommending restaurants, sending out destination manuals, and organising familiarisation trips for both agents and corporate buyers. Two-thirds also promote their services and destinations on a dedicated web site.

There is a great variety of types of operation among convention bureaux. A key feature is their funding structure. In this respect, some important characteristics distinguish bureaux in Europe from those in the USA. In Europe, local destination marketing has traditionally been undertaken directly by local or regional governments, whereas in the USA an 'arms-length' approach has been developed through the use of visitor and convention bureaux which are more independent of the public sector.

Although in the USA the largest proportion of bureaux funding still comes from local government, the contribution of the private-sector members (predominantly represented by local hotels, restaurants and travel companies) to bureaux's activities in the USA is generally higher, proportionally, than in Europe. In the USA, commercial enterprises contribute to convention bureaux financially through membership fees, joint-marketing expenditure, and 'in-kind' services, e.g. the provision of accommodation and meals for visiting journalists.

At the beginning of the 1990s, as their administration budgets became tighter, many European cities looked to the American convention bureau as a model for maximising commercial sector involvement in, and funding of, marketing activities. The question of whether the US model could be applied usefully to local destination marketing in Europe was researched by Richards (1993; p.43), who came to the following conclusion:

> It is difficult to see the US bureau system being transplanted directly into Europe. The key funding element of the US system, the Transient Occupancy Tax [a bed tax on hotel guests], is unlikely to be adopted as a universal measure [in Europe]. It is far more likely that certain elements of the American system could be adapted for use in Europe. The most useful aspects of the American model ... would seem to be:
>
> - a strong membership system which adequately represents the local visitor industry and provides a strong political lobby
> - a board of directors which effectively transmits the views of the members to the bureau
> - a clear set of annual and longer-term objectives, which can be used to generate performance indicators.

For Richards (1993; p.40), therefore, the advantage in the US bureau system lay mainly in the membership scheme and the financial contribution this provides:

> In the long term, however, it seems that the membership system is most financially valuable in providing a political lobby to secure and protect sources of public funding. The basic lesson for any UK or European organisation seems to be that the US bureau membership system is not a solution to short-term financial problems. Rather, developing a membership system should be seen as an investment in long-term political and financial gain, and a marketing advantage.

In most European countries, it is now generally accepted that convention bureaux effectively depend on a positive public/private sector partnership, underpinned by adequate public funding. Membership-based funding systems appear to be on the increase. In the UK, for example, the Meetings Industry Association estimates that 60% of bureaux are joint public and private sector funded, while the rest are funded entirely by local government (MIA, 1999).

Greaves (1998b; p.37) cites Tony Rogers, executive director of the British Association of Conference Destinations, on this issue:

> The trend is increasingly to establish a convention bureau at arm's length from the local authority as a way of increasing the partnership between the public and private sectors. Sometimes the private sector suppliers have the view that the local authority has ownership, but when they have a vested interest and are represented on the board, they have a much closer working relationship.

According to the same source, Rogers considers that this trend of private venues providing financial support will grow, especially as UK local authority budgets continue to either stagnate or dwindle.

Associations of destination marketing organisations

Although on one level individual countries and cities are in competition with each other in the meetings market, most understand that they have common objectives and shared concerns that can best be addressed through a cooperative and collaborative structure.

For this reason, a number of trade associations that include destination marketing organisations among their members have been created in different countries and world regions. Each serves its members' interests through a combination of joint promotion and marketing, lobbying, research and education and training programmes. A number of these have already been mentioned in this chapter, either as sources of data (e.g. the Meetings Industry Association) or authoritative comment on this industry (e.g. the British Association of Conference Destinations). Full details of these and some other key UK and international trade associations are given in Appendix A.

However, while the table in the Appendix concentrates mainly on UK and global associations, it is important not to overlook the fact that a number of world regions also have their own associations, whose objectives include marketing their region and providing advice to meeting planners and potential buyers.

For Europe, the Brussels-based European Federation of Conference Towns (EFCT) (www.efct.org) has members from 34 countries. In addition to the business tourism marketing activities it carries out on behalf of Europe as a whole, the EFCT has a number of other functions, not least of which is lobbying the EU for better conditions and recognition for conference suppliers.

Finally, on behalf of its ten member countries, the Asian Association of Convention and Visitor Bureaux (AACVB) (www.aacvb.org) was established in 1983 to promote Asian convention business and upgrade the level of professionalism in its membership. It strives towards regional cooperation in developing Asia's convention potential and 'promoting the region as an ideal convention destination' (Qu and Li, 1999).

Issues and trends

Much time and energy on the part of meetings-related associations, destination marketing organisations and the trade press is expended in making the effort to detect the most important trends shaping this vast industry. Demand for market intelligence of this kind is at least as great as its supply, with those planning investment in meetings-related facilities and services eager to know more about the dominant trends that are occurring in this sector of business tourism. But in such a diverse sector still characterised by partial and often contradictory data, identifying trends with a great deal of accuracy, based on convincing evidence, presents a considerable challenge. This chapter suggests some of the most apparent trends characterising the twenty-first-century meetings industry.

Level of demand

More or fewer meetings?

In Chapter 1, the link between the state of the economy and the general level of demand for business travel services was discussed. It is therefore logical to conclude that the level of demand for meetings of all types in the first few years of the twenty-first century will have reflected the broad changes in the state of the world's economy.

The level of demand for meetings can be measured in a number of ways, but one of the most straightforward is by estimating the number of such events held. Using this indicator of demand, it would be reasonable to expect that as the world economy at the turn of the century appeared to be heading for a global downturn, the number of meetings would begin to fall in many parts of the world. As is often the case, however, the evidence is ambiguous. While the number of association meetings appears to remain steady, the volume of corporate demand seems to be faltering.

In the UK, there were early indications of this trend in data included in the UK Conference Market Survey (MIA, 2000). This showed a marked drop in the number of corporate sector events, falling from an annual average of 12 meetings per company in 1998 to just over eight in 1999, the lowest number for several years. By the following year, however, the average had risen to 9.7 meetings per company, only to fall again to 9.2 meetings per company in 2002 (MIA, 2001 and 2002).

In his review of demand for events held in conference centres, Elzinga (2001; p.30) notes that from the mid-1990s, conference centres, specifically in the USA and Europe, benefited from the economic upswing as they allocated year after year more slots to the lucrative corporate market. But he concedes that 'as a first sign of the economic slowdown, fewer corporate meetings are being booked'. Attempting to put a positive spin on the situation, he adds: 'Conference centres are finding that a healthy business mix is important and that the less lucrative but more consistent association market is their most important business on a longer term basis.'

Smaller meetings

Clearly, the actual number of meetings being held is only one way of measuring demand. A number of surveys emphasise another quantitative trend: the move towards smaller corporate events, as meetings are attended by fewer delegates.

For Britain, the UK Conference Market Survey has recorded declining average attendance figures for corporate sector meetings, which fell, for example, from 138 delegates in 1999 to 111 delegates in 2001 (MIA, 2000 and 2002).

In part, this phenomenon is almost certainly an economy measure, as financially prudent businesses become increasingly aware of the transport, accommodation and other associated costs incurred in having several members of staff attend meetings, which might function equally well with fewer of their employees present.

However, again there is evidence that the situation in the association sector is quite different. ICCA (2001) data, which take into account only association meetings attended by between 50 and 10 000 delegates, show that the average number of participants per meeting has been increasing since 1993, when the figure stood at 638, to 815 in 2000.

An explanation for the apparent growth in the number of delegates attending one type of noncorporate meeting is provided by Rogers (1998; p.78). He links this phenomenon, in the UK at least, to changes within the country's industrial and commercial structures:

> Reduction in trade union membership since 1980 has led to trade unions merging which, in turn, has meant fewer trade union conferences (particularly affecting seaside destinations) but, paradoxically, with larger numbers of delegates than previously. Some resorts, the traditional hosts of many trade union conferences, have found that their conference venues are no longer big enough to accommodate their former clients.

Nevertheless, a number of commentators have pointed out trends in the market that could also, over time, exert a downward pressure on the average length of meetings in the association sector. One such trend is that emphasised by Chetwynd (1999; p.51): the rise of niche-knowledge and specialist conferences. She notes that specialist conferences have taken off in recent years, as smaller focus groups become increasingly popular in many industries. With specialist conferences, the emphasis is on the acquisition of knowledge, as opposed to the networking which tends to be a prime objective of large events. She explains:

> There are several reasons for this. Many [specialist conferences] are organised on the back of research or a recent report, which implies the imparting of new information or a new spin on old beliefs and data. A specialist conference will also attract a higher percentage of delegates who are steeped in the subject, and therefore more motivated to attend.

Supporting Chetwynd's view, Clark *et al.* (1997; p.82) mention an additional contributing factor, linking this trend with the apparent growth in the number of association meetings: 'Because of corporate downsizing, the education role once played by businesses is now being assumed by associations. At the same time, training needs are becoming more specialised, resulting in smaller but more numerous association meetings.'

Shorter meetings

There is convincing evidence that growing pressures on delegates' time and increasing focus on company profits have reduced the length of time made available for meetings. The UK Conference Market Survey has tracked this phenomenon since the late 1990s, and in its 2002 survey announced that the length of corporate meetings had continued to decrease, to an average of 1.3 days in 2001, down from 1.7 days in 1999 (MIA, 2002).

The situation regarding association meetings is similar. For the UK, the UK CMS noted that the average length of an association event *decreased* from 2.2 days in 1998 to 1.8 days in 2001. For the global association meetings market, ICCA (2001) data point to the same trend regarding the length of events. In 1992, the average length of large association meetings was 4.8 days, a figure that had actually fallen to 4.5 days by 2000.

Will the trend towards shorter meetings continue? A factor likely to add to the pressure to keep meetings shorter in the future is identified in research commissioned by the Professional Convention Management Association (PCMA) (www.pcma.org), an international association of professionals in the meetings industry. PCMA's research links the trend towards shorter meetings with recent developments in the workforces of many countries and considers how this could eventually affect the types of meetings employees wish to attend.

The suggestion is that downsizing, outsourcing and contingency work arrangements have created a workforce that is increasingly likely to identify more with their professions or occupations than with any employer. These workforce changes may help businesses become more flexible, but they also mean in many cases that employees are less loyal. The PCMA believes that this raises some fundamental questions, since, with relationships between them becoming less stable, employers and employees may become less willing to invest in each other. If the conference is no longer seen as a company benefit, then there may be a move towards employees themselves paying to attend meetings events. As the attendee will be more cost conscious and more demanding, time, especially if no longer compensated by the employer, will become more valuable. Consequently, the reasoning goes, attendees will want more intensive and concentrated programmes targeted at them (PCMA, 2000).

Growth in supply

Whatever the situation regarding changes in the profile of demand for meetings, there is little doubt as to the general trend concerning the supply of facilities for this market. What must appear clear to the inhabitants of many major cities is that investment in the infrastructure for meetings of all sizes continues apace. Most visible of all of these developments are the gleaming new conference centres that continue to be confidently unwrapped for the admiration of citizens and visitors alike in destinations the world over. Box 3.1 lists a few of the leading new developments to have been opened in Europe since the year 2000.

But to these new openings must also be added the considerable investment in refurbishment and renovations undertaken by cities with older conference facilities. Many 'first-generation' conference centres were, by the beginning of the twenty-first century, receiving a measure of much-needed reinvestment. An example of a UK conference centre in this position is the Brighton Centre, whose head of conferences has said (Goodhart, 1998; p.48): 'The Brighton Centre was built in the 1970s. Money needs to be invested in it if it is to compete with newer, smarter buildings. At the moment, we are managing to hold our own, but we were once the market leader and are struggling to retain that position a little.'

Some of the refurbishment has been undertaken by conference centres keen to be responsive to the changing trends in demand already discussed. Chetwynd (1999) provides the example of London's Barbican Centre, which undertook a major redesign of its meeting space in response to the apparent move towards smaller conferences. Its conference space, level 4, was reconfigured in 1999, as internal brick walls were replaced with partitions to allow for greater flexibility. As a result of the refurbishment, the Barbican's two conference rooms seating 170 delegates each became five rooms holding up to 80 people each.

Further examples of reinvestment and refurbishment are provided by Graf (2001b) in his survey of international conference centres' investment plans for the years 2002–5. Among the biggest spenders on structural alterations, extensions and refurbishment to their conference centres are The Bella Center, Copenhagen (US$40 million), Le Corum Palais de Congrès, Montpellier (US$45 million), and Rio de Janeiro's main conference centre (US$44 million).

In short, despite evidence of a slowdown in the world economy over the early years of the twenty-first century, this appears to have had very little impact on plans

Box 3.1

Growing investment in conference centres

June 2000

Forum Grimaldi in Monaco, including a new 1900-seat multipurpose auditorium and 13 000 m^2 of exhibition space. To be used for cultural events as well as conferences, allowing better space for both the Monte Carlo Opera and Ballet.

December 2000

Salzburg Congress – new state-of-the-art convention centre, including the Europa Hall, which seats 1350.

March 2001

Manchester International Convention Centre, part of a new cultural complex in the city centre. Cost £25 million. Includes an 800-seat auditorium and a 1825-m^2 exhibition and banqueting facility. Also intended as a venue for hosting events in the 2002 Commonwealth Games. The conference centre is part of the Great Northern Initiative, a regeneration scheme linking other major projects, such as the Great Northern Warehouse retail and leisure venue and the G-Mex Exhibition Complex.

2003

Phase 2 of ExCeL in London's Docklands.

to expand, refurbish or build completely new conference centres in cities the world over. Partly, this almost certainly reflects the desire of entrepreneurs to remain up-beat about market developments in order to protect the investments they have already committed to supplying facilities for meetings. However, it also illustrates clearly that the ability of infrastructural supply to adapt rapidly to changes in the state of the economy lags far behind that of the far more responsive demand for meetings, particularly in the corporate sector.

With such extensive new construction, refurbishment and renovations to conference centres, the key question necessarily arises: to what extent does a situation of oversupply already exist? Certainly, regarding the situation in Europe, the report *Business and Conference Tourism in the European Economic Area* is unambiguous, concluding that after the waves of development in the 1980s, the supply of conference facilities has reached an oversupply situation in certain areas (European Communities, 1996). When added to the worldwide expansion of meetings facilities, the overabundance of venues in Europe has undoubtedly contributed to the overall growth in competition, which will now be examined.

Table 3.7 Number of meetings per continent

Continent	1993–4	1995–6	1997–8	1999–2000
Europe	3295 (61%)	3554 (60%)	3667 (59%)	3476 (60%)
Asia	816 (15%)	996 (16%)	967 (16%)	890 (15%)
North America	685 (13%)	702 (12%)	691 (11%)	651 (11%)
Latin America	321 (5%)	311 (5%)	383 (6%)	355 (6%)
Australia/Pacific	179 (3%)	229 (4%)	275 (5%)	290 (5%)
Africa	142 (3%)	162 (3%)	181 (3%)	153 (3%)
Total	**5438**	**5954**	**6164**	**5815**

Source: ICCA (2001), www.iccaworld.com

Growth in competition

Expansion in supply has led inevitably to an intensification in competition, not only between venues but also between destinations active in the meetings market. This situation is apparent at all levels, from the local to the international, but it is perhaps illustrated most dramatically at the international level, where one of the trends to result from the growth in competition from other continents is, as UIA and ICCA figures reveal in Table 3.7, that Europe's overall share of the association segment of the market is no longer expanding.

While Europe and North America struggle to maintain their share of the international meetings market, one clear winner in the field is the Australia/Pacific region. Given that in 1990–1 this region hosted only 127 international association meeting events, the growth is shown to be all the more significant. Many of the factors favouring this region are the same as those which, since the 1990s, have been tempting growing numbers of leisure tourists to go there: relatively low airfares, novelty value, perceived value for money, and a clean and safe environment.

Nevertheless, it is important to see such growth in perspective and, notably, in a context that still sees almost three-quarters of the world's international association meetings being held in Europe or North America. The dominance of the countries in these two continents is clearly shown in Table 3.8.

As always, the USA appears at the top of the table, followed by the UK. What is worthy of note, however, is how Germany's ranking in third place is in danger of being threatened by the rise and rise of Australia, which, in ICCA statistics for 1995, held only ninth place.

Australia's prominent position is to be expected, given that, together with Japan, both countries account for a significant share of arrivals for both leisure and business tourism in their region of the world. Australia's success in attracting large meetings can be explained partly by the 'Olympics effect'. However, much of its international meetings market arises from the rapid expansion of business and travel links within the Asia-Pacific region itself, and the opportunities this brings Australia to host what are, in effect, regionally based meetings and trade shows (Dwyer *et al.*, 2001).

Table 3.8 Number of association meetings per country

Rank	Country	1998	1999	2000
1	USA	268	237	234
2	UK	186	166	193
3	Germany	178	165	161
4	Australia	111	111	152
5	Spain	174	163	144
6	France	160	142	141
7	Netherlands	124	105	126
8	Italy	144	133	116
9	Japan	117	98	102
10	Canada	92	89	91
11	Finland	88	106	85
12	Brazil	52	75	83
13	Sweden	108	77	81
14	Austria	102	81	78
15	Norway	45	64	72
16	Switzerland	61	60	63
17	Belgium	69	54	55
18	Hungary	46	72	52
19	Denmark	84	74	49
20	South Africa	49	48	46

Source: ICCA (2001), www.iccaworld.com

Although apparently secure in its number-two ranking, beaten only by the unassailable USA, the UK has no reason to be complacent, as despite hosting more international association meetings in absolute terms, its share of the total international conference market has been falling. Bray (2001) illustrates this trend using research published by the Office of National Statistics, which shows that 1999 and 2000 saw a sharp fall in delegate numbers arriving in the UK. A comparison between the first nine months of 2000 and the same period in the previous year indicates that the number of incoming visits to attend conferences in the UK fell by 11% from 679 000 to 605 000. (On a more positive note, however, it appears that those delegates who did visit the UK in 2000 appear to have spent more, as earnings from incoming conference business fell overall by only 2%, from £424 million to £417 million.)

Bray (2001) suggests a number of ongoing factors, which he believes may have militated against meetings planners choosing the UK for their international events, including the BSE ('mad cow disease') affair and the lack of a major purpose-built conference centre in London. He adds a few additional factors that arose later to damage further the image of the UK, including the fuel price protest and the foot and mouth epidemic. However, many commentators maintain that, in the early years of the new century, it is the strength of sterling that constituted the most discouraging feature of the UK as an international meetings destination. On this issue, Bray quotes the executive director of the British Association of Conference Destinations as saying that one of the real issues at the moment is competitiveness: the UK is perceived as being expensive, and there is a feeling that we are losing market share as a result.

For the UK meetings industry, however, a more encouraging note is struck by the data given in Table 3.9, which shows the capital in first place, a meteoric rise from its position in fifteenth place the previous year. Once more, the ICCA data demonstrate that despite the USA's dominance of the international meetings market as a country, it is the European capitals that account for the vast majority of places in the top 20 destinations in terms of cities. One key reason for this is mentioned in ICCA's analysis of these figures: of a total of 5075 international associations in the ICCA database, 65% are based in Europe.

The emphasis given here to the *international* meetings market must, however, be set in the context of the market as a whole. In the UK, as for most countries, the bulk of meetings held are domestic events. Providing the stable core of most

Table 3.9 Number of association meetings per city

Rank	City	1998	1999	2000
1	London	36	31	56
2	Madrid	78	49	55
3	Paris	47	36	55
4	Vienna	83	64	54
5	Sydney	32	42	49
6	Stockholm	58	42	48
7	Rio de Janeiro	18	37	47
8	Amsterdam	56	42	46
9	Barcelona	44	42	40
10	Helsinki	39	48	40
11	Singapore	43	46	40
12	Berlin	37	43	39
13	Edinburgh	35	36	39
14	Budapest	37	46	38
15	Melbourne	28	26	35
16	Copenhagen	64	55	33
17	Hong Kong	15	30	33
18	Oslo	22	24	31
19	Reykjavik	5	10	29
20	Lisbon	53	24	27

Source: ICCA (2001), www.iccaworld.com

countries' meetings market, domestic demand is not in the same category as the large international events tracked by UIA and ICCA. The vast majority of meetings held in the UK are local, regional or national events that do not consider overseas destinations. Melbourne, Washington and Prague are simply not in the competition to be the place that hosts the quarterly meeting of the Carlisle Rotary Club.

A buyers' market

There is growing evidence of a trend towards acknowledging that the market for meetings is becoming increasingly a buyers' market, and that many meetings planners are becoming extremely skilled in negotiating with venue suppliers. This particular trend is far from new. At the beginning of the 1990s, as the recession in the world economy put buyers in most markets in a position of power, one commentator remarked (Smith, 1990; p.75): 'Buyers are better informed about the nature of the market, better educated in knowing what they want, more aware that most things are negotiable under the right circumstances, and more determined to achieve their needs on satisfactory terms.' Consequently, even before the first economic slowdown of the new century, buyers were already in a favourable position, having learned much about the power of negotiating with suppliers.

Possible evidence of the effectiveness of planners' well-honed negotiating skills may be seen in the declining daily corporate delegate rates and 24-hour rates recorded in surveys such as the UK Conference Market Survey (MIA, 2001). According to this source, in 2000, average daily delegate rates for the corporate sector fell to £32.95 from £34.50 the previous year. While this could also be due to them trading down by, for example, using less costly facilities, anecdotal evidence seems to suggest that this is less likely to be the case: companies are keen to maintain standards while cutting costs.

The same source notes that association buyers also remain price-sensitive in their spending, with the average hotel room rate for their residential events down from £36 to £25 per night.

One technique used increasingly by meetings planners in their quest for better rates from suppliers is booking the venue closer to the actual date of the event. Since the early 1990s, they have understood that rather than be faced with the prospect of being left with unlet meetings facilities, venues and accommodation suppliers prefer to offer discounted rates.

One impact of this particular technique has been a significant shortening of lead times. Rockett and Smillie (1994; p.42), in their report on the European conference and meetings market, remarked:

> Most of the PCOs interviewed for this study identified booking lead times as the area of most dramatic change that has occurred in the market. It used to be taken for granted that the meetings business would book some six months to a year before the event date, but booking time has shrunk considerably.

One of the PCOs interviewed by the authors of the report described how he had arranged a meeting in Vienna for 500 persons four weeks before the event.

Fortunately for venue suppliers, such remarkably short lead times for large events are rare, as few meetings planners would leave themselves so little time to deal with the complex logistics of organising a meeting of that size. According to the UK Conference Market Survey 2002, corporate events were booked an average of 5 months ahead, although 55% of corporate events were booked within three months of the actual meeting (MIA, 2002).

The growing supply of meeting venues may also have contributed to meetings planners' ability to negotiate from a position of power. In the UK, the influence of this factor has been emphasised by Shallcross (1998; p.B-40), who links it with the decline in overall conference income recorded in one British Conference Market Trends Survey: 'This can be partly attributed to the trend towards smaller conferences. However, the growing number of competing venues ... may have an impact on this. As the pie gets bigger, more people come to the table and end up with a smaller slice.' He goes on to argue that conference organisers are in a stronger position than ever to negotiate rental rates, particularly for smaller events, due to the wealth of competing venues in the UK.

Confirming the continuation of this trend, the UK Conference Market Survey 2000 also notes that competitive pressures are mounting for conference venues and related service providers, with different types of venue attempting to gain market share by developing conference business at their premises. It points out that sporting venues in particular are becoming increasingly popular with organisers, and that many universities, museums and football clubs are other new entrants into the conference market (MIA, 2001).

However, the situation of buyers negotiating keenly against the background of an abundant supply of venues and conference destinations is far from being confined to only the UK or Europe. Regarding the US market, Judd (1995; p.180) notes:

> The position that cities find themselves in has not escaped the associations and groups that use convention facilities. The biggest associations already assume that they can persuade cities to give them convention space rent-free, and it can only get worse. In 1993, the Future Farmers of America, a youth organisation that has traditionally met in Kansas City, demanded that the city give it cash subsidies, lower hotel rates and other incentives. Since their annual convention brings 28,000 visitors to the city, the city's Convention and Visitors Bureau chair thought it was worth spending 'whatever it takes' to keep the group from going elsewhere. Such an approach can only become more common as tourism entrepreneurs and associations become more adept at playing cities off against one another.

Return on investment

Quantitative changes in the meetings market have already been discussed at the beginning of this section. But meetings appear to be changing qualitatively too. One major trend is the move towards more business-like events, with the emphasis on work and getting results. Rogers (1998) stresses this point, noting that meetings now have a much clearer business focus and are probably more intensive events than in the 1980s.

This emphasis on creating more business-like events is also evident from the findings of EIBTM's survey on the meetings market, as reported in Travel Industry Monitor (1997). The survey sample comprised over 100 respondents from association and corporate buyers in 12 countries organising an average of 15 events annually. It revealed that one indication of how seriously buyers were now taking their involvement in meetings was a marked increase in the level of interest in measuring the return on investment (ROI) achieved by the initiator. Reasons given by initiators and buyers for their increased focus on ROI were typically to 'maximise budget', 'ensure that event objectives were met', and 'to help maintain the reputation of meetings within the organisation'.

Ghitelman (1997; p.67), from his US perspective, emphasises the last point, observing: 'In the meetings industry, ROI is touted as a way planners can finally earn the respect of upper management. It is a way to address that often-heard planner complaint, "My role is not taken seriously enough in my organisation".'

However, despite the vast amounts spent on meetings, it appears that the percentage of initiators actually measuring the results of their investment is still low. In his investigation into event evaluation, Twite (1999a) quotes one PCO who states that only one in five of his clients actively measures ROI.

It is clear, however, that the growing number of clients who do evaluate the meetings they hold are convinced of the value of making the effort. But how do meetings planners demonstrate that their client's investment in a conference or seminar, for example, has been worthwhile? In the same article, Twite (1999; p.23) quotes the marketing operations manager of General Motors Europe, who uses post-event evaluation techniques to measure effectiveness:

> We have found that the best way to [get input from participants] is to design a questionnaire to see if they were interested in what we were telling them and if they understood the message we were putting across. For example, on a new product, there may be features or components that you are trying to explain to an audience, and if they haven't understood at the end of the first day, you can give them more information on the second.

Another PCO believes that companies should start with a clear, agreed brief that states precise and measurable objectives: '"To launch the new ABC" is hardly a measurable objective, whereas "To communicate the positioning, target audience, features, benefits and price structure of the new ABC to all customer-facing staff" would be more meaningful' (Twite, 1999; p.25).

Similarly highlighting the importance of setting objectives, Ghitelman (1997) describes, as one approach, the five basic steps to measuring ROI suggested by the professional association, Meetings Professionals International (MPI):

● Identify and meet with stakeholders (anyone with a direct interest in the outcome of a meeting) – find out what delegates want to hear about from the sponsors and what the sponsors want to say to the delegates.

- Establish measurable objectives – e.g. increase 'share of mind' of delegates, increase market share of the company's products.
- Determine measurement tools – e.g. a before-and-after telephone survey asking delegates about their attitudes, perceptions, opinions and belief toward the product/company.
- Develop the content of the event – identify speakers who can address the needs of delegates, then get the message across.
- Report the results – produce a report, with statistical data: not just reporting that a good time was had by all.

However, while this method appears sound, Ghitelman (1997; p.68) admits that there is a dilemma:

> Meeting planners are generally viewed as people who developed a set of logistical skills – negotiating room rates, arranging for food and beverage, and so on. They are not viewed as having a lot to contribute in the areas of strategic content or styles and methods of communication. But most meetings are held to communicate, change viewpoints or affect behaviour. This is not the job of meeting planners. In fact, most meeting planners are emotionally and intellectually comfortable inside their logistical box. It's hard for them to reach out and become professional communications consultants.

With rising cost-consciousness among buyers, it seems that meetings planners and intermediaries may increasingly have to step outside their 'logistical boxes' and take the initiative, by encouraging their clients to include the measurement of ROI in the brief. Only by doing so can the substantial sums of money being spent on meetings be proven to be money well spent.

Disintermediation

An earlier section of this chapter focused on some of the most important types of intermediaries linking buyers with suppliers. But as neither buyers nor suppliers are obliged to use intermediaries, many are, in fact, choosing to bypass the middlemen, preferring to deal directly with each other.

In Chapter 2, we showed that disintermediation is a growing practice in the individual business travel sector, as business travel agents are increasingly having to struggle to persuade buyers and suppliers that their role in the market is an essential one. Many believe that the meetings sector is demonstrating a similar tendency, and for the same reason – buyers and suppliers wishing to make savings on the fees and commissions they pay to intermediaries.

Nowhere is this trend seen more clearly than in the hotel conference sector, where many venue suppliers have been only too delighted to respond to their buyers' wishes to make savings on agents' fees. Upton (1999) is one commentator who has underlined this trend, describing how many conference buyers are seeking to deal directly with suppliers in order to make savings on the fees they pay to intermediaries for finding venues and organising the event. This is becoming increasingly possible, as a growing number of hotel chains are looking to increase their conference revenue by offering, along with direct sales, their own in-house events management services, which circumvent the need for clients to use any intermediaries at all.

Typical of this trend towards one-stop shops is the De Vere Hotels' brand, Priority One, which, as well as the meetings facilities themselves, offers 'creative input and expert consultancy on audio-visual support, people management, themed events, catering, delegate management and even crisis management' – in other words, many of the services traditionally provided by PCOs and other meeting planners.

What argument in support of their own role in the market can intermediaries put forward in the face of the apparent logic of buyers dealing directly with suppliers offering such a comprehensive service? Priority One and its like may satisfy buyers who know where they want to stage their conference, but for those who do not, it may be argued that the agent has an important role to play. Not surprisingly, agents are quick to defend their own *raison d'être*.

Upton (1999) cites one intermediary, whose argument is that buyers lose vital objective advice when booking direct:

> We have the knowledge of venues and continuous feedback from clients as to their service levels. A conference buyer may visit the venue and see the quality of the facility, but they won't know if the tea and coffee arrive on time. The efficiency of a conference venue is only as good as the banqueting or conference manager there, and generally we know them. We are also up to date on new products.

Although hotels are anxious to maintain ties with booking agents, there appears to be little doubt that a growing proportion of business will be generated directly between buyers and suppliers – on condition, of course, that suppliers can deliver on their promise of offering a more convenient and efficient service at a better price.

New technology

Scientific and technological advances have always been welcomed and used to the full by the meetings industry, and venues, for example, have been quick to seize the opportunities offered by developments in these fields. Recently, modern conference centres have been able to equip themselves with features such as high-performance simultaneous interpreting systems, sound reinforcement systems, projection facilities and sophisticated lighting systems, which even 20 years ago would have been inconceivable.

Information and communications technology continues to evolve at a breathtaking pace, but much of the debate in the meetings industry during the 1990s and into the twenty-first century has revolved around the issue of to what extent advances in new technology are an opportunity for this sector of business tourism, and to what extent they present a serious threat.

In particular, the potential of new technology to make travelling to meetings events no longer necessary has been discussed widely. The cost in time and money of attending meetings can be considerable; but when 'being there' was the only way of gaining access to the information and debate that most meetings offer, delegates and/or their employers were prepared to put up with the expense, inconvenience and time commitment in order to attend.

For more than a decade, however, advances in information and communications technology have made it possible for people to benefit from conferences and engage in face-to-face discussions without, in many cases, leaving their own offices. However, before considering how serious a threat this poses to those whose business it is to provide business travel and tourism facilities and services, some of the other trends that have arisen as a result of the application of new technology to the meetings industry will be reviewed.

The Internet

With the use of e-mail and the Internet being so widespread at work and home, these have become useful additional tools for the meetings organiser or planner. Use of the Internet for marketing meetings events is one example of an application of this technology to the meetings sector, as organisers can target directly any potential delegates using their e-mail addresses. It is already common practice for organisers of large events to set up a dedicated website for each event, with details of the venue and the programme, together with links to sources of information on, for example, leisure and recreational facilities at the destination.

However, the level of use of the Internet for this purpose varies and constitutes another difference between the corporate and association sectors. For the UK, this difference was emphasised in the UK Conference Market Survey 2001 (MIA, 2001), which recorded:

> Use of the internet to market corporate events remains low. Only 19% [of corporate planners] are marketing their events through the internet. In the association market, however, the internet is *de rigeur*. With their members spread across the country and further afield, the internet is growing in popularity for marketing – up to nearly 60% from 50% [in 2000].

Another probable explanation for this difference is that since corporate attendees have a vested interest in attending their events – and are often required to do so – corporate organisers do not need to market their events as strongly as their association counterparts, whose target audience has the choice as to whether to attend or not.

Actual registration for many events is also now possible via the Internet, streamlining planners' organisation and enabling them to keep delegates up to date with e-mailed messages about the forthcoming meeting. Specifically for this purpose, software designers have created a number of Internet-based registration systems for use by meetings organisers. For example, the www.myregtool.com, www.event411.com and www.seeuthere.com services enable organisers to manage delegate registration proceedings from any PC connected to the Internet. Most of these software packages allow the organiser to draft a registration spreadsheet, administer participation fees, monitor actual registration and, in some cases, even initiate 'e badging' of delegates enabling delegates to print out their name tag in advance on their own PC.

In a further application of the Internet to meetings planning, a number of websites now offer powerful search engines with extensive venue and other supplier listings, which claim to enable buyers to carry out their research and book venues online. Typical of such sites is www.businessmeetings.com, which is partnered by the business travel agency Rosenbluth International. The services it offers are described on the site's home-page as:

> A free service to search for any type of venue in any country in the world, view detailed information about the properties and then send a Request for Proposal direct to the venue to check availability and rates. You can make use of the extensive information we provide, to help the meetings planner, including access to independent destination reports and links to information on a variety of topics, from local weather to visas and embassies.

A growing number of hotel chains have also created websites that enable clients to make direct meeting room bookings with them. The *Conference & Incentive Travel* 2001 hotel survey showed that there had been a steady increase in the percentage of hotel websites offering this facility, from 48% in 1999 to 69% in 2001. Clearly, the growth in such websites is related directly to the trend towards disintermediation.

Research suggests that surfing for venues has become established practice among many in the meetings planners' profession: 25% and 37% of corporate and association meetings organisers, respectively, reported using this tool for identifying suitable venues in the UK Conference Market Survey (MIA, 2001). Interestingly, research conducted in the USA has linked this method to the shrinking lead times mentioned earlier. The Menlo Consulting Group (MCG; 1999; p.8) notes:

> The most noticeable trend in the corporate meetings segment is a shift towards meetings with planning lead times of three months or less. Technology is helping to shift the market in this direction. It is now possible for a corporate planner to search for a site [venue], select one, contact the hotel's sales force and sign a contract in the span of a single day. This trend shows no sign of slowing; 50% of corporate planners expect an increase in short-term meetings in the next 12 months.

Figure 3.4 shows the use of the Internet by both the corporate and association sectors.

The Internet clearly offers vast new potential to meetings buyers and planners, who appear to be increasingly aware of how this aspect of new technology can play a part in helping them reach their markets more effectively. However, there is considerably less evidence that those with responsibility for destination marketing have seized the opportunities with the same fervour. Most convention bureaux appear to maintain a competent website. But Yuan *et al.*'s (1999) study of the extent to which the full capabilities of the Internet are used by convention and visitor bureaux to augment their marketing efforts and to improve their performance across all facets of their business concluded that most CVB directors

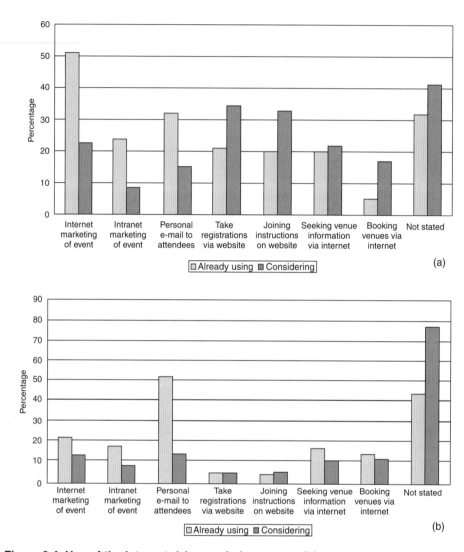

Figure 3.4 Use of the Internet: (a) association sector; (b) corporate sector

Source: *UK Conference Market Survey 2000*, published by the Meetings Industry Association.

had not yet recognised the potential of this technology. The study makes a number of sound suggestions as to how information technology may be integrated into CVBs' marketing and management efforts in such a way as to increase their efficiency and effectiveness.

It was stated earlier that not all of the services offered by new technology were receiving a warm reception by the meetings industry. One application of the Internet capable of causing obvious concern to facilities and services providers is virtual-conferencing, also known as electronic or web-cast conferences, which are increasingly being offered as an alternative to more traditional forms of meeting. In 1998, for example, the Union of International Associations included such events in its Congress Calendar for the first time.

Shallcross (1998; p B-52) describes how the virtual conference functions:

> Essentially, the virtual conference removes the role of geography and physical space from the conference experience. Delegates send and receive information, meet other delegates, interact, even buy and sell in a digital environment fashioned for the purpose. In other words, conventional conference centres become redundant.

He gives the example of the Environment '97 virtual conference organised by the Engineering Council. Attendance, he admits, was difficult to measure, but more than 8500 people registered online and the site was visited by many more people than actually registered. The organisers regarded the event as a success and the idea was extended to a safety conference in 1998 and another environment conference in 1999. The advantages of such a system for the initiator of the meeting include the potential for much wider participation than could be created for a traditional conference. The same advantage is offered by the videoconferencing technology, which we will now consider, before we assess the impacts of both Internet- and non-Internet-based systems.

Videoconferencing

Originally developed in the 1960s, videoconferencing was slow to achieve widespread acceptance due mainly to issues of cost and limitations of the technology. But more recent developments, including the extensive use of videoconferencing during the Gulf War, have meant that the system has been improved and costs have been diminishing significantly. The equipment needed to hold two-way on-screen discussions is no longer affordable only by heads of state and heads of major corporations.

Hotels, sensing the potential of videoconferencing to enhance their overall product, have led the way in installing the necessary technology in their premises. As long ago as 1994, Munro (1994) reported, for example, that Forte and Scandic Hotels had put videoconferencing lines into many of their properties, and that Hyatt planned to invest US$3.5 million in equipping many of its hotels. Videoconferencing rooms are now found in many residential management training centres, large companies and even educational establishments. In venues such as these, the use of videoconferencing tends to be limited to fairly small groups. However, a number of conference centres have also installed satellite-linked videoconferencing equipment, most often to enable keynote speakers who are unable to attend in person to address the delegates.

Given the availability and the potential of virtual-conferencing and videoconferencing, two key questions arise: to what extent is this technology being used, and is it being used to *replace* the traditional meetings to which delegates actually travel?

The UK Conference Market Survey 2000 provides some insight into this issue, at least for the UK, in reporting its findings that 'video-conferencing is being used by over 40% of corporate respondents in addition to meetings, but by just 10% instead of meetings' (MIA, 2001). If, however, destinations and suppliers can take encouragement from these figures, then they may feel more ambivalent about the same report's findings that 'nearly 66% of associations believe that "other" forms of communication will not reduce the number of face-to-face meetings, and 40% of corporates agree – although 37% are not sure; 14% of corporates specifically mentioned that video-conferencing is likely to reduce the need for face-to-face meetings in future'.

The situation in the US corporate meetings market echoes the MIA findings for the UK. Many companies have been experimenting with videoconferencing as a way to limit costs and eliminate hotel availability concerns. However, in one survey, only 32% of corporate planners said their company used videoconferencing – and then only for short meetings with few participants. As one planner explained, 'Video-conferencing replaces some small conferences of five people in the short-term, but it doesn't replace any longer-term meetings' (MCG, 1999; p.8).

Similarly, the PCMA (2000; p.1) research concludes that although the Internet is being used increasingly as a meetings planning and registration tool, the use of new technology as a replacement for business travel events is still mimimal: 'Although well over half of the convention industry now uses online registration, the proportions of respondents reporting using more sophisticated electronic technologies, such as virtual trade shows and video- conferencing, have remained distinct minorities – so far.'

In search of an explanation for this, the same report asks the following pertinent questions: 'Have structural limitations or a simple lack of computer know-how or equipment in the market stifled internet adoption in the short run? Or will these technologies remain "niche applications" that are not suited to the mainstream convention industry that sells the face-to-face experience?'

Most commentators would appear to favour the last, more optimistic outlook, basing their arguments on two key observations: the potential of new technology to enhance and complement aspects of 'real' meetings, and the essential value of face-to-face experience.

Shallcross (1998; p.B-53), for example, observes:

> Video-conferencing is being used as a resource to improve the quality and efficiency of existing modes of communication. Often the purpose of a conference is to bring together people who have common interests but do not have an established forum, and so, like virtual conferencing, video-conferencing is unlikely to impact significantly on conference activity in the short to medium term.

In support of his predictions, he cites an American Express survey of business travel managers which found that very few of them expected videoconferencing to replace the need to travel to 'make new contacts and clinch deals'.

Those who strongly advocate the use of the new technology as a substitution for travelling to meetings – telecommunications companies, for example – do not always realise or acknowledge that the value of a conference often extends beyond the simple transfer or sharing of information. And this is increasingly the case, according to Rogers (1998; p.185), who writes:

Conferences in the late 1990s are now much more active and participatory in style than was the case just a few years ago. The emphasis is on dialogue rather than declamation, networking and sharing rather than on passive listening, getting hands-on experience and forming workgroups so that conference themes can be understood and digested.

But perhaps the strongest argument against conferences being in danger of being replaced by Internet or videoconferencing technology is the very simple one suggested by Munro (1994): 'Delegates enjoy them!' – not only for the opportunities they provide to update knowledge and network with like-minded people, but also due to the fact that they are often located in cities of tourist interest, and offer other peripheral pleasures such as the social programme, the partners' programme and the type of pre- and post-conference tours discussed further in Chapter 7.

However, advances in information and communications technology ought not always to be seen as a threat to the meetings industry. In fact, it is believed by some that new technology may actually be generating demand for meetings, due to one of the impacts it has had on work patterns. Technological progress has made it possible for growing numbers of people to work productively at home, connected to their colleagues and clients by a telephone line and a computer link. With office rents in some cities at astronomical levels, one of the advantages for employers is clear. Employees may enjoy the freedom from commuting that remote working brings them. But, as Rogers (1998) has speculated, if the 'office-in-the-home' should become a more common feature of everyday life in the future, its end result may well be an increased demand for conferences as people respond to their gregarious instincts by coming together in regular meetings.

This chapter began with a reminder that humans are social animals. It is exactly because of this most human of characteristics that people the world over will always prefer to meet face to face, whenever possible, rather than push keyboard buttons and look at images on a screen. Because we all share the same basic need, in the words of the Wizard of Oz, 'to meet, confer and otherwise hobnob with my fellow wizards'.

Ethics and politics

This chapter concludes with an exploration of some of the ethical and political issues that are pertinent to the meetings industry. With the vast sums of money that are spent – and earned – by the various players in the meetings market, many of the ethical and political considerations surrounding this sector of business tourism are linked to the question of *who pays?*

Paying the piper and calling the tune?

The commercial sponsoring of one or more aspects of a meeting event is a controversial issue. This is a practice that, since the budget-strapped days of the early 1990s, has become increasingly widespread and sophisticated. There are many elements that can be sponsored by companies keen to have a presence at the event. For example, they can provide funds to pay for delegates' bags, badges, stationery, flowers on the conference stage, or coffee breaks and meals. And for the sponsor with more money to invest in the event, it can be spent on providing transport between hotels and the conference centre, free secretarial services for delegates, or the provision of staff to run press facilities or to welcome delegates. For example, at Globecom 96, an international conference and exhibition devoted to the future of telecommunications, British Telecom created a cyber cafe that enabled the many thousands of delegates who used it to send and retrieve e-mail and access the Internet free of charge.

However, sponsors are not necessarily drawn first to investing in funding aspects of events that attract large numbers of delegates. It can be more important to target events that, although comparatively small, attract the right type of delegate. Nicholas (1997) gives the example of the QEII Conference Centre's sponsorship of a coffee break at the 1997 conference of the Meeting Planners International association, quoting the conference centre's commercial director:

> There were only 95 delegates but they were some of the most important people to us and, having just finished a major building programme, we had new facilities to tell them about. Sponsoring the coffee break was a highly cost-effective way of promoting our new facilities. For a few hundred pounds, we had the opportunity to badge the coffee break, give out our brochures and to talk to everyone – after all, we had paid for their muffins.

Sponsorship's advantages for the event organiser are clear: the meeting is enhanced, at no extra cost to the initiator, by the addition of the type of added-value elements already mentioned. In return, the sponsor may receive a number of advantages, ranging from the tangible (having their brochure stands in key positions or a speaker on the programme) to the more intangible benefits that can result from having their logo displayed prominently: tacit endorsement by the meeting's organisers and close association with the aims and objectives of the event. Due to the advantages it is believed to bring, sponsorship has, in a short space of time, become so pervasive that many conferences would now not be able to go ahead without it.

But ethical questions provoked by the practice of sponsorship have also been raised. What appears to be a win–win arrangement for the organisers and the sponsors has, on occasion, been perceived as less than desirable by the delegates, particularly when it has become too crass or intrusive. In 1998, for example, the decision to allow the supermarket chain Somerfield to sponsor delegates' security passes at the Labour Party Conference was met with widespread outrage, especially when it was disclosed that the sponsor had paid £20 000 for the privilege of having its logo on the passes. (Three years later, at its party conference in Brighton, the Labour Party, apparently undaunted by this criticism, accepted sponsorship from a number of commercial concerns, including the McDonald's hamburger chain.)

Of more concern, perhaps, is the increasingly common practice whereby lead sponsors are given an opportunity to address the audience through providing a keynote speaker, Nicholas (1997) quotes the QEII conference centre's commercial director, who points out that views on this differ: 'It can be very useful for the sponsor if [the sponsor's keynote speech] is seen to give a considered view of the market … But it must be credible and useful – the audience must learn something from it. Otherwise it can have a negative effect.' Clearly, there is considerable scope for delegates taking objection to being addressed by sponsors whose financial investment in the event appears to have bought them the ability to put their point of view to the audience. Issues of objectivity and balance of conference content must be considered extremely carefully.

Nicholas (1997) also draws parallels between this practice and companies buying editorial with advertising: 'It has been tried and people are terribly uncomfortable with it. They treat that sort of thing with a huge amount of wariness and disdain. A speaker chosen by a sponsor is unlikely to be seen in a good light. I would go so far as to say that I think it is bad practice, because it could bring the integrity of an event into question.'

Paying the price of protest

A certain category of meeting has increasingly been accompanied by scenes of major disturbances and violence. These are the high-profile summits attended by world leaders and/or powerful financiers who meet to discuss issues of global significance, and whose presence at the destination attracts protesters eager to make their own voices heard. Box 3.2 lists some of the events that have been associated with violent protestations.

Meetings of this kind have often been held against a background of police and protesters fighting pitched battles in the streets, with the delegates meeting in fortress-like conditions. Public and media opinion has ranged from condemning all of the demonstrators as hooligans, to the belief that on each occasion a small, violent group manages to distract attention from the peaceful majority of demonstrators.

In the light of such potential hostility towards their meetings, some organisations have either cancelled their events outright – as happened with the World Bank conference planned to take place in Barcelona, June 2001 – or relocated them, in some cases moving them to places that are relatively inaccessible either geographically or financially. For example, the Asian Development Bank changed the location of its 2001 meeting from Seattle to Honolulu, where it was met by 'only' a few hundred relatively peaceful protesters, led by a small coterie of Hawaiian nationalists.

Increasingly, however, destinations where such sensitive meetings take place have felt it necessary to anticipate such disturbances in their streets by introducing stringent security measures. The city of Genoa was shut down for four days in July 2001 in a massive security crackdown on the anticapitalist, antiglobalisation protesters who travelled to be there during the G8 summit of world leaders. The airport, main train stations and key motorway junctions were all closed in an attempt to restrict access to the tens of thousands who planned to converge on the city. Despite such

Box 3.2

A riotous world

Seattle, November 1999: running battles at the World Trade Organisation Summit.

Washington, April 2000: more than 10000 anticapitalist protesters clashed with police in the shadow of the White House during a meeting of the World Bank and International Monetary Fund.

Prague, September 2000: 9000 'smash the IMF' protesters ran riot in Wenceslas Square, throwing petrol bombs at police.

Nice, December 2000: 20000 anticapitalist protesters fought pitched battles with riot police at the opening of the Nice Summit of European leaders.

Zurich, January 2001: after being prevented from protesting at the World Economic Forum in Davos, 1000 demonstrators rampaged through Zurich.

Quebec, April 2001: 20000 protesters clashed with police at the Summit of the Americas, which was discussing the creation of the world's largest free-trade zone.

Gothenburg, June 2001: three people were wounded by gunshots following massive disturbances during a meeting of European leaders.

Genoa, July 2001: 23-year-old protestor Carlo Giuliani was shot dead amid violent clashes with police during the G8 summit. More than 300 protestors were arrested. Scores of demonstrators were assaulted by the police.

Barcelona, March 2002: an economic summit of EU leaders was held amid unprecedented security. More than 8000 police officers, backed by military aircraft and naval vessels, were deployed to keep the peace. Riot police used batons to break up a crowd of 1000 protestors staging antiglobalisation demonstrations.

measures, the meeting was scarred by scenes of unprecedented violence and by the death of one protester, amid serious accusations of police brutality.

A number of important points of debate arise from consideration of all the stakeholders' rights and responsibilities in such circumstances. The right to protest peacefully is an essential part of democracy, and one of the responsibilities of the forces of order is to ensure that this right is respected. It is clear from events in Genoa, for example, that instead of protecting these rights, the Italian police used extreme violence against well-intentioned protesters.

Governments have a duty to protect their citizens and their property from the actions of the anarchists who are mainly drawn to such events by the opportunity they afford for violent disorder. But they also have a responsibility to ensure a forum for lawful protest and to stand firm against violent extremism. Asking international organisations to relocate their meetings to another country, as the Italian prime minister did after Genoa (Johnson, 2001), was widely regarded as an abdication of the responsibility to stand up to violence, and was damaging to the image of Italy itself.

Apart from being a moral duty, the obligation to let meetings of this type go ahead is also contractual in many cases. For example, when the United Nations Food and Agricultural Organisation moved its headquarters from Washington to Rome in 1951, this was conditional on a treaty signed by the Italian government, committing itself to 'ensuring that no impediment is placed in the way of full freedom of discussion and decision'.

The international outrage that followed the Italian Prime Minister's attempt to close his country to potentially sensitive meetings would appear to indicate that many believe that destinations that benefit handsomely from the financial benefits and enhanced reputation that high-profile meetings bring them should also be aware of the many responsibilities that this role entails.

Paying for politicians' vanity?

The cost of meetings of all types is an issue of considerable interest to those who pay the bills for the transport, accommodation and catering, venue hire, entertainment and all other aspects of this activity. For the corporate sector, shareholders' scrutiny of company accounts and the finance director's concern with the bottom line usually mean that there is an effective check on the worst excesses of meetings-related profligacy. In the association sector, where delegates are generally self-funding and one objective is to maximise attendance, setting costs at too extravagant a level would only serve to exclude some members and therefore be self-defeating. But there is growing concern in some quarters that the spending on government-related meetings in general, and intergovernmental meetings in particular, is not showing the same degree of restraint.

Pfaff (2001) is one commentator who believes that the scale of, and spending on, intergovernmental meetings has mushroomed out of control. He gives the example of world leaders' summits: these began in 1975, when Valéry Giscard d'Estaing, the then French President, suggested that the leaders of the five principal industrial countries spend a weekend in a government chateau to talk over common problems. This was turned into an annual affair when the entourages of the heads of government saw that it promoted not only useful conversations but also the political standing of government leaders in their own countries. It soon became the G7, and then the G8.

According to Pfaff (2001), the voters of smaller countries were presented with the sight of their prime ministers and presidents on seemingly familiar terms with American presidents, and American presidents were shown to American voters as free-world leaders receiving their respectful liege men. It suited everyone, but it soon ceased to perform its original function. The meetings were soon bringing thousands of officials to present to hundreds of journalists a final communiqué largely drafted before anyone had left home. A journalist himself, Pfaff writes: 'The journalists could more easily have written it up in their own offices. The real authors of the G8 outcomes are the officials who spend months in their national capitals negotiating the conclusions that their leaders then ratify at the summit meeting, in between receptions, dinners and spectacularly staged displays of national greatness, or egoism.'

He supports his argument with some sobering figures:

The Genoa summit was the anti-poverty summit. It decided to extend existing debt reduction measures for the developing countries and to give $US1.2 billion to fight disease. Simply organising [the 2000 summit] in Okinawa cost Japan $US766 million. Italy says it spent $US110 million. Property worth another $US20 million was destroyed by the wreckers among the demonstrators. Not counted in this is what it cost the US to bring a delegation of 600 people to Genoa, and other governments, their delegations averaging 350 each. If everyone had stayed at home, including the reporters, think how much could have been given to the poor countries.

The power of the delegate dollar

While few corporate and association meetings can match the spending levels of their high-profile intergovernmental counterparts, they are much more numerous and frequent in occurrence, and, as has already been noted, can have a considerable financial impact on destinations. It is clear that this can give meetings buyers and planners significant power over the voters and the governments of the cities and countries in which they hold their events.

What is interesting to note is that there have been occasions when buyers have actually used their spending power in order to either make a comment upon – or to directly influence – political decisions taken in the destinations proposed for their meetings. Some of the most effective uses of delegate dollar power have taken place in the USA (Rutherford and Kreck, 1994).

According to those authors, an early example of this occurred in 1987, when the then Governor of Arizona rescinded an executive order of the previous governor that had established a holiday for state executive branch workers in honour of the assassinated civil rights leader Martin Luther King, Jr. In the year following this decision, 48 conventions scheduled for Phoenix, the state capital, were cancelled, with an estimated loss of over $US15 million. When voters reaffirmed the holiday prohibition by a majority of 15 000 votes in 1990, the National Football League withdrew plans for the 1993 Super Bowl, with its estimated spending impact of $US200 million, and more meetings planners announced that their groups would boycott Arizona.

Similarly, business, tourism and hospitality leaders warned voters in Louisiana's 1991 gubernatorial campaign that electing former Ku Klux Klan and American Nazi leader David Duke would bring dire consequences to the state economy. Specifically mentioned was the potential loss of conventions, trade shows and sporting events. Finally, Rutherford and Kreck (1994) give the example of the howls of protest and threats of convention cancellations, which resulted directly from the state of Alaska's 1992–3 plan to shoot wolves from aeroplanes in order to enhance caribou herds.

It is clear that major meetings events take place within a context in which considerations of power and money loom large. The examples of cancellation and threats of cancellation described above demonstrate how consumer power in the sector of discretionary events can be used to influence politics and policies by registering protest loud and clear.

We have seen how public protestations over the extravagant amounts of money spent on lavish meetings of politicians are also beginning to make themselves heard. Politicians need to listen to these voices, particularly when they come from those who, through their taxes, subsidise such events. At the same time, however, our cynicism should not allow us to lose sight of the fact that political and diplomatic meetings still play a vital role in achieving and preserving peace between nations. It is often said that as long as countries are still talking, there is still hope of reconciliation; or as Winston Churchill put it, 'to jaw-jaw is better than to war-war'.

Case study

The Austria Center, Vienna

Context
For many years, Vienna has been ranked among the top cities for business tourism, in particular for the number of conferences and other types of meetings held there. The Austrian capital came top of the ICCA city league table for the number of international conferences held in 1999 – a total of 64 events. In the same year, it was placed third in the league table published by the UIA.

In all, 74 venues are listed in Vienna's official meetings guide, but in fact the number is much higher. The meetings industry as a whole forms an important part of the city's economy. In 2000, 9.9% of the overall number of room nights were generated by the meetings and incentives sectors. Conferences are also responsible for directly supporting some 5100–5200 jobs in Vienna (Vienna Convention Bureau: www.vienna.convention.at).

Background and ownership
With the opening of the Austria Center Vienna (ACV; Figure 3.5) in May 1987, Vienna added to its existing conference venues a facility with the necessary capacity and technical services for major international events. The construction costs at the time amounted to almost 240 million euros, but when the cost of the exhibition halls, which were added in 1993 and 1998, are taken into account, the costs rise to almost 250 million euros. Until 30 June 1985, all construction and start-up costs were covered by the Federal Government and the City of Vienna. As of 1 July 1985, all costs were taken over by the newly founded shareholding company ACC (Österreichisches Konferenzzentrum Wien, AG). Shareholders are:

- Republic of Austria
- Ministry of Finance and National Economy of the Kingdom of Saudi Arabia
- Kuwait Investment Authority for the Government of Kuwait
- Abu Dhabi Government, represented by the Abu Dhabi Fund for Development.

Also as of 1 July 1985, ACC handed over responsibility for operating and marketing the ACV to Internationales Amtssitz-und-Konferenzzentrum, Wien AG (IAKW AG), a shareholding company founded in 1971 by the Austrian Federal Government and the Vienna City Council (ratio 65:35). This company had been entrusted by a special Federal Act of Parliament with the planning, construction, maintenance, administration and financing of the Vienna International Centre (VIC; the seat of the United Nations) and the ACV.

In March 1986, a lease agreement was signed between the ACC and IAKW AG, under which IAKW AG retained responsibility for all matters relating to the operation of the centre. As of 1 August 1988, the Vienna City Council transferred its shares in IAKW AG to the Austrian Federal Government.

Facilities and services
The layout of the conference areas in the ACV enables a number of events to be held simultaneously. The building, which has an enclosed volume of about $500\,000$ m^3 and a net floor area of some $90\,000$ m^2, contains 14 conference halls on four floors, with a total of 9400 m^2 of hall space. Each area has its own conference rooms, offices and foyer with catering units.

▶

Case study *continued*

Figure 3.5 Austria Center Vienna
Source: Austria Center Vienna.

In addition, some halls can be divided using movable partition walls.

All halls have technical installations, including interpreting systems for up to nine languages, projection equipment and closed-circuit TV connections. The larger halls are equipped with stages of variable dimensions. Hall A has a 207-m^2 hydraulically operated lifting stage consisting of 11 platforms of adjustable height. The restaurant has seating for about 750 people. Movable partitions make it possible to divide it and run part of it as a self-service restaurant. In addition, there are buffets in the foyers for snacks during breaks.

The centre has spent 145 345 euros on the installation of an extensive computer network, particularly useful for IT industry meetings. This investment helps cut back on set-up and dismantling times, thus reducing costs for the client.

There are approximately 340 hotel rooms in the vicinity of the ACV in two four-star hotels. Delegates also use hotels in the city centre, accessible in less than ten minutes by underground, where there are 35 200 beds in the three-, four- and five-star categories.

Marketing and sales

ACV has three full-time sales representatives in-house, together with three external marketing offices in the key markets of the UK, France and Belgium, and the USA. In close cooperation with the Vienna Convention Bureau, they use the complete range of marketing tools: market research, mailshots, sales calls, attending trade shows and workshops, and carrying out presentations. Full use is made of the Internet (www.acv.at), and the centre has also produced its own CD-ROM.

The ACV is a member of the following organisations: MPI, ICCA, AIPC, Europäischer Verband der Veranstaltungs-Centren (EVVC; www.evvc.org) and the International Association for Exposition Management (IAEM; www.iaem.org). It is operating in a highly competitive environment, both within Vienna itself and beyond. The other two major venues in Vienna are the Hofburg Congress centre and Vienna Fairs (Wiener Messe). There are, in addition, four other main centres in provincial Austria: Graz, Salzburg, Innsbruck and Linz. The prime

Case study *continued*

objective of the ACV is to beat off national and international competition to keep Vienna among the most successful business tourism destinations.

Events at ACV

Since the ACV's opening in 1987 until the end of December 2000, 1921 events have been held there, attracting over 3.1 million attendees, of whom 541 000 came from outside Austria. In 2000, 94 major events were held in the ACV, attracting a total of 288 000 attendees, 41 000 of whom came from abroad. It is estimated that the revenue created by each incoming business tourist amounts to an average of 406 euros per day in the city. Table 3.10 gives a breakdown of the types of events that the ACV hosted in 2000.

Box 3.3 shows a month-by-month list of events held at AVC in 2001 and 2002, as well as some other events that were planned with long lead times.

Table 3.10 Austria Center Vienna: event categories

Type of event	Number
Corporate events	*45*
Meetings	31
Corporate functions	9
Product launches	4
Fashion shows	1
Association conferences	*19*
Conferences with related exhibitions	14
Conferences without related exhibitions	5
Public events	*12*
Dances	6
Cultural events	1
Consumer shows	3
Award ceremonies	2
Miscellaneous events	12
Specialised exhibitions	6

Source: Austria Center Vienna.

Box 3.3

ACV events, 2001 and 2002

January 2001

6	Schwebach Dancing School Ball
14	Ruefa Travel Fair
22	27th Gestrata Building Seminar
24	ERSTE Capital Management Seminar
24–25	ERSTE Bank Seminar
26	Confectioners' Ball

▶

Case study *continued*

Box 3.3 *continued*

February 2001
13–15   Exponet Vienna 2001

March 2001
2–6   European Congress of Radiology 2001 – Conference and Exhibition
10   Allgemeine Vermögensberatung – company seminar
11   Mormons Assembly
17–18   Herbalife 2001 Conference
24   Jubilee Broadcasting Concert
28–30   Publica 2001 Trade Fair

April 2001
4   Boehringer Ingelheim – Value Through Innovation Day 2001
27   Raiffeisen Landesbank (Mutual Bank) Annual General Meeting

May 2001
1–6   Systemisches Management – Conference and Exhibition
8   ERSTE Bank Annual General Meeting
9   Austrian Airlines Annual General Meeting
15–19   10th International Congress on Human Genetics – Conference and Exhibition
21   Austria Tabak Annual Shareholders Meeting

June 2001
11–14   Planet Tivoli EMEA 2001 – Conference
24–27   38th Congress of the European Renal Association/European Dialysis and
        Transplant Association – Conference and Exhibition

July 2001
3–8   26th Congress of the European Association of Transaction Analysis

August 2001
26–31   17th International Congress on Nutrition (Conference and Exhibition)

September 2001
6   Conference of the Austrian Railway Workers Union
8   Inline AG – Jürge Höllers Motivationtraining Vienna
8   Women's Conference of the Social Democratic Party of Austria
11   ARWAG Tenants' Meeting
16–21   45th General Conference of the International Atomic Energy Agency
16   Church of Jesus Christ Latterday Saints service
20   OMV AG Annual General Meeting

Case study *continued*

Box 3.3 *continued*

24–28 28th Congress of the International Railway Congress Association/European Congress of Ministers of Transport

29–30 BAUMAX 25th Anniversary Event

October 2001

2 Schmidt's upholstered furniture trade fair

4 Fidelity Investments conference

8–11 IIR-Bluetooth Congress – conference and exhibition

10–12 Austro Sicherheit – international trade fair and congress for security equipment, worker protection, service and technology

10–12 b@-sys – banking system trade fair

15–19 Public Service Union conference

19 Examination

20–21 Astra Zeneca – Atacand symposium

20 27th Youth Conference of the Austrian Trades Union Federation (ÖGB)

24 BAWAG World Savings Day gala

26–28 use.it2001 – trade fair for consumer electronics and information technology

30 Austrian Chamber of Business Trustees examination

November 2001

3–9 Deloitte European Congress

10–11 Austrian Chamber of Pharmacists conference

12 Economic Chamber of Vienna trade conference

13 IT Company Employees' Council Meeting

14–16 CWM 2001 and Collocation event – conference and exhibition

16–17 Janssen Pharmaceutica Psychiatry Standalone conference

23–25 17th Austrian Games Festival

28 Austrian Chamber of Business Trustees examination

December 2001

1 UN Women's Guild Bazaar

2–7 9th General Conference of the United Nations Industrial Development Organisation

10 Volksbanken AG Christmas party

13 Fernwärme Wien Christmas party

January 2002

5 Schwebach Dancing School Ball

12 Lower Austrian Farmers' Union Ball

13 Ruefa Travel Fair

18 Styrian's Ball

19 Upper Austrian Ball

25 Confectioners' Ball

▶

Case study *continued*

Box 3.3 *continued*

27   28th Gestrata building seminar

February 2002
12–14   Exponet Vienna 2002

March 2002
1–5   European Congress of Radiology 2002 conference and exhibition
14–15   Concrete Day 2002 conference and exhibition
16   Persian New Year celebration
22   ICCA Client/Supplier workshop

April 2002
7–8   Austria Hair Congress 2002
14–17   26th Triennial Congress of the International Confederation of Midwives

May 2002
3–5   Alcoholics Anonymous – Meeting of the German-speaking region
7   ERSTE Bank Annual General Meeting
23   Raiffeisen Landesbank General Meeting
26–31   16th World Congress on Safety and Health at Work

June 2002
21   Robert Bosch GmbH – General Meeting
30–3 July   18th Annual Meeting of the European Society of Human Reproduction and
            Embryology

September 2002
16–20   46th General Conference of the IAEA

October 2002
1–5   FDI 2002 Annual World Dental Congress
14–18   EMEA Remedy User Conference 2002 – conference and exhibition
26–30   6th Congress of the European Federation of Neurological Societies

November 2002
6–8   16th annual conference of the Construction and Woodworkers' Union
7–8   Bau-Software 2002 – trade fair
25–27   Care Innovation 2002

December 2002
4–8   European Medical and Biological Engineering Conference – EMBEC 2002

Case study *continued*

Box 3.3 *continued*

7–11 March 2003	European Congress of Radiology
28 September–1 October 2003	13th Annual Congress of the European Respiratory Society
11–15 October 2003	Annual Meeting of the European Association for Cardio-thoracic Surgery (EACTS)
1–5 December 2003	10th General Conference of the United Nations Industrial Development Organisation
5–9 March 2004	European Congress of Radiology
23–28 August 2004	15th Annual Congress on Archives – ICA
5–10 September 2004	20th Congress of the Transplantation Society
4–8 March 2005	European Congress of Radiology
8–11 June 2005	European Congress of Rheumatology – EULAR 2005

Questions

1 What features of the city of Vienna might explain its considerable success as a conference destination? Are there any features of Vienna that might make it less attractive as a destination? Refer to the decision-making criteria mentioned in this chapter.

2 From the information given in Box 3.3, identify one or more examples of each of the categories of events mentioned in Table 3.10.

3 What patterns can be observed, regarding (a) the themes of the events held at the ACV, and (b) their seasonality?

4 What observations can be made concerning the local/national/continental/global nature of the events held at the ACV?

Case study

Meeting in Madrid

The event

The initiator for this event was one of the world's leading professional services firms, with global representation. In March 1999, it brought together 1300 of its management consultants (known as 'partners') from 47 different countries to meet for the first time at a three-day conference entitled 'Together to change the world'.

The objectives behind the meeting were described as follows by the company's London director: 'The aim of the event was to get the partners in one place at the same

▶

Case study *continued*

time in order to communicate the company's future plans and targets. We have a huge geographical spread and it was also a great networking opportunity. Our business relies on personal connections and the event encouraged like-minded people to meet.'

Organisation of the event

Twelve months before the event, the company appointed several UK-based agencies to handle the event management and logistics. The reason for using UK-based agencies was their reputation of being able to handle large groups. The Delegate Group (www.delegate-group.co.uk) was given responsibility for researching venues and destinations, and for organising accommodation and social programmes; Caribiner International (www.caribiner.com) was appointed to handle the production, staging and logistics; and the company's own preferred incumbent travel supplier, American Express Corporate Services (www.americanexpress.com/corporateservice/) organised the travel and flight arrangements. The Spanish ground handler ITB Viajes worked on behalf of The Delegate Group, assisting it with the organisation of hotel accommodation and transport in Madrid and the social programme.

The Delegate Group

One of this agency's main tasks was to select the destination and the venue according to the criteria identified for it by the client. The company wanted a continental European destination, partly on the basis that since there is always the danger of an overly US or UK emphasis for such a large international company, that message would have been reinforced by choosing a US/UK destination for the meeting.

Following its research, The Delegate Group pitched the three options of Vienna, Madrid and Lisbon. Madrid won for three main reasons, identified by the agency's Managing Director as follows:

- Madrid is considered to be a crossroads in Europe.
- Madrid provided good flight accessibility, with the fewest time changes for the greatest number of delegates.
- Madrid came in at about 50% the price of Vienna and had a better standard of accommodation than Lisbon.

The Delegate Group was also aware that its client had a large European office in the city of Madrid.

However, the principal deciding factor was the venue, the Palacio Municipal de Congresos, considered by The Delegate Group to be one of the finest conference centres in Europe. The Palacio delivered fully on its promises: in addition to its first-class auditorium, it provided facilities for the considerable on-site administration required, together with the necessary breakout rooms for the event itself; the availability of extensive on-site telecommunications services was also a major benefit.

Another key role played by The Delegate Group was finding suitable accommodation for those attending the event. What should have been a relatively straightforward task proved more complicated by the fact that due to the internal reorganisation of the client company, the final date of the meeting was not settled until just four months before the actual event, which left the hotel and venue bookings late, particularly for such a large group. Moreover, unlike major convention cities in the USA, European hotels do not easily accommodate such large numbers of delegates under one roof, so delegates had to be placed in ten hotels scattered around the city. This added to the pressure on the different supplier agencies, who had to transport the groups around Madrid.

ITB Viajes

To provide them with local assistance, The Delegate Group appointed the ground handler ITB Viajes, whose valuable knowledge of the right people to make things happen proved to be a major asset. For example, ITB was able to get a government meeting moved in order that the event could take place in the Palacio on the required dates. Both agencies collaborated on the organising of the social programme, which was planned to create further networking opportunities for the delegates, most of whom were attending without their partners. On the first evening, the group was split into five subgroups and dinner was organised at local restaurants. The delegates were split into categories according to their roles in the company rather than according to the hotels in which they were staying. The social highlight of the event was the gala 'Fiesta!' at the Palacio del Negralejo. This Andalusian-style complex was taken over with three 'houses', each themed on a different Spanish region: La Mancha, the Mediterranean and the Basque country. A Spanish cultural theme featured artisans, folk dancing, music and typical sports, as well as a gala dressage demonstration of white Andalusian horses and a human

Case study *continued*

tower. A 20-minute fireworks display set the scene for dinner.

American Express Corporate Services

AECS handled the reservations of all flights and despatch of tickets. The agency operated a 24-hour service for two and a half months dedicated entirely to this event. It then moved the staff from its Essex office to Madrid and set up a satellite-driven booking station in the conference centre.

Caribiner International

With delegates coming from so many countries, the three UK-based agencies had to work together closely to overcome the logistical challenges. In order that the client would only have a single point of contact, Caribiner International's head of logistics was appointed to coordinate the event.

Caribiner International's in-house database system proved crucial for the smooth running of the event. Every delegate's itinerary was different, and there were constant changes being made to travel arrangements in the lead-up to the event. Caribiner was able to keep abreast of all changes by updating the database online. The agency also produced all the print items, IT support and registration arrangements.

This agency was also given overall control of production for the conference. Making an impact was key to the success of the event, which Caribiner decided should open with a 40-piece orchestra. The agency's project director explained the rationale behind this: 'We used the opening of the event to draw a parallel between business life and that of an orchestra. You can play an instrument on your own, but when you play together, the sound can be beautiful. The principal challenge was the

intellectual nature of the audience and the content of the meetings.'

The content of the meeting meant that Caribiner's skills in production organisation were used to the full. Over two days of the event, 86 video programmes were shown on the auditorium's central screen.

The conference comprised a number of plenary sessions, an exhibition and 21 breakout rooms running simultaneously with 67 wrap-around meetings, the theme of which varied according to the job function of each delegate. Around 55 of the partners took to the stage to make speeches. They were then joined by guest speakers, including a video link to the chief executive of Nokia, one of the company's clients, who was in Helsinki at the time, and David Frost as the celebrity guest speaker.

Assessment of the event

From the point of view of the agencies, this was a complex event to organise, especially as it involved so many intermediaries working together. Caribiner's head of logistics emphasised that it is very rare for companies that are normally competitors to work together in this way. But he admitted that despite some hiccups on site, all agencies worked together well and enjoyed the experience.

The initiating company's director confirmed this: 'The agencies formed a kind of consortium for the event. We brought all their skills together and got the best out of each of them.' He added, crucially, that the meeting achieved its targets: 'Relationships were formed and feedback from the partners was very positive. They were very impressed by the organisation and Madrid.'

The Delegate Group has gone on to use the same destination on other occasions for worldwide events, since, from its point of view, one thing that the 1999 event proved was that Madrid works.

Case-study based on an article by Roberta Etter in *Conference & Incentive Travel*, May 1999, Haymarket Marketing Publications.

Questions

1 What features made this event typical of a corporate meeting, and in what ways did it have more in common with an association meeting?

2 What important intermediaries may have been involved in persuading The Delegate Group to choose Madrid as the venue? Consider organisations operating at city level, country level and the European level. Say as much as you can about the role and functions of each.

3 How might the return on investment for this event have been measured more accurately?

References

Boyer, P.S., Clark, C.E., Kett, J.F., Salisbury, N., Sitkoff, H. and Woloch, N. (1993), *The Enduring Vision: a history of the American people*, Lexington, D C Heath & Company.

Bray, R. (2001), 'Sterling takes the blame', *Financial Times*, 11 May.

BTF & BTAC (1999), *Business Tourism Leads the Way*, London, Business Tourism Forum.

Carey, T. (2001), 'Of boxes and centres', *Tagungs Wirtschaft*, July.

Chetwynd, C. (1998), 'Rooms with a view', *Marketing Week*, 26 February.

Chetwynd, C. (1999), 'The specialists', *Marketing Week*, 13 May.

Clark, J.D., Evans, M.R. and Knutson, B.J. (1997), 'Selecting a site for an association convention: an exploratory look at the types of power used by committee members to influence decisions', *Journal of Hospitality & Leisure Marketing*, Vol. 5, pp. 81–95.

Cossardeaux, J. (2000), 'Les maines vantent l'impact économique des centres de congrés', *Les Echos*, 16 March, p. 6.

Creevy, J. (2001), 'Market contenders', *Conference & Incentive Travel*, June.

Dwyer, L., Mistilis, N., Forsyth P. and Roa, P. (2001) 'International price competitiveness of Australia's MICE industry', *International Journal of Tourism Research*, Vol. 3, pp. 123–39.

Elzinga, D. (2001), 'The major trends impacting conference centres', *Tagungs Wirtschaft*, July.

European Commission (1996), *Business and Conference Tourism in the European Economic Area*, Brussels, European Commission.

Eurostat (2000), *Methodological Manual for Statistics on Congresses and Conferences*, Brussels, Eurostat.

Fighiera, G.C. (1985), 'Le caractère saisonnier des réunions', *Revue de Tourisme*, Vol. 40, pp. 14–19.

Gazette Officielle (1998), 'France Congrès: un outil pour mesurer le poids économique de la filière congrès', *Gazette Officielle du Tourisme*, No. 1419, pp. 4–6.

Ghitelman, D. (1997), 'Taking measures', *Meetings & Conventions*, July.

Goodhart, L. (1998), 'Symbolising city strength', *Conference & Incentive Travel*, July/August.

Gosling, J. (1998a), 'Strictly business', *Conference & Incentive Travel*, July/August.

Gosling, J. (1998b), 'Dynamic solutions', *Conference & Incentive Travel*, October.

Gosling, J. (1999a), 'A different choice', *Conference & Incentive Travel*, January.

Gosling, J. (1999b), 'Ship to shore, *Conference & Incentive Travel*, July/August.

Graf, B. (2001a), 'From temple of vanity to perfect communications centre', *Tagungs Wirtschaft*, July.

Graf, B. (2001b), 'Priority for core meetings business', *Tagungs Wirtschaft*, July.

Greaves, S. (1998a), 'Selling the world', *Conference & Incentive Travel*, June.

Greaves, S. (1998b), 'Competing for business', *Conference & Incentive Travel*, September.

Greaves, S. (1999), 'Continental drift', *Marketing*, 25 February.

Greenhill, S. (2000), 'The UK conference market – the buyers' perspective', *Insights*, September.

ICCA (2001), *The Statistics of the International Meetings Market 1993–2002*, Amsterdam, ICCA, (www.iccaworld.com).

Inskeep, E. (1991), *Tourism Planning: an integrated and sustainable development approach*, New York, Van Nostrand Reinhold.

Johnson, J. (2001), 'The prime minister's fear of the summit', *Financial Times*, 8 August.

Judd, D.R. (1995), 'Promoting tourism in US cities', *Tourism Management*, Vol. 16, pp. 175–87.

Kotler, P., Bowen, J. and Makens, J. (1996), *Marketing for Hospitality and Tourism*, Upper Saddle River, NJ, Prentice Hall.

Lau-Thurner, U. (2001), 'Exclusive caterers and not enough breakouts', *Tagungs Wirtschaft*, July.

Lawson, F. (2000), *Congress, Convention and Exhibition Facilities: planning, design and management*, Oxford, Architectural Press.

Leask, A., Fyall, A. and Goulding, P. (2000), 'Revenue management in Scottish visitor attractions' in Ingold, A. and McMalion-Beattie, U. (eds), *Yield Management: strategies for the service industries*, London, Cassell.

Leask, A. and Hood, G. (2000) 'Unusual venues as conference facilities: current and future management issues', in Jones, D. (ed.), *Proceedings of the Convention/Expo summit VIII*, Las Vegas, University of Nevada.

MCG (1999), *Quantifying Offshore Business Tourism*, London, British Tourist Authority.

MIA (1999), *UK 1999 Conference Market Survey*, Broadway, Meetings Industry Association.

MIA (2000), *UK 2000 Conference Market Survey*, Broadway, Meetings Industry Association.

MIA (2001), *UK 2001 Conference Market Survey*, Broadway, Meetings Industry Association.

MIA (2002), *UK 2002 Conference Market Survey*, Broadway, Meetings Industry Association.

Mill, R.C. (1992), *The Tourism System: an introductory text*, Englewood Cliffs, Prentice Hall.

Munro, D. (1994), 'Conference centres in the 21st century', in Seaton, A.V. (ed.), *Tourism: the state of the art*, Chichester, John Wiley & Sons.

Nicholas, R. (1997), 'The logo motive', *Marketing Week*, 4 December.

Olliver, A. (2002), 'Familiarity breeds success', *Meetings & Incentive Travel*, March.

Oppermann, M. (1996a), 'Convention destination images; analysis of association meeting planners' perceptions', *Tourism Management*, Vol. 17, pp. 175–82.

Oppermann, M. (1996), 'Convention cities: images and changing fortunes', *Journal of Tourism Studies*, Vol. 7, pp. 10–19.

Paine, A. (1993), 'The university conference market', *Insights*, May.

PCMA (2000), *Nonconventional Behaviours: long range trends influencing the demand for conferences and convention services*, Birmingham, AL, Professional Convention Management Association.

Pemble, A. (1998), 'Highly qualified', *Conference & Incentive Travel*, September.

Pfaff, W. (2001), 'We could have done without the Genoa circus', *International Herald Tribune*, 26 July.

Qu, H. and Li, L. (1999), 'The comparative analysis of Hong Kong as an international conference destination in Southeast Asia', in Lockwood, A. (ed.), *Proceedings of the Eighth Annual CHME Hospitality Research Conference*, Guildford, University of Surrey.

Richards, G. (1993), *The Operation of Visitor and Convention Bureaux in the United States: implications for Europe*, London, British Travel Educational Trust.

Rockett, G. and Smillie, G. (1994), 'The European conference and meetings market', *EIU Travel & Tourism Analyst*, Vol. 4, pp. 36–50.

Rogers, T. (1998), *Conferences: a twenty-first century industry*, Harlow, Addison Wesley Longman.

Rutherford, D.G. and Kreck, L.A. (1994), 'Conventions and tourism: financial add-on or myth? Report of a study in one state', *Journal of Travel and Tourism Marketing*, Vol. 3, pp. 49–63.

Ryan, C. (1999), 'The use of a spatial model to assess conference market share – a New Zealand example', *International Journal of Tourism Research*, Vol. 1, pp. 49–53.

Seaton, A.V. and Bennett, M.M. (1996), *Marketing Tourism Products*, London, Thomson Business Press.

Shallcross, W. (1998), 'The British conference market', *Insights*, January.

Shone, A. (1998), *The Business of Conferences*, Oxford, Butterworth Heinemann.

Smith, G.V. (1990), 'The growth of conferences and incentives', in Quest, M. (ed.), *Horwath Book of Tourism*, London, Macmillan.

Smith, G.V. (1991), 'Professional organisations in the European meetings industry', *International Journal of Hospitality Management*, Vol. 10, pp. 119–26.

Travel Industry Monitor (1997), *Travel & Tourism Intelligence*, June.

Trelford, S. (1999), 'London calling', *Marketing Week*, 24 June.

TTI (2000), 'The MICE industry', *Travel & Tourism Intelligence*.

Tuppen, J. (1996), 'Tourism in French cities', in Law C.M. (ed.), *Tourism in Major Cities*, London, Routledge.

Twite, P. (1999), 'Listen and learn', *Conference & Incentive Travel*, June.

Upton, G. (1999), 'Capturing the middle ground', *Marketing*, 25 February.

Wakely, S. (1997), 'Training and management centres', *Conference & Exhibition Factfinder*, June.

White, S. (1998), 'The conference business deserves better research', *Conference & Incentive Travel*, October.

Witt, S.F. and Moutinho, L. (eds) (1995), *Tourism Marketing and Management Handbook*, Hemel Hempstead, Prentice Hall.

Yuan, Y.Y., Fesenmaier, D.R., Xia, L. and Gratzer, M. (1999), 'The use of internet and intranet in American convention and visitor bureaus', in Buhalis, D. and Schertler, W. (eds), *Information and Communication Technologies in Tourism: proceedings of the International Conference in Innsbruck, Austria*, Vienna, Springer.

Chapter 4

Incentive travel

Objectives

On completion of this chapter, you should be able to:

- *understand the use of incentive travel and the advantages it offers;*
- *appreciate how incentive trips are designed, including the roles played by all suppliers;*
- *discuss the main trends affecting incentive travel.*

◗ ● Incentive travel in the twenty-first century

- Forty-two employees of Laser, a London-based company selling TV advertising space, spent a weekend based in the Dutch coastal resort of Noordwijk, a short drive away from Schiphol airport. Saturday was spent on team-building games, followed by a gala dinner in the evening held on a 'Welcome to Holland' theme. The next day was spent exploring Amsterdam, and included evening entertainment aboard a paddle steamer, which was reserved exclusively for Laser. Before flying home the following evening, the participants were able to enjoy a day at the beach, playing golf and tennis, riding and driving go-karts.
- Thirty-six senior managers of American Electronics flew from the USA to Madrid's Hotel Ambassador for a three-day incentive trip. Activities included a treasure hunt around the city and a visit to one of the company's factories in Guadalajara, just south of Madrid.
- Twenty-five Total Oil sales employees and their spouses travelled to Sun City and then on to Londolozi, one of South Africa's most exclusive game reserves. They spent four days on photograph-safaris, and ate each evening in the hotel's award-winning restaurant.

● ● ● ● Introduction

That noisy group of passengers at the front of the plane, all dressed in Bermuda shorts and Hawaii shirts, and drinking and laughing together all the way to Rio de Janeiro: are they travelling on business or for pleasure? They could be on an incentive trip; in which case, the answer would be 'both'.

With its strong emphasis on lavish fun, entertainment and indulgence, incentive travel is the form of business tourism that most resembles the type of leisure travel normally undertaken by individuals in their own time, unconnected with the workplace. Nevertheless, despite their superficial similarity to holidays and short breaks, incentive trips represent a distinctive travel product, which, due to its definite work-related purpose, belongs firmly in the category of travel for business.

General definitions describe this form of business-related travel in terms of its usage, one of the most commonly quoted being that used by the Society of Incentive & Travel Executives (SITE): 'A global management tool that uses an exceptional travel experience to motivate and/or recognise participants for increased levels of performance in support of organisational goals.'

Incentive travel, then, is basically composed of memorable and enjoyable trips paid for by the traveller's employer, with the explicit aim of encouraging employees to meet challenging business objectives through reaching or exceeding individual and/or group targets. These targets may occasionally involve non-sales aspects of the company, such as reducing staff turnover; but overwhelmingly incentive travel is used with the basic objective of increasing sales.

Contests play an important role in incentive programmes, as they are often used to determine who within the company or sales team will be rewarded with the travel prizes on offer. For this reason, those on incentive trips are often referred to as 'incentive travel winners' or 'award winners'. This type of reward often takes the form of group travel – participants travel with other award winners, and often with their own spouses or partners.

Incentive programmes typically involve special entertainment, food and beverage functions, and either spectator or participative events, such as visits to a theatre or rafting or shooting. They may also include an actual work element, such as a conference or seminar, or simply a visit from a member of the company's senior management team who gives the participants a congratulatory pep talk.

Although most of these elements characterise the vast majority of incentive trips, there are differences of detail between national markets. In some developing markets (e.g. India), the incentive travel award may be a simple, off-the-shelf package or even an airline ticket, possibly with some accommodation thrown in. A not insignificant proportion of the US incentive travel business is in the form of individual incentives (e.g. for couples or foursomes), using an incentive travel package in much the same way as a catalogue or merchandise item (BTF & BTAC, 1999). However, the more traditional form taken by most incentive travel awards is that of group travel and a made-to-measure programme of activities and entertainment.

● ● ● ● The effectiveness of incentive travel

Widely recognised as a useful management tool, incentive travel is generally considered to be an effective means of rewarding and motivating employees. Its effectiveness can be explained partly by its popularity with the award winners themselves. Experience suggests that no matter how frequently participants travel on business as part of their job, incentive travel is still regarded by them as a highly desirable prize.

However, travel prizes are clearly not the only method available to management as a means of motivating their workforce to achieve corporate objectives. Alternative performance-related rewards that companies may extend to their highest-achieving staff include:

● cash bonuses
● vouchers or merchandise awards
● profit-related pay schemes.

O'Brien (1997a) has estimated that only one in four major international corporations uses incentive travel programmes to reward their personnel. As incentive travel programmes tend to be funded from companies' sales or marketing budgets, this means that they have to compete internally for funding against other sales and marketing projects as well as against the other types of motivational tools mentioned above.

What arguments can be advanced to demonstrate the advantages of using travel as opposed to the other forms of reward? There are advantages to both the employer and the employee.

Advantages for the employer

Witt *et al.* (1992) described typical objectives that companies may have for their involvement in incentive travel programmes:

● To facilitate communications and networking opportunities, particularly with company executives.
● To foster corporate culture and social interaction.
● To generate enthusiasm for the following business period.
● To foster loyalty to the company.

It can be argued convincingly that most of these objectives are attained more easily through rewarding staff with a group incentive trip than by simply supplementing their salary by the equivalent cost of the trip. The camaraderie and company loyalty generated by the trip and its shared memories can go far in strengthening participants' positive feelings towards their employer. Through participating in an incentive trip, colleagues, who may in the workplace be in competition with each other, are able to relax together and generate a measure of team spirit.

The highly visible aspect of incentive trips also gives them the potential to motivate the non-winning section of the workforce after they have taken place. This can happen when the award-winning employees return to their jobs with fascinating descriptions of their incentive trip; other colleagues are, as a result, stimulated to strive harder to win the next incentive prize. For the company, this represents a lasting benefit that would not arise from simply giving the most productive members of staff a cash bonus, for example, since the recipients would be less likely to discuss that type of reward at any length with their colleagues.

Advantages for the employee

As well as meeting the company's objectives, travel as a reward also owes much of its effectiveness to the fact that it has the potential to respond to some of the individual employee's own intrinsic needs. For example, unlike many other rewards, a travel prize has a considerable amount of trophy value attached to it. Social status is increased, not only because the winner is recognised as a top salesperson, but also because he or she may be one of the few who have experienced the unique award, such as staying in a medieval castle in Scotland or visiting a particular foreign country. It has been argued by the supporters of incentive travel that any reward giving this type of recognition to its recipient provides a long-lasting, positive reinforcement, an element that adds to its motivational value.

For example, it has been suggested by Ricci and Holland (1992) that, for the individual, an incentive trip has the potential to harness each of the four categories of travel motivation described by McIntosh (1984):

- physical motivation (rest, health, sport, etc.)
- cultural motivation (the desire to experience other cultures)
- interpersonal motivations (to meet and visit people)
- status and prestige motivators.

It is clearly upon the fourth category of travel motivators that incentive travel builds most strongly. The enhanced attention and status accorded to award winners fulfils a basic need for recognition and acceptance.

Another advantage for the award winners, it is often claimed, is greater acceptance by their partners and other family members of the additional time and effort that must be worked in order to achieve the award. When family members also go along on the trips, there can be greater tolerance for the long hours needed to achieve a reward. This point will be developed further in the later section on the organising of incentive programmes.

With so many benefits arising from its use, the effectiveness of incentive travel as a motivator is not in doubt. However, commentators differ on the question of whether travel is always the most powerful motivational tool available to employers. While some (e.g. Witt *et al.*, 1992; Hastings *et al.*, 1988) have concluded that travel-based incentives are more effective at motivating employees than other forms of reward, others are much less convinced that this can be demonstrated unambiguously in quantitative terms. This crucial issue will be explored further later in this chapter.

Quantifying incentive travel

Incentive travel still remains one of the least recognised and most poorly measured segments of the business travel market. One of the difficulties involved in collecting data on incentive travel arises from the question of what exactly constitutes an incentive trip.

While explaining concisely the use of incentive travel awards within companies, the definitions provided at the beginning of this chapter are of limited value when it comes to identifying which corporate events may be classified as incentive trips and which belong in other business tourism categories, notably conferences and seminars. A company organising a three-day event in Monaco, for example, for some of its highest-achieving employees may describe it as a seminar or conference, even though there is clearly a high incentive element involved, reflected in the choice of venue and the, no doubt, highly enjoyable programme of activities.

In addition, the task of identifying incentive events is made even more complicated by the way in which a variety of motivational elements are increasingly being introduced into many types of corporate meetings. These may range from gala dinners to theatre visits or team-building activities designed to entertain delegates and create a team spirit among them. A former editor of *Conference & Incentive Travel* magazine underlines this trend (White, 1999; p.3):

> As corporate conferences incorporate more incentive elements, the line between business and motivation becomes less defined. The classic interpretation of a travel incentive ... is based on a level of achievement through sales, culminating in a group travel reward. Perhaps in the future, there will be no distinction, and all events will have an incentive component.

In fact, the lack of clarity concerning the exact dividing line between incentive travel and other forms of business travel is not without its benefits. It serves, for example, a useful purpose within companies using this method of rewarding their staff. As company accounts are increasingly scrutinised for evidence of excessive corporate largesse, the fact that incentive trips may be presented as other types of events makes them less likely to attract the unwelcome attention of shareholders and tax authorities.

The Business Tourism Forum (BTF) report notes the trend of companies deliberately camouflaging their incentive awards by avoiding that particular term: 'In other markets, "study trips", "off-shore" conferences and other titles are used to disguise the award. The need to emphasise a conference or educational aspect of an incentive travel award is becoming more prevalent in many parts of Europe' (BTF & BTAC, 1999).

It is this lack of precision in identifying incentive travel events that must be borne in mind throughout this chapter when regarding the quantitative data presented. For example, given the difficulty involved in isolating incentive events from other forms of business travel, the estimate of the Horwath Axe report on business travel in Europe that incentive trips accounted for only 2.4% of all travel for work-related purposes (CEC, 1996) is very likely to have been a considerable underestimation.

●●●● Buyers

In this section, the main consumers of incentive travel will be investigated. It is important to distinguish here between those who pay for the trips, the companies, and those who go on incentive trips, i.e. the award winners who are the end consumers.

Looking at buyers in terms of industry sectors, there is little change from year to year in who constitute the biggest spenders on this form of business tourism. In general, the major buyers of incentive programmes remain as they always have been: the automotive, financial services, pharmaceutical, office equipment, electronics and consumer durables sectors (*The European*, 1995). The fact that these industries all operate in extremely competitive sectors, where maintaining or increasing market share demands constant exhortations to greater efforts on the part of the salesforce and management, makes these types of business the natural consumers of the vast majority of incentive trips.

The trade magazine, *Conference & Incentive Travel*, carries out regular surveys in which UK-based incentive travel agencies are asked to name the industry sectors that provide them with the most business. The results of one such survey are shown in Figure 4.1. In terms of end consumers, an earlier survey found that sales staff and dealers account for 80% of business for the agencies, confirming the overwhelming use of this type of award with those selling their companies' products and services (Twite, 1999).

Considering the main buyers in national terms, it is the country that first used travel to motivate employees that still consumes the most incentive travel products.

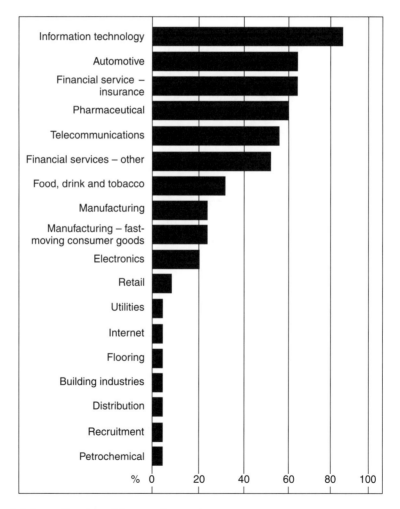

Figure 4.1 Incentive travel buyers by sector

Source: Conference & Incentive Travel, February 2002.

The origins of incentive travel as a modern motivation tool are attributed to the US company National Cash Registers of Dayton, Ohio (now part of AT&T). In 1906, the company awarded 70 salespeople diamond-studded pins and a free trip to company headquarters. In 1911, the winners got a free trip to New York. (Ricci and Holland, 1992). It is back to those humble trips that today's multimillion-dollar incentive travel industry may trace its genesis.

Today, the US incentive travel market remains the largest in the world, and it is still recognised widely that the major trends and developments affecting incentive travel tend to originate in the USA and then spread to other countries.

Europe is the next largest user of incentive travel, although this motivational tool did not cross the Atlantic until the 1970s, being used first in the UK and then about ten years later in continental Europe. Most of the European incentive travel market is still generated by the UK, followed by France, Germany and Italy. Nevertheless, the Scandinavian countries, Austria, Belgium and Spain are all fast developing as outbound incentive travel generators.

However, even between individual European countries, there are a number of interesting differences in the ways in which incentive travel is used. O'Brien (1997b) points out two of these. First, whereas the French, Italian and German incentive travel industries have always capitalised on their own domestic destinations, the UK domestic market is relatively small because many UK companies do not regard the home market as an appropriate destination for their major incentive programmes.

Second, in the case of the Scandinavian countries, O'Brien notes that the elitism implied by incentive travel goes against the work ethos, particularly in Sweden. Consequently, when travel is offered as an incentive, the award tends to be offered to practically everybody in the company and resembles more a company outing rather than an incentive trip.

●●●● Intermediaries

In this section, the question of who organises incentive travel programmes and how they do so for maximum effect will be explored. This sector of business travel, perhaps more than any other, is one where the use of intermediaries is widespread. Whereas there are members of staff in most companies who would have a go at arranging a seminar or conference if need be, there are far fewer who would dare to venture unaided into the organising of an incentive programme.

O'Brien (1997b) has estimated that, in Europe, only one in five companies handles all incentive travel arrangements in-house, most opting to have their incentive programmes organised using the services of an external agency.

A range of external agencies providing five different levels of incentive-related services was identified by Ricci and Holland (1992). The range serves to illustrate the various elements that constitute the planning and management of an incentive travel programme:

- Full-service incentive marketing companies, which handle promotional materials, administration, travel and merchandise fulfilment.
- Full-service incentive houses, which are similar to incentive marketing companies but specialise in incentive travel rather than merchandise rewards.
- Incentive travel fulfilment houses, which primarily arrange incentive travel trips with some incentive promotion services.
- Travel agents with an incentive division where the agency specialises in providing incentive travel programmes but offers no marketing services.
- Retail travel agencies, which offer typical travel arrangement services and can assist with incentive trips.

Intermediaries offering the more complete range of incentive-related services often reflect this in the names by which they are known: incentive travel agencies, incentive travel companies or incentive travel houses. To these may be added more recent arrivals on the scene: performance improvement companies, such as Maritz, Inc., who propose a range of rewards, including travel, to motivate their clients' workforces.

Agencies active in this field vary from one-person businesses to vast multinational conglomerates for whom incentive travel is only part of their business. An example of the latter is the UK-based events management agency, TMO, with an incentive travel turnover of over £25 million in 2001, out of a total turnover of almost £33 million (Creevy, 2002). However, only a small minority of incentive travel intermediaries have an annual incentive travel turnover on this scale. The vast majority are small and medium-sized agencies doing much smaller volumes of business. According to research undertaken by *Conference & Incentive Travel* magazine, half of the top 25 agencies in the UK in 2001 had fewer than 50 members of staff (ibid).

Nevertheless, an earlier survey's author quotes the divisional managing director of another major player in this sector, Maritz Travel, who believes that the future will see increasing consolidation among incentive travel agencies, with a few large agencies coming to dominate the market. He also sees increasing demand for services from full-service agencies who can offer clients a comprehensive package providing everything necessary to take their incentive programmes through from beginning to end (Twite, 1999).

In the following section, the process of organising and implementing an incentive travel programme is investigated.

Organisation of incentive programmes

The actual process of implementing an incentive programme means that considerable long-term planning is required to ensure that corporate objectives are met in full. Some incentive programmes can last for up to a year, and it is not unusual for companies to be planning large-scale incentives two years in advance. The majority of incentive travel programmes, however, are planned up to 12 months in advance (O'Brien, 1997b).

The full incentive travel organisation package will involve the agency in under-taking an initial analysis of the client's business and the types of travel rewards most appropriate to their company. This phase is crucial. The key characteristics of the prize must be inspirational and aspirational, for if the agency fails to identify a destination that fully inspires the company's employees to make a considerable extra effort in order to win the chance to visit it, then the programme is unlikely to succeed.

Incentive travel agencies will therefore begin by establishing a shortlist of possible destinations with the client. This will be based on employees' aspirations as well as other factors, such as budget and where the company's recent incentives were held. In order to achieve maximum effectiveness, a company's incentive reward system should be tailored to fit the needs and desires of its employees. To determine what employees both desire and need, a number of methods may be used. Shinew and Blackman (1995) identify these as:

- administering a structured data-collection instrument, such as a questionnaire containing both open- and closed-ended items;
- systematically observing employees' reactions to different rewards;
- asking the employees directly which rewards are most valued.

Variety is an important factor. US companies tend to rotate incentive destinations to maintain participant interest, e.g. London may only be considered a suitable destination for a major incentive once every four years (O'Brien, 1997a).

Organising the incentive programme will also involve at an early stage conducting research into whom, within the company, should be targeted for motivation by the prospect of winning the travel award. Often, the result of the research will be that it appears appropriate to offer more than one incentive product to a company's employees. Shinew and Backman (1995; p.292) explain why:

Offering a single set of rewards to an entire workforce potentially reaches only a portion of the target group. Therefore, the motivational component of incentive programmes may be maximised by offering reward options targeted toward specific segments of the workforce. For example, option one may be a trip to Disneyworld that involves both spouses and children…whereas a second option for childless employees might be a trip to Paris.

Multiple-tier awards is an alternative strategy. This approach encourages limitless performance levels and, therefore, bears broad motivational appeal. For example, level one may award the incentive trip to the qualifier whereas level two includes the qualifier and his or her family. Another possible application would be where level one is a domestic trip while level two is an international trip. The multiple-tier approach motivates the employee who has already qualified for the trip to continue striving for the next objective.

The same authors point out that the identification of specific variables that may influence an employee's level of attraction toward particular rewards has received only limited attention in the literature on incentive travel. One of these variables is almost certainly the attitude of the employee's spouse or partner towards the incentive programme and the prizes available to winners.

The vast majority of employees interviewed by Shinew and Backman (1995) indicated that the support of their spouse/partner was a major consideration to them in their decision as to whether to participate in their employers' incentive programmes. These findings suggest that management might wish to consider the influence of spouses when planning an incentive programme. For example, when attempting to determine the attractiveness of potential incentive travel destinations, the company may benefit from surveying both the employees and their spouses. Further, sending travel brochures home with employees may serve to increase the incentive programme's motivational effect. Moreover, there may be greater family tolerance for the long hours needed to achieve the incentive reward if there is enthusiasm for the trip being offered.

A further advantage of including award-winners' spouses and partners is emphasised by one incentive travel organiser based in Monaco (Collis, 2000; p.115):

> The partner helps to push the executive to achieve his or her targets if they know they're going to Monte Carlo as well. If the other half is along, it makes for a much more sane and balanced approach. It's the difference between dancing the night away and drinking the night away, which is what happens when you have all men together. We had a nightmare experience with an incentive for the business unit of a company that didn't bring partners. It was an office party for three days. Not a good idea!

In designing the actual award, therefore, the agency must also advise the client company on whether the travel is to be undertaken by the winning employees only or whether it should include others, notably their partners and other members of their families. In his survey of the European incentive market, O'Brien (1997b; p.B-20) noted that only one-quarter of all trips were limited to employees only. 'In most cases, the winner's spouse or partner is permitted to travel with him/her, and in 20% of cases, companies also invite other family members as well. Family members are invariably paid for by the company.'

Once the actual incentive programme prize has been agreed upon, the agency will then carry out a promotional campaign within the company to advertise the competition and the prize. The rules of the competition will be announced to those members of staff selected to participate. Throughout the duration of the incentive programme, the agency will monitor employees' performance and periodically send them reminders of the desirability of the prize in order to continue to spur them on to greater achievements. These reminders are known as 'teasers', and may take the form of brochures or photographs of the destination being sent to employees at work or to their homes. Even more creative teasers have been used. An agency once sent small bottles of sand to participants to remind them that the prize they were competing for was a trip to an exclusive oasis resort in the Sahara.

The final task to be undertaken before the actual trip is to choose and nominate the winners. Announcing the winners is often done at an in company event, such as a reception or lunch, in order to make maximum impact.

Parallel to these activities, agencies will design and plan the details of the actual trip. The following section examines the crucial question of what the successful incentive trip should be.

Design of incentive trips

To the outsider, they may look like extravagant up-market holidays, but behind the fun and joviality of most incentive trips lies a lengthy period of detailed planning and designing of the travel award in order to ensure that the company's objectives are met to the full.

The principal difference between incentive travel and personal travel is that, in the former case, a company (i.e. a form of external control) is planning, organising, and promoting the anticipation and fulfilment of the reward experience (Ricci and Holland, 1992). Furthermore, a basic tenet is that incentive trips must consist of experiences that individuals cannot achieve on their own: there is no such thing as an off-the-peg incentive trip, and the skill of the incentive agency lies in ensuring that they design a travel experience which, every time, surprises, delights and impresses the – often very demanding and well-travelled – incentive programme winners.

The characteristic features of incentive trips include the following:

- *Uniqueness*: no single event should be like any other. Itineraries should not be predictable, but rather, full of surprises and special events. Innovative ideas are the life-blood of this sector, and organisers have to continuously produce creative and original elements to delight participants. The unexpected arrival of the company's managing director by hot-air balloon for the final evening's gala dinner, for example, would be a memorable way to conclude an incentive trip.
- *Use of fantasy or exotic experiences*: incentive trips often include the opportunity for participants to try out novel sporting activities, such as clay-pigeon shooting, falconry or hang-gliding. A skilled incentive travel organiser will be able to include in the programme some activities that the participants will not have already tried but may have always wanted to.
- *Exclusivity*: at the end of the trip, the participants should have the impression that they have had privileged access to exclusive places and people. If a tourist attraction, such as Madame Tussauds, is visited, then it must be unlike the visits made by the general public; for example, a champagne breakfast held there before opening time, or a behind-the-scenes look at how the wax models are made. Use is often made of celebrities to achieve this effect. For example, guided tours of the destination are all the more memorable if the guide is a well-known actor or sportsperson who happens to live there.
- *Activities*: few incentive trips leave participants to lie on the beach for days on end. Activities and sports are included as a way of making the trip more

memorable and dynamic. Given that award winners are, almost by definition, often competitive by nature, much use is made of competitions and team games, such as beach Olympics, mini-hovercraft races and talent competitions.

Clearly, organising the transport, accommodation, and the entertainment and activities that constitute an incentive trip involves the agency in a vast amount of detailed negotiation and logistical arrangements. Their allies in this task are the same DMCs who assist conference organisers with the details of the ground programme, as described in Chapter 3. These agencies use their local knowledge and contacts to turn the incentive travel agency's ideas into reality.

In the same way as PCOs do, incentive agencies tend to work in partnership with their appointed DMCs, who may be thought of as the creative packager of the travel experience as well as being the logistics manager ensuring that all visitor arrangements run smoothly. In the UK and Ireland, DMCs tend to be small companies that specialise in particular inbound country markets. The world of the DMC is a secretive one, as their business contacts are effectively their core asset (O'Brien, 1997b).

Suppliers

Following on from the preceding investigations into the demand for incentive travel and the role of those intermediaries who design and plan incentive programmes, this section explores the supply of incentive travel services.

One distinguishing feature of incentive travel is that unlike, for example, the conference or exhibition sectors, there are no specific infrastructural facilities required for destinations active in the incentive market. Nevertheless, in common with the other forms of business travel already covered in this book, incentive travel makes use of the services and facilities of every sector of the tourism industry, including accommodation, transport, tourist attractions, and recreational resources. However, perhaps for more than any other form of business tourism, it is vital for incentive travel suppliers to fulfil the very high expectations of their clients, with faultless standards of service and attention to detail. Clearly, given their use of luxurious, top-of-the-range facilities, incentive travel clients represent a market that offers high rewards to suppliers. But this is on the strict condition that those suppliers consistently produce an impeccable standard of service at every stage. Some examples of the extra effort needed by suppliers to compete favourably in this market are given below.

Hotels

Given incentive travellers' taste for the best in everything, they constitute a lucrative market for hotels active in this sector. Many hotels, by their very design, are well suited to responding to the need for a fantasy or exotic element in incentive trips. For example, at the Hyatt Regency Waikoloa in Hawaii, guests are transported to their rooms by boat via canals through tropically landscaped grounds.

Many large hotel chains have dedicated incentive departments whose role it is to persuade incentive travel organisers that their hotels have everything that is required to satisfy their clients. But even smaller, independent hotels can also attract this type of business – on the condition that they are prepared to make the extra effort required. In her advice to hoteliers interested in breaking into the incentive market, Briggs (1993; p.28) make the following points:

> Don't make the mistake of thinking that all an incentive group needs is high room rates, a box of chocolates and a bottle of ordinary champagne in the rooms. It takes creativity and imagination to justify those rates...Firstly be sure you can deliver the goods and that your staff can be relied upon to offer a high level of service. You will need to develop a range of services and people you can contact to help you provide new experiences for incentive guests. It doesn't have to be a grand fireworks display in the grounds of your nearest stately home. It could equally be talented magicians performing at each table or a Body Shop massage/makeover for each guest. If you ... leave the actual packaging up to incentive agents and other professional organisers, you still need to develop a list of suggestions and contacts which show that your hotel is the ideal location for an incentive group, to demonstrate that you understand their needs.

However, this is not a market without disavantages for the hotel sector. One particular difficulty is underlined by O'Brien (1997b; p.B-26):

> A dilemma facing the European hotels industry concerns the future for incentive travel rates. With strong demand for hotel rooms from business travellers, hoteliers are trying to maximise revenue yield from key customer segments...However, hoteliers have had to come to terms with the fact that the incentive rates quoted some 12–18 months ago now reflect a low yield compared with existing rates achieved from the independent business travel sector.

Solving this dilemma to the satisfaction of all parties involved may prove to be a considerable challenge for the industry, as long as lead times still stretch to one or even two years.

Transport

There can be no incentive travel without some form of transport being used, and, as in the case of hotels, this market provides transport operators with an opportunity to sell their most expensive products and make healthy profits. But, again as for hotels, transport operators' chances of success in the incentive sector depend entirely on them making an extra effort to meet – and exceed – the expectations of their passengers.

In this sector, the transport element is often not seen simply as a means to an end – getting to the destination – but as part of the incentive experience itself, characterised by pleasure, exclusivity and uniqueness. For this reason, many operators make the effort to use the journey as an opportunity to make their incentive passengers feel special. For example, a company using the Eurostar as transport for its incentive trip has a wide range of unique benefits to choose from to make its award winners feel privileged. These include in-carriage branding with the company logo, on-board entertainment, personalised on-board welcome messages, as well as gifts as a souvenir of their Eurostar trip.

It is the airline sector that is used most frequently to convey incentive winners to their destinations. One indicator of the importance of incentive groups to airlines is the fact that, by 2000, dedicated conference and incentive departments had been established in 60% of the airlines responding to a *Conference and Incentive Travel* magazine survey (Roberts, 2000). However, on the down side, it was found that in the majority of cases these departments were staffed by only one person, which meant that some agencies were experiencing delays in getting vital quotes for the airlines' group rates from these departments.

The conclusion of the survey was that the key feature required of the airlines, by incentive travel organisers, was flexibility. One example of the need for this arises in the question of passenger lists. Clearly, passengers' names are not available until the winners of the incentive programme have been selected, and, as with group travel of any kind, there can always be last-minute changes to the list of those travelling. This can be a major problem for incentive travel organisers if they are dealing with an airline that requires final passenger lists weeks or even months before the actual flight – as many do. However, on the positive side, the respondents to the survey showed that they were responding to the need for flexibility: 32% of them allowed name changes less than three days before travel – an increase from the previous year's 12% of airlines offering such a service.

Another specific need for flexibility arises from the need of incentive trip organisers to be able to book seats well in advance. A total of 85% of airlines were found to allow reservations one year in advance of travel, double the percentage of the previous year's survey. Finally, incentive travel organisers are known to appreciate dedicated group check-in facilities for their award winners, and 90% of airlines claimed to offer this facility (Roberts, 2000).

Destinations

The other key supply-side elements in the incentive market are the destinations that are used for trips of this kind. Clearly, there are considerable benefits to cities and countries chosen as destinations for this form of business-related travel. On a per capita basis, incentive travel almost certainly provides the greatest spending levels of all forms of business travel, with the concomitant economic benefits for suppliers. But destinations' images are also enhanced when the experience of incentive groups is a wholly positive one. Elliott (1997) emphasises this point, with the example of Australia as a destination: 'If an incentive or other programme is successful, it can have favourable repercussions, as when the President of the lingerie company Charle Corporation, Mr Masaharu Hayashi, endorsed Australia as a first-class destination to his corporate peers, following an incentive visit of 4,500 Japanese saleswomen to Sydney in 1992, spending A$10 million.'

So which destinations most successfully attract incentive events? O'Brien (1997b) confirms that the USA and Europe remain the key geographic destinations for incentive travel programmes, although the Far East and Australia, Eastern Europe and the Caribbean are becoming increasingly popular incentive destinations:

> With its geographical variety, rich supply of heritage and cultural resources, as well as its relatively high levels of security, the importance of Europe as a destination for incentive trips is generally acknowledged. Not only is it the main destination for incentives organised for European companies, but it has, since the 1960s, also been the primary international destination for US incentive groups.

A number of European countries are widely used as destinations by the US incentive market, although, as the research undertaken by the Menlo Consulting Group indicates (MCG, 1999), Europe tends to be reserved for experienced winners, who are most likely to have won other trips closer to home in the past.

For the outbound US incentive market, the same research showed that although Europe is important as an overseas destination, short-haul destinations dominate the international incentive market. The sun and sand destinations perform particularly well in this segment: 44.2% of incentive travellers visited the Caribbean, Bermuda or Hawaii on their most recent international incentive trip. Although technically a domestic destination, Hawaii represents an offshore oasis to many Americans and has a similar appeal to that of the Caribbean islands for incentive planners. One in five incentive travellers visited nearby Canada, Alaska or Mexico on their last incentive trip (MCG, 1999; p.20). Table 4.1 indicates the most popular overseas destinations for US incentive trips.

Nevertheless, despite the fact that one in four US outbound incentive programmes has Europe as its destination, the use of Europe as a destination for incentive trips by the US market has developed along quite different lines to its use by European companies. Consequently, the characteristics of the American incentive market for Europe differ considerably from the characteristics of the intra-European market for incentive travel. Those differences are summarised in Table 4.2.

Table 4.1 Destinations visited by US award winners on recent international incentive trips

Destination	Percentage
Caribbean, Bermuda or Hawaii	44.2
Canada, Alaska or Mexico	20.2
UK	7.7
Other Europe	18.3
Asia or South Pacific	3.8
Other	5.8

Source: MCG Inc. (1999) and BTA, *Travelstyles: Americans as international travellers*.

Table 4.2 European and US incentives in Europe

European market	US market
Companies organise several incentive trips per year, with smaller groups	Companies organise one or two larger trips per year
Higher work input: seminars, workshops, etc.	Minimum work input: mainly a leisure experience
Shorter lead times	Longer lead times
More adventurous, lesser-known destinations and activities	Standard international destinations: capitals known to Americans
Average four nights; more likely to be over a weekend	Average seven nights
Lower budget per participant: three- and four-star hotels	Higher budget: four- and five-star hotels
Emphasis on activities and ground programme	Emphasis on quality of accommodation
DMCs play a more limited role in organising	DMCs play a fuller role

Source: Based on O'Brien, K. (1997b), 'The incentive travel market to the UK and Ireland', in *Insights*, September, published by the English Tourism Council (Tel: 0208 563 3362).

Clearly, some of these differences may be explained through the cultural distinctions that exist between the two markets. For example, Americans, particularly if they are relatively unfamiliar with Europe, are most likely to be motivated by the opportunity to visit capital cities with attractive images, such as London, Paris and Rome. But since many European award winners are already well-travelled within the continent as a whole, they are likely to be attracted to more unusual destinations offering the opportunity to engage in new activities, e.g. a jeep safari in Cyprus or ice-fishing in Lapland.

Other contrasts between the US and the domestic use of Europe as an incentive destination are due to geographical factors. The US market makes more use of DMCs, for example, because, being remoter from Europe itself, Americans are more dependent on intermediaries on the spot to research and organise the details of the programme. Similarly, since they spend more time travelling in order to reach Europe than native Europeans do, their trips are, on average, longer. For Europeans themselves, short two- or three-day incentives in their own continent are perfectly feasible.

For the European domestic and outbound market, the debate among incentive travel organisers tends to revolve around the long-haul/short-haul destination decision. Some agencies believe that even the most impressive short-haul programmes lack the impact and motivating factor of unusual and exotic long-haul destinations. Overfamiliarity with European cities is one hurdle to overcome. If such destinations are to be chosen as places in which to hold incentives, then they must demonstrate that they can be as effective at motivating staff as long-haul destinations are.

However, there are many in the industry who do not agree that further is necessarily better. In the report of an industry forum held to discuss this issue, Doyle (2001; p.21) quotes one incentive organiser: 'We get a lot of calls from people saying that the last thing they want to do on an incentive is get on a plane for seven or eight hours, because they do that all the time with their job. You can organise short-haul incentives that will get people talking just as much as long haul.' Another contributor to the same forum introduced a new variant on the debate: the 'short long-haul trip'. 'Places like Dubai, for instance, are really coming into their own. They're not too far to get to and you can pack a lot into just three or four nights. You always have [airline] seats available, and there are enough carriers to get people there.'

Whether long-haul, short-haul or domestic, however, the difficulty for all destinations active in this market is that, of all forms of business travel, it is generally agreed that incentive travel is the most fickle. Novelty and fashion are major factors in the destination decision-making process, and today's hot new place to send incentive groups can be tomorrow's tired cliché.

But, above all, to be effective, the destination must succeed in motivating those who are competing to win the travel award. A basic requirement is that the destination should be perceived as being safe and politically stable. Any hint of danger or political volatility can disqualify an incentive destination overnight. As the authors of the BTF report point out, anticipating with some accuracy the impacts of the events of September 11 (BTF & BTAC, 1999; p.21): 'Incentive travel is most susceptible, however, to geo-political problems. War or an escalation of terrorist acts could easily wipe out the segment in a particular year, and it is not as resilient as other business tourism sectors – the incentive travel programme can take anything up to 18 months to build up again after the perceived danger disappears.'

Issues and trends

Market growth

Commentators generally agree that after the recession and the Gulf War of the early 1990s, the rest of that decade witnessed overall growth in the incentive market worldwide. Generally speaking, observation suggests that demand for incentive travel programmes tends to follow economic growth patterns, although, as O'Brien (1997a) points out, it usually lags some 12 months due to companies' budgeting cycles.

Interviewed in 1997, the international president of the SITE and senior vice president with Marriott Hotels emphasised the general expansion in incentive programmes, especially outside the USA, indicating that some of the growth could be accounted for by the fact that more countries were recognising the value of using incentive travel as a motivational tool (Murray, 1997; p.18):

A decade ago, more than half of all incentive programmes originated in the United States. The figure is now less than 43% ... Europe's share is now 27%. This is a business that prospers when times are good, and today everyone is bullish ... As an industry, our number one task is to ... show that promotions can be effective in bad times as well as in good.

In the same year, the Travel and Tourism Intelligence survey of incentive travel in Western Europe also forecast growth in the market in other European countries, such as Austria, the Benelux countries and Spain, which it considered were set to join the UK, Germany, France and Italy as major generators of demand for this form of business tourism. The same survey estimated that, ten years after its publication, Eastern Europe would also represent an important market for incentive travel (O'Brien, 1997a).

Commentators have also noted that some of the growth in the market witnessed during the 1990s was due to new end users increasingly being considered to be worthy recipients of travel awards. For example, according to a former executive director of the Incentive Travel and Meetings Association, incentives such as luxury spa weekends are also being geared more towards women as premier prize-winners. He also predicts that women could potentially represent up to 50% of the market (*The European*, 1995). Companies also appear to be increasingly aware of the importance of motivating not only those 'out in the field' selling their products but also those on whom their sales staff depend for support back at base, such as secretaries and administrative staff.

There is a strong likelihood that this growing trend towards using incentive programmes to motivate non-sales staff may have originated in the recession of the early 1990s, when, according to Juergens (1991), many companies began using travel awards to encourage behaviours that reduce costs, such as cost-saving suggestions, improved work habits and reduced employee absenteeism.

Nevertheless, even against a background of general growth in the market, the level of demand for incentive travel is in part affected by the performance of its principal customers in the market. This in turn is subject to a number of factors in the wider market environment, including changes in government legislation. For example, in the UK in 2000, the automotive sector operated in a context of extensive consumer and government pressure on prices and from additional European legislation. As a result, 'for many manufacturers, the result has been an exercise in back-to-basics and a reappraisal of the way they sell cars, even questioning whether using incentives is relevant any more' (Fisher, 2001; p.31). The same source discusses how that year's slump in IT company share prices led to cancelled incentive events and considerable uncertainty about marketing budgets for the following year. On the positive side, he adds that incentive demand from the UK pharmaceutical industry was still buoyant, despite the fact that such companies were having to come to terms with the cost of branded drugs and centralised buying from the National Health Service.

Cost-consciousness

Although, as has already been stated, demand for incentive travel is correlated strongly with economic prosperity at both company and national levels, the 1990s did not witness a return to the lavish spending levels of the 1980s. Instead, prudence and cost-consciousness came to characterise spending in incentive travel, with a desire to get the fullest possible value for money being a major consideration.

O'Brien (1997b; p.B-17) notes the trend towards companies getting better value from their spending on incentives: 'Most companies using incentives have reduced average expenditure levels per participant and have shifted the perception of the trip away from a frivolous perk to a well-earned reward.' He reported that expenditure levels were still high but had been pruned back, and companies had sought to reduce travel programme costs in a number of ways. Trip duration had been shortened, and incentive travellers were more likely to be participating in some form of work-related activity during their trips. Reduced ground-handling costs were being achieved by offering participants 'free' days or unescorted opportunities for shopping.

O'Brien, while acknowledging growth in the market, emphasises that this has been achieved against a backdrop of tighter negotiations with suppliers to reduce average travel costs. This echoes a similar trend noted in Chapter 3 concerning the nature of buyers' and intermediaries' negotiations with suppliers of facilities for meetings: their growing skill in getting more for either less or at least the same amount of expenditure.

Some commentators have claimed that Europe as a destination for short-haul incentive trips has benefited from the ethos of cost-consciousness. According to the Horwath Axe business and conference tourism survey for the European Commission, European companies' incentive trips, having favoured long-haul destinations in the 1980s, were returning to the European and, in particular, Mediterranean regions (short- or medium-haul trips) by the mid-1990s. The survey report noted that due to the costs incurred and the economic context of recession, companies tended to favour less prestigious and expensive destinations, putting emphasis instead on the quality of the organisation and content of the incentive programme. To this end, it claims, European destinations have had the opportunity to reposition themselves in this market segment (CEC, 1996).

These findings were echoed by a former executive director of the Incentive Travel and Meetings Association: 'One trend is companies being more prudent with their incentive spend, compared with the pre-recessionary 1980s...The long-haul market has shown no real sign of growth, but many more companies are providing incentives either domestically or within Europe to a broader range of staff rather than just the very top achievers' (*The European*, 1995).

Return on investment

Even in an era of cost-consciousness, however, incentive travel remains a high-spending form of business tourism. One justification for the generous levels of expenditure on this activity is that incentive programmes are generally claimed to be 'self-liquidating', meaning that the extra profit they generate for the company, in the form of extra sales, economy measures or greater productivity, covers the expenses of the programme (Shinew & Backman, 1995).

But, do companies really take the time to find out whether this happens in practice? Do they know if their corporate objectives are being met effectively through the use of incentive travel?

It would appear that although several anecdotal and a few empirical reports exist, there is a scarcity of comprehensive, empirical-based research that examines adequately the impact and effectiveness of travel rewards in achieving corporate objectives.

The research undertaken by LaForge (1990) illustrates this. In order to ascertain the most common evaluation methods used, he conducted a survey of companies that use travel incentives awards for their staff. Respondents were asked which statements would best describe the evaluation approach expected by their top management at the close of an incentive travel programme. Over 50% indicated that only a summary review of objectives and results would be expected, and 31% indicated that simply assuring management that the trip was enjoyed by all and that goodwill was gained for the company was sufficient.

His findings are confirmed by the international president of the SITE (Murray, 1997; p.18):

> The number of companies which seek to evaluate the success or otherwise of a campaign by investigating the return on their investment (ROI) remains the exception rather than the rule... What is known for certain from our own research is that whenever our members either offer, or present, an ROI, they are almost always retained to carry out a second incentive and motivational programme the following year.

Nevertheless, he also identifies some interesting national differences in the approach to ROI, since although in the USA 'less than one quarter of clients of SITE members demand an analysis of whether the returns justified the expenditure, in Europe the figure is 50% and in Canada in excess of 80%'. Again, cultural differences may explain the differences between the USA and other countries. Since as a management tool incentive travel has been established firmly in the USA for many decades, it may well be that its effectiveness is widely accepted, while elsewhere it is still under pressure to prove itself as a worthwhile investment for companies.

Another question arises concerning ROI: could companies equally achieve their objectives by spending the cost of the incentive programme on other types of motivational tools, such as cash bonuses or merchandise, instead of travel?

Quantitative evidence demonstrating travel as the most effective form of reward is scant and has still to be proven conclusively many years after Ricci and Holland (1992) first stated that reviews of consumer behaviour, psychology, management and travel literature had failed to locate empirical studies documenting the superior reward value of travel.

Some studies even suggest that the opposite may be true. For example, based on empirical research on a major life insurance company, the Shinew and Backman (1995) study examined the effectiveness and attractiveness of travel, merchandise and cash awards as incentives in the workplace. The results indicated that the two travel-related rewards (incentive trips and sales conference trips) received the highest attractiveness ratings. Interestingly, however, when respondents were questioned on the capacity of each of the award options to motivate them to increase their productivity, it was found that it was the prospect of winning cash that was the greatest productivity motivator for the employees surveyed, albeit by a narrow margin.

It is perhaps in the quest to add value to incentive programmes that, increasingly, work-related elements are being included in trips. Confirming this, a 1996 survey of European and US usage of incentive travel noted that incentive travel programmes were no longer solely leisure-based trips. It found that over 50% of all incentive trips involved a conference or meeting, and over 40% of all incentive trips involved either a site, factory or business visit of some kind. The survey concluded that the main differentiating factor between the US and European incentive travel markets was that, in Europe, companies deliberately built in work inputs in order to achieve better value from the incentive travel budget (BTA *et al.*, 1996).

Impact of new technology

As for the other sectors of the business travel market, advances in communications and IT have provided considerable opportunities for improving the way incentive travel is planned and organised. In the field of incentive travel, the Internet in particular appears to offer considerable potential for improving participation and information flow.

The work of incentive travel agencies has already been affected particularly. As most agencies prefer to negotiate personally with suppliers, the Internet is rarely used for actually booking transport and accommodation. However, it has proved to be a useful tool for venue research. By visiting the websites of some hotels, for example, agencies can check rates, room capacities, location and availability to see if the venue is worth pursuing.

But it is commonly expected that new technology will have its greatest impact in the areas of incentive participation and programme management. Programme management costs can be reduced, for example, by agencies posting information for participants on a dedicated website rather than producing a printed brochure, with the added advantage of instantaneous data transmission. A number of agencies have been quick to introduce online participation for the incentives they organise. The incentive agency World Event Management, for example, has a dedicated incentive registration site within its own website. Participants log on to the site with a password and access the particular incentive programme in which they are competing, in order to check on the latest details (Greaves, 2000; p.26):

> Monthly performance results are posted on the web page, and as the date of the trip itself draws closer, the site can be used to keep motivation levels high by providing updates on the programme, including pictures of the destination and hotel, weather reports and the itinerary...Nearer the date of the incentive, winners can access flight and hotel information and input their dietary and medical requirements.

Nevertheless, it has already been recognised that there are limits to the use of new technology for the purposes of registration and programme management. Much depends on who the participants are and how comfortable they are with technology.

Greaves (2000; p 28) quotes one incentive travel organiser: 'Companies in the IT, telecommunications and finance sectors will turn to the Internet because they feel comfortable with it and use it for on-line financial transactions. But others are holding back – 45% of our clients are from the automotive sector, and they are still behind in technological developments.'

It would appear that the paperless incentive programme is not yet set to become reality. As will be seen in Chapter 5, the same limitations apply in the case of registration for trade fairs and exhibitions: the rate of adoption is determined by the extent to which the targeted participants have the skills and the equipment required to give them access to the new technology.

Product development

Of all sectors of business tourism, incentive travel is undoubtedly the most fickle and sensitive to changes in fashion. This is seen most clearly in the changing trends in destinations for this type of product. Choice of destinations for incentive travel is influenced by many factors, including, as has been discussed, budget. However, novelty value is also a key element. New destinations and new types of incentives are important factors in the constant revitalisation of the concept of incentive travel as a motivational tool. Given that award winners are often people who also travel extensively for work-related purposes, incentive travel organisers are constantly on the look-out for new destinations or new ways in which to package well-known places.

Given the considerable profits to be made from catering to the incentive travel market, there is no shortage of destinations trying to break into this sector. Due to the luxurious and extravagant nature of incentive trips, those responsible for organising and designing them are targeted particularly by destinations who generally recognise that participants on incentive trips generate a significantly higher spend per head than other business tourism sectors (CEC, 1996).

Many commentators have raised the question of whether Europe will continue to enjoy its current generous share of the world's incentive market in the face of growing competition from regions such as the Far East, Australia and South Africa. According to O'Brien (1997a), these destinations have begun targeting the European incentive market in earnest. He points out that both flight and accommodation costs associated with long-haul travel, for example to the Asia-Pacific region, were falling by the mid-1990s, making long-haul travel for all purposes an increasingly competitive product. He expresses the belief that in the long term, larger aircraft offering both lower seat rates and faster journey times will make the long-haul markets more competitive in incentive travel.

On the benefits side for Europe, however, the same author notes that South Africa, as well being a popular incentive destination, also offers business potential for European destinations, since it is now considered as a new incentive travel generating market, with particular interest in the UK. By way of contrast, the Asia-Pacific incentive travel market does not yet extend to Europe, since most incentive trips offered by companies in that world region tend to be short in duration – typically three days (O'Brien, 1997a).

As well as new destinations, new types of incentive programmes are evolving constantly. Ricci and Holland (1992, p.294), in their discussion of what they term 'the growing "lifestyles concept" of incentive travel', provide evidence of what was arguably the most important trend in incentive travel design of the 1990s: the move away from sybaritic indulgence towards activities and the great outdoors:

> There is a trend away from the resort hotel with the fine dining and jacuzzi for some segments of the incentive market, because some clients have already done enough of that. They are seeking a different quest such as a hunting-photography safari, an Alaskan adventure, a fishing holiday on a quiet lake in an isolated setting and rustic but comfortable accommodation, or a South American rainforest trip.

Clearly linked to a new generation of management's attitude to healthier living and desire to spend time in pollution-free environments, this trend, if it continues, opens up the possibility of new types of destinations entering the market on the supply side. As examples, a detailed case for the use of Canada's wilderness areas as an incentive destination is made by Witt *et al.* (1992), and the case study at the end of this chapter describes Iceland's assets as a venue for this form of business tourism.

Its novelty value, while it lasts, no doubt also explains the popularity of the Channel Tunnel as an element in incentive programmes. O'Brien (1997a) expresses the belief that it has stimulated new forms of incentive travel and has the market potential in the medium to long term to stimulate large group incentives to multiple incentive destinations. Noting that the fixed link has created the one-day incentive for Belgian, French and UK groups, he suggests that the success of the Eurostar and the Channel Tunnel is indicative of how the uniqueness of a new transport system can itself stimulate new types of incentive events through the mere fact of their novelty and topicality.

The other incentive phenomenon of the 1990s was the rise of cruising as an incentive travel option for the Western European market. Cruising had been popular with the US market for many years, but it was not until the 1990s that European incentive organisers saw the attractions of cruise ships for incentives. Much of their appeal stems from the economic benefits that cruising offers. Since it is possible to make block bookings on cruise ships 12 months ahead of the incentive programme, and on guaranteed, all-inclusive rates, the incentive planner has the security of knowing that costs are controlled firmly, especially as food and beverages are usually contained within the negotiated rates. The supporters of the use of cruises as incentive prizes claim that these guaranteed rates distinguish the cruising market from other types of incentive programmes. One cruise company manager emphasises this point: 'One, often-forgotten element that sets cruises apart, is that with ever-increasing lead times, prices for exclusive charters are fixed, as opposed to land-based events where prices can be variable' (Buchanan, 2001b; p.66).

Other apparent advantages include the fact that the logistics of hosting an incentive group on board a cruise ship are very much simpler than an equivalent land-based incentive. Once a group has embarked on to the ship, it may visit up to five different countries in the space of a seven-night cruise without all the aggravation of travel, airports and transfers. All ships have built-in entertainment and sports facilities, dozens of different meal services per day, and plenty of distractions for the most demanding passengers. But a key advantage for incentive organisers is that they, literally, have a captive audience.

Going one step further, the factor of exclusivity can be added to that of audience captivity for companies prepared to charter an entire cruise ship for their award-winners. Gosling (1999) describes this use of incentive cruises as a growing trend, quoting a Cunard Line sales manager who maintains that the real growth end of the incentive market is in full-ship charters. The manager stresses the advantages of exclusivity over sharing a ship with other passengers, pointing out that the itineraries can be custom-made for the client and the ship's programme can be tailored entirely towards the group. The same manager also claimed that chartering was cost-effective, especially when compared with a land-based programme.

There does appear to be a compelling argument in favour of using cruise-based products for the incentive market. However, it will be interesting to monitor the development of this trend to determine whether O'Brien (1997a) was correct in his prediction that, as cruising becomes more of a mass-market activity, it might lose its popularity as an incentive travel product, being no longer sufficiently exclusive and aspirational to motivate employees.

Limits to growth

The increasing use of incentive travel during the 1990s would appear to indicate that companies are accepting that recognising and rewarding employees for a job well done is not a superfluous or magnanimous gesture, but rather a highly effective management tool that confirms accomplishment and reinforces commitment.

However, several decades of experience of using incentive travel have shown that this motivational method is not without its own potential problems. Shinew and Backman (1995) suggest that incentive reward programmes may result in a number of undesirable or unanticipated outcomes, including:

● reduced cooperation among employees before, during and after a contest period;
● decline in morale because the contest was perceived to be unfair;
● post-contest sales slumps.

According to the same authors, there is also the danger that rewards will lose their extra incentive value if used too often, thereby becoming a routinely expected component of the compensation package.

More seriously, perhaps, they believe that incentive reward systems may also fail to reward the behaviours that have the greatest impact on the long-term success of the organisation. The difficulty arises from the fact that the organisation of incentive programmes tends to be led by ease of measurement. As management often seeks to establish simple, concrete and quantifiable standards against which performance is measured, this approach, according to Shinew and Backman (1995), may result in the rewarding of behaviours that have limited application to overall organisational effectiveness while excluding those that are more complex. While the activities of a company's salesforce may be relatively straightforward to quantify, general cooperation among colleagues and the creativity of the R&D department are examples of behaviours that may not be rewarded simply because they are difficult to measure. They may, however, be just as important to a company's survival and prosperity as its sales record.

Another commentator sees the continuing growth of the incentive market as being under threat from two internal factors relating to employee performance and company expenditure. Gold (1996) first points out that the incentive market is driven by companies' convictions that their employees could do better, i.e. that they are not working to their full capacity. The theory behind incentives of any kind is that employees can be urged on to even greater achievements on behalf of the company if they are inspired or rewarded by travel products. But, he claims, in the increasingly competitive world of modern commerce, where employees are under more and more daily pressure to achieve better results, higher sales figures, etc., it is no longer the case that there is a great deal of unused potential in the system. As a growing number of those in employment are finding that they have to work full-out just to hold on to their jobs, the incremental returns from sending staff on incentive trips may diminish to the extent that such awards are no longer cost-effective.

Second, the same author predicts that companies may in the future choose to invest in other means of making their employees more productive. He maintains that one problem with incentive travel is the short-lived nature of the benefits it brings. Accordingly, he sees the greatest threat to the use of incentives coming from in-service staff training, which, he claims, is increasingly considered, by management, as the most effective way of increasing employees' productivity.

Ethical issues

An area for some concern is the impact of incentive travellers on destinations and host communities' quality of life. The positive and negative impacts of incentive travel are, of course, similar to those of the leisure tourism they so closely resemble, which are well documented in the general literature on tourism. The benefits that incentive travel offer to the image and economies of destinations have already been mentioned in this chapter. But side by side with these can arise the negative externalities generated by incentive travel. At the destination, these are created by two features of incentive trips: they are often attended by large numbers of visitors, and they are often characterised by lavish and highly visible levels of spending.

Group travel of all kinds has the potential to create logical problems for organisers and destinations. This is particularly true of groups that come and go after a short period at the destination. As Elliott (1997) states, incentive tourism poses a major challenge for management because of the great numbers of people involved very intensively for a short period. Skilful visitor management can help meet the challenges involved in moving around large groups of visitors; but the other potentially negative impact involves a more insidious influence on the destination.

Focusing on the potential impacts of incentive travel on host communities suggests that these may be exacerbated by the fact that this form of business travel is more conspicuous than many of the other types considered in this book. For example, in the case of travel for conference or trade fair attendance, visitors spend most of their time indoors, engaging in activities that are related to their work. By contrast, the lavishly funded and, occasionally, frivolous activities indulged in by incentive travel award-winners run the risk of contrasting severely with the lifestyles and values of those living in some of the destinations chosen for incentive trips.

For example, how do the ordinary inhabitants of Grenada feel when their local beach is taken over by an incentive group for an evening's rum-soaked 'Caribbean party', to which they are most definitely not invited? Ricci and Holland (1992; p.295) take up this point: 'The blatant luxury, conspicuous consumption and indulgence of many incentive rewards may be repulsive to some people. The historical image of exclusive bacchanalian flings of spoiled aristocrats troubles the conscience of true believers in equality, openness and democracy.'

It is a fact that extravagant leisure enjoyed by a privileged few has been around since ancient times. It would be unfortunate if the public image of incentive travel in the twenty-first century were to become associated too closely with that particular tradition.

Outlook

There is general agreement that, at the end of the twentieth century, the incentive travel sector was enjoying a period of buoyant growth. According to the *Study of the Incentive Merchandise and Travel Marketplace 2000* (Incentive Federation, 2001), there was steady growth in the US incentive market, with prospects for further growth. The study found that total expenditure for merchandise and travel items used by US companies for incentive programmes had increased to $US26.9 billion in 2000 from $US22.8 billion in 1996. The study also identified a 6% increase in the number of responding companies that say they used incentives as a motivational tool, rising from 26% in 1996 to 32% in 2000.

But at the turn of the century, most industry commentators were acknowledging that while incentive travel in the USA was nearing maturity in marketing terms, in Europe the market was still in the growth cycle and remained a huge potential market for this form of business travel. As the Howarth Axe survey of business travel in Europe had concluded a few years earlier, regarding incentive travel, Europe currently constitutes a considerable demand generating resource that remains significantly underexploited (CEC, 1996).

The extent to which that demand can be exploited depends on a number of external factors operating in the market environment. As the size of European company budgets available for expenditure on incentive travel is determined largely by the state of the economy in general, this must be the main consideration to be taken into account in predicting the outlook for the expansion of incentive travel everywhere.

Moreover, given the continuing dominance of the USA on the demand side of the market, the purchasing power of the dollar against other currencies is clearly a key consideration, in particular in its scope for having an impact upon the inbound US market to Europe.

Not all factors are economic, however. Political stability is a key requirement of this market, as it is impossible to motivate employees by the prospect of sending them or their families to a destination affected by civil unrest or conflict. The wide-scale cancellation of incentive trips to many destinations after 11 September 2001 came as a reminder that incentives are a nonessential form of travel, which can only be effective where security reigns.

How long will it take for the incentive travel sector to recover from the 2001 terrorist attacks on the USA? It is to be hoped that the upbeat words on this topic spoken by David Riddell, of SITE, at the end of the 1990s, will still prove to be true (Murray, 1997; p.19):

> Travel will be the incentive king in the 21st century. The world is getting smaller, as everywhere becomes more accessible. As a result, everyone wants to go everywhere. And, if by working harder, they can travel to the most distant points of the globe – at someone else's expense – that will be an important motivator to bigger achievements. What is more, every year, more companies will realise that travel as an incentive can produce measurable results.

Case study

Iceland as an incentive destination

The place

A relatively recent newcomer to the business tourism market, Iceland is beginning to make its mark in the corporate marketplace, and incentive travel is one of the markets the country has been targeting seriously since the 1990s.

Although only a short flight away from continental Europe, Iceland, with its lunar landscapes and extreme daylight patterns, can give visitors the impression that they have travelled to another planet. On all sides, the country is surrounded by the fishing grounds of the Atlantic, and deep underground lies the island's geo-thermal water supply, which is tapped to heat homes, offices and greenhouses as well as scores of health-giving pools.

In the promotional literature of the Iceland Convention & Incentive Bureau (IC&IB, 2000), the assets of Iceland as an incentive destination are described as follows:

> Hotels, conference facilities, support services and modern comforts are on a par with the rest of Western Europe.

Case study *continued*

What makes Iceland stand out as a venue is its unique natural beauty and pure environment. Dramatic volcano and glacier scenery – and action-packed incentives are there, waiting to be enjoyed by future visitors.

Raw forces of nature – glaciers, volcanoes and the ocean – have been forging and shaping the face of Iceland for 20 million years, and are still hard at work. The uninhabited interior is a vast adventure playground for incentives, alive with challenges and rewards.

A friendly country with an outstanding reputation for stability and personal safety, Iceland is just 2–3 hours by air from the European continent and only 5–6 hours from the east coast of the United States.

We have a clean capital city, fresh air, long summer nights, low crime level and good food. The development of advanced horticultural methods using thermal heat means that vegetables are available in abundance throughout the year, while there is a wide selection of fresh fish, seafood and lamb. The adventurous can even try birds such as puffin and guillemot.

The enthusiastic claims of the IC&IB are supported by a travel organiser, Jayne Byott, who organised a visit for 150 employees of a UK pharmaceutical giant to Iceland in the summer of 2000, staying at the Loftleider Hotel and holding meetings in Reykjavík's City Theatre (Murray, 2000): 'This is one of nature's still undiscovered wonderlands. Everyone should seek it out.'

The activities

Much of the attractiveness of Iceland for incentive organisers lies in its natural resources and the use that can be made of them to entertain award-winners. Following a familiarisation trip for journalists and events organisers, the verdict of one travel writer was very positive (Murray, 2000):

Upon arrival, most incentive groups are taken to the Blue Lagoon, to bathe in the geothermal pool. It is as though you are being enveloped in the arms of someone who wants to cuddle you. Almost instantly, you feel good all over, rejuvenated, the stresses of the everyday world soothed away. And for members of groups, there is an extra. Drinks can be served to them as they stand up to their necks in the warm water. There are few more congenial starts to any visit.

Everyone is taken to see the geysers that shoot warming water high into the air every few minutes. And everywhere,

there are vast, seemingly endless, fields of moss-covered lava – reminders that the whole of Iceland was created by a long-ago volcanic eruption that literally hurled it from the depths of the ocean.

Nor can those of us who have driven snow-mobiles on a glacier ever forget that feeling of exhilaration. There is more excitement river rafting down the glacial river Hvita or whale-watching.

Two years previously, Goodhart (1998), another writer, was equally impressed by some of Iceland's other qualities: 'Another advantage is that language is not a barrier. Many Icelanders speak perfect English. The people are Germanic in their organisational skills and Swiss in their precision timing, and organisers would be unlucky to encounter many hitches in their itinerary.' Goodhart went on to quote Catherine Hadfield, events coordinator for Black & Decker, who accompanied her on the trip: 'We want something that people would never do themselves. Iceland is quite different, so you can get people excited about it. It is an amazing place, with mad landscapes. One minute you can be walking on a moon-type surface and the next snowmobiling round the glaciers.'

The market

How can Iceland be used as a destination for business tourism? Its rich natural resources are undoubtedly a huge asset, but is that enough? Murray (2000) identifies some obvious gaps in the facilities: 'There are good hotels, such as Icelandair's Loftleider and the larger Radisson SAS property ... but meeting and incentive planners on inspection visits quickly notice that the other top international names are missing. There is no convention centre, although the university can offer a tiered auditorium seating almost 1,000.'

Murray (2000) goes on to quote Nicholas Fisher, special events manager at Business Events, part of Carlson Wagonlit, who:

... was full of enthusiasm for the country's attractions, which left him wondering why he had not been there before ... Iceland has almost everything except a 5-star hotel or a property with more than 250 rooms. This inevitably means that any large incentive group cannot be accommodated in a single venue and certainly not to the standard to which many top salesmen and women and senior executives have become accustomed.

▶

Case study *continued*

Goodhart (1998) visiting Iceland two years earlier heard similar comments from incentive organisers, including Tim Gasson, managing director of Absolute Corporate Events, whose verdict was: 'I think it is a very unusual destination that currently is underused. I would choose it for a three- to four-day, activity-based, mid to upper level incentive group, but not for top executives, who expect a luxury hotel and want modems in their rooms.'

Whatever its perceived limitations, however, Iceland is earning a reputation as a novel and exciting destination for incentives, with European countries providing most of its customers. Murray (2000) reports that Iceland Incentives, a local DMC, in 1999 handled a record number of groups from the UK, including Volvo, Sony and GE Capital Finances. He goes on to quote Matthias Kjartansson, managing director, saying: 'Britain is our best overseas market and has overtaken Germany.'

Promotion and organisation of incentive trips

The challenge of promoting Iceland as an incentive destination is the responsibility of the IC&IB, which was established as a non-profit-making organisation in 1992. It was set up by leading members of the Icelandic travel industry, along with leading hotels, conference centres and professional events organisers.

The role of the IC&IB is to market convention facilities and incentive opportunities in Iceland at an international level. Its services are provided free of charge, and are listed in the IC&IB's own promotional literature:

- Assistance with corporate meeting and conference preparation.
- Information on meetings facilities, availability of accommodation and flights.
- Suggestions for incentives, special events, spouse programmes and safaris.
- Organisation of inspection visits.
- Information about suppliers of services for conferences and incentives.
- Promotional material and bid support for conferences.
- List of events.

Much of the promotion of Iceland abroad, other than in Frankfurt, New York, Italy and France, where there are ITB representatives, is handled by Icelandair, who clearly has a strong interest in companies choosing Iceland as a business tourism destination.

Perhaps in Iceland more than in any other destination, incentive programme organisers rely heavily upon the DMCs. Their specialised skills and expertise in organising entertainment for groups in the often extreme climate and alien landscape of Iceland make them particularly necessary to incentive agencies. Six of the members of the Convention Bureau are DMCs.

Future developments

Goodhart (1998) gave her impression of Iceland's future as an incentive destination:

Reykjavik is now reasonably well established as a conference destination, particularly among pharmaceutical companies and legal firms. Its pretty wooden houses, painted in pastel colours, good selection of high quality restaurants and lively nightlife means that groups can enjoy a stimulating couple of days in the city.

What the DMCs are now trying to push are some of the country's other towns such as Hveragerdi, Akureyri and Husavik. The advantages are clearly peace and quiet, cheaper prices and dramatic scenery. The disadvantage is that most towns, apart from Hveragerdi, are a short flight away from the International Airport, which is itself a 45-minute drive from Reykjavik.

Iceland is not yet considered a year-round destination, which has much to do with the fact that in the winter, there are only four hours of daylight. The other aim of the DMCs is to lengthen the season, which currently runs from May to September. In July and August, hotels are usually so full of tourists and special interest parties that conference and incentive groups cannot be accommodated. Prices are hiked in these two months and organisers would do better to look at the shoulder periods.

Two years later, another gap in Iceland's business tourism resources also seemed about to be filled when plans were announced to build a major convention complex with seating for 1500 in the same hall, plus a five-star hotel. All going according to plan, the first convention was due to take place before 2004.

Case study *continued*

Questions

1 What are the characteristics of Iceland that make it (a) suitable and (b) unsuitable as an incentive destination for the North American market in particular?

2 What features of Iceland make it a particularly suitable destination for European incentive groups?

3 What predictions can reasonably be made for the future of incentive trips to Iceland from other European countries, in the light of current trends in this sector?

Case study

Golf developments in Scotland

A day's game on a prestigious golf course is widely considered to be an effective way to entertain or reward employees who have achieved outstanding results.

Hart (2001) enthuses: 'Even for try-harder weekend hackers, who love golf but dislike the pomposity that ostensibly goes with it, the opportunity to stroll around a course in the company of colleagues, with preferably a well-known pro or two in attendance, is too good a chance to miss.' He adds that in addition to the team- and character-building aspects of the game, golf offers the extra advantage that it can be enjoyed by participants of virtually any age. It is also said to offer the kind of privileged lifestyle that surrounds the 'nineteenth hole', invoking an esoteric worldliness as well as an added aura of exclusivity for spouses or non-players.

Golf is a sport that Scotland gave to the world, and to play on a Scottish golf course is the dream of golfers from Tokyo to Seattle. This fact has by no means escaped the attention of those with responsibility for promoting Scotland as a business tourism destination. The Scottish Convention's Bureau's publication, *Incentive Scotland*, boasts: 'You're never far from a golf course wherever you go. Championship venues like St Andrews, Royal Troon, Turnberry, Prestwick, Gleneagles and Carnoustie, amongst many others, provide an irresistible challenge to the experienced and inexperienced golfer alike.'

But behind the hype and all the joviality at the nineteenth hole, there is, according to some, a more sinister aspect to the rapid development of luxury golf courses, all the way from Florida to Fife, via the Algarve.

Burnside (2001) believes that the environmental and social impacts of corporate golf developments have been ignored or passed over for too long. His argument is that these facilities have highly damaging impacts, due directly to the vast doses of fertilisers, herbicides and pesticides required to provide golf courses with perfect turf. These, he argues, are known to be seriously damaging to human and animal health as well as the environment; and the landscapes they create are 'entirely artificial, and altogether impoverished environments, often in areas of real natural beauty or ecological interest'.

Burnside's native Fife, considered by many to be the spiritual home of the game of golf, has more than 40 courses, occupying more than 2000 hectares. He believes that although the older courses were developed on natural dune slacks, many of the new developments, with their executive homes, hotels and conference facilities, and their heavy management styles, utterly transform the landscape; and many are in inappropriate locations. Burnside claims:

Evidence from the US suggests that there is a clear link between golf courses and other invasive 'developments'. In Fife, for example, just outside St Andrews – a town which noticeably lacks a green belt – the first phase of two large-scale luxury courses, with the apparently obligatory conferencing and hotel facilities, was opened in September 2001, at a cost of £50 million. The St Andrews

▶

Case study *continued*

Bay complex, part of the luxury American Chateau Elan group, boasts two championship courses with what are described as 'pristine fairways' as well as a 209-room hotel, a luxury spa and a 1,500 m² fully-flexible conference centre, comprising two boardrooms and nine conference rooms.

There may be an important land-use issue at stake in Fife as elsewhere. Burnside observes that other golf developments in the UK have smuggled 'executive' housing estates and driving ranges on to what was once prime farmland or local recreational resources under the cover of 'employment creation'. But, he ripostes, golf is a noticeably seasonal employer, with its requirement for waiters, grounds workers and other casual staff during the summer months, and so contributes relatively little to the local economy.

He concludes: 'There are too many courses in this country, and new developers arrive every year. These courses can create pollution and destroy native landscape, while providing no more than low-paid seasonal employment, as the vogue for grouse-shooting, deer-stalking and other forms of land use did before them.'

Buchanan (2001a), in a less polemical article on this topic, quotes the general manager of the St Andrews Bay complex, who, understandably, is more enthusiastic about the development: 'There have never been enough five-star bedrooms in this corner of Fife and the directional sell for St Andrews has been sadly lacking when it comes to incentives. We are here to change all that.'

This case-study incorporates material from the article 'Bunkered by Mr Big' which appeared in *The Guardian* newspaper on 28 July 2001 © John Burnside.

Questions

1 What arguments might be used to respond to Burnside's antipathy towards golf developments in Scotland?

2 How might golf-based incentives be affected by current trends in this sector?

References

Briggs, S. (1993), 'That special break: making incentives work for you', *Caterer and Hotelkeeper*, 10 June.

BTA *et al.* (1996), *Incentive Travel Usage and its Impact on the UK and Ireland*, London, British Tourist Authority and the UK national tourist boards.

BTF & BTAC (1999), *Business Tourism Leads the Way*, London, Business Tourism Forum.

Buchanan, G. (2001a), 'Regional rewards', *Conference & Incentive Travel*, June.

Buchanan, G. (2001b), 'Business on board', *Conference & Incentive Travel*, July/August.

Burnside, J. (2001), 'Bunkered by Mr Big', *The Guardian*, 28 July.

CEC (1996), *Business and Conference Tourism in the European Economic Area*, Brussels, European Commission.

Collis, R. (2000), *The Survivor's Guide to Business Travel*, London, Kogan Page.

Creevy, J. (2002), 'Changing times', *Conference & Incentive Travel*, February.

Doyle, C. (2001), 'Setting the agenda', *Conference & Incentive Travel*, June.

Elliott, J. (1997), *Tourism Politics and Public Sector Management*, London, Routledge.

The European (1995), 'The executive love of the travel perk', *The European*, 30 November–6 December.

Fisher, J. (2001), 'Cryptic statistics', *Meetings & Incentive Travel*, June.

Gold, J.-P. (1996), 'Un marché en plein mutation', *Tourisme d'Affaires*, Les Cahiers Espaces, February.

Goodhart, L. (1998), 'Solving the mysteries', *Conference & Incentive Travel*, September.

Gosling, J. (1999), 'Ship to shore', *Conference & Incentive Travel*, July/August.

Greaves, S. (2000), 'Making the web work', *Conference & Incentive Travel*, April.

Hart, J. (2001), 'Are the venues up to par?' *Meetings & Incentive Travel*, June.

Hastings, B., Kiely, J. and Watkins, T. (1988), 'Sales force motivation using travel incentives: some empirical evidence', *Journal of Personal Selling and Sales Management*, Vol. 8, pp. 43–51.

IC&IB (2000), *Iceland – For a Change*, Reykjavik, Iceland Convention & Incentive Bureau.

Incentive Federation (2001), *A Study of the Incentive Merchandise and Travel Marketplace 2000*, Westfield, NJ, Incentive Federation, Inc.

Juergens, J. (1991), 'Our survey says: new trends continue to develop with incentive travel users', *Successful Meetings*, April.

LaForge, A.E. (1990), 'Incentive Travel Survey', *Successful Meetings*, April.

McIntosh, R. (1984), *Tourism: principles, practices, philosophies*, New York, John Wiley & Sons.

MCG (1999), *Travelstyles: Americans as international travellers*, Palo Alto, CA, Menlo Consulting Group.

Murray, M. (1997), 'Incentives mean business', *Hospitality*, November/December.

Murray, M. (2000), 'Iceland's warm welcome', *Incentive Travel & Corporate Meetings*, February.

O'Brien, K. (1997a) 'The West European incentive travel market', *Tourism and Analyst*, Vol. 1, pp. 40–52.

O'Brien, K. (1997b), 'The incentive travel market to the UK and Ireland', *Insights*, September.

Ricci, P.R. and Holland, S.M. (1992), 'Recreation as a motivational medium', *Tourism Management*, September.

Roberts, S. (2000), 'Fight for the skies', *Conference & Incentive Travel*, May.

Shinew, K.J. and Backman, S.J. (1995), '*Incentive travel: an attractive option*', *Tourism Management* Vol. 16, pp. 285–93.

Twite, P. (1999), 'Agency survey', *Conference & Incentive Travel*, February.

White, S. (1999), 'Editorial', *Conference & Incentive Travel*, February.

Witt, S.F., Gammon, S. and White, J. (1992), 'Incentive travel: overview and case-study of Canada as a destination for the UK market', *Tourism Management*, September.

Chapter 5

The exhibitions industry

Objectives

On completion of this chapter, you should be able to:

- *distinguish the different types of exhibitions and their uses;*

- *understand the advantages of exhibitions as a sales and marketing medium, and understand the advantages for the destinations where they are held;*

- *understand the roles of the main players in this market;*

- *appreciate the characteristics of a successful exhibition destination;*

- *discuss the various trends in the exhibition market.*

❯ ● ● Exhibitions in the twenty-first century

- 7900 exhibitors and 782 000 visitors, 130 000 of them from outside Germany, travelled to Hanover for the CeBIT exhibition, the world's largest trade fair for IT, telecommunications and office automation products.
- 48 500 hotel and catering professionals attended Hotelympia at London's Earls Court exhibition centre to review the latest developments in their industry and take advantage of face-to-face interaction with existing and potential new suppliers of catering equipment, food and drink, hotel furnishings and technology.
- 30 000 visitors attended the tenth Entech Pullutec trade fair at the Bangkok International Trade and Exhibition Centre; 150 manufacturers of environmental protection and pollution control equipment, from 24 different countries, exhibited their products over an area of 4500 m².
- 75 000 brides- and grooms-to-be visited the National Wedding Show in four locations: London Olympia, Birmingham NEC, Glasgow SECC and Manchester GMEX; 900 exhibitors presented wedding-related goods and services, from dresses and flowers to chauffeur-driven limousines and honeymoon holidays in exotic locations.

● ● ● ● Introduction

Practically any product or service imaginable, from an offshore oil rig to a time-share investment, if it can be bought and sold, will have its own regular exhibition or exhibitions somewhere in the world. These events are 'shop windows', where, on a regular basis, those who produce the products or services can display them, explain them, and sell them to potential customers.

Exhibitions of this type, also known as 'expositions', are marketplaces of products and services – usually lasting from a few days to a week – that bring together two groups of people: those with something to sell (the exhibiting companies and organisations) and those who attend with a view to making a purchase or getting information (the visitors). Both groups create a high level of demand for travel services, catering and accommodation at the destination. They are usually joined by another group – people in the print and broadcast media, since exhibitions are often extremely newsworthy events, with exhibitors often choosing them as occasions on which to launch new products, for example.

Generally speaking, exhibitions may be divided into two categories: trade fairs/shows and consumer fairs/shows. The former are business-to-business events, usually restricted to those seeking to purchase products or services for use in their businesses or professions, e.g. printing equipment, forklift trucks, or specialist software packages for accountants. Consumer fairs are generally open to the public, and feature any products or services that people are prepared to purchase, from cars and kitchen appliances to holidays and investment opportunities.

The same exhibition may be open to both the trade and the public, sometimes on separate days, with often the first day or two being restricted to professionals and the press. However, both types of exhibition differ in the patterns of travel they stimulate. Public exhibitions attract large numbers of visitors, but most of them attend for only one day and are drawn mainly from the local or regional area. Very large or specialised trade fairs, on the other hand, generally attract visitors and exhibitors from a number of countries, and are regarded as important stimulators of inbound tourism for the host nation.

Trade fairs and exhibitions often become regular, usually annual or biennial, events held in the same location, or in rotation between a number of cities.

The global impact of travel for the purpose of attending an exhibition is considerable. Europe alone hosts over 3000 large trade fairs every year, attracting millions of visitors and hundreds of thousands of exhibiting companies to the cities in which they take place (Ladkin, 2000).

Uses of exhibitions

The main purposes of exhibitions are to generate sales, promote new products, maintain or create industry contacts, and to act as places that facilitate the exchange of ideas and information between exhibitors, industry experts and visitors. Thus, from the point of view of those exhibiting at trade/consumer shows, these events are a key component of their communications and marketing mix.

Exhibitions are generally recognised to be a cost-effective way of communicating information between buyers and suppliers. Without this important form of two-way communication, the supporters of exhibitions maintain, the efficiency of trade would be diminished severely. As an advertising medium, exhibitions are said to play a vital role in the marketing of goods and services. In this way, they can be used to stimulate domestic trade and promote exports when they are attended by foreign visitors.

Advantages to visitors

Exhibitions offer a number of advantages to both exhibitors and visitors. For visitors seeking to make a purchase or find out about a particular product, consumer and trade fairs bring together under one roof an extensive range of goods or services of direct interest to them. Such events represent a form of three-dimensional advertising where the product can be seen, handled, compared, assessed by demonstration, and (depending on the product) even smelled and tasted. One trade fair organiser has expressed this particular advantage vividly: 'When you're buying something expensive, there are times you've just got to kick the tyres.'

In addition, since exhibitions also offer visitors the chance to have face-to-face discussions with those who are highly knowledgeable about the product or service on sale, they are able to get authoritative answers to their technical questions from these experts. Many trade fairs in particular include a series of seminars or conferences of interest to those attending, often with the participation of one or more luminaries in the specialist field. For the potential visitors, these can represent important added value, further encouraging them to attend.

Advantages to exhibitors

For the companies who exhibit, having a presence at an exhibition seldom comes cheap. The stand – or 'booth' in the USA – has to be hired or bought and set up. It has to be manned by staff, whose travel and accommodation costs have to be paid. Nevertheless, the advantages to exhibitors are clearly considered to be worth the investment. Klein (1999; p.1) describes those advantages:

> In many industries, the trade show has become a must-seize market opportunity. It's a time to meet prospective customers, get valuable feedback on your product or service, and close sales. A trade show enables you to develop trust and rapport with your customers. Once you have that, you can leave voice-mails and e-mails with a face behind them.

> Despite the outlay of time and money, a trade show is still a very economical way to build your business. A national survey done by Data & Strategies Group Inc. showed that closing a sale with an exhibition lead costs an average of $625 and takes 1.3 follow-up calls. Compare that with the average $1,117 cost and 3.7 phone calls needed to close a sale otherwise. And … you see immediately what customers think of your product.

It is this cost-effectiveness and the opportunity that exhibitions give companies to actually meet their customers or potential customers face to face that explain partly the ongoing appeal of trade fairs as a marketing and sales technique. But there are other advantages. Beyond actual sales or generating potential leads, these events also provide companies with the opportunity to increase their visibility in the market, to improve their image, and to gain immediate feedback on new products or services.

Further reasons for companies spending so much on attending these events year after year are linked to the fact that trade fairs are places where competing companies and organisations can also meet each other face to face. This means that exhibitions give exhibitors an ideal opportunity to analyse the competition, which they often do by visiting each others' stands as 'mystery shoppers', to take note of new products, staff knowledge and behaviour, etc.

Secondly, as Klein (1999; p.1) points out, exhibitors tempted to cut costs by staying away from these events do so at their own risk: 'If you think you can skip the whole affair because all your deals are done elsewhere, think again. Trade shows become a gossipy society unto themselves, where your competitors might float rumours in your absence that your company is ready to bite the dust.' This suggests that simply by being there, companies are able to defend themselves against rumours of their being in such financially dire straights that they cannot afford to attend – *les absents ont toujours tort*!

Advantages to destinations

Whatever the reasons behind the popularity of exhibitions, the economic benefits generated by these events for the places where they take place are considerable. Many of these benefits arise from the spending of the exhibition organisers, visitors and exhibitors on travel, accommodation, recreation and entertainment at the destination. National or international exhibitions, in particular, may have considerable impact on the host economy through the number of visitors and exhibitors staying in serviced accommodation for several days. As we also saw in the case of travel for conferences and other types of meetings (Chapter 3), the ancillary spending on this form of business tourism brings benefits to a wide range of suppliers operating at the destination. In addition, cities often use the hosting of large international exhibitions as a way of creating for themselves the image of a centre of industrial or commercial expertise.

These advantages provide part of the explanation for the extensive investment in exhibition facilities undertaken by cities during the second half of the twentieth century. This issue will be explored further in the section on suppliers, but it is important first to consider who the buyers are in this market.

●●●● Buyers

Exhibitors

In the exhibitions sector, there are two types of end users – exhibitors and visitors – each with their own specific requirements from the events they attend.

The exhibitors in this market are primarily those companies and organisations who pay to display their wares at such events. From multinational manufacturing groups to one-person businesses selling craft jewellery or consultancy services, all sizes of companies in all sectors of industry and commerce are served by specialist exhibitions promoting their particular product or service. The sheer diversity of such events and those who exhibit at them can be seen from the list in Box 5.1, which shows many of the larger exhibitions that took place in the UK over a two-month period during spring 2001.

In some sectors – e.g. high-tech, manufacturing, transportation, communications and wholesale goods – trade shows are the preferred venue for doing business, and a considerable proportion of such companies' sales and marketing budgets are spent on exhibiting at the relevant events.

Before making a decision to participate in an exhibition, companies usually seek information on the organiser's track record and verify attendance figures of previous events and the extent to which the event is supported by the industry sector. Once

Box 5.1

Major UK exhibitions, 23 February–29 April 2001

Evening Standard Homebuyer Show, Olympia, London

Holiday Show, NEC, Birmingham

Asian Wedding Fair, Wembley Centre, London

International Confex, Earls Court 1, London: leading annual forum for the meetings, events, corporate hospitality and support services industry

Hirex, NEC, Birmingham: hire equipment and services

Sailboat and Windsurf Show, Alexandra Palace, London

Incentive World 2001, Earls Court 2, London

Daily Mail Ideal Home Show, Earls Court, London

Sewing for Pleasure, NEC, Birmingham

Glassex, NEC, Birmingham: glass technology and fabrication exhibition

ETF 2001, ExCeL, London: electrotechnical trade fair

Commercial Vehicle Show, NEC, Birmingham

Spring Graduate Recruitment Fair, ExCeL, London

IFE 2001, ExCeL, London: international food and drink trade exhibition

The London Garden Show, Alexandra Palace, London

National Custom and Sports Car Show, Doncaster Exhibition Centre

Amateur Gardening Spring Show, NAC, Stoneleigh

Harrogate Spring Flower Show, Great Yorkshire Showground, Harrogate

Source: Access All Areas, February 2001.

the decision to attend has been taken, in order to get the maximum benefit from their attendance, most exhibitors undertake some form of promotional activity to draw attention to their presence at the event. This could take the form of:

● notifying existing and potential customers of their participation in the event using direct mail or e-mail;
● undertaking advertising in the relevant trade or consumer publications;
● organising some activity to draw visitors to the stand, e.g. live demonstrations of their products, a competition (such as a prize draw), or featuring a celebrity (occasionally termed an 'attractor').

Visitors

Also called the 'audience' for the event, the visitors are those who invest their time and money to attend the exhibition, either as a trade buyer or, in the case of consumer shows, as a member of the public. Their experience must be of the highest quality; if it is not, they will vote with their feet and leave in a disgruntled frame of mind, and will not return or recommend the event to friends or colleagues.

For this reason, provision must be made for their various needs: refreshments, toilets and rest areas, as well as telephones, adequate signage and printed show guides. In addition, those exhibitions laying claim to international status need to provide an interpreter service, an overseas visitors' lounge and multilingual information staff. Professional visitors, in particular, are likely to judge an exhibition by the quality of these various services.

Suppliers

Venues

The basic requirement for the hosting of an exhibition is the venue, the hall in which the event can be held. The venue owners' role is to provide covered space with access for transport to deliver on site, visitor reception facilities, carparking, and support services ranging from catering to first-aid, from security to cleaning.

Of all the venues used for exhibitions, the large purpose-built exhibition centres are the most visible. Used for the hosting of major trade fairs and consumer shows, these vast exhibition complexes, situated in and around major cities and conurbations, are able to provide the extensive surface areas required by large, international events, such as the annual World Travel Market in Earls Court, London, covering 14 acres of exhibition space, at which most countries in the world are represented as potential holiday destinations.

The location of exhibition centres is generally chosen to facilitate public access for the large numbers of visitors who attend such events. Clearly, city-centre locations, such as London's Earls Court and Olympia, make access very straightforward, but the vast area that most exhibition centres cover makes the cost of siting new facilities in city centres prohibitively expensive.

Lawson (2000; p.21) describes the range of sites that may be used:

New exhibition centres may be sited in the city, using redundant railway stations and sidings or in disused industrial or docklands ('brown' land sites), or on low value agricultural land, disused airports or exhausted mineral workings. In every case, however, this must be part of a regional development plan with provision for easy access from the international airport and city, junctions to the main highway network and an integrated system of frequent and fast public transport designed to carry the large numbers of public likely to attend. Good landscaping and associated development (business, research and/or science parks, hotels, shops, institutional and commercial buildings, recreation facilities) are important in generating an attractive image and viable services.

Exhibition centres may be owned and managed by the municipal authority or private-sector entrepreneurs, such as property companies. Some are part of multi-purpose complexes – Wembley, for example, includes a conference hall, exhibition halls with a total floor space of 17 000 m^2 and Wembley Arena. But, even when an exhibition centre is a stand-alone facility, it can usually also be used to host other types of events (conferences, entertainment events, etc.). Indeed, many exhibition centres depend on these other types of activity for essential income, in the same way as conference centres often do (see Chapter 3).

Exhibition centres are not the only type of facility suitable for trade fairs and consumer shows. Agricultural shows, for example, require extensive outdoor areas for the animals and farm machinery they exhibit, and air shows, such as the biennial event at Paris Le Bourget, where civilian and military aircraft are on display, need airports as venues.

In Chapter 3, we emphasised that exhibitions are often run in association with a conference on the same theme. For this reason, this type of exhibition is also hosted in conference centres and hotels, which often have dedicated exhibition space included on their premises.

In terms of where most of the world's facilities for exhibitions are situated geographically, the developed countries, with their established industrial bases and financial resources to invest in exhibition infrastructure, lead the way. Many of the cities of the USA, Japan and, increasingly, South-East Asian countries have developed the type of large, specialised trade fairs that appear on the global exhibition calendar each year.

But many of the world's most successful countries in this sector are to be found in Europe, and international trade fairs in particular are the jewels in Europe's exhibition crown. Among the thousands of trade fairs and consumer exhibitions held worldwide, some 1500 may be characterised as being of major international interest. They are located in 200 cities, about two-thirds of which are in Europe (Lawson, 2000). However, far from those European cities being spread evenly across the continent, the main exhibition venues are found in a limited number of regions situated at the heart of the European continent. Those regions are indicated in Figure 1.2, together with the main conference destinations of Europe (see Chapter 1).

Germany, France and Italy have long been at the leading edge of the trade fair concept in Europe. As a result, these countries are not only the most experienced at running such events but also have the largest venues. Each of these countries recognised from an early stage that trade fairs were an important source of import and export opportunities, and their head start has meant that they now have a more sophisticated and developed exhibitions infrastructure in terms of size and location. They also have a history of hosting large trade fair events, which over time have become major national and international events (Ladkin, 2000).

Another explanation for the success of France, Germany and Italy in this sector stems from the way in which their exhibition centres are funded. All three countries rely heavily on public-sector support to build and operate exhibition centres. The importance of this cannot be overestimated, in a market where, reflecting a similar situation to that of the conference centres described in Chapter 3, few exhibition centres generate sufficient funds to survive on a full commercial basis.

The best example of this approach to exhibition centre development and funding is Europe's (and the world's) leading trade fairs country, Germany, where cities such as Hanover and Munich dominate the market for large-scale events in this sector. Germany offers a number of competitive advantages for exhibition organisers and visitors: its long experience in staging world-class events, its favourable geographical location, and its good transport links and communications facilities. However, it is generally accepted that an important part of the reason for Germany's success is that most exhibition facilities are owned by city and state governments, who carry most of the property costs and employ their own fairs organisers. This means that the exhibition centres are not under pressure to reap profits from ticket sales or the amount of space they rent, but instead are recognised as important instruments for boosting the local economy. That helps Germany to outcompete the UK, for example, where property owners expect a decent return (*The Economist*, 1996).

However, as Dempsey (1996) has pointed out, an uncertain future hangs over fairgrounds in Germany because the cities and states may soon no longer be able to afford to continue to subsidise or own them and thus insulate them from genuine competition. With many German local authorities running overall deficits for most of the 1990s, they were under growing pressure from the federal authorities in Bonn to privatise or contract out certain services, from refuse collection to the maintenance of swimming pools and playgrounds. According to Dempsey, there is every reason to suppose that in the years ahead, the running of exhibition centres will be subject to the same discipline. Barber (2001) notes the same tendency, pointing out that although in the decades following the Second World War Germany's federal states, its big cities and even the federal government were inclined to pour public money into the trade fair business, increasingly German industry is coming under pressure to change its ways.

In contrast, the UK relies to a much greater extent on private investment than public funding of exhibition centres. One consequence of this is that there are far fewer venues capable of handling large-scale international trade fairs in the UK than in several other European countries. Examples of UK venues that do host large international exhibitions are the National Exhibition Centre (NEC) in Birmingham, operated jointly by Birmingham City Council and Chamber of Commerce, and Earls Court in London. Each is in the market for hosting large-scale exhibitions; indeed, the NEC managed to entice the 2003 International Textile Machinery Show (ITMA) to the UK away from its usual continental venues.

ExCeL in London's Docklands, which opened in 2000 with a total construction cost of £250 million met entirely from private capital, is also capable of competing in the market for these events. It will be in an even stronger position to do so when phase two of its development is complete in 2003; however, to put it in perspective, even when that phase is completed, the entire site will only be half the size of the NEC.

With the supply of large exhibition centres in the UK being so limited, Becket (2000) has remarked that major British exhibition organisers are increasingly having to organise events overseas: 'That is not just because it is cheaper to set up such events outside Britain, but because there is inadequate space for all the new exhibition ideas being brought to market. The main London halls such as Olympia and Earls Court are solidly booked for the high seasons of January to June and September to November.'

However, many believe that it is not only the UK's lack of available space for large international exhibitions that discourages such events from choosing British venues. One of the most prominent voices in the exhibitions industry is the executive director of United Business Media International Ltd (UBMI), an exhibitions operation that stages several hundred shows every year, in every continent. He speaks for many in the industry when he says that the UK exhibition sector needs to develop to remain competitive, including cost, transport, exhibition capacity and the integration of exhibitions with other events. Of these factors, cost would appear to be the most crucial (Gartside, 2001a; p. 15):

> The UK remains a very expensive place to put on shows. Venues and contractors within the UK have to continue to drive down their costs to compete at international levels. The cheapest country [in which to hold an exhibition] is the Netherlands. If we give the Netherlands a [price index] rating of 100, France scores 110, Germany 115, Italy 140 and the UK 150. So before we've done anything else, just to hire the venue and provide the service for our exhibitors, we're facing half as much cost again as the Netherlands.

On the more positive side, however, the same commentator emphasised that London and the UK have attractive images as exhibition destinations, adding that international shows in the UK will have better attendance from the USA and often Asia.

Another feature of the supply of exhibition facilities in Europe is that, in any given country, it tends to be concentrated heavily within a limited number of cities. Ladkin's (2000) report reveals that in Italy, France, Spain and Austria, the largest two venues in each country account for between 50 and 60% of events held there. This concentration is greatest in the UK, where 85% of all UK trade fair events take place in the top two venues – the NEC in Birmingham and Earls Court in London. In contrast, Germany's largest venues account for just 26% of events, and collectively the five largest German venues account for only 57% of that country's events. This is explained by the fact that in addition to its very large venues, Germany has a network of smaller regional exhibition centres.

Taken together, the leading 40 European trade fair cities account for 80% of all exhibitors and just under 70% of visitors. Within this, four leading trade fair cities – Paris, Milan, Hanover and Cologne – dominate the market (Ladkin, 2000).

Exhibition contractors

The exhibition contractors are those firms that produce services and facilities for exhibitors, exhibition organisers or the venue. The term 'contractor' covers the companies that offer any of the many different elements that are vital to participating in any exhibition, including lighting, flooring and furnishing, signage, freight handling and electrical services. However, perhaps the most obvious service that exhibition contractors provide is the hire and installation of exhibition stands. These can be either individually designed and customised on behalf of the exhibitor or provided as a standard modular unit or shell scheme. In either case, however, a contractor is usually engaged to construct, install and subsequently demount the stand. It is the stand contractor's responsibility to ensure that the structure of the stand is safe and that it complies with the detailed regulations supplied by the exhibition organiser, as well as those imposed by local authorities or fire officers.

Contractors may be nominated by the exhibition organiser or engaged directly by the exhibitor on the basis of past experience.

In the UK, the interests of exhibition contractors are served through their own association, the British Exhibition Contractors Association (BECA) (www.beca.org.uk), which, formed in 1913, is among the oldest established trade associations in the UK. From the point of view of the exhibitions industry as a whole, one of the most valuable services provided by this association is the BECA Bond, its Association Guarantee of Completion. Through this bond, exhibitors who appoint a full BECA member as their contractor have the guarantee that their stand will be finished and ready on the event's opening day. If the contractor becomes insolvent within seven days of the start of build-up, BECA will arrange for another contractor to complete the contract.

Intermediaries

Exhibition organisers

Exhibition organisers are essentially promoters and primary risk-takers. They may be private entrepreneurs, subsidiaries of publishing houses, or trade/professional associations. They vary greatly in size, from one-person operations to huge multinational conglomerates. Lawson (2000) notes how horizontal integration has led to the creation of large exhibition organiser groups – often with interests in publishing and other media.

Exhibition organisers are responsible for the production of events, from their conception to their completion. Within the exhibition organising team, there are three main roles, which the Association of Exhibition Organisers (AEO, 2001) describes as follows:

Marketing
The marketing team is responsible for researching the relevant sector of the industry at which the exhibition is aimed, in order to:

- find out if there is sufficient demand for the show (in the case of a new event);
- create leads for the sales team to follow up and convert;
- assess where the marketing team should focus its promotional activity.

The marketing team must then create a campaign, the nature of which will depend on whether the show is a trade or consumer event. The marketing executive will use a combination of magazine or journal adverts, posters, direct mail and other promotional devices to maximise publicity and attract as many visitors as possible to the event.

Sales

Sales professionals are responsible for all non-ticket revenue, from selling stand space to arranging sponsorship. However, their main task is to sell the conceptual package of the exhibition to potential exhibitors in the hope that they will buy stand space for the event.

Operations

The operations team is responsible for everything other than the sale of the stand space and the marketing of the event. It must book the venue, make sure all the necessary contractors are hired, and ensure that all required services are provided for exhibitors and visitors. Operations staff coordinate the build-up of the event and make sure that everything is in place ready for the opening of the show. During the event, the team liaises with exhibitors, contractors and visitors to ensure that everyone is satisfied. It must also be ready to deal with any difficulties that may arise. After the event, the operations team coordinates the smooth and efficient breakdown of the event.

In the UK, the AEO (www.aeo.org.uk) is the trade body for those who 'conceive, create, develop, manage, market, sponsor, supply or service trade exhibitions and consumer events'. The AEO undertakes a variety of activities on behalf of its members and the exhibition industry in general. These include developing a code of conduct, training and recruitment, lobbying, networking and information, industry research, and publishing a series of booklets for exhibitors such as *How to Exhibit* and *Measuring Exhibition Success*. The AEO also runs an exhibition industry promotion campaign entitled 'Exhibitions Work' (www.exhibitionswork.co.uk). This campaign seeks to heighten the profile of exhibitions and assist marketers in using them to their maximum potential, as well as to increase visitor attendance. In addition to its website, it is supported by an enquiry line and a series of printed guides that make a convincing case for using exhibitions as a powerful, cost-effective marketing medium. Figure 5.1 shows one of the advertisements put out by the campaign.

It is interesting to note that in the USA, a trade body, the Centre for Exhibition Industry Research, has also taken the initiative by launching an information campaign with similar aims: 'Exhibitions: You have to go to know' (www.gotoexhibitions.com). Using the website along with advertising and public relations, the Exhibition Industry Promotion Campaign is a 'multi-faceted programme communicating the value of exhibitions to business leaders and decision makers'.

Figure 5.1 AEO campaign advertisement

Source: Inside Communications Ltd.

Issues and trends

Growth

In common with other sectors in the business tourism industry, the demand for exhibitions tends to track the general state of the national and global economy. This was particularly apparent when the European trade fairs market, which had performed well in the latter part of the 1980s, suffered a considerable decline in mainland Europe in 1993–4. However, by 1996, the industry was once again restored to healthy growth rates (Ladkin, 2000).

One measure of the state of the market in Europe is provided by the research undertaken by the European Major Exhibition Centres Association (EMECA; www.emeca.com), which brings together in its membership 19 European major exhibition centres, most of which have an area of over 100 000 m² of exhibition space, a strong investment profile and an international dimension. The EMECA member venues and their exhibition capacities are given in Table 5.1.

Table 5.1 EMECA members venues

City	Total gross exhibition area (m²)		
	1997	**1998**	**1999**
Barcelona	141 100	141 100	141 100
Basel	142 800	142 800	133 000
Birmingham	158 000	158 000	190 000
Bologna	135 000	150 000	150 000
Brussels	114 362	114 362	114 362
Düsseldorf	203 900	203 900	205 200
Frankfurt	290 280	291 532	291 500
Leipzig	106 600	139 600	139 600
London	104 500	104 500	104 500
Lyon	92 657	92 657	92 657
Madrid	102 600	102 600	102 600
Milan	362 991	372 215	372 215
Munich	125 000	155 000	155 000
Nuremberg	133 000	133 000	133 000
Paris	212 140	226 000	226 000
Paris-Nord	164 058	164 058	190 600
Utrecht	181 380	170 207	162 780
Valencia	198 295	198 295	198 295
Verona	108 200	108 200	108 200
Total	**3 076 863**	**3 168 026**	**3 210 609**

Source: EMECA.

It is clear that the gross exhibition area provided by EMECA venues has increased significantly as additional capacity has been added and continued large-scale modernisation programmes have taken place. Has there been an increase in demand to match this increase in European supply of exhibition space? One of EMECA's activities is carrying out studies and surveys of exhibition activity in Europe. According to this research, over the 1994–9 period, the number of exhibitions increased significantly (+17.50%); during the same period, there was a marked growth in exhibitor participation (+19.12%) and visitor attendance (+33.21%). Table 5.2 demonstrates the recent growth in this sector in Europe in terms of the number of exhibitions, exhibitors and visitors.

The EMECA figures suggest that by 1999, Europe was still in a growth situation for exhibitions, but that growth rates were declining. The number of exhibitions increased by 3% between 1997 and 1998, but only by 1% in 1998–9. Visitor numbers increased by 10% and 2%, respectively, while supply increased by 3% in 1997–8, slowing to 1% in 1998–9. However, the amount of actual space rented, measured in exhibition days, fell by 3% in 1999, reversing a 14% rise in 1998 over the previous year.

Within the UK, exhibition business at the end of the twentieth century was reported to be particularly buoyant. Investment in the exhibition business among the marketing community was found to be running at record levels, and the spend on exhibitions, based on Chartered Institute of Marketing figures, was expected to reach £964m by 2002, a rise of 22.2% since 1997 (Zappaterra, 1999).

The AEO's data in Table 5.3 give details of more than half of the UK exhibitions held in venues of 2000 m^2 and over, excluding all one-day public events.

The progression indicated in both the numbers of visitors and the number of events being held appears to confirm the picture of a buoyant market in the UK. But the declining number of visitors per exhibition points to another trend in the market: the move towards smaller events. As will be explained in the next section, this trend is not confined to the UK.

Table 5.2 Growth of exhibitions in Europe

	1997	1998	1999
Facilities			
Exhibition hall capacity (m^2)	3 076 863	3 168 026	3 210 609
Key numbers			
Exhibitions	1 151	1 186	1 202
Exhibiting companies	392 176	411 651	419 961
Visitors	38 083 672	41 769 057	42 795 697
Business volume indicators			
Total gross exhibition area rented (m^2)	28 815 585	31 195 336	32 613 080
Total gross exhibition area rented (days)	398 503 162	453 426 365	439 389 905

Source: EMECA.

Table 5.3 UK exhibition demand 1991–9

	1991	1992	1993	1994	1995	1996	1997	1998	1999
Number of visitors (millions)	9 392	9 153	9 516	10 280	9 705	10 392	10 757	10 994	10 096
Number of events	660	672	671	691	733	710	841	843	817
Visitors per exhibition	14 230	13 620	14 181	14 876	13 240	14 636	12 790	13 042	12 357

Source: Exhibition Venues Association (EVA).

Smaller and shorter events

Not only have fewer visitors on average being attending exhibitions throughout Europe, but those events have been shrinking in size. Ladkin's (2000) report on the European exhibition market indicated that a long-term trend was the declining physical size of trade fairs: in Europe, the average size of exhibition events declined from 19 000 m² in 1990 to 14 900 m² in 1996.

There is general agreement within this sector that the trend for smaller exhibitions underlies the increasingly specialised nature of trade fair events. Indeed, it is widely thought that much of the growth in this sector may be attributed to increased diversification and interest in niche events. In the same way in which conference themes are becoming more specialised, trade shows are also becoming more focused. Lawson (2000; p.20) remarks that 'the trend in trade shows and exhibitions is not only to create sales, contacts and market orientation, but also to exchange ideas and information between experts, exhibitors and visitors. Exhibitions are becoming more specialised … and aimed at distinct target markets.'

Part of the objective in holding more focused events is to make them more efficient and productive. Becket (2000) quotes an exhibition organiser on this subject:

> After years of trying to get more people to our exhibitions, we are now trying to reduce the number of people attending. With the casual visitors – what stand organisers call the 'tyre-kickers' and leaflet collectors – now happily diverted by the Internet, the exhibition space can be used for more serious commerce. The time is long past when you wander into a large exhibition hall, start in one corner and systematically work your way round the exhibitors. Now people want to be able to set up meetings before they leave their home countries and have the whole visit organised before setting foot over the threshold.

An example of the trend towards smaller, niche-knowledge, specialist exhibitions is provided by an annual luxury jewellery exhibition held in the UK, which delegates attend on an invitation-only basis. The managing director of the exhibition's organisers, the Event Organisation Company, explains how it works (Chetwynd, 1999):

> We identify the key European players and send them personal invitations with letters. This is followed up with phone calls, always in the language of the delegate. We have to make the exclusivity work, forming a virtue out of necessity because there is no

great volume at the top end. To encourage delegates to make the most of networking opportunities at the exhibition, the company puts on restaurant-quality catering. There is also a dinner in the evening in first class restaurants, with delegates divided into groups according to region and type of activity, with a mix of buyers and sellers.

If this trend continues, what will be the implications for the future design of exhibition facilities, particularly in Europe? In their survey of the exhibitions industry, consultants Touche Ross (1994; p.2) noted that it was no longer the case that exhibition activity was concentrated in so-called 'blockbuster' exhibition centres in central Europe: 'In future, quite the opposite trend is likely to prevail, with a focus on quality rather than quantity, and on specialisation rather than volume, with central Europe threatened to be left with an oversupply of very large, inefficient, inflexible, exhibition centres.' The consultants also noted a fundamental change in the nature of exhibitions, with 'a trend towards niche marketing, the integration of other media, and the need for exhibitions to become more involved in buyer education, as product life-cycles reduce. This requires a new type of exhibition centre designed for flexibility of use and integrated with conference and seminar facilities' (Touche Ross, 1994; p.3).

The president of EMECA appears to support this view, expressing in an interview his belief that 'instead of huge German-style volume trade fairs, people want exhibitions that they can walk through in a day. Niche is the future' (Daneshkhu, 2001).

Return on investment

For exhibitors, participating in a trade fair or consumer show means investing substantially in preparation, promotion, stand design and build, as well as the many staff expenses incurred by their employees who work at the event. How can they be sure that this spending on exhibitions is bringing them a worthwhile return on investment? Do most of them know whether the same resources might be invested more profitably in other sales promotion techniques?

In the field of US travel trade shows, the transatlantic equivalent of shows such as the World Travel Market in Europe, Pizam (1990) found that the majority of exhibitors – state tourist offices – used only rough methods of measuring the effectiveness of their participation in these events. One of the most commonly used methods was found to be the measuring of the amount of literature distributed by exhibitors to visitors. But it is clear that this is something of a blunt instrument, as pointed out by the managing director of exhibition organisers, Pinewood Consulting, who firmly dismisses this particular evaluation technique (Zappaterra, 1999; p.36):

> Judging success by the number of leaflets handed out at a stand is meaningless if most of the people are just going to dump the mound of literature they've gathered into some cupboard, never to be seen again. We recommend that our clients don't indiscriminately hand out leaflets, but instead have all the literature ready to send out as soon as the show is finished and people are back in their offices.

The question of return on investment is a complex one in the exhibitions sector, as in other forms of marketing, and many exhibitors shrink from evaluating the success of their attendance because they believe that it is too inexact a science. Nevertheless, most of them are also aware that funding for participation in trade fairs has to compete with spending on other sales promotion techniques, and that rigorous evaluation is often required to demonstrate the effectiveness of this technique and to convince senior management of its worth at the next marketing budget round.

Pizam (1990) proposes a number of exhibition evaluation methods, classifying them into techniques to be used before, during and after the event.

Before the event

One of the methods that may be employed before attendance at any trade fair is a quantifiable technique for deciding which events are worth attending. This is based on assigning a relative weight of importance to each marketing objective and combining it with an 'impact rate', an estimation of the extent to which specific trade shows fulfil each of the potential exhibitor's own marketing objectives. Clearly, this technique depends on the exhibitor setting objectives in the first place, since without these, effectiveness cannot be measured realistically. Pizam suggests some examples of possible objectives:

- To increase awareness of the product by 10%.
- To contact 70% of the possible audience.
- To make 50 follow-up appointments.

The chief executive of Caribiner Europe, a company active in exhibitions organising, agrees that the evaluation strategy has to start well before the exhibition (Zappaterra, 1999; p.35):

> The starting point with any evaluation is to determine why you're exhibiting and what you're researching. A good way of doing this is to write down your top three objectives. With something like the Motor Show, the most important day is the press day, when an 'attractor' on the stand might get a company an appearance on *Top Gear*. So if you know that that is your objective, you can tailor your stand not to visitors, but to the press and its wider audience.

However, setting objectives that please everyone within the company or organisation represented at an exhibition often proves to be very difficult. This is demonstrated by the experience of one trade fair specialist, the head of marketing at Academy Expo, an exhibition and events agency. He points out that getting the sales department and the marketing department to agree can be problematic: 'Sales will judge the show on the number of leads, whereas the marketing department's objectives – things like promotion of brand values, brand reinforcement, good PR and so on – will be measured over a longer period' (Zappaterra, 1999; p.35).

Pizam (1990) also lays great emphasis on the use of trade fair audits in selecting which events to attend. Such audits, usually prepared by independent organisations, contain information on past attendance and characteristics of the visitors. One use to which a reliable audit may be put is to allow the potential exhibitor to estimate what Pizam calls 'exhibit efficiency', defined as 'the percentage of the audience with a high interest in seeing an exhibitor's products'.

During and after the event

An evaluation technique commonly used during and immediately following trade fairs involves the counting of enquiries and leads. This can take the form of exhibitors collecting visitors' business cards and classifying them as to what type of follow-up is required: a sales call, special literature, or investigation of a problem or complaint, for example.

Another possible post-exhibition activity suggested by Pizam (1990) is calculating the cost per enquiry by dividing the direct costs of exhibiting at the event by the number of visitors with whom contact has been made. However, he suggests that a more accurate measure of effectiveness is arrived at by calculating the cost per visitor reached. This is estimated by dividing the costs of exhibiting by the number of visitors who not only stopped at the stand to talk to a salesperson but also remembered doing so 8–10 weeks after the show *and* indicated an ongoing interest in the exhibitor's products. Clearly, this method depends on an audience survey being undertaken, which in itself involves more time and expense for the exhibitor.

Although estimating the return on this type of investment remains an inaccurate science, continuing spending on this form of business travel depends on efforts being made to justify the considerable financial investment it entails. But Zappaterra (1999; p.36) cites one exhibition organiser who highlights a potential problem: 'Good evaluation and research might show that maybe you'd be better off not exhibiting at all. For example, if past visitors' lists show that the people you most want to reach didn't attend, then a series of roadshows targeting those people could be a lot more beneficial.'

Information technology

Most exhibition organisers have been quick to recognise the opportunities that the application of information and communications technology (ICT) to the exhibitions sector has created.

Becket (2000) describes one of these opportunities, the use of websites to market exhibitions to potential exhibitors and visitors:

> Most of the organisers are now setting up their own web sites, which means that a four-day exhibition becomes a four-month promotional event. It actually involves a far greater range of participation and selling. Exhibition organisers can put on the internet a lay-out of the hall showing how the exhibition is being planned, and sell stand space. They can also organise sponsorship deals and sell advertising via the Web.

The online registration of visitors is another technique that is growing in use and that offers the advantage of being both faster and more convenient than postal registration. The commercial director of the QEII Conference and Exhibition Centre in London explains another advantage (Becket, 2000):

> We saw this trend starting to take off about 18 months ago. The major benefit of online registration to [exhibition] organisers is that they can keep updating their information. They can...keep people informed constantly. It makes the event much

more lively and interesting. The take-up of events using the internet is probably about 25 30%...It really does depend on the type of event being staged. If there is a fee attached, then online registration is a suitable option.

After visitors have registered online, website hyperlinks can be used to lead them to other relevant information. For large events, exhibitors and visitors can access a map of the show highlighting routes, locations and specific areas of interest. Smith (1999; p.44) quotes a representative of exhibition organisers, Brintex, who believes that the benefit for visitors is the simplicity of the registration procedure, while the advantage to the exhibition organiser is a higher number of actual visitor conversions. 'It is one thing getting delegates to sign up but another to actually visit the show. With online registration, once we have captured their e-mail details, we can keep in touch with them far more closely.'

Further tools may be added to the show's website, of which online diaries allowing visitors to make advance appointments with the exhibitors they wish to see, are one of the most useful. Such a system was used extensively in connection with the Meetings & Incentive Travel show at ExCeL in 2001: Appointment Scheduler, an online appointment system booked timed meetings for visitors with exhibitors.

However, despite the considerable advantages of online marketing and registration, it is generally accepted in the exhibitions sector that it is important to examine the profile of the delegates and consider whether they are sufficiently ICT-oriented before choosing this option. A key question must be: do they have access to the Internet? Enthusiasm for online registration will vary according to the nature of the event. For example, while exhibition organisers Venture Marketing's Insurance & Financial Services Technology trade show witnessed a seven-fold increase in visitors registering online (from just 7% to 49% in one year), its safety and security event, the UK Security Show, registered only 4% take-up of online registration in 1999 (Smith, 1999).

Figures such as these mean that most organisers will not consider converting totally to online registration and stand-booking. They understand that ICT extends the reach of their shows and makes things happen more efficiently; but until the use of e-mail and the Internet becomes almost universal, none of them will use it exclusively for marketing and registration purposes: the risk of excluding potential customers remains too high.

Going one step further is the use of ICT to generate online sales of exhibitors' products – a technique that is still at an early stage but growing. An example of this is described by Smith (1999; p.44): Web service provider Just Results has introduced e-commerce to exhibitions by creating a giant digital supermarket where exhibitors are able to sell their services and products over the Web all year round.

The first customers for this service are the organisers of the trade show, Mail Order Live, held at the NEC. This show, according to Just Results, marked the first time that an exhibition organiser set up free online shops for its clients, the exhibitors. Each exhibitor received free web space within Mail Order Live's 'shopping mall' web pages during the show, with the option of paying £35 per month to stay online afterwards. Just Results claimed that the scheme not only created an opportunity for exhibition organisers to generate extra revenue, but also provided closer contact with exhibitors throughout the year.

But if products can be viewed, described and sold via the Internet, then why should potential buyers go to the trouble of travelling to these events at all? And why should exhibitors go to the considerable expense of sending staff and merchandise to an event half way across the world when a virtual online trade show offers so many advantages, including:

● it is open to a global audience;
● it is open 24 hours a day, seven days a week;
● it can last all year, not only for a few days.

Paralleling the concern of those in the meetings industry who worry that advances in ICT might obviate the need for delegates to travel, anxiety has been experienced by some in the exhibitions industry over the possibility of the virtual trade fair taking away their business. Will exhibition visitors continue to attend or will they prefer to 'e-ttend' – peruse a range of products on screen and get e-mail answers to their questions about these without actually leaving their homes or offices?

The conclusion appears to echo that given in Chapter 3 concerning the impact of virtual and videoconferencing: a virtual trade fair is a complement to a live show rather than a direct competitor. Friedmann (2000; p.25) describes how organisers can use virtual trade shows to enhance the live event and extend its life:

> An online show can begin operation several months before the actual show. Research shows that 90% of show attendees have purchasing power but fewer than 10% have made contacts with exhibitors prior to a show. Visitors to the virtual show can make contact with companies ahead of time, which will greatly increase trade show effectiveness for both buyers and sellers. [Virtual] booths can include interactive demos, live online seminars, downloadable brochures and e-commerce capabilities. [By] using Webcasting for broadcasting audio-visual transmissions across the internet, virtual shows are able to feature convention seminars and keynote speeches from the actual trade show.

Friedmann quotes the results of a survey (*Tradeshow Week*, 29 November 1999), which revealed that in the USA, 25% of exhibitions also offered online versions of themselves.

Klein (1999) is one of many commentators who see virtual exhibitions as no real threat. She maintains that the exhibition industry prematurely predicted its own demise because of the Web, and that the rise of the virtual office has served only to reaffirm the importance of the human touch in doing business. Klein's belief, shared by many commentators, is that because ICT is having the effect of increasingly isolating people from each other in other domains of their work and leisure lives, these people are now even more motivated to attend trade fairs and consumer shows for, among other things, the human contact they bring.

Or, as the slogan of the previously mentioned Center for Exhibition Industry Research promotional campaign puts it, 'There are some things you just can't dot.com'.

More environmental awareness

It has been recognised for some time that gathering many thousands of people together for an exhibition is far from being an environmentally friendly act. There is the pollution generated by their travelling to the event in the first place. In addition, once at the venue, they are part of an event that may consume the equivalent amount of power to that required to run a small city, with all of its attendant CO_2 emissions. However, it is undoubtedly the sheer *waste* produced by exhibitions that creates the most serious impact on the local environment. And even though most exhibitors, exhibition organisers and the visitors themselves may be unaware of this, the contractors certainly know exactly how much waste is produced, since it is part of their job to get rid of it after the event.

As the director of BECA has put it: '[The contractors] after all, are responsible for hurling miles of used carpet, tonnes of packaging, reams of unused brochures and thousands of square metres of unwanted display material into the skip after the UK's 800 exhibitions every year' (Gartside, 2001b; p.38).

In response to the need to have more effective environmental policies for the exhibitions sector, BECA formed in 2001 a think-tank with the aim of fostering sustainable business practices. With the eye-catching acronym SEXI (Sustainable Exhibition Industry), one of the think-tank's first tasks was to examine waste management procedures in the industry, with a view to determining the extent to which recycling of waste could replace the use of landfill. The SEXI think-tank has other approaches to the problem of waste to consider: an examination of production processes within the exhibition contracting sector to identify where waste streams can be eliminated or their environmental impact reduced, and an evaluation of more environmentally sound materials for exhibition stand design.

Case study

National Starch & Chemical

Company background and products

National Starch & Chemical (www.nationalstarch.com), a member of the ICI group of companies, is a leading manufacturer of adhesives, speciality chemicals, resins, electronic materials, and speciality food and industrial starches. The company's products serve to adhere, bind, thicken, protect, strengthen and texturise a vast number of objects used in the home, in offices and in industry. They include, for example, key ingredients in food products, computers, paper, and beauty products such as lotions and hairsprays.

National was founded more than a century ago and now operates a global network of more than 125 manufacturing

and customer service centres located in 36 countries in six continents.

The company has its headquarters in New Jersey, USA, but it is organised around a number of global or regional divisions with a presence all over the world, including a number of European countries. These divisions are shown in Table 5.4, with some examples of the products of each division to demonstrate the wide range of markets served by National.

From the adhesive that sticks cereal boxes together to the ingredients that improve the taste and appearance of microwave meals, from the glue that keeps the pages of this book from falling out to the additive that determines

Case study *continued*

Table 5.4 Divisions of National Starch & Chemical

Adhesives	Speciality synthetic polymers	Electronic and engineering materials	Speciality starches
Used in	*Used in*	*Such as*	*Such as*
Non-wovens, e.g. disposable nappies	Personal care products, e.g. hairsprays, conditioners, mousses, sunscreens, skincare preparations	Conductive and non-conductive adhesive pastes for semiconductor packaging, microelectronic and opto-electronic assemblies	Speciality food starches, e.g. binders for meat, fish products and pet foods; coating agents to control texture, crispness and appearance in battered foods
Food and consumer packaging			
Envelopes	Industrial specialities, e.g. antiscalants for water treatment, deflocculants for oil-drilling applications	Speciality coatings and process lubricants for electronics, automotive, aerospace, appliance and other industries	Products that influence the expansion, texture and eating quality of cereals and snacks
Bookbinding			
Building components			
Automotive components	Emulsions, e.g. pigment binders in paints, coatings for carpets	Epoxy, silicone and acrylic adhesives for the electronic, fibre-optic, aerospace and medical markets	Strength additives for enhancing bulk and softness in paper tissue and towel manufacturing
Footwear			
	Construction materials, e.g. additives in cement mixes, flooring compounds and wallpaper adhesives		Starch additives to improve strength and printability for paper and board

Source: National Starch & Chemical.

how quickly shampoo comes out of its bottle, National products touch the lives of everyone, even if they are mostly unaware of it. For, like business travel itself, the need for most National products is driven by derived demand: products required by manufacturers because they are inputs that are necessary elements in the course of producing other goods.

National's use of exhibitions

Since most of the company's products are sold to other manufacturers, National makes full use of business-to-business trade shows to market its products to its customers and potential customers. Its use of exhibitions is determined by the annual communications plan of each division, which is, in turn, based on that division's objectives for the year. The marketing staff's task is to determine the optimum mix of marketing techniques for their

product range. In addition to trade show attendance, this will normally also include advertising, public relations, give-aways and collateral material, such as brochures, videos and multimedia products. Approximately 30% of National's marketing communications budget is spent on trade show attendance.

However, much depends on the particular product to be marketed. For example, in the case of the market for packaging adhesives, there is a vast number of potential buyers of National's products, making advertising in the trade press a worthwhile investment for the company as a way of reaching its clients.

By contrast, in the much more specialised non-wovens industry (manufacturers of personal items made from non-woven materials, e.g. disposable nappies, feminine hygiene products, adult incontinence products, surgical gowns), there is a small number of key players who are

▶

Case study *continued*

National's potential and actual customers. For that reason, advertising is not as cost-effective as face-to-face activities such as meeting clients at specialist exhibitions.

In Europe, for each product division there are one or two key trade shows that are absolutely imperative for the company to attend: the company aims not only to be present but to make a high impact. For example, it is vital for the company's speciality starches division to have a stand at DRUPA (the world's largest printing and graphics arts trade show, held in Düsseldorf every five years) in order to promote adhesives for bookbinding and other paper-converting applications. At such an event, National would make its presence felt by using a stand offering over 100 m^2 of exhibition space.

At the other end of the scale, there are a number of smaller, subregional events that National may attend on a trial-and-error basis, only repeating the experience if the show has led to new contacts and new business. This category would include the growing number of exhibitions in Central and Eastern Europe. However, even at these 'second-division' events, National would aim to have an eye-catching presence by using a stand that was more than simply the basic, standard-issue shell scheme.

Steve Gunn is National Starch & Chemical's European marketing communications manager. It is part of his responsibility to oversee National's use of exhibitions, and to ensure that the company derives maximum benefit from its investment in this form of marketing. His belief in the value of exhibitions is unwavering: 'We use exhibitions as an integral part of our marketing communications programme and find them particularly beneficial when entering new markets and geographic regions. They are a quick and effective way of raising your profile and testing new business opportunities, providing you think it through.'

Gunn identifies the three unique benefits of exhibitions as follows:

- Firstly your visitors arrive with a unique mindset which is keen to know about new development, new opportunities and new products. Compared to when they are busy sitting at their desks, visitors are simply much more inquisitive. They have come to the exhibition because they want to find out about new opportunities and an exhibition provides them – all in one place.
- Secondly we often find that a wide range of decision-makers attend exhibitions. It obviously benefits us to influence as many people as we can within an organisation and at an exhibition we often develop new contacts in companies with whom we are already doing business.

- Finally it is important that we can demonstrate the effectiveness of products in use. At an exhibition we can arrange quite complex demonstrations of our products which simply would not be possible within the constraints of a normal sales call.

Gunn stresses that exhibition attendance is not only about getting new sales leads. It is also about building relationships with other exhibiting companies, who are not necessarily National's direct competitors, to their mutual benefit. For example, at the DRUPA event described above, the owners of a stand demonstrating a bookbinding machine might be persuaded by National to use their adhesive in the machine and to display a sign directing interested visitors to the National stand.

The key objective is to attract visitors to the stand. To achieve this, Gunn emphasises the importance of either having the National stand located close to a stand that is likely to draw crowds – e.g. a working machine display – or having something eye-catching happening on the National stand itself to stop visitors in their tracks. Displays and demonstrations are used widely. For example, when National's food-related divisions attend food shows such as the Food Ingredients Europe (FIE) show, which rotates between Paris, Frankfurt and London, there are demonstrations and give-aways of products such as fat-free ice-cream and fibre-enriched pasta made using National ingredients.

To visually demonstrate a product such as an adhesive provides more of a challenge, but National often overcomes this by having a machine on its stand demonstrating the product in action. For example, a machine gluing labels on to bottles using one of National's adhesives is far more arresting than simply displaying pots of glue. Customer involvement is a useful technique too. On one occasion, passers-by were invited to stop at a National stand to tug at the pages of a book bound using one of the company's adhesives to test their strength against the glue's.

In general, National has a three-step approach to exhibitions, covering before, during and after the exhibition. Gunn believes that this approach offers the best chance of success:

- Before the exhibition, decide what the key themes of your presence there are to be. Make sure that you keep a focus on these key themes and that your messages and style are consistent in your pre-show mailings, your stand design and your exhibition

Case study *continued*

give-aways. 'Often we reflect the design of a key promotional campaign throughout our participation, from press ads and pre-show mailings right through to stand literature and give-aways.' It is also important to make sure that everyone who will be manning the stand is up to speed not just on the stand design, layout, key messages and so on, but also on how to be most effective when on the stand. If the objective is to collect sales leads, then National ensures that everyone on the stand understands this and has the paperwork and whatever is necessary to capture the information and the customers' interest in a structured manner that makes it easy to follow up on afterwards.

- At the exhibition, National takes advantage of every opportunity to provide an eye-catching three-dimensional feature. This may be a new product demonstration or a continuation of themes introduced in its preshow marketing campaign. Something large and new, colourful, moving or unusual seems to work best as far as grabbing attention goes. Frequently, National will also take the time to arrange social or business gatherings with its own international colleagues at the event. 'With so much pressure on people's time, we don't get the chance to meet up perhaps as often as we should and exhibitions are a good opportunity to build relationships with our colleagues from our overseas offices.' Events can also be organised for key customers and prospects.
- Thirdly, quick and effective follow-up of leads is required. 'If someone has registered interest in receiving additional information or even a product trial, there is nothing more frustrating for him or her than having to wait a month before hearing anything! This can negate all your up-front time and investment in steps one and two.'
- Immediately after the show, it is important to review what has worked well and what has not. Gunn conducts a review of the event's success against the objectives he had and uses this, combined with information from the organisers about visitor demographics and so on, to make a decision about future participation.

National Starch & Chemical at Pakex

Organised by Reed Exhibition companies, Pakex (www.pakex.co.uk) is the largest and most prestigious packaging exhibition in the UK. It is held at the NEC in Birmingham every three years. At the five-day event in 2001, National was one of the 1442 companies who came from 34 countries all over the world to exhibit at Pakex. Most were manufacturers of speciality packaging material, such as plastic film, injection-moulded packaging and blister packs.

The exhibition, which covered 78 000 m^2 of net floor space and 43 500 m^2 of exhibition space, was visited by 29 962 people, including 12% of buyers who attended on more than one day. Coming from 80 countries in total, including South Africa, Japan, Taiwan, Argentina, Israel, the USA, the Netherlands, Germany, Sweden, Saudi Arabia and Brazil, they were decision-makers and buyers who attended in order to do business with the exhibiting companies. Visitors came from a range of industries whose products require packaging, but food, confectionery, brewing and beverage sectors accounted for some 82% of the visitor base, with companies such as McVitie's, Tesco, Asda, Mars, Nestlé and Sun Valley in attendance. The cosmetics, pharmaceuticals and automotive sectors were also represented.

Some 87% of the visitors came from the UK, 9% from the rest of Europe, and 4% from the rest of the world. Pakex's own research found that 32% of all visitors had direct purchasing responsibility over £100k. In addition, 67% of the audience was at chairman, managing director, director or manager level, indicating that the exhibition succeeded in bringing key players with money to spend.

In 1998, National attended the Pakex event in order to promote its adhesives, which are used for packaging-related purposes, e.g. jar and bottle labelling and carton sealing. Figure 5.2 shows the National stand at Pakex.

How did National maximise the impact of its attendance at Pakex? A few of the techniques used are set out below:

- *Posters*: there was a series of posters on display along the wall of the walkway leading from the station to the exhibition hall. Based on the theme 'Packed with...', the posters were used to alert visitors to National's presence at Pakex and to draw attention to some of the company's packaging-related products. Designed to direct visitors to the National stand, the posters are shown in Figure 5.3.
- *Product launch*: during the exhibition, National made the most of the media interest in the event by launching a new 'all seasons' labelling adhesive, ETICOL 700, which can be used at a range of temperatures.
- *Press releases and newsletters*: to alert the press to the product launch and other company developments, National issued a number of press releases in advance of, and during, Pakex. An example of such a

▶

Case study *continued*

Figure 5.2 National Starch & Chemical's stand at Pakex
Source: Association of Exhibition Organisers.

press release, describing the qualities of National's PALLETFIX 321 product, is shown in Figure 5.4. Many exhibitors distribute brochures at exhibitions, but in addition to this National produced an exhibition newsletter for visitors to its stand. In a broadsheet format to give it more of the appearance of something carrying current and topical information, the newsletter was produced in colour and in a number of languages. It carried short articles that encouraged visitors to ask for further information at the stand itself.

- *Media packs*: National produced public relations media packs for the trade journalists attending the event. Some of these were distributed through the pigeon holes set aside for journalists in the exhibition's media room. Others were taken by National's staff directly to the key trade journals' stands, where editors were invited in person to visit National's own stand.
- *Reception for journalists*: National held a reception on its stand for members of the press, who were able to

see for themselves a number of demonstrations of National products in use.

- *Post-exhibition review*: after Pakex, National conducted a review of the leads that the trade show had generated for it by reviewing those who had visited its stand. This revealed that the types of leads were split three ways, approximately equally:
  - one-third were existing customers of National, contact with about half of whom was expected to lead to new business;
  - one-third were possible new customers for National, with long-term potential;
  - one-third were a variety of types of visitor, from consultants to allied suppliers.

The last word goes to Steve Gunn, who oversaw National's use of Pakex: 'Exhibitions can take considerable resources if you are to do them well, but if you have clear objectives and understand their role in the marketing mix then a bit of planning is all that is needed to make them extremely beneficial.'

Case study *continued*

Figure 5.3 National Starch & Chemical's poster campaign
Source: National Starch & Chemical.

Case study *continued*

NEWS RELEASE
Date: 27 March 1998
Editorial contact: Steve Gunn, tel: +44-(0)1494-467515

National Starch & Chemical
A member of the ICI Group

For immediate release .....

Pakex 98

Europe's most exciting
packaging event
March 30 - April 3
NEC England

A revolution in palletising: PALLETFIX 321 - the finest water-borne palletising adhesive

PALLETFIX 321 is a unique, new palletising adhesive that is waterborne. It bonds simple, recycled, sized and tough virgin papers and boards with clean release and is already fieldproven with a leading branded consumer goods company.

Apart from the obvious environmental benefits, PALLETFIX 321 will also please retailers because it will eliminate the problem of sticky hot melts transferring to the shelves in their retail outlets.

Key benefits of PALLETFIX 321

- It can be extruded, brushed, or sprayed.
- It provides a secure bond that 'cracks' apart without fibre tear.
- Once 'cracked', it leaves a rubbery nonsticky residue.
- It makes the containers restackable by virtue of its nonslip residue.
- It doesn't burn!
- It doesn't fume!
- It ensures lower maintenance costs and effort than hot melts.

For further details contact National Starch & Chemical, Galvin Road, Slough, Berks SL1 4DF. Tel: 01753-501321. Fax: 01753-539338.

- - *Ends (141 words)* - -

National Starch & Chemical European Operations, Windsor Court, Kingsmead Business Park, London Road, High Wycombe, Bucks HP11 1JU, England. Tel: +44-(0)1494-467500 Fax: +44-(0)1494-467560 Direct line: +44-(0)1494-467515

Figure 5.4 National Starch & Chemical's press release

Source: National Starch & Chemical.

Case study *continued*

Questions

1 Identify the various different players in Pakex: who are the organisers, buyers, visitors and intermediaries?

2 Find out if Pakex has any competitors; if so, where are the competing exhibitions?

3 What techniques could have been used to evaluate further the success of National Starch & Chemical's participation in Pakex?

Case study

CeBIT, Hanover

How an offshoot of the Hanover Fair developed into the world's largest trade show for information and communications technology and also the largest trade show of any kind, anywhere in the world

The German city of Hanover, with more exhibition space than the whole of the UK, has long established itself as a premier-league trade fair destination. Every year at the Hanover Exhibition Centre, thousands of suppliers and users from all over the world come together at CeBIT (www.cebit.de), the world's leading showplace for information and communications technology (ICT) and office automation. But the launch of the first CeBIT on 12 March 1986 was the outcome of a long and complex decision-making process.

The products and services of the computer industry had long been a key feature of the Hanover Fair (Hanover Messe), the world's biggest trade show for capital goods, organised by Deutsche Messe AG, one of the world's foremost exhibition companies.

By the late 1950s, the office equipment industry (as it was then called) already ranked as the third largest exhibitor group at the Hanover Fair. The fair reflected the electronics boom in the 1960s and provided the launching pad for numerous technological innovations. In 1965, for example, Heinz Nixdorf

(who was later to become one of Germany's best known entrepreneurs) launched his revolutionary 820 Universal Computer at the Hanover Fair.

In 1970, Deutsche Messe AG underscored the importance of office equipment at the Hanover Fair when it opened a new hall (Hall 1) to accommodate this sector, adjacent to the northern entrance of the exhibition centre. This massive building complex consisted of three levels: an underground garage with parking space for 2000 exhibitors; a ground-floor exhibition hall covering a total area of 70 300 m^2; and a roof level with 750 prefabricated cabins. In 1984, Hall 1 found its way into the *Guinness Book of Records* as the world's largest single-storey exhibition hall.

The inauguration of the new hall coincided with the search for a name for the part of the Hanover Fair dedicated to this fast-growing category of exhibitors. One suggestion was CeBOT – the German acronym for Center for Office and Organisation Technology. However, the Exhibitors' Advisory Committee decided in favour of CeBIT – Center for Office and Information Technology, not least because the syllable 'BIT' (the smallest unit of information handled by a computer) alluded to the growing importance of electronic data processing in the 1970s, and even more so in the 1980s, when PC manufacturers travelled in vast numbers to the Hanover Fair to exhibit their products.

▶

Case study *continued*

Nevertheless, in 1970 no-one could have foreseen the extent to which the data processing market would divide into more and more segments and grow at a breathtaking rate. As a result, the vast capacity of Hall 1 was soon filled to bursting point with exhibitors. At the end of the 1970s, Deutsche Messe AG decided to allocate also Halls 2 and 18 to CeBIT. At the beginning of the 1980s, CeBIT extended further, into Hall 3. However, demand for exhibition space continued to exceed the capacity available, as more and more data processing and software companies, as well as the growing group of PC manufacturers, wanted to use CeBIT as a platform at which to present their products. The original title, Center for Office and Information Technology, had now become the World Center for Office, Information and Communications Technology.

Nevertheless, numerous potential exhibitors were still excluded from CeBIT for the simple reason that Deutsche Messe AG was unable to offer them stand space at the exhibition. By 1980, the ICT product category at the Hanover Fair was outranked only by electrical engineering in terms of the number of exhibitors. In spite of the allocation of additional halls, it was not possible to reduce the long waiting lists of willing exhibitors. Nor was it possible to meet the demand for additional stand space on the part of established exhibitors. A split between CeBIT and the Hanover Fair appeared inevitable.

In November 1984, Deutsche Messe AG finally announced that, with effect from 1986, the Hanover Fair – CeBIT would take place annually as a discrete event in March, followed one month later by a separate trade fair, Hanover Fair – Industry. In 1985, the last amalgamated Hanover Fair underlined the urgent necessity of separating off CeBIT as a trade fair in its own right. Compared with 1970, the number of IT exhibitors had increased two-fold to 1308 – and a further 870 companies were on the waiting list. The rented stand space had grown two and a half times to 130 600 m², while the number of visitors had risen almost five-fold, to 293 000. With almost 7000 exhibitors and over 800 000 visitors, the 1985 Hanover Fair had reached its absolute capacity limits.

The decision to create a separate trade show for exhibitors of office technology and ICT was far from non-controversial. At the 1985 Hanover Fair, the separation of CeBIT was the principal topic of discussion. The pros and cons were still being debated hotly in the immediate run-up to the CeBIT premiere in 1986. The advocates of the split pointed to the extended exhibition space and improved infrastructure. The opponents argued that an independent CeBIT devoid of a broader industrial background would lose some of its appeal.

Exhibitors, visitors and Deutsche Messe AG thus looked forward to the CeBIT premiere with a mixture of suspense and trepidation. The moment of truth came on 12 March 1986, when 2142 exhibitors presented their products, systems and services on a net display area in excess of 200 000 m². In that year, the display category 'Telecommunications' was included in the CeBIT line-up for the first time – with 190 exhibitors. At CeBIT 2001, the telecommunications section boasted over 1100 exhibitors on a total display area of more than 107 000 m².

With 334 400 visitors, the first independent CeBIT got off to an encouraging start. Nevertheless, the debate about the split continued for a number of years. Many believed that the creation of a separate CeBIT show was the most momentous decision ever taken by Deutsche Messe AG and one of the biggest operations ever carried out in the international trade fair industry. CeBIT soon carved out a stronger and stronger position in the trade fair market, due in no small part to continuous refinements to the concept by Deutsche Messe AG. The major show categories became even more clearly defined, and exhibitors took advantage of the increased space capacity to present their products in multiple show sectors.

CeBIT rapidly developed into the largest and most important IT event of the year. The number of exhibitors and visitors increased continuously, despite freak weather conditions on two occasions. For example, two days before CeBIT '87 opened its gates, a sudden blizzard swept over the city of Hanover, leaving one metre of snow in its wake. The show nonetheless got off to a punctual start, thanks to the tireless efforts of countless

Case study *continued*

helpers. 'SnowBIT', as the fair was nicknamed that year, attracted 406 474 visitors.

By the beginning of the 1990s, the Hanover Exhibition Center (now completely at the disposal of CeBIT) was becoming more and more cramped, even though Deutsche Messe AG had begun to replace some old exhibition halls with new buildings. The halls were full to overflowing, and the waiting list of companies wishing to exhibit at CeBIT began to lengthen again. CeBIT was also facing another challenge: by 1995, the number of members of the public visiting the event had risen to 218 000 – 29% of the total attendance.

In an attempt to enable CeBIT to retain its character as a trade show for those in the IT industry, moves were taken to 'reprofessionalise' the event. First, admission prices were raised significantly. Second, the duration of CeBIT was reduced to seven days, in line with exhibitors' wishes. In addition, Deutsche Messe AG announced the creation of a new consumer show targeted at distributors and private users of PCs, multimedia and the Internet. This offshoot was to be called 'CeBIT HOME, the World of Home and Consumer Electronics'.

The premiere of CeBIT HOME in 1996 attracted 632 exhibitors, who occupied 52 248 m^2 of display space. A total of 215 000 visitors attended the show. In 1998, CeBIT HOME brought together 586 exhibitors on 48 370 m^2, and visitor attendance stood at 175 000. CeBIT HOME 2000 was scheduled to take place in Leipzig in order to make way for EXPO 2000 in Hanover. However, the event had to be cancelled due to the poor response from exhibitors.

Since 1996, the number of private visitors at CeBIT has declined continuously and amounted to only 12.6% in the year 2000. Accordingly, industry professionals accounted for 87.4% of total visitor attendance. During the seven days of CeBIT 2000, more than 780 000 visitors travelled to the Hanover Exhibition Centre to attend the event. This persuaded the CeBIT trade fair committee and the Executive Committee of BITKOM (the German Association for Information Technology, Telecommunications and New Media, Berlin/Frankfurt) to agree to a proposal by Deutsche Messe AG to extend CeBIT from seven to eight days beginning in 2002. A decisive reason for prolonging CeBIT was the sharp rise in visitor attendance and the large number of foreign visitors (approximately 130 000 in 2000), the argument being that exhibitors would be able to use the extra day to exploit this enormous potential and build international business relationships.

Its organisers claim that CeBIT has become the unchallenged international showcase for information and telecommunications technology, and that among its competitors, CeBIT is the only trade fair that has recorded sustained growth. CeBIT 2001 not only set a new record of 8106 exhibiting companies, but also had the highest number of foreign firms in attendance (3060 from 62 nations) of any trade show in the world. In fact, CeBIT is not only the largest trade fair for the IT industry, but also the largest trade show of any kind, anywhere in the world. Table 5.5 shows the development of CeBIT.

Tables 5.6 and 5.7 show the distribution of suppliers per product group and per country.

The success of CeBIT and the globalisation of the international trade fair industry have prompted Deutsche Messe AG to organise versions of CeBIT in three of the world's most promising markets for ICT: Turkey, Australia and China. The starting point was 'Bilişim', a CeBIT event held in Istanbul in September 2000, which has since become an annual event. The next element in this global CeBIT strategy is the trade fair, 'CeBIT Australia', which was first run in Darling Harbour, Sydney in May 2001. Finally, Deutsche Messe AG's plans to stage regular ICT trade fairs in China began with the first 'CeBIT Asia' show in Shanghai in August 2001. To accommodate this trade fair, the International Expo Center in Shanghai's Pudong Special Trade Zone was constructed as a joint venture between Deutsche Messe and Düsseldorf and Munich exhibition centres. This venue now boasts four exhibition halls with a gross covered area of 45 000 m^2, plus 10 000 m^2 of open-air exhibition space, making it one of the largest exhibition sites in Asia (for further details, see www. messe.de).

Case study *continued*

Table 5.5 The development of CeBIT

Year	Number of exhibitors			Net exhibition space (m^2)			Number of visitors		
	German	Foreign	Total	German	Foreign	Total	German	Foreign	Total
1970	508	130	638	49 455	5 880	55 335	55 400	5 500	60 900
1971	542	130	672	49 337	5 920	55 257	37 200	5 000	42 200
1972	551	132	683	50 093	6 223	56 316	90 000	9 600	99 600
1973	557	132	689	50 565	6 356	56 921	96 100	12 800	108 900
1974	654	136	790	55 687	7 104	62 791	86 600	19 900	106 500
1975	491	140	631	52 506	7 478	59 984	88 400	13 600	102 000
1976	502	143	645	55 464	7 550	63 014	90 500	21 800	112 300
1977	531	156	687	56 828	7 841	64 669	135 100	23 900	159 000
1978	563	159	722	67 935	7 685	75 620	116 200	15 800	132 000
1979	667	189	856	78 179	11 784	89 963	123 900	20 200	144 100
1980	685	205	890	82 432	13 804	96 236	154 700	29 500	184 200
1981	683	229	912	87 253	13 576	100 829	142 000	27 000	169 000
1982	689	293	982	96 045	18 329	114 374	165 900	36 400	202 300
1983	697	344	1 041	97 760	19 270	117 030	200 900	47 100	248 000
1984	821	391	1 212	108 074	20 718	128 792	237 800	52 200	290 000
1985	934	374	1 308	111 784	18 920	130 704	243 200	49 800	293 000
1986	1 462	680	2 142	169 084	33 801	202 885	271 392	63 035	334 427
1987	1 467	781	2 248	168 926	36 752	205 678	336 992	69 482	406 474
1988	1 750	981	2 731	179 238	38 850	218 088	387 879	98 002	485 881
1989	2 026	1 188	3 214	188 326	42 831	231 157	413 660	97 491	511 151
1990	2 557	1 576	4 133	214 742	49 289	264 031	480 104	80 956	561 060
1991	2 863	1 751	4 614	225 750	55 505	281 255	487 723	90 833	578 556
1992	3 357	2 045	5 402	247 388	59 183	306 571	557 309	91 596	648 905
1993	3 562	2 190	5 752	249 089	60 614	309 703	558 411	102 273	660 684
1994	3 567	2 278	5 845	242 149	64 408	306 557	576 738	105 811	682 549
1995	3 669	2 442	6 111	251 901	65 774	317 675	653 939	101 387	755 326
1996	3 957	2 592	6 549	261 784	76 282	338 066	518 181	88 759	606 940
1997	4 250	2 659	6 909	271 923	80 650	352 573	506 090	100 072	606 162
1998	4 502	2 737	7 239	283 237	88 186	371 423	556 419	122 141	678 560
1999	4 521	2 891	7 412	304 300	94 613	398 913	576 442	121 877	698 319
2000	4 934	2 958	7 892	318 801	98 643	417 444	651 414	130 596	782 010
2001*	5 046	3 060	8 106	330 900	100 711	431 611			

* Preliminary figures

Source: CeBIT.

Case study *continued*

Table 5.6 Number of suppliers according to product groups

Product group	Number of exhibitors			Net rented space (m²)		
	2001*	2000	1999	2001*	2000	1999
Information technology	1 368	1 438	1 382	108 308	111 789	106 595
Data processing systems	229	273	311	44 476	47 332	48 774
Tower/palmtop PCs	70	82	82	7 939	8 239	9 657
Computer components and extension units	238	249	253	9 479	10 191	10 292
Peripheral equipment and OEMs	367	314	312	25 757	23 995	20 545
Accessories, maintenance and waste disposal	178	197	152	6 260	8 644	4 985
Multimedia hardware	286	323	272	14 397	13 388	12 342
Network computing	448	430	401	20 384	19 707	18 946
Engineering, design, manufacturing, planning, automatic data collection (hardware)	378	391	347	12 774	13 423	12 063
Software	3 035	2 947	2 744	93 110	90 172	86 108
System, operating and development	181	211	215	9 555	10 526	11 774
Application (branch- and task-oriented)	1 638	1 577	1 530	49 690	48 864	47 744
For engineering, design, manufacturing, planning, ADC	443	457	461	15 776	15 764	16 122
For multimedia	96	131	131	1 820	2 033	1 975
For Internet and online services	348	274	195	7 527	5 116	3 021
For municipal and public administration	277	248	178	7 673	7 075	5 107
For telecommunications	52	49	34	1 069	794	365
Consulting and services, online services	615	473	421	21 634	16 361	11 360
Information technology services and consulting	231	154	113	4 986	3 720	1 819
Internet services	213	133	113	8 602	4 665	2 798
Other consulting and services	171	186	195	8 046	7 976	6 743
Telecommunications	1 112	1 063	1 080	107 669	97 095	96 044
Office technology	391	405	408	45 678	47 203	46 467
Banking technology	196	193	200	9 169	8 923	10 028
Card technology and security equipment	212	213	185	8 048	8 040	6 776
Research and technology transfer	351	339	244	4 837	4 730	4 526
Total number of exhibitors/m²	**8 106**	**7 892**	**7 412**	**431 611**	**417 444**	**398 913**
Special displays				1 095	1 870	1 870
Total CeBIT	**8 106**	**7 892**	**7 412**	**432 706**	**419 314**	**400 783**

* Preliminary figures

Source: CeBIT.

Case study *continued*

Table 5.7 Exhibitors and exhibition space according to countries

Country/region	Number of exhibitors			Net exhibition space (m²)		
	2001*	2000	1999	2001*	2000	1999
Argentina	1	4	8		24	32
Armenia	4			14		
Australia	26	27	37	332	429	449
Austria	75	68	69	2 961	2 230	2 417
Bangladesh	7	10	14	28	52	35
Belarus	15	13	20	83	84	88
Belgium	78	70	78	3 099	3 148	2 818
Brazil	6	3	15	121	77	80
Bulgaria	10	7	1	68	50	20
Canada	37	30	29	692	836	774
Chile			1			
China, People's Republic	24	30	17	447	550	408
Colombia	7	11	12	54	52	53
Czech Republic	20	19	18	501	438	371
Denmark	44	34	33	1 536	1 442	1 665
Ecuador		2			8	
Egypt	9	9	6	125	125	60
Estonia		1	1		70	12
Finland	61	52	47	1 573	858	1 083
France	107	111	118	5 066	5 423	5 829
Georgia	4			48		
Great Britain	333	324	314	10 683	10 273	10 137
Greece	20	14	13	571	679	607
Hong Kong (SAR)	85	77	74	1 659	1 532	1 497
Hungary	4	17	18	114	288	210
Iceland	8	8	8	70	70	70
India	23	25	21	289	387	314
Indonesia		1	1		6	20
Ireland	32	27	33	801	578	810
Israel	106	84	85	2 694	2 531	1 808
Italy	88	81	96	4 404	4 716	4 709
Jamaica		1			4	
Japan	34	34	43	1 944	2 141	2 730
Jordan	6	7	6	40	40	36
Kuwait		1				
Latvia	5	7	7	50	58	48
Lebanon	1					
Liechtenstein	1	1				

Case study *continued*

Table 5.7 *continued*

Country/region	Number of exhibitors			Net exhibition space (m²)		
	2001*	2000	1999	2001*	2000	1999
Lithuania	6	5	2	72	52	46
Luxembourg	17	15	12	650	639	364
Malaysia	20	30	15	257	373	191
Mauritius	1	1		20	20	
Mexico		3	3		79	63
Monaco	1	1		24	24	
Nepal		5	2		20	24
Netherlands	98	109	121	11 639	12 954	9 269
Norway	19	17	20	915	813	837
Pakistan	5	5	7	60	60	60
Poland	15	14	13	718	651	427
Portugal	11	9	12	322	297	282
Romania	14	13	1	102	75	
Russia	75	63	63	1 024	902	655
Singapore	36	40	42	787	1 076	973
Slovakia	1	1	1	45	25	25
Slovenia	8	10	8	182	163	147
South Africa	1	2	4		21	20
South Korea	98	66	38	2 791	2 473	1 838
Spain	50	45	55	1 357	1 224	1 161
Sri Lanka	1			25		
Sweden	111	111	89	7 101	6 434	5 327
Switzerland	121	131	113	5 349	5 680	5 283
Taiwan	529	507	510	13 951	13 222	13 057
Thailand	9	9	9	67	62	110
Tunisia	1			18		
Turkey	10	10	13	242	316	414
Ukraine	41	46	41	320	374	393
United Arabian Emirates	1	2	2	16	25	57
USA	478	478	451	12 574	11 390	14 382
Vietnam	1		1	16		18
Total	**3 060**	**2 958**	**2 891**	**100 711**	**98 643**	**94 613**
Germany	5 046	4 934	4 521	330 900	318 801	304 300
Grand total	**8 106**	**7 892**	**7 412**	**431 611**	**417 444**	**398 913**
Special displays				1 095	1 870	1 870
Grand total CeBIT	**8 106**	**7 892**	**7 412**	**432 706**	**419 314**	**400 783**

* Preliminary figures

Source: CeBIT.

▶

Case study *continued*

Questions

1 During the first few years of the 1990s, the IT industry was operating in the context of a recession in the world economy. Is there any evidence of this in the CeBIT data given in Table 5.5?

2 It was mentioned that, among its competitors, CeBIT is the only trade fair that has recorded sustained growth. Find out which events are CeBIT's principal competitors. How do they compare with CeBIT in size and rate of growth?

3 Use the data presented in Tables 5.6 and 5.7 to describe recent developments in exhibitors attending CeBIT.

References

AEO (2001), *Career Opportunities in the Exhibition Industry*, Berkhamsted, Association of Exhibition Organisers.

Barber, T. (2001), 'Strengths and weaknesses on display: Germany', *Financial Times*, 11 May.

Becket, M. (2000), 'People just want to go on meeting like this', *Daily Telegraph*, 10 January.

Chetwynd, C. (1999), 'The specialists', *Marketing Week*, 13 May.

Daneshkhu, S. (2001), 'Flexibility becomes keyword', *Financial Times*, 11 May.

Dempsey, C. (1996), 'Leipzig changes ways', *Financial Times*, 14 February.

The Economist, (1996), 'Messe business', *The Economist*, 20 January.

Friedmann, S. (2000), 'Virtual trade shows thrive on the web', *Convene*, 5 January.

Gartside, M. (2001a), 'Exhibitions now!' *Access all Areas*, February.

Gartside, M. (2001b), 'Waking up to waste', *Access all Areas*, July/August.

Klein, K. (1999), 'Trade secrets', *Business Week's Frontier*, 16 August.

Ladkin, A. (2000), 'The European exhibition market', *Travel & Tourism Analyst*, Vol. 2, pp. 49–63.

Lawson, F. (2000), *Congress, Convention and Exhibition Facilities: planning, design and management*, Oxford, Architectural Press.

Pizam, A. (1990), 'Evaluating the effectiveness of travel trade shows and other tourism sales promotion techniques', *Journal of Travel Research*, Vol. 29, pp. 3–8.

Smith, W. (1999), 'Easy entrance', *Marketing Week*, 22 July.

Touche Ross (1994), *Royal Victoria Dock Proposed Exhibition Centre Demand: Specification Study (Executive Summary)*, London, Touche Ross & Co.

Zappaterra, Y. (1999), 'Proving your worth', *Marketing*, 25 February.

Chapter 6

Corporate hospitality

Objectives

On completion of this chapter, you should be able to:

- *define corporate hospitality and assess its role within the marketing mix;*
- *explain the reasons for its growth;*
- *explain the challenges associated with attempts to measure its effectiveness;*
- *define the roles of corporate hospitality suppliers and organisers;*
- *identify external and internal issues that affect the corporate hospitality sector;*
- *assess the ethical issues associated with the use of corporate hospitality.*

● ● ● Corporate hospitality in the twenty-first century

- Fosters entertained 800 invited guests to the Melbourne Grand Prix, providing them with food, opportunities to meet celebrities, and as much beer as they could drink.
- Plough Lane Landscaping of Wiltshire hosted an evening of go-karting near Swindon for 15 site managers from local housing development companies. The guests competed in a 'grand prix', with prizes ranging from a case of champagne to a wooden spoon, and then enjoyed a meal out at a nearby steakhouse.
- The *Travel Trade Gazette* entertained travel recruitment organisations to a day at the races, providing them with entry passes to Royal Ascot and limitless beer and wine throughout the day.
- CAT publications played host to 600 guests for a summer party at Chelsea Football Club's ground. Activities included a range of sports activities and games on the famous Stamford Bridge pitch before an evening of food, wine and entertainment in the club's hospitality suite.

● ● ● ● Introduction

Three days before the start of the annual Wimbledon tournament, lorry-loads of Pimms are delivered to the labyrinth under Court Number One, where the 1500 extra catering staff recruited for the fortnight will later work through the night hulling 27 000 kilograms of strawberries. The signs are unmistakable: two weeks of corporate hospitality partying at Wimbledon are about to begin.

Corporate hospitality is exactly what the name suggests: hospitality extended by companies. Also known as corporate entertainment, this form of business travel involves companies inviting their guests to attend, at no charge, a memorable event or organised activity, usually lasting one day or less. Such events can be either *participative experiences* – e.g. inviting the guests to take part in a golf day, sailing or clay-pigeon shooting – or *spectator events* – e.g. invitations to prestigious performances of operas or ballet, or to a World Cup final or a day drinking Pimms and champagne and eating strawberries at Wimbledon.

Corporate hospitality events may be classified into the types of activities shown in Table 6.1.

Whatever the event or activity, however, the entertainment that companies lavish upon their guests is inevitably highly generous, and the pleasure quotient very high. It would be a rare corporate hospitality event at which champagne or fine wines did not flow liberally before, during and after.

But despite the emphasis on fun and excitement, the objectives behind this corporate largesse are entirely serious and connected closely to the host companies' business objectives. What are the uses of corporate hospitality and who are its fortunate recipients?

Table 6.1 Classification of corporate hospitality events

Sporting events	Take-part events	Shows	Trips and tours
Grand Prix	Rallies	National summer shows	Daytrips
Horce racing	Racing circuits	Flower and garden shows	Shopping days
Regattas	Helicopter rides	Indoor events (e.g. Earls Court and Olympia)	Overnight stays and weekends
Tennis tournaments	Flying lessons		
Golf tournaments	Clay-pigeon shooting	Theatre	Mini-cruises
Football matches (domestic and international)		Premieres	Round-trip flights
		Exhibitions	Extended stays
Rugby matches			

Source: Adapted from Burton, J. (1999), *Business Development and Account Management*, London, GBTA. Reproduced with the permission of the Guild of Business Travel Agents.

Uses of corporate hospitality

Corporate hospitality is a valuable tool used by companies to forge and foster relationships with key players, both internal and external to the company, and to raise awareness of the company or brand in influential circles. 'Relationship management' is the phrase used to describe the technique of forming close bonds with those people who are important to the competitiveness and profitability of companies. Along with other marketing techniques, such as advertising and public relations, corporate hospitality can be a highly effective method of establishing and maintaining a positive image for the companies who invest in it, and ultimately improving their business performance.

Five main groups may be targeted:

- *Actual and potential customers and suppliers*: this is the group most often invited to enjoy corporate hospitality. 'When the right event and the right mix of people are brought together [corporate entertaining] performs a valuable function in building relationships between clients and suppliers' (Greaves, 2000; p.35). Sixty per cent of companies surveyed in 2000 by Sodexho expressed the belief that 'nurturing relationships with clients could not be secured in any other way' (Greaves, 2000; p.35).
- *Intermediaries and agents*: who are likely to buy or recommend the host company's products or services.
- *The financial community*: including investors and potential investors.
- *Key 'influencers' or advocates*: i.e. the general media and trade journalists, and local and national politicians.
- *Members of the local community*: who are likely to affect or be affected by the host company's operations.
- *'Internal' customers*: the company's own staff.

When corporate hospitality events are organised for a company's own staff, there is inevitably a significant level of similarity between these events and the incentive travel awards described in Chapter 4. The employer may have similar aims and objectives: motivating staff or rewarding them for achieving their sales targets; partners and spouses may be invited along; and the event will provide an opportunity for colleagues to relax together. However, one key distinction between incentive travel and corporate hospitality is that while an incentive trip usually includes at least one overnight stay, the latter rarely does. Since the use of business travel to motivate staff has been dealt with in detail in Chapter 4, this chapter will deal specifically with the more usual use of corporate hospitality – as an external marketing technique.

In general, an organisation may aim to achieve one or more different results by investing in corporate hospitality, for example:

- to create a positive and favourable impression of itself with a target audience;
- to develop a relationship with, and the allegiance of, a target audience;
- to stimulate potential customers and advocates to aspire to future guest status;
- to use the corporate event as a showcase for its own products and services.

A successful example of the use of corporate hospitality is seen in the case of Unipart, Europe's leading independent logistics and automotive parts company. Unipart has used corporate hospitality for many years to build goodwill with a variety of bodies, from local authorities and government ministers to chairmen of supplying companies. The great diversity of venues and events used reflects the different groups of guests the company chooses to entertain.

In the past 20 years, Unipart has held dinners at Blenheim Palace, the Guards Museum and the Foreign Office. The company has also invited 30 guests, including the heads of Honda and Rover, to the Henley Regatta and taken its contacts in the City to the Henley Music and Arts Festival. For 800 garage owners and their families, Unipart has organised fun days out at the Waddington Air Show, while heads of car companies and their partners have been entertained with several days flying at Château d'Oex in Switzerland.

A representative from the company describes Unipart's philosophy regarding corporate hospitality: 'Every penny has to work and we drag so much value from it. There is no definitive measurement but it builds a rapport and an opportunity to talk freely in a social environment. It opens doors, and clients understand our ethos. There is no price to be put on that' (Upton, 1998; p. 30).

The types of objectives that companies have for corporate hospitality indicate that it may be used as a tool to achieve results of the type that, more generally, relationship marketing aims to deliver. Relationship marketing has been defined as marketing 'based on relationships, networks and interaction, recognising that marketing is embedded in the total management of the networks of the selling organisation, the market and society' (Gummeson, quoted in Lovelock, 2000; p. 149).

In general, relationship marketing is used by companies to move their targets to the top of what has been called the 'ladder of loyalty', so that they become

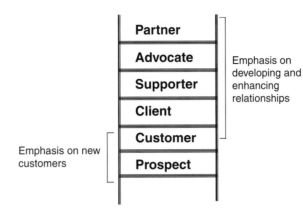

Figure 6.1 The ladder of loyalty

Source: Based on Christopher, M., Payne, A. and Ballantine, M. (1991), *Relationship Marketing*, London, Butterworth-Heinemann, in Palmer, A. (2001), *Principles of Services Marketing*, 3rd edn, McGraw-Hill, Maidenhead. Reproduced with the permission of McGraw-Hill.

advocates or even partners of the company. Figure 6.1 illustrates this in diagrammatic form.

A major aim of relationship marketing is achieving customer retention – converting customers into loyal clients. Corporate hospitality, as a relationship marketing tool, can be a highly effective way of doing this. This type of client is important to companies for a number of reasons:

● It is generally more profitable for a company to retain existing customers rather than constantly recruiting new clients.
● Loyal customers are likely to be repeat purchasers, the value of whose purchases may increase over time.
● The word-of-mouth advocacy of loyal clients is valuable, since the people with whom they associate often belong to the same target market segment.
● Once an organisation has built a relationship with customers, their tolerance of a one-off difficulty or service failure will be greater.
● Once a relationship has been established with a customer, the operational costs of dealing with that customer will be reduced because (1) details of their needs and preferences are likely to be held on a system, and (2) the customer's experience of the organisation will mean they usually require less help during the buying process.

Palmer (2001) classifies three levels of relationship marketing: tactical, strategic and philosophical. Corporate hospitality and entertainment is used at all three levels.

Tactical relationship marketing is a form of targeted sales promotion made possible through advances in market information collection and analysis. Focusing more on the lower rungs of the ladder of loyalty, potential customers are targeted with an offer designed to appeal specifically to them, so that a relationship with the company can be initiated. A mailshot from a credit card company offering an introductory very low rate of interest for new cardholders is an example of such tactical relationship marketing. A prospect who takes advantage of such an offer may develop into a loyal and long-term client.

Although a somewhat risky investment in some cases, corporate hospitality is occasionally offered at this level. For example, a travel agency and cruise company may co-fund an evening's hospitality for 'known cruisers' in a particular locality. The evening would provide the opportunity for guests to become clients of either or both the agency and cruise company, and subsequent, more strategic relationship marketing strategies could be used to entice them further up the ladder. When corporate hospitality and entertainment are used at the tactical level, its budget is generally comparatively modest and may extend to little more than cheese and wine and the screening of a film on cruises. But occasionally other factors, such as the public relations value of local newspaper coverage and the improved product knowledge of travel agency staff involved in the evening, may help to justify higher investment.

Strategic relationship marketing involves the creation of a more formal tie between an organisation and its selected public, with both parties benefiting from the union. 'Through a process of mutually rewarding co-operation, mutual dependence and shared risk, the relationship is likely to show greater stability and endurance' (Han *et al.*, 1993). An example of a successful strategic relationship marketing arrangement in the travel industry is that of the shipping company P&O's shareholders' scheme, where all shareholders enjoy price reductions on travel with that company. Not only does this help tie them into using P&O; it also ensures they book early to qualify for their reductions, making the task of P&O's yield management department an easier one.

Examples of corporate hospitality being used to reinforce a strategic relationship are common in business travel itself. Business travel agencies occasionally organise hospitality and entertainment packages for the bookers from their major corporate accounts. Such packages could include a free daytrip by air to a short-haul destination, with a meal arranged at the destination. Time could be allocated during the day for a brief presentation to the travel bookers and, possibly, an update on the agency's booking procedures; but the majority of the day would be devoted to giving the guests a good time, thus strengthening the relationship between them and the agency. The desired outcome of the day from the point of view of the host business travel agency would be for the company bookers to move up to the 'advocate' rung of the ladder of loyalty.

Philosophical relationship marketing has been described as the refocusing of marketing strategy away from products and their lifecycles towards the lifecycles of customer relationships, involving the 'integration of a customer orientation, competitor orientation and interfunctional co-ordination ... using all employees of an organisation to meet (profitably) the lifetime needs of targeted customers better than competitors' (Han *et al.*, 1993). Organisations striving to achieve this focus regard the creation of effective relationships with *all* of their publics as pivotal to their business success. Corporate hospitality, tailored carefully to meet – or exceed – the expectations of the different publics with whom relationships are being sought

Figure 6.2 A typical example of lavish corporate hospitality
Source: Reproduced with the permission of Legoland, Windsor.

or strengthened, is used widely at the philosophical relationship marketing level. Indeed, most of the spending – and certainly most of the lavish spending – on corporate hospitality occurs at this level (Figure 6.2).

However, as has been indicated, a company's clients and intermediaries are only two of the audiences that it may choose to target with corporate hospitality. As well as being used to develop a long-term bond between seller and buyer, corporate hospitality is also used by companies as a method of strengthening links with key people and organisations in the business environment, in such a way that they become active supporters of the company. The support that these links can create can be crucial for the survival and prosperity of companies. For example, it is clearly in the interests of an airline to have the support of not only its customers and intermediaries, but also:

● the media (including the trade press)
● influential business bodies (e.g. ITM)
● travel trade bodies (e.g. GBTA)
● investors
● suppliers
● airports

- governments and any other organisation that could have some influence on its sales and operations.

The following section examines the organisations that make corporate hospitality possible through the facilities and services they supply to the market.

Suppliers

The suppliers in this market take the form of a great variety of organisations, large and small, operating in a great diversity of fields. It is a market with many attractive features for suppliers, not least the fact that this is one of the most high-spend, high-yield sectors of business-related travel and hospitality. For many suppliers, particularly the venues, corporate hospitality also represents a means of using spare capacity to increase their revenues, quite considerably in many cases.

Most corporate hospitality events comprise three main elements: the venue, the entertainment/activity and the catering. In many cases, the venue already includes all of the services and facilities required to provide for the comfort and entertainment of the client's guests. However, a considerable number of ancillary services are often required, such as marquee hire, security staff, lighting, and floral arrangements for decoration. An event held in the grounds of a stately home, for example, will call for the services of a number of different suppliers.

Additionally, guests may be provided with transport to and from the venue as well as souvenir gifts to take away with them. Given that the aim of corporate hospitality is to create a positive and lasting impression on guests, successful coordination of all these supply elements is necessary to produce the desired outcome. Each of the main elements will be considered in turn.

Venues

Prestige events in famous venues are generally considered to be among the most effective occasions at which to offer corporate hospitality. In the UK, for example, the British Grand Prix, Wimbledon and Royal Ascot have been described as the 'stalwarts of the industry' (Greaves, 2000; p.35). Sodexho, a major player in the organising of corporate hospitality events, includes Glyndebourne, the Chelsea Flower Show, Royal Ascot, Wimbledon, the Henley Regatta, the British Open Golf Tournament and the Pink Ribbon Charity Ball in its own list of exclusive high-profile UK corporate hospitality events. The respondents to the Sodexho 2000 survey voted as their top events Royal Ascot, Glyndebourne, Celebrity Golf Day, race days at Newbury and Cheltenham, World Cup football in Moldova, the Variety Club dinner and the Royal Tournament. Internationally, the Formula One Grand Prix circuit has been widely acknowledged as 'the most exclusive place to entertain a VIP corporate guest' (Levy, 1999; p.24).

Clearly, sporting venues and events are widely considered to be highly suitable for the corporate hospitality market, and their popularity shows no sign of waning. Football, in particular, is regarded as a very attractive option, as witnessed by the many companies who hire boxes at Premier League club games to entertain clients. The growth in demand for corporate hospitality at football grounds has been described as an 'explosion' by the sales manager for Tottenham Hotspur, at whose ground up to 4800 guests can be entertained privately in the club's 120 boxes and small lounges. He adds, 'Big companies have corporate seats with more than one football club, depending on where they have offices, factories or clients' (Croft, 2001; p. 66). In the same article, the marketing manager for Keith Prowse, another corporate hospitality agency, confirmed the hierarchy of matches for companies seeking the most prestigious events at which to entertain their guests:

1 FA Cup final.
2 FA Cup semi-final.
3 European matches.
4 Premiership matches.
5 England international games.
6 'The rest'.

However, investment in corporate hospitality at football matches is neither restricted to large companies nor to the top football clubs. Small and medium-sized companies are now being targeted, and often a local allegiance will be exploited. Swindon Town Football Club, for example, offers corporate hospitality packages to match a range of corporate budgets, ranging between £40 and £100 per guest (Figure 6.3).

The motivation for football clubs being willing suppliers to the corporate hospitality market is first and foremost financial. This market represents for them a key income generator whose arrival could hardly have been more timely. Following the 1989 Taylor Report into the Hillsborough football stadium disaster, all Premier League and First Division clubs were obliged to have all-seater stands, increased security and crowd safety measures. It is the revenue generated through selling corporate hospitality to businesses that, in no small measure, helped fund these costly yet vital improvements.

It is interesting to note in passing that some sporting venues carry such kudos that they can even earn revenue from companies by attracting them when there are no events or games taking place. 'Organisations like Chelsea Football Club and the Harlequins Rugby Club are not only offering match-day hospitality. They are taking the idea one step further, saying "come and use our famous facilities for your conferences, dinner-dances, product launches and fun days"' (Campbell, 1998; p.31). The use of such venues has advantages for both suppliers and buyers. From the clubs' perspective, they are generating profits at a time when the grounds would otherwise be unused, and the infrastructure for accommodating guests is already in place – parking, catering, toilet facilities, security, etc. From the buyers' perspective, they can entertain their guests in the well-equipped hospitality suites

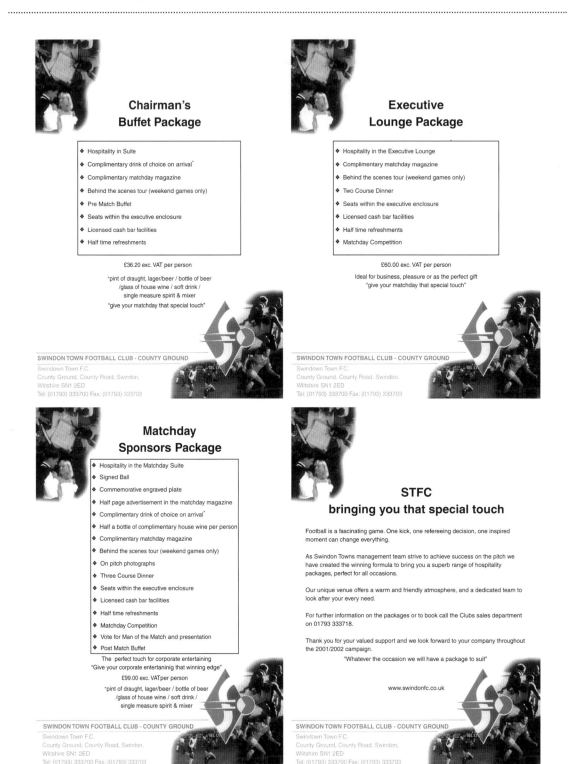

Figure 6.3 Swindon Town Football Club promotional material
Reproduced with the permission of Swindon Town Football Club.

and additionally offer them the chance to use the 'hallowed turf' for activities, games or predinner drinks.

But despite the apparent dominance of sport, a significant share of corporate hospitality spend is accounted for by both cultural and participative events, as seen in the case of Unipart at the beginning of this chapter. The choice of venue, event or activity inevitably depends on whom the companies are targeting and for what purpose. The key is clearly getting the right people to attend the right event, and at times a box at an opera may well be more appropriate than a go-karting event or a rugby international.

Entertainment

It is clear that very often the venue and the entertainment provided are practically synonymous with each other. Anyone receiving an invitation to the Royal Opera House would reasonably expect there to be a performance included in the evening's proceedings. However, when the event is held in a venue where there is no particular performance or game to be watched, entertainment may be booked specifically for the guests: after-dinner speakers, comedians, musicians, magicians, and circus acts such as jugglers and acrobats are among those most commonly found.

Activities are used in the more participative forms of corporate hospitality, and these are generally matched to the age, interests and personality of those attending. These can range from adrenalin-filled sports such as quad bikes, kayaking and gorge-scrambling to the slightly gentler hot-air ballooning, wine and cookery events with celebrity chefs, or spa days. Challenging activities in particular provide the advantage that companies can get to know their guests in a different way, as barriers tend to be brought down when people step outside their comfort zone and participate in something new together.

Catering

Although at many of the venues used for corporate hospitality it is not their primary function to offer a catering service, most understand quickly that the provision of quality food and beverages is a vital ingredient for the corporate entertainment market. In some cases, venues establish their own catering operation; others, such as Madame Tussauds, when it is closed to the general public, buy in the services of outside caterers. Indeed, in new or refurbished sports venues, the catering needs of the corporate hospitality sector are often amongst the first considerations. At Kempton Park racecourse, for example, £9 million was spent on new facilities, including a grandstand with an adjustable conference and dining area for up to 500 people (Campbell, 1998); and in 2001, Chelsea Football Club announced plans to build its own hotel on site (Croft, 2001).

Whatever the supplier's role in providing services and/or facilities for corporate hospitality events, it is clear that with so much at stake, an excellent track record is a vital qualification for any supplier. This is particularly important given that this is a sector where there are no rules of entry and which is therefore open to anyone keen to have a go at attracting corporate hospitality business. Concern over this situation has been voiced by a number of those active in this market, including the chairman of Global Event Solutions, who sums up the situation in the industry: 'It needs to be far more professional. A farmer with a field and six quad bikes can go into corporate hospitality; he is baling hay one minute and running bikes the next' (Upton, 1998; p.30).

Although the three main elements of the corporate hospitality package have been considered separately, it is, of course, the synthesis of all three that leaves the lasting impression upon guests. Very often, there are several suppliers contributing to a corporate hospitality event, and it is the responsibility of the intermediary to coordinate the various elements, from the catering contractors to those providing the important ancillary services. The full role of the intermediaries will be described in the following section.

Intermediaries

Due to the considerable expense involved in paying for the hire of the various facilities and services, levels of financial investment in corporate hospitality events are generally high. But the buyer company also invests much of its reputation in the corporate hospitality event going well, and this can mean taking a considerable risk: by offering corporate hospitality, an organisation is putting itself on show to the people it values. If something goes awry, it is those valued guests who will witness the failure, to the considerable embarrassment of the host. For these reasons, buyers are all the more insistent that the planning of the event itself should be meticulous and rigorous.

This is precisely why most companies entrust the planning and organisation of corporate hospitality events to specialist intermediaries – external agencies whose role it is to design the event and liaise with the various suppliers. That leaves the host company to concentrate on its guests, without having to worry about the many logistical aspects of the event.

Intermediaries in corporate hospitality include:

- specialist agencies dealing exclusively with the organisation of corporate hospitality events;
- agencies also operating in associated sectors, such as product launches, conferences, team-building exercises and incentives;
- business travel management companies offering a corporate entertainment service in addition to their other services;
- in-house corporate hospitality organisers employed by the venues themselves to package specific programmes for corporate clients.

The size of intermediary organisations varies from one-person operations to multinational conglomerates for which arranging corporate hospitality is just one element of a much wider portfolio of business. However, regardless of their size, it is their experience of this sector that enables the best among them to avoid the types of problem that can arise during a corporate hospitality event. There are many possible pitfalls, of which three examples are:

- too few or too many guests arrive on the day;
- the robust humour of the after-dinner speaker is offensive to some of the guests;
- some of the guests have already been entertained at the same venue by another organisation and remember that the service was better on that occasion, e.g. a company asks its guests to make their own way to Glyndebourne, while on the previous occasion a competitor company flew them there in a helicopter.

Meticulous planning on the part of the intermediary should ensure that situations such as those cited above do not arise to threaten the success of an event. Prior research is considered to be an imperative stage in the organisational process: analysing the client's corporate objectives, finding out about competitors' activities, and getting to know the guests' profile and their previous corporate hospitality experience should form the foundation of the event.

In addition to sound research, it is generally accepted that certain fundamental conditions must be fulfilled for corporate hospitality events to achieve their objectives successfully (Sodexho, 2001):

- Making sure that the target guests attend.
- Achieving a good mix of people, both guests and employees.
- Finding the appropriate venue.
- Excellent organisation.
- Providing high-quality catering and service.
- Providing enjoyment and fun for guests.
- Creating an original, exclusive, interesting and memorable event.
- Finding the right event for the right people.

The corporate hospitality and entertainment field is widely recognised to be steeped in tradition, protocol and even snobbery at times, but intermediaries worth their salt are aware of this and act accordingly in the interests of their clients. They are generally prepared to take care of anything from the big issues – the budget, choosing the event, tickets, guest list, catering, seating plan, transport, disabled access and toilets – to the finer details, such as a cloakroom service and making umbrellas available in case of rain.

However, most buyers and intermediaries realise that a successful corporate hospitality event is not simply one that goes off without a hitch: it is equally important to distinguish the event with creative extras to make it memorable for the guests. As in the case of incentive travel, corporate hospitality only works if guests recall the experience – with pleasure. And just as incentive travel winners are often well-travelled people who are hard to impress, so too are many of those invited to corporate hospitality events often blasé about attending yet another prestigious performance at the Royal Opera House or another FA Cup final. Such a level of audience sophistication demands that events offer guests an experience that is entirely unique and special. It is in designing these experiences that the creativity and imagination that distinguish the most talented intermediaries from their merely competent competitors come into play.

In a sector where so much is at stake, it is not surprising that the success of the different components of the supply chain should also depend to a large extent on trust between buyers, intermediaries and suppliers, based on the total credibility of the last two. To establish credibility with potential buyers, intermediaries and suppliers can adopt several approaches, including gaining recognised accreditation and providing financial guarantees.

Recognised accreditation can be gained within industry in general (e.g. ISO 9002 or Investors in People) or within this particular sector, e.g. by becoming members of professional organisations such as the Corporate Hospitality and Events Association (CHA; www.cha-online.co.uk) or the Association for Conferences and Events (ACE; www.martex.co.uk/ace). Through the work of the CHA in particular, those responsible for booking events have become much better educated in choosing quality events and professional suppliers.

One way of providing a financial guarantee is to become a fully bonded member of the CHA. This association's protective bond scheme was introduced after the sector suffered negative publicity during the 1998 World Cup football championships in France, when many corporate hospitality buyers were devastated by the news that the agencies from whom they were expecting to receive match tickets had failed to obtain them. An editorial from *Conference and Incentive Travel* magazine later that year highlighted the scale of the disaster for corporate hospitality buyers and agents (White, 1998; p.3):

> As World Cup euphoria gripped the country, thousands of disappointed fans were unable to watch the matches live. It is not the first time that tickets for major sporting events have not materialised but the World Cup is probably one of the most publicised ticketing disasters for some time.
>
> The corporate hospitality industry is once again the butt of people's anger. Corporate packages for the major matches were selling for several thousand pounds and one of the primary reasons for the high demand was the opportunity to watch a live game; however, many corporate guests were disappointed. During the World Cup a number of hospitality agencies ceased trading, unable to source tickets from their suppliers.
>
> Attracting guests to corporate hospitality can be a tough call and this year demand for Wimbledon, Ascot and the Grand Prix was down as companies clamoured for the all-elusive football tickets. Having secured a package for an estimated £2,000 per head, only to discover that the tickets were not available, is a disaster. Not only is the failure to supply tickets a stinging indictment of the cowboy nature of the industry, it is also a serious embarrassment for companies who have invited their top clients to the World Cup. And to cap it all, there is no protection for the corporates who purchased the tickets and packages.

It is time that the corporate hospitality industry created a protective bond for the business to safeguard corporate clients. By having an accredited bond hospitality agents would be protected from collapse and it would act as an insurance against non-delivery. This calls for financial commitment on the part of agencies but in the long run it will raise standards across the industry.

The calls for a protective bond were indeed heeded by the industry. All members of the CHA who have been trading as agents for over three years are now bonded up to £300 000 (a similar scheme to those of the Air Travel Organizer's Licence (ATOL) and the Association of British Travel Agents (ABTA)), ensuring that buyers' investments in corporate hospitality are protected.

Issues and trends

Growth in corporate hospitality

Although the use of corporate hospitality is now widespread in many sectors, according to Sodexho (2001) it is only recently that companies have really appreciated its value as a strategic marketing tool; its greatest growth, according to this major hospitality company, being in the last two decades of the twentieth century.

While it is generally accepted that this sector is enjoying a period of robust growth, the statistics are inevitably somewhat approximate. One reason for the ballpark nature of the available data is that since corporate hospitality is linked so closely with other forms of business travel – often taking place in close association with, for example, incentive programmes, team-building programmes and entertaining guests at trade fairs – the task of isolating accurate and meaningful statistics is far from straightforward. In addition, many companies, fearful of appearing to be too extravagant in the eyes of shareholders and employees – particularly those facing austerity measures or the threat of redundancy – prefer not to publish their spending on this potentially sensitive item too explicitly.

There is general agreement, however, that in the UK at least, corporate hospitality represents a growth sector. Its value was estimated at £600 million in 2000 (Greaves, 2000) and between £700 million and £1 billion in 2001 (Sodexho, 2001). So what are the reasons for this growth?

Its increasing use within an organisation's marketing may be attributed to a range of factors, including:

● *Increasing competition*: competition for customers has never been more intense. One impact of globalisation has been to introduce more competition into many companies' existing markets. Companies thus need, more than ever, to distinguish themselves from their competitors; one way of doing this is to have a positive presence at events that reflect their brand and appeal to the lifestyle of their target customers. When the downturn in the economy in the early years of the twenty-first century added to the competition faced by many companies, many of them responded by increasing their spend on corporate hospitality. An example of this is provided by Gannaway (2001; p.35), who quotes a representative from the bank, Kleinwort Benson, a buyer of corporate hospitality: 'If business is difficult and times are hard, that's when you should spend money on corporate hospitality. You need it to generate work rather than sit back and say times are tough.'

- *More service-based industries*: the shift in focus in many developed economies from a manufacturing to a service industry base has intensified the need for these new industries to adopt a more marketing-oriented focus. As discussed in Chapter 2, since it is not possible to patent successful service ideas and practices, an innovation of one service company may be imitated soon after by others, resulting in a number of companies with fairly undifferentiated products competing in the same marketplace. Developing relationships with clients is seen as a means of creating loyal customers and discouraging existing clients from defecting to other service providers. A distinctive and effective corporate hospitality component within a company's marketing strategy can be a powerful means of establishing a strong bond with key customers.

- *Reduced opportunities for face-to-face communications*: one of the paradoxes of modern business is that the huge advances in communications and IT, with the dominance of electronic systems such as e-mail and preprogrammed telephone responses, have reduced the amount of personal contact between an organisation and its customers. Corporate hospitality can be used to re-establish that personal link. The value of spending time in person with clients is perhaps greater now than it has ever been. As the Sodexho (2001) report emphasises, 'Meeting and greeting people face-to-face may seem a quaint notion in this techno-dominated age, but companies neglect it at their peril'. The fact that most people in work are under increasing pressure to be productive and efficient means that there is an even more compelling argument for creating time out for face-to-face networking. Upton (1998; p.29) quotes the publicity and sponsorship manager of Cornhill Insurance: 'These hospitality opportunities are crucial to us; we try to build new relationships and keep existing ones. Business lunches do not last three hours nowadays. [By using corporate hospitality], we are able to get alongside our customers and have a dialogue for the whole day.'

- *A growing and improving range of corporate hospitality products*: at the same time as more organisations have recognised the value of using corporate hospitality as part of their marketing mix, its suppliers and organisers have seized the opportunity to develop and improve their products and the level of professionalism with which they market them. The range of events and activities now available to potential buyers of corporate hospitality is immense, and corporate hospitality suppliers are becoming increasingly adept at winning new business – and keeping it.

- *Growth in the customer base for corporate hospitality*: growth is also due in part to demand-side changes. Croft (2001; p.66) is one of many industry observers to notice that an increasing number of smaller companies are using corporate hospitality as part of their marketing mix. He cites, as an example, the sales manager for Tottenham Hotspur: 'Ten years ago, it was just big companies which used corporate hospitality facilities at football matches; now small companies are doing the same. Further growth in our market will continue to come from small to medium-sized companies. It's more difficult to sell to blue-chip businesses as they have to go through 40 levels of management to get approval.'

Smaller events

In common with many of the business-related events considered in this book, corporate hospitality events are displaying a tendency to becoming smaller and more intimate. The director of the CHA has remarked that this form of entertaining is becoming more targeted and focused than ever before: 'Group sizes are smaller so that the hosts have a better opportunity of mixing with their guests' (Barnard, 2001). The trend to smaller events, with more host–guest interaction, has also been emphasised by other commentators: 'Long gone are the marquees for 50. Instead, companies buy a table for ten and ensure than the client/supplier ratio is more equal' (Greaves, 2000; p.35).

Becket (2001) expands upon the effects of this change of emphasis regarding the types of events organised, quoting representatives of the agency, Elegant Days and the caterer Sodexho: 'Where they used to invite 500 people but spend only £120 or so a head, companies now invite 15 to 20 and will spend anything up to £1,000 a head on them. A corollary of concentrating on the few important guests is that most recipients are no longer first-timers and are therefore more discerning about the function. That means they generally want something new.'

Many commentators emphasise the importance of making sure that clients and their guests have time together for contact and conversation. For this reason, tennis, golf matches or horse-racing, for example, which give time for socialising and networking in the lulls between the action, may be chosen in preference to taking guests to Glyndebourne or Covent Garden, where there would be far fewer opportunities for conversation.

Return on investment

With so many of its objectives being long term and qualitative, ROI on corporate hospitality is considered by many to be more difficult to estimate than the ROI on any of the other forms of business travel covered in this book. For example, in response to the question, 'How do you measure the cost-effectiveness of this form of marketing?', Upton (1998; p.29) insists: 'The bottom line is that you cannot. Despite the huge spends behind it, corporate hospitality is the least scientific of all aspects of marketing which, when set against a backdrop of ever-increasing accountability, is even more surprising.' She goes on to claim that, in her view, no one appears to question whether it is working. She supports her assertion with the example of Global Event Solutions, a branch of multinational travel management company BTI Hogg Robinson. The company chairman maintains that repeat business and client testimonials are regarded as a measure of success of their investment in corporate hospitality (Upton, 1998; p.30): '[Corporate hospitality] is a tried and tested formula, a known quantity. There is cachet and credibility attached to attending an event; you feel valued if you are asked. It is a strong client-retention statement, but no-one can demonstrate whether it is effective or not in financial terms.'

Certainly, most buyers and organisers appear to accept that to conduct an analysis of the ROI for corporate hospitality, particularly in the short term, would be a dauntingly complex procedure. A study conducted by Total Research (Luckhurst, 1997) revealed that 66% of the blue-chip companies questioned did not attempt to evaluate the effectiveness of their corporate hospitality expenditure. Even at a time when much marketing expenditure is being challenged rigorously, most buyers appear to accept that since one of the main desired outcomes of corporate hospitality is the establishment of sustained relationships, measurement can only be made realistically over the long term. Shorter-term methods of evaluation have been described variously as 'gut-feel' or 'anecdotal', based on an impression of the feedback received during or just after the event.

However, some buyers do take a more rigorous, systematic approach to measuring ROI. Luckhurst (1997) describes the telephone survey carried out by one such organisation, the firm of accountants Ernst and Young. Follow-up telephone calls were made to guests who had attended a dinner hosted by the company at the Monet and Bonnard exhibitions in London. Forty-nine per cent of the guests said that they now associated the firm with 'quality' and 'culture'; 33% believed the event had created a more favourable impression of the company; but 27% were honest enough to admit that it had made no difference at all. With the other 73% of guests influenced positively by the event, however, the buyer considered the event to have been a thoroughly worthwhile investment.

Assessing the impact on the general public of investment in event sponsorship is a more straightforward procedure than measuring the returns from the corporate hospitality that can go with it. Cornhill Insurance, for example, takes the time to evaluate the impact of its investment in the sponsorship and corporate hospitality deal it has with test match cricket: £9 million over three years to sponsor six annual test matches earns the company the opportunity to entertain 2250 business contacts over 24 days. The company's publicity and sponsorship manager describes the effectiveness of the deal (Upton, 1998; p.29):

On the sponsorship side, Cornhill's objective is brand visibility and brand awareness, which are measured with standard tracking and research on name awareness. In 1978, pre-cricket, the company's unprompted awareness was only 1%, when it was insuring 3% of the population. In 1998, Prudential is the best-known insurer, but Cornhill is in third place, despite the fact that it is not the third biggest insurer. We get our awareness well above our true station in life, and it is coming from cricket.

Corporate hospitality and sponsorship

Companies with large budgets often combine corporate hospitality with sponsorship deals, a spin-off from which is the corporate hospitality it affords. By establishing a formal link with the corporate hospitality venue or event through sponsorship, a company can increase its presence considerably.

Effectively, sponsorship of, and offering corporate hospitality at, particular events and venues, are activities that reinforce each other's impact for those companies in a position to combine the two. For example, companies that sponsor a particular football team can enjoy the twin advantages of:

- being associated in the minds of spectators with a game and team they admire, thanks to advertising on the players' kits and around the stadium;
- impressing VIPs through their access to the corporate entertainment facilities at the ground as well as the chance to meet the players, etc.

But although football may provide the most obvious examples, other sports and cultural activities also attract sponsorship deals combined with corporate hospitality. Hewlett Packard, for example, works in partnership with Formula One racing teams, providing sponsorship for them as well as entertaining their own clients at Grand Prix events. In 1998, One2One invested £2 million in sponsoring the British Golf Masters over a three-year period, enabling the company to entertain 500 key business contacts during the five-day event (Upton, 1998).

In the world of business travel, American Airlines provides an interesting example of this practice. The airline has focused on identifying events and exhibitions that appeal to business travellers over the North Atlantic. Its consumer marketing manager has explained that the philosophy behind its sponsorship policy is for the airline to be associated with 'high quality arts events which would reflect our brand value' (Terazono, 2000). By sponsoring events such as the Jackson Pollock exhibition at the Tate Gallery in 1999 and the English National Opera's summer 2000 Anglo-American programme, the airline was aiming to achieve two goals. First, since many of those attending the events (200 000 visitors at the 1999 exhibition, for example) were potential passengers for the airline, American Airlines' sponsorship will have encouraged them to assimilate the link between the airline and the exhibition through advertising on leaflets, sponsorship notices, etc. Second, by using the events to offer corporate hospitality to VIP guests, the airline was providing a more memorable experience for those guests who will have also seen the evidence of American Airlines' sponsorship.

In addition, from a financial perspective, the cost of sponsorship may be offset more easily than the cost of corporate hospitality. A theoretical value can be attached to, say, logo exposure on pamphlets or numbers of people seeing the company name in particularly favourable locations over set periods of time. By doing this, the cost of sponsorship can be compared with exposure provided by other promotional activities, such as one-off advertisements. This way, sponsorship often appears as the leading promotional technique, with corporate hospitality being presented as an effective means of reinforcing the impact of that sponsorship.

More participative events

A number of commentators have remarked that corporate hospitality involving guest participation is gaining ground at the expense of more traditional spectator events. Guest involvement in activities is regarded increasingly by companies as a vital key to their events' success, as confirmed by Gannaway (2001; p.27): 'New generation corporate hospitality does not revolve purely around the passive pleasures of watching big names run around with various sized balls while plying guests with copious amounts of alcohol. The new style of corporate hospitality is about inspiring and challenging delegates, turning them into participants rather than spectators of an event.'

Companies understand that amid guests' rising expectations for corporate hospitality, their events have to be differentiated sufficiently from those of their competitors if they are to succeed in tempting those they have invited to attend. Original, interactive events appeal to the wish for self-development of guests. They also offer the advantages not only of being more memorable but also of bonding participants and their hosts, reinforcing the relationship between them. This is particularly true of events that provide a novel experience shared by hosts and guests. Gannaway (2001; p.31) provides the example of a corporate hospitality day at Heathrow Airport during which hosts and guests took turns on a £10 million British Airways flight simulator. The organiser of the event sums up the appeal of the activity: 'This is the sort of thing people dream about doing and guests are bowled over by the experience of landing a 747. That shared experience really brings people together and breaks down barriers.'

New technology

The advances in information and communications technology (ICT) described in other chapters of this book have only recently had a significant impact on the corporate hospitality market. But ICT is increasingly making its presence felt on how corporate hospitality is bought and sold. According to Becket (2001), the CHA found in 2001 that 42% of buyers were browsing the Internet for information on corporate hospitality products, while in the previous year this research technique was 'hardly used at all'. As a result, an increasing number of venues, event organisers, agencies and caterers have put their brochures online, and a few have ventured as far as even doing business via their websites.

However, as Sims (2001; p.41) points out, as far as venue-providers are concerned:

The evidence so far is that the internet is being used in tandem with more [traditional] sales techniques rather than instead of them. The web is an important shop window exposing your venue to a national and international audience, but there is no sign yet that the corporate entertainment industry is ready to abandon brochures, familiarisation visits or exhibition stands.

But Sims reserves particular praise for a few venues that, in his opinion, have produced websites of excellent value to corporate hospitality buyers and agents. Sodexho's website (www.corporatehospitality-online.co.uk), with its full details of packages available at Henley and a number of other premier venues, is held up as an example worthy of imitation. Others mentioned are www.spurs.co.uk, the official website of Tottenham Hotspur Football Club, with its informative links to 'hospitality' and 'corporate' leading to details of corporate facilities at White Hart Lane (with plans for a virtual tour); and www.polo.co.uk, Ascot Polo Club's site, offering clear links to everything the event planner needs – hospitality packages, prices, and an e-mail link to the general manager to speed up the booking process.

Increasing numbers of female participants

Throughout this book, the need for suppliers to cater for growing numbers of female business travellers has been a recurrent theme. Growing numbers of women at managerial levels have also had an impact on the corporate hospitality market.

One trend linked to this development are the signs that companies are now looking for more variety and a better mix of corporate hospitality events. Sport still accounts for the great majority of corporate hospitality events, but there is growing interest in, for example, inviting guests to first-night shows and theatrical events. Events365, a corporate hospitality organiser, co-sponsors events so that it can then sell tickets for opening nights. For example, the company organised an event at the opening night of the stage musical *Saturday Night Fever* for 150 guests, and opening parties for *Dr Doolittle* and *Cirque du Soleil*. Upton (1998; p.30) quotes the company's sales and marketing director on the growing need for variety: 'For some clients, Wimbledon is absolutely the right event; or some heavy drinking at the rugby on Saturday. But with more women rising through the ranks, you need to offer a broader appeal.'

Ethical considerations

With such considerable funds being spent by companies on giving their guests a thoroughly enjoyable time, the question inevitably arises as to at what point the bona fide use of corporate hospitality as a marketing tool amounts to outright bribery of the guests by their hosts. In recent years, concerns have been voiced, not least by the English Law Commission, over the need to distinguish clearly between acceptable and unacceptable corporate hospitality, the latter consisting of gifts of hospitality, which are, in effect, bribes in return for which the recipients are expected to provide the host company with something of value, such as a contract or useful inside information.

Given the extensive part that corporate hospitality now plays in business life, Chetwynd (1998) believes that a growing number of legal minds are of the opinion that the time is propitious to review the relevant legislation that dates back to the nineteenth and early twentieth centuries – the Prevention of Corruption Acts 1889 and 1916.

Essentially, what are under scrutiny are the intentions and expectations of those providing the hospitality, but in fact the provider *and* the recipient of the hospitality may be guilty of corruption, either by offering/conferring an advantage or by obtaining/soliciting the same. The view of the marketing manager for ACE Corporate Management, a corporate hospitality intermediary, is that 'if a company is prepared to give another company business on the basis of corporate hospitality, it is fundamentally corrupt' (Chetwynd, 1998; p.47).

In March 1998, a Law Commission report (No. 248) proposed measures to curb corruption in the public and private domain. According to a legal journalist writing on this issue (Lewis, 2000; p.3):

> On the subject of corporate hospitality, the Law Commission commented that one must not be too puritanical. The object, after all, is to make friends. It is a valuable opportunity to cement working relationships. However, they recognised that what is proffered can exceed the boundaries of acceptable graciousness. Bribery can 'simply be dressed up as hospitality'. In these blatant instances, benefits may be obviously unrelated to proper business activities, or of disproportionate expense. The Law Commission report accordingly recommended that these truly corrupt practices masked as promotional activities should be censored.

But how is the law to recognise the point at which corporate hospitality crosses the line into corrupt territory? In the same article, Lewis suggested that there were a number of key pointers to help determine when the advantage offered is no longer above board. One of the most important features of these is the business content of the event. She observes three levels:

- Taking clients to lunch is unlikely to be construed as imposing an obligation on guests to reciprocate with work. Wining and dining is part of negotiation rituals and will not raise eyebrows unless extravagant.
- At the next level, there are specific events like hiring pods at the London Eye or flying guests to Euro 2000. While it will be hard to demonstrate continuous business discussion, provided that an element of business exists, these freebies continue to have a fig leaf of respectability.
- It is when invitations extend to partners or when hosts are absent that occasions become more difficult to condone. Instead, the impression can be created that hospitality is a pure gift. The motive could come under the microscope. An all-expenses-paid trip could be misconstrued – and may need to be disclosed to the Inland Revenue as a benefit in kind, since under Section 154 of the Income and Corporation Taxes Act 1988, benefits provided for employees or their families 'by reason of their employment' are taxable in the same way as if provided by their employer.

It is important to note that the above legislation is part of UK law. Clearly, cultural differences come into play in determining the point at which corporate hospitality becomes unacceptable: what may be a legitimate part of business culture in one country may be viewed as totally corrupt in another. And while some companies allow their employees to use their own discretion over the acceptance of corporate hospitality, others set policies for their staff, in order that they may protect themselves from accusations of corruption. IBM, for example, provides its employees with strict guidelines: hospitality may only be accepted from current, not prospective, suppliers; only invitations to sporting or cultural events with a value not exceeding US$100 may be accepted; and no overnight stays should be involved. The employee must always be accompanied by the supplier at whatever event has been organised. And finally, if the IBM employee's spouse or partner is invited, then they may only go if paid for by IBM (Chetwynd, 1998).

Conflicting markets

For many suppliers, corporate hospitality is only one aspect of their product and service portfolio. Although its rewards are substantial, the needs of any supplier's corporate hospitality market must nevertheless be balanced against the needs and expectations of its other clients. This chapter began with the example of Wimbledon as a highly popular venue for corporate hospitality. But, in recent years, the organisers of Wimbledon have been accused of reserving a disproportionate number of seats for corporate clients at the expense of members of the general public wishing to purchase tickets to watch the tennis matches. Wimbledon is by no means the only sports venue to be criticised for giving too much priority to corporate hospitality customers. According to Upton (1998), the popular image of corporate hospitality has come to be one of hundreds of true supporters being delayed or denied access to a particular event only to see empty seats as the revellers stay in the marquee imbibing rather than watching the action. O'Hara (2001) describes how, at Wimbledon, Tim Henman once complained to the umpire when he was forced to play to a half-empty centre court because the corporate guests were in their marquee drinking champagne instead of taking their seats to watch the match.

It has become clear that sports clubs who ignore the reactions of their supporters to corporate hospitality extravagance do so at their peril. For although corporate hospitality is a lucrative aspect of many such clubs' finances, the loyalty and revenue provided by members of the public are also essential. Experience has shown that football clubs, for example, are not always sufficiently aware of the danger of antagonising fans who notice that the best views and best facilities are reserved for corporate guests, and that occasionally the lavish boxes are partly filled with people whose attention is clearly not focused on the game in play. The most high-profile example of corporate hospitality controversy in football was seen in 1999, when more than 4000 season-ticket-holders at Newcastle United's stadium took legal action over plans to move them from what they (the fans) claimed were their guaranteed seats in order to make way for corporate hospitality facilities.

Clearly, greater sensitivity on the part of football clubs and other sports grounds active in the corporate hospitality market is required. Explaining the role that this activity plays in their own finances might also help. Croft (2001; p.66) quotes Tottenham Hotspur's sales manager, who, while admitting that there is some resentment from certain section's of the club's fan base at the idea of corporate hospitality, stresses that without the extra revenue, fans' tickets would cost a lot more: 'If corporate guests weren't bringing in the millions, then we would have to find that money somewhere else'.

By trimming players' salaries perhaps?

Case study

Legoland, Windsor

A visitor attraction originally designed with children and families in mind, Legoland, Windsor (Figure 6.4) also provides an excellent example of a venue well positioned to operate in the corporate hospitality, conference, events and exhibitions markets. Purely as a visitor attraction, it already possesses certain ingredients that are key to attracting the corporate hospitality buyer, including:

- easy road and rail access from London and the Home Counties;
- proximity to the motorway network and even Heathrow Airport;
- plenty of on-site parking;
- built-in entertainment from the attraction itself;
- an attractive setting within sight of Windsor Castle;
- a reputation as an interesting attraction;
- a service-oriented workforce.

For a tourist attraction vulnerable to seasonal visitor fluctuations, the targeting of complementary high-value markets has become standard practice, especially when so much is already in place to attract those markets. By offering tailored extras to meet the needs of clients, and by opening an additional facility called the Pavilions, Legoland has provided a novel setting for a large corporate hospitality event at the same time as adding to its own visitor numbers and revenue.

If the guests enjoy themselves, then the venue should also benefit from their decision to return as paying visitors with their own families, or simply from their positive word-of-mouth recommendations to friends and relatives. Also offered as the venue for large conferences, exhibitions, meetings and seminars, the Pavilions, a huge luxury marquee, can be used as the base for corporate entertainment in the form of fun days, dinners, and dinner dances for groups of between 100 and 500 guests. For corporate hospitality buyers seeking to entertain smaller groups, Legoland offers other facilities such as its JFK Drawing Room and Terrace in the Mansion House, where capacity ranges between 50 and 200, depending on the meal arrangements required.

Legoland offers corporate hospitality buyers a wide range of packages to suit their particular needs. Many combinations are possible, meaning that different guest groups can be targeted. As well as entertaining their guests in one of the two hospitality areas in Legoland, buyers can purchase exclusive use of a themed area or individual rides within the park. A wide range of extra entertainment can be arranged, including themed evenings, comedians, magicians, a casino, bands, photographers, gifts and competitions. Menu prices range from around £17 per person for lunches to around £30 per person for dinners, with child prices available for all occasions except the themed evenings.

Case study *continued*

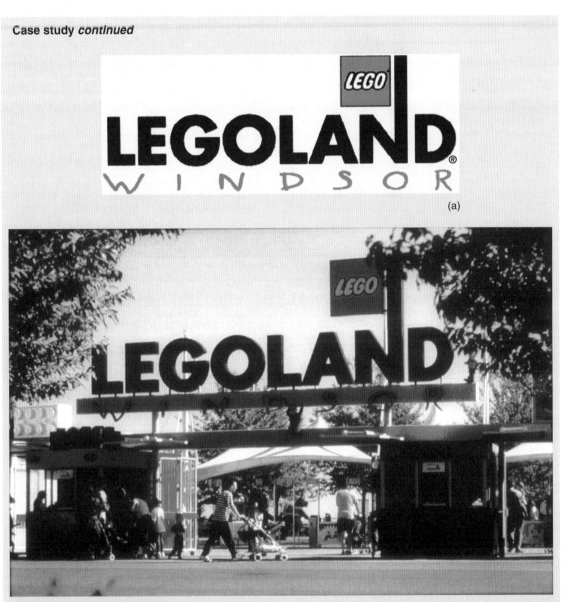

Figure 6.4 (a) Legoland logo; (b) Legoland
Source: Reproduced with the permission of Legoland, Windsor.

Questions

1 Consider the ways in which Legoland's marketing of its attraction for business tourism events will differ from its marketing to leisure visitors.

2 What challenges may be faced by Legoland in welcoming corporate hospitality guests and paying customers simultaneously, and how could these challenges be addressed?

References

Barnard, T. (2001), 'Frequently asked questions', www.cha-online.co.uk, Corporate Hospitality & Event Association.

Becket (2001) 'Corporate hospitality: lifetime clients who love the high life', *Daily Telegraph*, 12 February.

Campbell, F. (1998), 'Grounds for appeal', *Business Travel World*, September.

Chetwynd, C. (1998), 'Corrupt hospitality', *Marketing Week*, 5 November.

Christopher, M., Payne, A. and Ballantyne, M. (1991), *Relationship Marketing*, London, Butterworth-Heinemann.

Croft, M. (2001), 'Perfect pitch', *Marketing Week*, 29 March.

Gannaway, B. (2001), 'Entertainment in action', *Conference & Incentive Travel*, September.

Greaves, S. (2000), 'Building bridges', *Conference & Incentive Travel*, May.

Han, S.L., Wilson, D.T. and Dart, S.P. (1993), 'Buyer–supplier relationships today', *Industrial Marketing Management*, Vol. 22, pp. 331–8.

Levy, M. (1999), 'Fast and furious Formula One', *Conference & Incentive Travel*, May.

Lewis, P. (2000), 'The fine line between a free lunch and bribery', *The Times*, 12 December.

Lovelock, C. (2000), *Services marketing: People, Technology, Strategy*, 4th edn, Upper Saddle River, NJ, Prentice Hall.

Luckhurst, J. (1997), 'Measuring up', *Marketing Week*, 14 August.

O'Hara, M. (2001), 'The free lunch brigade', *The Guardian*, 26 June.

Palmer, A. (2001), *Principles of Services Marketing*, 3rd edn, Maidenhead, McGraw-Hill.

Sims, J. (2001), 'Marketing mix is a recipe for success', *Corporate Entertainer*, Winter/Spring.

Sodexho (2001), 'Corporate hospitality supplement: survival guide to the season', *Sunday Business*, 20 May.

Terazono, E. (2000), 'American Airlines: emphasis put on cultural links', *Financial Times*, 2 June.

Upton, G. (1998), 'Hosts with the most', *Marketing*, 20 August.

White, S. (1998), 'Hospitality agents need to safeguard corporate clients', *Conference & Incentive Travel*, July/August.

Chapter 7

The business and pleasure interface

Objectives

On completion of this chapter, you should be able to:

- *understand the ways in which business travel can increase the level of leisure and recreational activity in destinations;*

- *appreciate the potential benefits that adding pleasure to business travel brings to suppliers and events planners;*

- *understand the decision-making process that leads to business travellers choosing to add leisure activities to their trips;*

- *understand the roles of key players in stimulating and facilitating leisure add-ons to business trips.*

● ● ● ● Combining business travel with pleasure in the twenty-first century

- Delegates attending TIAFT 2000, the Helsinki-based conference of the International Association of Forensic Toxicologists, chose from a number of post-conference tours including a three-day Lapland Arctic Safari, a one-day cruise to Tallinn, Estonia, and a three-day trip to St Petersburg by train.
- The website home page for the 35th World Vegetarian Congress, held in Edinburgh, contained links to the event's organised social programmes: a whisky-tasting evening, a gala banquet and ceilidh, and a 'Nicht on the Toun' pub crawl.
- In its bid document for the European Congress of Clinical Chemistry, the Marketing Manchester convention bureau included a range of ideas for partner programmes and social programmes, based on the city's attractions and surrounding countryside.

● ● ● ● Introduction

This book began by outlining a number of contrasting characteristics between leisure travel and business travel. However, although tourism and work are usually perceived as two opposite fields of human activity, academics' and tourism professionals' attention is being focused increasingly on those situations in which work-related and leisure-oriented activities are combined. This final chapter focuses on the important links between the two and, notably, how business travel generates additional leisure activities at the destination.

Uriely's (2001) research into the interface between travel and work is set in the framework of his typology of travellers who combine work with tourism, as shown in Table 7.1.

Our concern in this chapter will be primarily with the activities of those whom Uriely calls 'travelling professional workers'. The ways in which such tourists endeavour to combine business travel with pleasure is the theme of this concluding chapter.

It is worth reiterating at this point that almost all business travel includes elements that are practically indistinguishable from the activities of leisure visitors to the destination: enjoying a restaurant meal, visiting local attractions, relaxing in the hotel sauna, shopping for gifts – these are all examples of pursuits in which both types of visitor may engage. The difference is, of course, that in the case of the leisure visitor, such activities are central to the motivation behind making the trip, while for most business travellers, they are incidental and peripheral to the main reason for visiting the destination.

Nevertheless, incidental and peripheral though they may be, leisure elements do play an important role in motivating the business traveller. In the case of discretionary business travel, they provide an extra reason for attending the conference or trade fair,

Table 7.1 Types of travelling workers and working travellers

Dimensions of comparison	Working tourists		Travelling workers	
	Working-holiday tourists	**Non-institutionalised working tourists**	**Migrant tourism workers**	**Travelling professional workers**
Work and touristic motivations	Work is grasped as a recreational activity that is part of the tourist experience	Work in order to finance a prolonged travel	Travel in order to make a living and have fun at the same time	Travel in order to exercise work Engage in tourist-related activities as a by-product of the excursion
Work characteristics	Unskilled but usually recreational manual labour Extraordinary work Unpaid work	Unskilled and usually unpleasant manual labour Occasional work Low-paid and non-prestigious work	Skilled or semiskilled work in the tourism economy Repetitive seasonal employment Unsecured and low-paid employment	Professional, official role, or business-related work Repetitive, career-related work Prestigious and well-paid work
Demographic profile	Middle-class young adults	Middle-class young adults	Lower-middle-class or working-class single and unattached adults Periodically unemployed in their home societies	Middle- or upper-middle-class adults

Source: Uriely, N. (2001) '"Travelling workers" and "working tourists": variations across the interaction between work and tourism', *International Journal of Tourism Research*, Vol. 3, pp.1–8. © John Wiley & Sons Limited. Reproduced with permission.

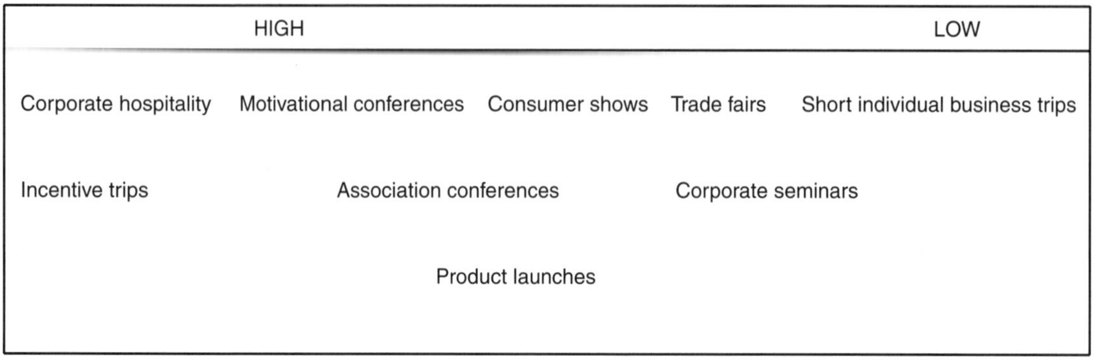

	HIGH				LOW
Corporate hospitality	Motivational conferences	Consumer shows	Trade fairs	Short individual business trips
Incentive trips		Association conferences		Corporate seminars
		Product launches		

Figure 7.1 Business tourism: pleasure quotient

for example; and for all types of business travel, leisure activities at the destination compensate in part for the visitor spending time away from home. Indeed, for some forms of business travel, the leisure and pleasure element is absolutely central to the reason for making the trip in the first place: incentive travel and corporate hospitality, composed almost entirely of leisure, recreational and cultural pursuits, only achieve their objectives if participants thoroughly enjoy themselves.

It is possible, therefore, to classify the various examples of business travel according to their pleasure quotient – the extent to which the elements of leisure and enjoyment are generally a feature of the particular type of event or trip. Figure 7.1 demonstrates this.

Combining business with pleasure

Travel for business-related purposes can increase the level of leisure and recreational activity at the destination in four main ways:

● Through business travellers extending their visit to the destination – adding a number of days before or after – in order to enjoy the cultural/shopping/sightseeing resources of the destination.
● Through business travellers being accompanied by guests (usually spouses/families) who engage in leisure tourism activities while at the destination. This may be through an official, organised guest programme, or independently.
● Through business travellers themselves engaging in leisure or recreational activities as part of the social/networking/relaxation element of the event attended.
● Through business travellers who have been impressed by the destination returning with their spouses/families for holidays/short breaks, or encouraging others to do so.

Each of these activities will now be explored in turn.

Extenders

It is not difficult to understand why business travellers should choose to extend their visits by a few days before or after the business event in order to enjoy the destination's attractions. They are often professional people with high levels of disposable income and interest in experiencing new places. Those whose employers have paid for them to attend may consider that since they have not personally paid for the business aspect of the trip, it is reasonable for them (the business travellers) to fund a leisure tourism extension out of their own pockets. For long-haul visitors in particular, visiting a particular city on business may be a once-in-a-lifetime opportunity to enjoy the destination's attractions before or after the actual event.

There is ample evidence to suggest that business trips are being extended in order that the travellers can participate in cultural or sports activities. Collis (2001) quotes the managing director of Unmissable.com, an Internet-based supplier of 'ready-to-go experiences and activities': 'People going away on business trips to, say, Italy or Spain, contact us to see if we can get them tickets for football or the theatre. We're seeing a lot of people going on cookery courses, bungee jumping or white-water rafting.'

The practice of extending business trips in this way is highlighted by the research undertaken by Doyle and Nathan (2001), which suggests that frequent travellers often view short extension breaks as a trade-off for intensive travel and working long hours. Their conclusion is that seasoned travellers often try to direct their work travel to either places they already like or places they would like to explore, and that they regard these breaks as a chance to see a place or to experience a different way of life. In other words, there is a breed of business traveller who habitually regards business trips as potential triggers for a short leisure break, part of which – the actual travel element – is financed by his or her employer.

For the self-employed, Rutherford and Kreck (1994) indicate an additional motivating factor for combining business and pleasure travel: the tax-deductibility of the business and professional portion of the trip. However the obverse of not having to pay taxes on the business aspect of a trip is that extenders could find themselves liable for paying tax on the leisure part of the trip. *The Guardian* (1998) solemnly warned its readers: 'You could be liable for part of the costs [of a business trip]. If you attend a conference and you stay for an extra day, for instance, the private element of the trip is taxable to you. To avoid a tax charge, the social part of any trip must be purely incidental, or you will have to declare it on your tax return.'

The Saturday night rule almost certainly encourages extensions of this type. This is the rule according to which many airlines charge passengers spending a Saturday night at their destinations only a fraction of the cost of the fare paid by those who do not. Anecdotal evidence suggests that companies may be persuaded to pay for the extra hotel accommodation of those employees who agree to spend the weekend at the destination before or after the date of their meeting, when they realise the savings to be achieved by paying for airfares for trips including a Saturday night.

Opinions differ over which type of individual business traveller is the more likely to extend business trips: the more experienced and more senior business traveller or their less senior and less seasoned travelling colleagues? On the one hand, as suggested above, more seasoned travellers may be more adept at directing their business travel plans to take in places they wish to visit for personal reasons. But many believe that it is those who are less used to work-related travel who are more likely to take advantage of business trips by extending them for pleasure. One such commentator is the managing director of Worldwide Escapes (www.worldwideescapes.com), a travel company that organises customised weekend breaks for business travellers in Asia and South America. She is quoted by Collis (2001) as saying: 'It's not so much frequent business travellers but people who may not travel a great deal who want to take advantage of weekends away. My guess is that high-level people are more dedicated to work and don't necessarily take a weekend off.'

Guests

Although the classic image of the business traveller is the solitary road warrior venturing alone into the world on their particular mission, many choose to go accompanied by a partner, spouse and/or other members of their family. As well as the obvious advantage of familiar company that this arrangement offers, there is also that suggested by Williams and Shaw (1991), who expressed the belief that an overseas business trip with a spouse is an added bonus that can sometimes help justify the long hours put in on the company's behalf. Clearly, this echoes one of the advantages associated with including spouses and partners in the type of incentive programmes discussed in Chapter 4.

Drache (2000) indicates a further benefit of business travellers taking guests with them, pointing out that sharing the hotel room, rental car, etc., and using air miles to book the second seat, for example, means that for the business traveller, being escorted by a spouse or some other person far from doubles the outlay.

Measuring exactly what proportion of individual business travellers visit their destination accompanied by a guest would be a problematic (and indiscreet) undertaking. However, efforts have been made to measure the proportion of conference delegates who take a guest with them for the duration of the event. Estimates vary, but not too wildly. For the UK, the BTF & BTAC (1999) report claims that national and local surveys suggest that 20–30% of delegates may bring accompanying persons, while for the US market, Opperman (1996) has estimated that approximately one-third of association attendees in North America are accompanied by spouses.

Clearly, for conferences, a determining factor in the question of whether delegates are accompanied will be the inclusion, or not, of an organised, parallel programme of activities to entertain their guests while the delegates participate in conference sessions. Guest programmes – of activities ranging from sightseeing and shopping to cultural visits and guest celebrity speakers – are an established staple of many association gatherings in particular. The change in their nomenclature reflects the evolution in social mores of the past 50 or so years, as they have changed from 'wives' or 'ladies' programmes through 'spouse programmes', to the current 'partner', 'accompanying persons' or simply 'guest programmes'. Box 7.1 shows the accompanying persons programme that guests of delegates to the 2001 National Association of Pension Funds (NAPF) conference in Brussels were able to follow.

Box 7.1

Accompanying persons programme for the NAPF conference, 2001

Accompanying persons
We hope that the allure of Europe's cultural capital will encourage many accompanying persons to join us. Over the three days, they will be whisked off to see the Medieval, Gothic Revival, Art Nouveau and Art Deco architectural delights of the city. The plethora of theatres, museums and exhibitions will keep them busy – not to mention the shopping!

Monday 22 October
Full day excursion to Antwerp
Participants will leave the hotel at approximately 0900 for a leisurely coach transfer to Antwerp, the diamond city. The excursion commences with a guided tour of the city. There are many sights to see, including some fine churches and distinguished museums – reminders of its auspicious past as a centre of a wide trading empire. Participants will enjoy lunch at Dock's Café located on the river Scheldt – a spectacular building decked out in precious metals with a magnificent view of the ships going by. The afternoon promises to be a voyage of discovery as participants are led on a fashion walking tour of the city. Focusing on contemporary design, architecture and history, the tour depicts Antwerp's originality and passion for style.

Tuesday 23 October – morning
Culinary walk through Brussels
Belgium is renowned for its culinary delights – waffles, chocolate, mussels, shellfish ... Brussels is one of the capitals of gastronomy with an abundance of fine restaurants and a good cook in most household kitchens. Discover the origin of Belgium's culinary traditions on a walking tour in the sidestreets of downtown Brussels. A tasting of some of the 'delights' is of course obligatory!

Or

Brussels and its 'Art Nouveau' secrets
Participants will leave the hotel at approximately 0900 for a relaxing bus tour through the areas of Brussels where Art Nouveau has left its signature. In honour of the king of Art Nouveau, a visit to the home of Victor Horta is an unforgettable experience, with its sublime pursuit of volume and light, the ingeniousness of its decorative and domestic detail, and the nobility of its spirals and materials.

▶

Box 7.1 *continued*

Tuesday 23 October – afternoon
Brussels, the medieval heart, the whole story
This bus tour allows participants to absorb all the interesting sights there are to see in Brussels! First stop is Laeken, where participants can admire the Royal Castle, the Royal 'Serre', the 'Heizel', Brupark and its surroundings, the Chinese Pavilion, the Japanese Tower… plus plenty more! A walking tour in the medieval heart of Brussels will follow, where the Grand Place, the Town Hall and Cathedral stand.

Wednesday 24 October – morning
Planet Chocolate
A visit to Belgium would not be complete without a tour of Planète Chocolat! Belgium produces 172 000 tons of chocolate per year and has 2130 chocolate shops. Participants will enjoy a guided tour of the chocolate factory followed by a tasting of the final product.

Source: NAPF; www.napf.co.uk

Even at intergovernmental summit meetings, there are often social get-togethers and cultural/shopping trips planned for those who are still called the 'first ladies' – when they are not excluded for security reasons, that is, as happened in Genoa in 2001.

Social programmes

We stressed in Chapter 3 that one aspect of conferences that was lost when video-conferencing was used to replace live events was the social aspect. Smith (1990; p.70) quotes Alvin Toffler in this respect: 'People go to conventions for three reasons – to get information from the platform; to meet colleagues and exchange views – networking; and for recreation, the change in routine, the social programme.'

Although much of the social aspect of conferences and trade fairs is incidental – meeting colleagues, making contacts, finding leads, for example, over coffee or in the conference centre or exhibition hall bar – it is nevertheless commonly regarded as a vitally important aspect of such events.

For this reason, efforts are often made by conference organisers in particular to add social programme elements to events, especially when they extend over three or four days. Excursions and gala evenings are typical of the type of social events that can be included in conference programmes to help delegates – and their guests, if included – relax together. For the three-day NAPF conference mentioned above, the social programme included an optional preconference golf tournament or excursion to Bruges; a lavish cocktail party to celebrate the twentieth anniversary of the European Federation for Retirement Provision, a Brussels-based trade association; and a black-tie gala evening of dinner and dancing amid the sumptuous surroundings of the Concert Noble venue in the heart of Brussels.

Returners

Many business travellers complain that they often see very little of the destinations they visit. For the corporate business traveller visiting a city overnight, their experience of it may be limited to a few glimpses through the taxi window on the way from the airport to the hotel, and back again the next day. However, longer business trips, particularly those including excursions and guest programmes of the kind described above, may succeed in tempting the business visitor to return to the destination for leisure purposes. This will be conditional on:

● the experience having been a positive one;
● the visitors not being overfamiliar with the destination (through frequent business or leisure visits),
● the business visitors not leaving believing that they have done it all already during their business visit.

Accessibility and degree of familiarity are clearly important factors. Well-visited destinations such as the UK may have to try harder to tempt frequent business visitors back as holidaymakers or short-break tourists. Even so, the Conference Delegate Expenditure Research Study undertaken by Systems Three (1998) on behalf of the UK national tourism boards found that 39% of overseas delegates attending UK conferences indicated that they would return to the destination for leisure purposes. But this might be compared with Rogers' (1998) reporting of the findings of the Sydney Convention and Visitors Bureau's Convention Delegate Study, which found that in one year, 72% of overseas delegates attending conferences in Australia were visiting the country for the first time. Before the conferences, only one in three had considered visiting the country, whereas afterwards, two-thirds wanted to return on holiday within the following five years. Clearly, the intentions expressed in such surveys are not always carried through into action, but the surveys undertaken on this issue demonstrate with clarity the potential of business trips to generate subsequent leisure visits.

● ● ● ● The benefits of combining business with pleasure

The benefits to business travellers of extending their trips or taking a partner with them have already been mentioned. But adding pleasure to business-related activities also has potential advantages for other stakeholders.

Destinations and suppliers

The positive economic impact of business travel on destinations was a major theme of Chapter 1, which emphasised how the spending on the organisation of large business-related events such as conferences and trade fairs, as well as the spending of the business visitors themselves, were sources of considerable amounts of revenue for suppliers. But, one of the induced impacts of business tourism on the destination arises when business visitors add leisure travel and recreation activities to their visits before, during or after the actual event attended, providing extra income to cities and businesses operating in them.

Additional hotel room-nights and additional food and beverage consumption, even during slack seasons, are only part of the potential increase in profitability to be reaped from business visitors adding tourism and recreational activities to their primary travel purpose. Extra spending in shops and on visiting tourist attractions also arises from business visitors' activities in the destination, as well as the activities of those accompanying them. For the host community as a whole, this means the prospect of an enhanced tax base and extra employment on top of that created by the strictly business element of the trip.

There is a general awareness of this type of incremental spending. For example, for the UK it has been noted that in addition to the spending of conference delegates themselves, 'as a significant proportion of overseas conference delegates bring partners and, in some cases, families with them, the total value of conference visitors is in reality substantially higher' (BTF & BTAC, 1999). But how often is this incremental spending adequately measured and demonstrated? It is clear that whenever it is measured, it can be used effectively to add weight to arguments seeking to justify, for example, further investment in conference facilities and Convention and visitor bureaux (CVB) marketing activities.

Moreover, the extenders segment also offers cities the chance to increase considerably their reputation as tourist destinations, since business visitors extending their trips, if satisfied with their experience, are more likely to become valuable ambassadors as they encourage others to visit the destination or to return themselves for a longer holiday.

Initiators and planners

For those who initiate and plan discretionary business travel events, the advantages are clear. Particularly when they organise events where attendance is optional and/or at the attendees' own expense, the opportunity to extend the trip and/or bring a guest may boost attendance. This will be the case particularly when potential attendees (and their guests) have been made well aware of the destination's tourism and recreational attractions at the time when the decision as to whether to book is being made. Partners and spouses may play a role here, as anecdotal evidence suggests that they may actually encourage potential delegates to attend – accompanied – if the destination appeals to them.

However, guests are not universally welcomed by those who initiate and plan business travel events. Companies, in particular, are increasingly looking at guest attendance at residential corporate events as a distraction, especially if teamwork or team-building elements are included in the event's programme. In particular, when the event brings together staff who are spread over several strategic business units, it can serve a valuable social function by, for example, introducing

London-based staff to people from the provincial offices who, until the event in question, were no more than voices on the telephone.

Matthews (2001) quotes the sales and marketing director of Sodexho Prestige, specialists in corporate hospitality and events management:

> In the past couple of years, partners have begun to be excluded from most company events, not just for cost reasons, but also because they can detract from the company's own *esprit de corps*. While a small number of firms still extend an invitation to partners, they usually have to pay something for the privilege – a clear sign perhaps that outsiders aren't really all that welcome.

The sales and marketing director estimated that of the 80 000-plus events organised by Sodexho for companies in 2001, fewer than 20% involved partners.

However, there is at least one convincing argument in favour of including guests, and, as was mentioned in the case of incentive travel, this is based on the civilising effect that their presence can have. The managing director of an events management service explains (Matthews, 2001):

> Having partners is an insurance policy against no-shows and bad behaviour. Staff invited without partners to a do that will probably cost between £30,000 and £250,000 often won't bother to turn up, and, if they do, they will probably behave in an appalling manner. Having their partner there tends to rein them in and prevents them from doing something stupid.

But taking guests on business-related trips is often regarded as part of the same controversial work life/home life interface, of which inviting colleagues into one's family home for dinner or going to the office Christmas party with a partner are other equally fraught manifestations. And even when guests are included in the invitation, it appears that neither they nor the business travellers they accompany are necessarily enthusiastic about combining work and private lives in this way. The range of opinions on this issue is demonstrated in the (admittedly unscientific) sample of comments shown in Table 7.2.

Table 7.2 Pros and cons of including guests on business trips

Cons	Pros
'Why do companies feel they have to include the spouse? It's humiliating; you're never treated like a human being in your own right.' (Journalist)	'Accompanying my husband to conferences is one of life's pleasures.' (Corporate wife)
'I would never dream of taking my husband on a business trip. I mean, what would he do?' (Consultant)	'You don't have to rush back home.' (Publisher)
'I'd rather enjoy myself with the man in my life when I'm relaxed – at home.' (Travel writer)	'It makes the executive's life a bit easier at home and is relatively inexpensive.' (Corporate travel administrator)

Source: Collis, R. (2000), *The Survivor's Guide to Business Travel*, London, Kogan Page.

The decision-making process

While the linkages between business travel and leisure tourism have long been acknowledged, very little research has attempted to demonstrate this important connection empirically. A rare and notable contribution to this topic is the research undertaken in the state of Washington by Rutherford and Kreck (1994).

While Rutherford and Kreck focused on the quantitative issues of calculating the proportion of delegates adding leisure tourism and recreational activities to their conference trips, and estimating the actual amounts they spent on these activities, a complementary quantitative approach to the subject was proposed by Davidson (2001). His research agenda is aimed at reaching an understanding of the decision-making process that determines whether conference attendance leads to business trip extensions. He first considers the characteristics of those delegates most likely and least likely to take advantage of the leisure and recreational facilities of the conference destination. He then discusses the types of conference most and least likely to attract delegates who extend their stay and/or bring guests. Finally, those types of destinations most likely to attract extenders and their guests are considered.

Delegate characteristics

The likelihood of delegates deciding to extend their visit and/or bring a guest is most probably determined by a combination of characteristics, the most important of which will include whether the delegate is:

- foreign/native to the destination;
- self-funded/funded by the employer;
- familiar/unfamiliar with the destination;
- with/without friends and/or family members at the destination;
- single/in a relationship;
- accompanied/unaccompanied on the trip.

It is possible to speculate that attending an overseas conference in particular adds an incentive to extending, particularly if the delegate is unfamiliar with the destination. Similarly, if the trip has been funded by the delegate's employer, for example, then the delegate may be more likely to spend their own money on an extension to the visit. Regarding the delegate's relationship status, it is reasonable to expect that someone travelling alone may feel under pressure to return to their partner more or less immediately after the event itself if they have not brought that person as their guest.

Conference characteristics

In conjunction with the delegate's own characteristics, the features of the conference itself must be taken into account. These will include:

- the type of meeting (association or corporate);
- length of conference;
- timing – days of the week, e.g. proximity to a weekend;
- timing – month of the year, e.g. during school holidays;
- timing: proximity to sporting/cultural event;
- degree to which excursions are already included in the official programme;
- inclusion of a guest programme in the conference.

The most important of these characteristics is almost certainly the first, with delegates' propensity to extend and bring guests being generally greater in the more 'relaxed' association market. Indeed, as Oppermann (1996) was quoted as saying in Chapter 3, the association meeting sector resembles to a large extent the leisure travel sector, since potential conference delegates are like tourists with a wide choice of different events at different locations, at varying costs and at different times.

Nevertheless, the other factors must also play a part in the decision-making process, in particular the timing of the conference. Midweek conventions may discourage delegates from extending when this means taking a day or two's leave from work. On the other hand, the temptation to extend and/or bring a guest will be increased when a pre- or post-conference extension offers the delegates the possibility of attending a famous cultural or sporting event at the destination. Finally, conferences offering a number of excursions and tours built into the official programme may leave delegates with the impression that they have sufficiently experienced the destination and that little extra would be gained by extending.

Destination characteristics

Factors about the destination affecting the decision to extend a visit include:

- image, including perceived level of expensiveness and security;
- distance from delegates' places of residence: long-haul?
- ease and cost of transportation in and around the destination;
- amount of tourism information provided by DMOs/hotel/conference organisers.

Ryan (1999) argues convincingly that distance from the delegates' places of residence might be an attracting rather than an inhibiting factor to travel and extend, particularly if the destination has not been not previously visited. It is certainly the case that the opportunity to accompany their partner on a business trip to Australia might excite more interest on the part of a UK resident than a trip to Frankfurt or even Paris, which might already be familiar to them.

But although all of the above factors may be taken into account by delegates considering extending their visit, image almost certainly plays the determining role. As discussed in Chapter 3, conference destination images and their relevance to destination selection have occasionally been analysed from the point of view of meeting planners. However, it is clear that in the context of the potential delegates' decision-making process, much more research is required that focuses on the image that these players, the ultimate customers of both association events and conference destinations, have of the destination itself. Since the attractiveness of the destination as perceived by potential business visitors will play a role in determining whether the association delegate will actually attend the event, and whether they will be accompanied by guests and/or extend their visits, both meeting planners and destination marketing organisations need to understand how the destination is perceived. It follows that in cases where the destination either has no particular image or has a negative image, then the destination marketing organisation must take steps to correct this situation.

The roles of key players

It is apparent that there are considerable benefits to be gleaned from business travellers extending their trips and/or bringing guests with them. In this section, we suggest how three key players – destination marketing organisations, meeting planners and hotels – can contribute to expanding this market.

Destination marketing organisations

In addition to the needs of meeting planners and the initiators of the events, DMOs also need to consider the extenders and guests markets at all stages of their involvement with a meetings event, from familiarisation visits onwards. This will include providing full and enticing information on possible ideas for extensions, as done, for example, by the Hawaii Visitor and Convention Bureau (HVCB), which adapts the information to suit the potential tourist. Foster (1998) quotes a representative of the HVCB:

> Meeting planners booking dates at Hawaii's new convention centre are keeping to the national average of about four days. What sets Hawaii bookings apart is the average time delegates are planning to stay in Hawaii: almost nine days. Almost everybody is doing pre- or post-convention travel, largely on the Neighbor Islands. Many planners are including information about such travel in the information packets they prepare for delegates. The HVCB has been supplying information and photos of the various islands for planners to use. Clients who are making their first visit to Hawaii may want to stay on Oahu and experience its many sights and attractions. Agents can catch the interest of Hawaii-savvy delegates with upscale Neighbor Island resorts or niche packages.

Information is clearly part of the solution to encouraging business visitors to stay longer in order to enjoy the destination's attractions. This means DMOs emphasising the leisure attractions of the city or area they represent when dealing with enquiries from planners and buyers of business travel events. Buyers and their intermediaries are increasingly requesting this type of information. Greaves (1998; p.38) quotes a Newcastle city conference officer, who describes how her remit is expanding, with customers no longer asking the bureau simply to source a suitable venue, but also demanding information on appropriate social programmes as well:

They want ideas and details on rugby matches, the Newcastle races, visits to brew eries and comedy stores and the best restaurants and bars. In the past, the conference brochure has been mainly venue-oriented, but a new one will be launched at Confex next year which will have a much greater social slant to meet this growing need.

As Figure 7.2 shows, convention bureaux can also market destinations on the strength of their business and leisure mix.

Part of the DMOs' strategy must also be to create a greater general awareness of the potential and actual added value to be gained from business visitors' incremental spending on leisure and recreation. Crucially, this spending must be

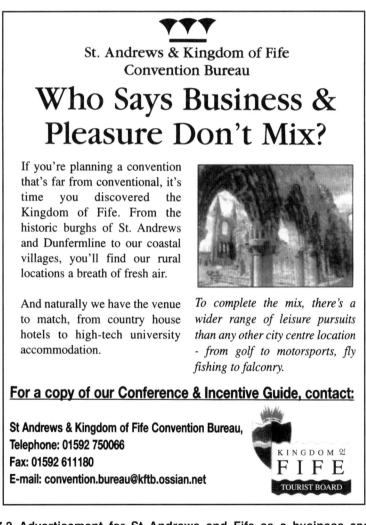

Figure 7.2 Advertisement for St Andrews and Fife as a business and leisure destination

Source: St Andrews & Kingdom of Fife Convention Bureau.

included in any survey of business visitors' impact on the destination's economy. Rogers' (1998) example of the Sydney Convention and Visitors Bureau's Convention Delegate Study, mentioned earlier in this chapter, incorporates calculations of indirect and induced impacts as well as the direct effects of business visitors' spending. The annual study seeks to illustrate the cascading effect of conference business, with other regions of the country benefiting as delegates extend their stay in order to travel and see some of the sights and attractions of other Australian cities. The research found that international delegates were spending an average of 10.7 nights in Australia, three nights of which were devoted to pre- or post-conference touring.

How many DMOs are in a position to provide such comprehensive data on their business travel visitors' activities and intentions? Such facts provide valuable support when a case is to be made for additional funding for marketing activities, for example, or to alert other professionals to the potential value of the extenders market.

Meetings planners

Meetings planners such as professional conference organisers have a role to play in arranging pre- and post-conference tours, adding enticing guest programmes to the events they organise, and actively marketing these as part of the event package. With destination management companies, they can identify hotels that will offer a few days' accommodation either side of the main event at delegate rates, and attractions that will provide special deals to business visitors.

Regarding guest programmes, the days when most of these seemed to be organised with the Stepford Wives in mind are mercifully long gone. Much progress has been made in the professionalism with which planners organise guest programmes. Most meeting planners now agree that guest programmes are no longer the exclusive domain of wives or even women. For those who are still unconvinced, the following extract may provide a salutary lesson (Letts, 2000; p.27):

> Mark, who is in his late forties and works in the media, is the boyfriend of Roland, a successful City financier. A couple of years ago, when Roland was working for Merrill Lynch, he won a performance-related bonus: a first-class trip to a company symposium outside New York. 'Bring your partner', said Merrill. So he did.
>
> 'They were very sweet about it, really,' recalls Mark. 'While Roland spent the mornings in meetings, I was included in the spouses' programme. There I was, stuck with all these power wives, learning how to bake chocolate cakes and become a proper Merrill Lynch spouse … At night they left gifts on everyone's beds. They gave me a Louis Vuitton scarf and a handbag.

But for successful guest programmes, factors other than gender come into play. Many planners say that guests' expectations are higher, and the pressure is on to organise increasingly innovative programmes. Many participants now have their own careers to nurture, and they are increasingly demanding programmes of substance that will enrich their lives, contribute to professional development, help them cope with modern stresses, give them an insider's look at a destination, and possibly provide a little pampering.

What can meetings planners do to create programmes that satisfy guests and boost participation? Crocker (1999) encourages them to adhere to two fundamental principles of meeting planning: know your group and study its track record. Planners charged with designing a guest programme need to know the ages, level of sophistication, and socioeconomic profiles of participants. It is also essential to take into account where groups have visited previously, and what they liked and did not like about earlier programmes. Crocker's further recommendations for a successful guest programme include:

- appeal to the group's interests (antiques, churches …);
- make it educational (local culture/cuisine, investments, retirement planning …);
- make it relevant (dovetailing with the topic of the actual conference);
- spotlight the destination (the things the city is famous for);
- enrich the basics (do something for the group that they could not do on their own);
- be gender-inclusive (choose topics of mutual interest, e.g. financial planning).

Hotels

Those managing hotels at the destination have an interest in business guests extending their visits in the same city in which the business event has taken place. It has already been mentioned that hotels can help by offering additional room-nights at conference rates. This will be particularly in their own interest if it persuades business visitors to stay over into weekend periods, which are generally quieter for hotels. Extenders can provide a market for a hotel's onsite facilities, such as its golf course, beauty parlour and health suite. But if hotel management can forge links with other suppliers, such as theme parks, theatres or museums, to create attractive packages for business visitors and their guests, then they will have even more success in creating extenders out of business visitors.

Finally, it is worth noting that cross-selling of this kind by hotels is an effective marketing technique that can operate in both directions. As well as using the presence of business guests in their premises to generate leisure short breaks, many hotels market their business facilities such as seminar rooms and incentive packages to their leisure guests. On the most basic level, this can take the form of leaving brochures in guests' rooms or in reception, giving details of the conference suite, day delegate rates, and so on. However such marketing is carried out, it serves as a reminder that the relationship between leisure tourism and business travel is a wholly symbiotic one. Success in one segment may not guarantee success in the other, but destinations and suppliers are increasingly coming to understand the importance of endeavouring to make the most of both leisure and business visitors.

References

BTF & BTAC (1999), *Business Tourism Leads the Way*, London, Business Tourism Forum and Business Tourism Advisory Committee.

Collis, R. (2000), *The Survivor's Guide to Business Travel*, London, Kogan Page.

Collis, R. (2001), 'Escaping the grind', *International Herald Tribune*, 6 July.

Crocker, M. (1999), 'Great expectations: no longer can assumptions be made about what your attendees' guests want, or even who they are', *Meetings & Conventions*, June.

Davidson, R. (2001), 'Adding business to pleasure: conventions and tourism', in Jones, D. (ed.), *Proceedings of the Convention/Expo Summit IX*, University of Nevada, Las Vegas.

Doyle, J. and Nathan, M. (2001), *Whatever Next ? Work in a mobile world*, London, Industrial Society.

Drache, A. (2000), 'Travel tips for the savvy taxpayer: mix pleasure with business and keep the deductions', *Financial Post – Canada*, 13 June.

Foster, C. (1998), 'Conventional wisdom', *Travel Agent*, 6 July.

Greaves, S. (1998), 'Competing for business', *Conference & Incentive Travel*, September.

The Guardian (1998), 'End of line for corporate entertainment?', *The Guardian*, 10 October.

Letts, Q. (2000), 'Painting the city pink', *London Evening Standard*, 3 February.

Matthews, V. (2001), 'When two have to become one', *Financial Times*, August 2.

Oppermann, M. (1996), 'Convention destination images; analysis of association meeting planners' perceptions', *Tourism Management*, Vol. 17, pp. 175–82.

Rogers, T. (1998), *Conferences: a twenty-first century industry*, Harlow, Addison Wesley Longman.

Rutherford, D.G. and Kreck, L.A. (1994), 'Conventions and tourism: financial add-on or myth? Report of a study in one state', *Journal of Travel and Tourism Marketing*, Vol. 3, pp. 49–63.

Ryan, C. (1999), 'The use of a spatial model to assess conference market share – a New Zealand example', *International Journal of Tourism Research*, Vol. 1, pp. 49–53.

Smith, G. V. (1990), 'The growth of conferences and incentives', in Quest, M. (ed.), *Horwath Book of Tourism*, London, Macmillan.

Systems Three (1998), *The Conference Delegate Expenditure Research Study*, London, Systems Three.

Uriely, N. (2001), '"Travelling workers" and "working tourists": variations across the interaction between work and tourism', *International Journal of Tourism Research*, Vol. 3, pp. 1–8.

Williams, A.M. and Shaw, G. (eds) (1991), *Tourism and Economic Development: Western European experiences*, London, Belhaven.

Appendix: Key business travel associations

Name	Contact	Membership total	Membership basis	Target membership (who is eligible for membership)	Mission statement	Unique selling point	Membership fees	Membership benefits
European Society of Association Executives	Website: www.esae.org	255	Individual and organisation	All staff employed in associations of all types in all countries in Europe	To enhance the reputation and standing of all members	The only pan-European organisation serving the needs of all professional staff employed in the not-for-profit sector	Individual: €250/year Corporate: €1200/year	Dual ESAE/ASAE membership; networking and information exchange; website services
The Meetings Industry Association	Website: www.meetings.org	650	Organisation	Venues with meeting facilities and suppliers to the industry	To improve the performance of the UK meetings industry	Members are committed to minimum standards included in the Meetings Magna Carta	£250–£775	Regular promotion to 7000 corporate and association buyers, networking at national and regional events
Association of British Professional Conference Organisers	Website: www.abpco.org	33	Individual	Professional conference organisers	Develop and enhance the professional status of conference organisers	Membership is exclusive to professional conference organisers	£95 + VAT (associative members) £295 + VAT (full members)	Recognition, training, networking
Meetings Professionals International	Website: www.mpiuk.org	18 000	Individual	Planners and suppliers	The pivotal force in positioning meetings as a primary communications vehicle	The leading global community that is committed to shaping the future of the meeting and event industry	US$305	Expand professional knowledge and profit from continuous professional education

Organisation	Website	Number	Membership basis	Membership	Aim	Benefit	Fee	Services
International Congress and Convention Association (ICCA)	Web site: www.icca.nl	628	Corporate	The entire meetings industry	Maximising business opportunities for members	An online database of 1700 meeting planners	€2200 (membership fee) + €1400 (one-time conference fee)	Educational programmes, concerted promotional campaigns, access to ICCA database
International Special Events Society (UK Chapter) ISES	Website: www.isesuk.org	110	Individual	Event organisers, event suppliers, caterers, venues, theming companies	To uphold the integrity of the special events profession	Experience, expertise and ethics	US$345	International contacts and UK networking
Incentive Travel & Meetings Association ITMA	Website: www.itma-online.org	220	Company basis	Event-organising companies and their suppliers	To advance the professionalism and profile of the industry	Representing the interests of a worldwide membership	£75–£1500	Industry recognition, statutory bodies and legislation representation and advice, networking, education and motivation
Association for Conferences and Events (ACE)	Website: www.martex.co.uk/ace	450	Company	Organisations involved in the creating, marketing, organising, accommodating and servicing of conferences and events	To provide an information centre and forum for member organisations	Provision of accurate information free from hype	£80–£180	Insurance scheme for events, business promotion opportunities, discount on services and facilities for members, networking events

Name	Contact	Membership total	Membership basis	Target membership (who is eligible for membership)	Mission statement	Unique selling point	Membership fees	Membership benefits
British Association of Conference Destinations (BACD)	Website: www.bacd.org.uk	96	Company	Conference destinations in the British Isles for full membership	To be the lead body for the destination industry	One-stop access to 90 conference destinations throughout the British Isles	£595–£995	Marketing and business development, representation and lobbying
Society of Incentive & Travel Executives (SITE)	Website: www.site-intl.org	2000	Individual	Key players in the design, promotion or delivery of incentives and motivational events	Fosters networking and professional development among individuals and businesses	Only international association dedicated to incentives, travel rewards, and motivational events	US$395 annual dues	Targeted and tiered education, global resource network
Hotel Booking Agents Association (HBAA)	Website: www.hbaa.org.uk	38	Company	Any agency whose majority income is derived from hotel commissions or management fees relating to hotel and conference bookings	To enhance the professionalism of the HBA and its dealings with both the hotel industry and corporate buyers	The only association aimed exclusively at HBAs	£50–£300	No structured programme

Source: Reproduced with the permission of *Meetings & Incentive Travel* magazine, copyright © CAT Publications Ltd, June 2001 (amended).

Glossary

Academic venue	Educational institution, such as a university, which lets out its facilities for meetings
Aspirational	Capable of inspiring (added effort)
Attractor	Celebrity or key industry figure whose presence at the stand attracts interest
Audience	Used here to describe those who visit exhibitions to buy/get information on products
Award-winner	Participant in an incentive trip
Bid process	System by which several destinations tender to host a particular event, usually an association meeting
Blockbuster	Extremely large exhibitions
Booth	American word for an exhibition stand
Breakout rooms	Meeting rooms used in the venue when a conference breaks up temporarily into smaller groups for discussion
Business-to-business event	Exhibition for professionals and trade only
Business tourism	Travel for the purpose of attending meetings, incentive trips, exhibitions
Business travel	Generic term covering all types of work-related travel
Buyer	(a) The organisation that initiates and pays for the meeting; (b) the person who has responsibility for identifying a suitable venue
Buying centre	Collection of individuals who have an impact on the decision determining the choice of destination/venue

Chapter	Local group of members of an association with a wider geographical coverage
Conference desk	Part of a destination marketing organisation with responsibility for marketing the destination's meetings venues
Conference production company	Intermediary dealing with the technical aspects of producing a meeting event
Congress	Large meeting, usually attended by delegates from a number of countries
Consumer show	Exhibition open to the general public
Contractor	Supplier of elements, such as stands, necessary for exhibition attendance
Convention	Large association meeting (mainly US usage)
Convention bureau	Marketing organisation established to attract meetings to the destination; usually joint private/public sector funding
Converted venue	Facility originally built to serve another purpose and subsequently converted into a meetings venue
CRS	Computer reservation system
Delegate	Someone in attendance at a large meeting
Derived demand	Demand for goods and services that are necessary inputs into the production of other goods and services
Destination management company	Intermediary based at the destination where the event is to be held and responsible for organising the accommodation, excursions, transfers, etc.
Discretionary	Allowing an element of choice (of destination)
Electronic conferencing	Participation in a meeting via the Internet
End consumer	In business travel, the person who undertakes the trip/attends the event

Final demand	Demand for goods and services that are ends in themselves
Flag carrier	National airline of a country (but not necessarily government owned), e.g. Air France, British Airways
Fun day	Organised day out at a venue, with entertainment and catering supplied
GDS	Global distribution system – on which travel agencies can book flights, car rental, hotels, rail travel, etc.
Ground handler	*see* Destination management company
Guest	Someone who accompanies a delegate to an event but who does not participate in the main programme; often a spouse or partner
Hybrid event	Event combining two or more forms of business tourism, e.g. a conference with an accompanying exhibition
IATA	International Air Transport Association
Implant	Satellite branch of a travel agency within the premises of a corporate client
Incentive commission	Extra commission paid by a supplier on achievement of sales targets
Incentive travel house	Intermediary specialising in designing and organising incentive programmes
Intermediary	Agency bringing together suppliers and buyers
ITM	Institute of Travel Management, a UK-based organisation for corporate travel managers
Keynote speaker	High-profile or influential speaker given prominence in the conference programme
Lead time	Time between when a booking is made and the date of the actual event
Load factor	Percentage of seats filled in an aircraft
Management fee	Fee charged by travel agents to clients to cover the costs of servicing their travel account and to generate a profit

Management training centre	Venue specialising in the hosting of training seminars, often residential
MICE	Acronym describing the business travel sectors: meetings, incentives, conferences and exhibitions
Multiple-tier award	Incentive award offering various levels of travel experiences, according to the level of achievement
NBTA	National Business Travel Association, a USA-based organisation for corporate travellers
Niche event	Small but specialised exhibition aimed at a very specific market
No-frills airlines	Low-cost airlines such as easyJet, Ryanair, Buzz and Go
Nondiscretionary	Allowing no element of choice (of destination)
Oneworld	International alliance of major airlines, including British Airways, American Airlines, Cathay Pacific and Qantas
OPODO	Combined Internet direct reservation site for nine major European airlines
ORBITZ	Proposed combined Internet direct reservation site for major US airlines
Outplant	Travel consultants within an agency dealing exclusively with an account
Override commission	*see* Incentive commission. Extra commission paid once targets have been achieved
PCO	Professional conference organiser: an intermediary hired by the buyer to deal with the detailed organising of all or part of a large meeting event
Premium air travel	Business- and first-class air travel
Product launch	High-profile corporate event held to launch a new product or service, with sales staff, dealers and the press invited
Prospect	Potential client
Purpose-built venue	Facility designed specifically to be used as a meetings venue

Rebates	Discounts given to corporate clients to attract their business
Relationship management	Technique of attempting to form closer bonds with people who are external to the company, but who are nevertheless important to its success
Residential training centre	*see* Management training centre
Self-liquidating	Incentive programme that pays for itself through the increased sales etc. achieved by the participants
Seminar	Small meeting, usually corporate, held for training purposes or to formulate strategy
Slots	Departure or arrival platforms at airports
SMERF	Social, military, educational, religious and fraternal segments of demand for meetings
Star Alliance	International alliance of major airlines, including Lufthansa, Air Canada, United Airlines and Varig
Summit	Conference bringing together influential figures, often heads of state, to discuss an issue of far-reaching importance
Supplier	Company or organisation producing goods or services required by business travellers, e.g. transport, accommodation
Syndicate rooms	*see* Breakout rooms
Teaser	Reminder sent out to those competing in an incentive programme to remind them of the desirability of the prize for which they are competing
Teleconferencing	Practice of using video, audio and/or computer facilities to enable a meeting between people who are physically distant from each other to take place; the technology involved in this practice
TIA	Travel Industry Association of America
Transaction fee	Fee charged by travel agents to clients to cover the costs of processing a transaction and to generate a profit

Trophy value	Prize's capacity to impress the winner's peers
Unusual venue	Facility used occasionally as a meetings venue but which has a different principal function, e.g. as a museum, theme park or stately home
Venue-finding agency	Intermediary specialising in the identification of suitable venues corresponding to a list of criteria supplied by the client
Videoconferencing	*see* Teleconferencing
Virtual conferencing	Using the Internet to view the proceedings of a conference, send questions to speakers, download papers, etc.
Web-cast conferencing	*see* Virtual conferencing

Index